The Solaris Effect

Art & Artifice in
Contemporary
American Film

The . . . .

SOLARIS
EFFECT

. . . .

Steven Dillon

UNIVERSITY OF TEXAS PRESS
 AUSTIN

Requests for permission to reproduce
material from this work should be sent to
    Permissions
    University of Texas Press
    P.O. Box 7819
    Austin, TX 78713-7819

    www.utexas.edu/utpress/about/bpermission.html
⊗ The paper used in this book meets the
minimum requirements of ANSI/NISO z39.48-1992
(R1997) (Permanence of Paper).

Library of Congress Cataloging-in-Publication Data
Dillon, Steven, 1960–
The Solaris effect : art and artifice in contemporary
American film / Steven Dillon. — 1st ed.
    p.   cm.
Includes bibliographical references and index.
ISBN-13: **978-0-292-71345-1**

1. Motion pictures—United States.   I. Title.
PN1993.5.U6D47 2006
791.430973—dc22
                2006014047

To my parents

Contents

....

Preface   *ix*
Acknowledgments   *xiii*

1   Tarkovsky's *Solaris* and the Cinematic Abyss   *1*

2   Steven Soderbergh's Tinted World   *21*

3   Aronofsky, Sundance, and the Return to Nature   *45*

4   *Mulholland Drive, Cahiers du cinéma,* and the Horror of Cinephilia   *77*

5   Spielberg's *A.I.:* Animation, Time, and Digital Culture   *105*

6   Cinema against Art: Artists and Paintings in Contemporary American Film   *141*

7   A Plague of Frogs: Expressionism and Naturalism in 1990s American Film   *173*

8   Situating American Film in Godard, Jarmusch, and Scorsese   *209*

Notes   *233*
Bibliography   *253*
Index   *261*

Preface

··

Like Mount Rushmore, this book has several faces. For now, I will begin by taking a postcard picture, by stepping back and looking at all four heads at once. Later on, like Cary Grant and Eva Marie Saint in Hitchcock's *North by Northwest*, we will roam over the nostrils and chins of these big heads, through lots of overly enlarged details. First, a brief view of the mountain, before we go scrabbling about among the sculptures and the rocks.

This book is, on the one hand, or one face, a survey of contemporary American film from 1990 to 2002. *The Solaris Effect* contains substantial descriptions of about sixty films. These descriptions ought to stand on their own, as probes and forays into a fascinating decade of cinema. There is still relatively little critical work on directors such as Steven Soderbergh, Darren Aronofsky, Todd Haynes, Harmony Korine, and Gus Van Sant. This book treats Soderbergh and Aronofsky at length, and tends to emphasize small-budget independent American film at the expense of blockbuster Hollywood film. Yet more canonical figures like Martin Scorsese, Robert Altman, and Steven Spielberg also make detailed appearances. One way to read *The Solaris Effect* is as a modest supplement to Robert Kolker's *Cinema of Loneliness*.[1] Kolker surveys major figures (Kubrick, Spielberg, Scorsese, Stone) in a nearly definitive manner, but omits anyone not admitted to his limited pantheon. For instance, Kolker does not even mention David Lynch.

The Solaris Effect is deliberately sculpted. I organize my look at contemporary American film around ideas of art and artifice. Since both political eco-consciousness and digital CGI-consciousness developed and increased in the 1990s, American film stands as a particularly interesting place to reflect on *art*. Many of the canonical figures (Scorsese, Kubrick, Altman) readily don the mantle of artist, and younger directors, too, often directly explore regions of art, of creativity, of making and representation.

My chapters often go back and forth between the sculptures and the rock, between art and nature. How do science fiction films like Spielberg's *A.I.* and Aronofsky's π represent the relationship between nature and artifice? How do the winners of the Sundance Film Festival regard the apparent oppositions between nature and culture, wild and tame, river and bridge? If independent film casts off the glossy artifices of big-budget Hollywood, does it then go to the natural world for an authentic alternative, a ground of truth?

To organize this discussion of nature and art in contemporary American film, I use Andrei Tarkovsky's *Solaris* (1972) as a model. *Solaris* is philosophical science fiction that relentlessly explores the relationship between the powers of nature and the powers of art. Tarkovsky himself is usually taken for a cinematic naif, regarded often as an innocent lover of the natural world. But one of the many subplots of *The Solaris Effect* consists of an argument on behalf of Tarkovsky's cinematic self-consciousness. This self-consciousness is also called self-reflexivity. When Tarkovsky takes a picture of the natural world, he does so self-consciously, not innocently.

Hence my other theoretical hero is Jean-Luc Godard. The four heads of *The Solaris Effect* rest on the two sturdy shoulders of Tarkovsky and Godard. Godard's practice helps explain what we might mean by cinematic self-reflexivity. From time to time, I will invoke examples from early (New Wave), middle (politically militant), and late (post–*Sauve qui peut [la vie]*, 1980) Godard. By the end of the book I hope to have contributed to an understanding of what we might mean by self-reflexive cinema. I also hope to have significantly complicated the apparent opposition between naive Tarkovsky and hypersophisticated Godard. Both are extraordinarily self-reflexive filmmakers, and late Godard—philosophical, lyrical, slow, with a surprising number of landscapes—is never too far away from the cinematic worlds invented by Tarkovsky.

And so these descriptions of American film will turn prescriptive. The final head on the hill is the head of critical judgment. I will argue that American film must work self-reflexively. American film must acknowledge not only that it exists *as* a film, but also that it is located, that it is situated in the United States. Film is a major artifact of American cultural imperialism, now more than ever, and American film must always acknowledge its own origin. Unless one's aesthetics are sheerly relativistic or completely generous, critical judgments must have criteria. My aesthetic criteria are what I take to be Godardian. Late Godardian politics are not dogmatic (especially compared to those from middle-period Godard), and they are attended by an enormous range of social and cultural issues. But Godard's films are always *placed*, situated, not only in the history of film, but also in a global landscape. It may surprise some readers how often American films, too, concretely situate themselves on a global map.

The monument, or hydra, thus looks something like this:

1. A survey of American film from 1990 to 2002 (with a rare example from 2003)
2. The categories of nature and art as organizing principles of the survey
3. Film art evaluated according to its cinematic self-reflexivity
4. A critical judgment that American films, in the end, will have more chance of aesthetic success when they are self-reflexive, that is, when they refer to themselves not only as film artifacts, but also as being located on a global map

As will be evident in the chapter on David Lynch, I am a great fan of French film criticism, especially that represented by the journal *Cahiers du cinéma*. My writing does not look very much like that of any *Cahiers* critic, but it has been strongly influenced by the whole history of the magazine and the work of many of its writers. I am still much moved by the early cinephilia of Godard and Truffaut, and consider myself a crazily enthusiastic cinephile in many respects. But the politically militant *Cahiers du cinéma* of the late 1960s and the 1970s has also made a strong impression on me. In its more recent incarnations, *Cahiers* has returned to a more openly enthusiastic mode, but with a political and philosophical awareness of what such enthusiasm entails. I see much of this book as following in the contradictory, figurative, self-aware, multifaceted spirit of *Cahiers du cinéma*.

Hitchcock liked to conclude his films with landmark set pieces. When his films find themselves at Mount Rushmore or the Albert Hall or the British Museum or the Statue of Liberty, the monuments lend their grandeur to the chase (here, at last, is a location worthy of the narrative), at the same time that a blackly ironic humor descends upon the landmark. It is thrilling and thrillingly funny to see Cary Grant scurry over Abraham Lincoln's giant head. When famous landmarks are used for a playground, a kind of witty desecration takes place. Hitchcock does not destroy the landmark, like a terrorist, or like the aliens in *Earth vs. the Flying Saucers* (Sears, 1956). Instead, Hitchcock teases the landmark, vibrating the statue rather than toppling it.[2]

Movies are monuments that are there and not there. Where are they? The photographed face both is and is not that person. These four Solaris faces are not presidents, they are residents. The faces of American film look at us and tell us where they are. The faces are cut into a dark hill.

Acknowledgments

· ·

Thanks again to my editor, Jim Burr, for his suggestions, and for making the editorial process run so smoothly. Kip Keller copyedited the manuscript masterfully. I took seriously the many substantial comments by an anonymous reader for the Press, and I hope that the book was improved as a result. I appreciate very much the enthusiastic response by Winston Wheeler Dixon, and I have been sustained by the continued encouragement of Marshall Brown. I benefited from working through some of these films with my students in a 2002 first-year seminar, Contemporary American Film. Laura Tomaselli showed herself to be an especially astute critic of film in that course. I also learned from conversations with Lee Davis while directing his senior thesis on Lynch's *Blue Velvet*, and from Megan Taylor while directing her senior thesis on Godard's *Contempt*. Kathy and John Williamson made the book possible.

The Solaris Effect

· ·

Tarkovsky's *Solaris* and the Cinematic Abyss   I

···

> *The image, sir, alone capable of denying nothingness,*
> *is also the gaze of nothingness on us.*
>
> —GODARD, *In Praise of Love* (2001)

Film Theory, or Film as Theory

Psychoanalytic theory rose to such prominence in film studies because film seemed to demand an analysis of fantasy. Flowing across the screen, projected through the dark, come these dream images—idealized desires and ego-building identifications. Yet even as we watch and inhabit these fantasies and dreams, we have the underlying consciousness that these dreams are not true, that they are constructions, that "this is only a movie." Lacanian theory, with its centralized concept of "lack," seems perfectly fitted to address itself to this dream screen, a screen both full of desire and perpetually absent.[1] Dozens of models for cinematic fantasy have been offered over the past forty years, from the description of the "cinematic apparatus" by Jean-Louis Baudry (1970), which emphasized the ideological delusions of film, to Marc Vernet's *Figures de l'absence: De l'invisible au cinéma* (1988).[2] Even Richard Allen's recent critique of Lacanian film theory, *Projecting Illusion: Film Spectatorship and the Impression of Reality* (1995), still finds the category of fantasy useful in treating the problem of cinematic illusionism.[3] So many models of cinematic fantasy have been offered, indeed, that one can easily sympathize with a vehement call to end such studies: "Film theory should be less a theory of fantasy (psychoanalytic or otherwise) than a theory of the affects and transformations of bodies."[4] Here Steven Shaviro, in a brilliantly polemical book, would like to announce the end of Lacanian theory and the beginning of a criticism inspired by Gilles Deleuze and Georges Bataille.

The present book intends, nonetheless, to continue the investigation of cinematic fantasy. The simultaneous fullness and emptiness of the cinematic experience seems fundamental, and worthy of further critical discussion. Movies themselves repeatedly stage this problem and always have. But instead of turning to Freudian models and language to aid our understanding, I will turn to films—above all, to Andrei Tarkovsky's *Solaris* (1972), one of the most profound cinematic dreams ever conceived. Taking Tarkovsky's film as a model for the beautiful and infernal absence created by cinema will substantially augment what psychoanalytic analyses have offered so far. To show that *Solaris* has something important to say about cinematic experience is to underscore both the power of cinematic self-reflexivity and the complexities of cinephilia. Psychoanalytic explanations tend to reject cinematic self-reflexivity, as we shall see, and to refuse to occupy the place of the cinephile. By contrast, *Solaris* presents a self-reflexive narrative of cinematic love that does not reduce the film to a fetish.[5]

I will argue, furthermore, that Tarkovsky's film has a particular relevance to American film of the 1990s, where amidst a cultural landscape of virtual reality, fantasy takes on an unprecedented significance. Recent films like David Lynch's *Mulholland Drive* (2001) and Steven Spielberg's *A.I.* (2001) turn out to be contemporary versions of Tarkovsky's masterpiece. And it is no coincidence that Steven Soderbergh made his own version of *Solaris* in 2002. Chapter Two will show that Soderbergh's famously varied career has been directed toward *Solaris* for some time.

Marc Vernet begins his book *Figures de l'absence: De l'invisible au cinéma* with snippets from three of the most important French writers on film:

Mitry: L'image n'apparaît pas comme "objet," mais comme absence de réalité.
Bazin: la présence-absence du représenté
Metz: la signifiant imaginaire[6]

These three phrases emphasize what may be a fundamental aspect of the cinematic image. The cinematic image is both present and absent.[7] But different kinds of cinema mark this phenomenon in different ways. Classical Hollywood cinema is typically characterized by "invisibility" and "transparency," by a continual refusal to acknowledge that the film is actually a film. After modernist filmmakers like Godard took the lead, ideological criticism from the 1970s vigorously argued that film was required to identify itself as film through gestures of self-reflexivity.[8] Vernet's *Figures de l'absence* circles back around, making the case that even classical Hollywood film is, after all, full of devices that call attention to the cinematic apparatus. Vernet studies devices such as "the look at the camera," superimpositions and dissolves, and the use of offscreen space in order to argue that all kinds of film, not just Godard's, continually remind the spectator that "this is only a movie."

But I want to insist on differences. Clearly there is a felt difference between the self-reflexivity that occurs in Minnelli and Hitchcock on the one hand and in Godard on the other. Vernet wants to level the field counterintuitively, a project that provides a fresh, new look at certain films, but may blur the distinction between what is self-conscious in some films and not others. Self-reflexive films overtly break cinematic illusionism in ways that most classical Hollywood films do not.[9] Cinema's "absent presence" is therefore still a problem, an ongoing question, which in my view not all contemporary American films face up to equally. It is this fundamental and paradoxical experience of cinematic presence that I call the Solaris effect and that I wish to explore in this book. And so I begin with films instead of psychoanalysis.

Self-reflexivity stands as a crucial reason for my turn away from psychoanalysis. Psychoanalytic approaches to film tend not to be very good at processing cinematic self-reflexivity. As Richard Allen argues, the viewing subject in Lacanian studies of film is treated essentially as if he is unconscious.[10] If self-reflexivity shocks consciousness or leads to self-consciousness, then a psychoanalytic explanation of such an effect is going to have some difficulties. In *The Imaginary Signifier*, for example, Christian Metz spends a good deal of time working through the shadowy forms of reality that are captured on the screen. Here is a typical characterization by Metz of cinema's penchant for absence:

> What is characteristic of the cinema is not the imaginary that it may happen to represent, but the imaginary that it *is* from the start, the imaginary that constitutes it as a signifier (the two are not unrelated; it is so well able to represent it because it is it; however it is it even when it no longer represents it). The (possible) reduplication inaugurating the intention of fiction is preceded in the cinema by a first reduplication, always-already achieved, which inaugurates the signifier. The imaginary, by definition, combines within it a certain presence and a certain ab-

sence. In the cinema it is not just the fictional signified, if there is one, that is thus made present in the mode of absence, it is from the outset the signifier.

Thus the cinema, "more perceptual" than certain arts according to the list of its sensory registers, is also "less perceptual" than others once the status of these perceptions is envisaged rather than their number or diversity; for its perceptions are all in a sense "false." Or rather, the activity of perception which it involves is real (the cinema is not a phantasy), but the perceived is not really the object, it is its shade, its phantom, its double, its *replica* in a new kind of mirror. It will be said that literature, after all, is itself only made of replicas (written words, presenting absent objects). But at least it does not present them to us with all the really perceived detail that the screen does (giving more and taking as much, i.e. taking more). The unique position of the cinema lies in this dual character of its signifier: unaccustomed perceptual wealth, but at the same time stamped with unreality to an unusual degree, and from the very outset. More than the other arts, or in a more unique way, the cinema involves us in the imaginary: it drums up all perception, but to switch it immediately over into its own absence, which is nonetheless the only signifier present.[11]

This is a long, complicated passage, but a good example of how Metz works through the presence and absence of cinema with his semiotic and psychoanalytic tools.

But for Metz *all* films are "fiction films," which inevitably embody these complex psychoanalytic forms of signification. Thus Metz only barely touches on attempts to "defictionalize" film, that is, on gestures that interrogate or reflect on the cinematic medium in the course of the film.[12] Metz's framework, in fact, cannot tolerate self-referentiality, or it does so by simply absorbing it back into the fictive pool of everything. For Metz the laws of cinematic expression come from outside the cinema, and whatever a film could say about itself would stand only as one more element of its fiction. But it seems to me that films can quite usefully talk about themselves and about the nature of cinema, and in terms that are just as rewarding as those offered by Metz. Moments of cinematic self-reflexivity are not necessarily obvious or obviously praiseworthy; it still takes an interpreter to identify moments of self-reflexivity and evaluate their content. Metz seeks out rules of cinematic signification, yet without much interest in what the cinema itself might have to say about those rules. It is very odd to note that although *The Imaginary Signifier* was written at the height of Godard's radical period (1973–1976), there is not one reference to him in the entire book.[13]

And self-referentiality is equally cannibalized by Deleuze. Godard is now, to be sure, a central hero for Deleuze, and the turn between the "movement-image" (*Cinema 1*) and the "time-image" (*Cinema 2*) occurs right at the French New Wave, with Godard leading the way.[14] Yet "modern" cinema in Deleuze has to do with "direct time," not with self-consciousness or self-reflexivity. Indeed, in Deleuze's terms, self-reflexivity is again pushed to the brink of impossibility. If "the essence of cinema has thought as its higher purpose, nothing but thought," then how is cinema to refer to itself?[15] Deleuze's scatterings of the object continually reject both the "self" and the "reference" that would be required to make up this cinematic "self-reference." Deleuze's deconstructive monism, which rejects the conceptual oppositions of body and thought, presence and absence, will not linger long over films that may or may not talk about themselves.

Nonetheless we will frequently take heed of one of Deleuze's most important contributions, which is to reverse the potentially tragic separation of photography and world by affirming that break as the beginning of creative thought.

> The link between man and the world is broken. Henceforth, this link must become an object of belief: it is the impossible which can only be restored within a faith. Belief is no longer addressed to a different or transformed world. Man is in the world as if in a pure optical and sound situation. . . . Only belief in the world can reconnect man to what he sees and hears. The cinema must film, not the world, but belief in this world, our only link. The nature of cinematographic illusion has often been considered. Restoring our belief in the world—this is the power of modern cinema (when it stops being bad).[16]

Many descriptions of cinematic absence have an elegiac or melancholy tone.[17] But since Deleuze rejects the absence and loss of psychoanalysis, his whole attitude and tonality is decisively different. His writings on cinema make for an instructive counterweight to the usual nostalgic and melancholy forms of cinephilia. Yet Tarkovsky has much to say, as well, about nostalgia, melancholy, and love.

Whether following Lacan or Deleuze, most general theories of film have not proved consistently useful; they are spectacular, or fascinating, but students of film these days usually do not have a theory.[18] Even more so, general theories of art are always too full of inconsistencies and omissions to seem very convincing. No general remarks seem applicable to all films or all art. To avoid unnecessary generalizations, therefore, I will discuss art and film on a much more limited scale, by aiming Tarkovsky's *Solaris* at one recent period of American film. This book studies self-reflexivity in American film from 1990 to 2002. Western art (painting, sculpture) was inarguably and unapologetically self-reflexive for almost the entire twentieth century. Self-reflexive art comments on its medium, on what art can possibly be. Self-reflexive art also places itself in a historical context, in among other artworks.[19] My argument is that late twentieth-century American film needed to acknowledge its medium, its place in cinematic history, or else risk failing as an aesthetic object. Such an aesthetics is openly prescriptive, but most aesthetics are. What I mean by cinematic and historical self-reflexivity will be explained by the dozens of examples that make up this book.

One might think that contemporary American film would be the last place to look for art and self-reflexivity, but there are many important directors who have sustained ideas about style and expressivity. Indeed, American films specialize in artifice, and contemporary directors often comment cinematically on their use of technology and their stylistic choices. Realistic films may be an option elsewhere in the world, although even films like Abbas Kiarostami's *Taste of Cherry* (1997), which shows us the cameras and crew at the end, or Carlos Reygadas's *Japón* (2002), which makes the main character an artist, foreground their cinematic medium.[20] Yet because of the way the film industry works, and because of its overdetermined place in film history, realism is very rarely a plausible approach for contemporary American film. For instance, almost all American movies these days are financed with stars; a producer who can get a star or two has a chance of getting some money. But with a star in a picture the film already looks unreal; what ever else the movie might seem to be about, it is certainly about celebrity and performance. Many American films take this aspect into account, therefore, and do not try to pretend that Jack Nicholson or Nicole Kidman are not actually there. American films from the 1990s that pretend that stars are not there, when they are, do not make sense.

Similarly, American films made in the 1990s ought to have acknowledged that they were, indeed, films. American culture during 1990s was more technology conscious than it had ever been before, and digital technology slowly took over the film industry. An American film that does not want to admit that the camera is even present thus lacks minimal credibility. Often, the stylistic alternatives open to American films are given as a choice between artificial Hollywood and more naturalistic or more honest independent film. But naturalism has almost always failed in recent American film. The choice is really between different kinds of artifice. The emptiness of blockbuster Hollywood films, filled wall to wall with digital effects and GameBoy characters, gives artifice a bad name. Just as Godard once said, too provocatively no doubt, that he preferred watching a James Bond movie to the philosophical pretensions of Antonioni, action movies by John McTiernan make more cinematic sense, in many respects, than the naturalistic pretensions of John Sayles.[21] McTiernan at least makes movies, but Sayles makes movies that would rather not be movies.

Godard, we should also point out, not only makes films, he makes theories of film. Godard's example shows that films can think about film, and can start us thinking about film, as rewardingly as psychoanalysts, philosophers, or novelists. Godard regarded his early films as extensions of his film criticism, and his work has consistently obliterated the distinction between theory and practice. His films show us what the problems of cinema are; they teach us what to look for. Most film historians would agree with this description of Godard's critical significance, and in *The Solaris Effect* I will invoke Godard as often as Tarkovsky.

But I will also treat Tarkovsky as others would treat Godard, as someone whose films rise to the level of film theory. I want to insist on the novel idea that Tarkovsky investigates the possibilities and problems of cinema as deliberately and as searchingly as Godard. Tarkovsky's *Solaris* is an extraordinary meditation on cinema, and we can use that film as a model for critical interpretation. Whereas most critics see Godard and Tarkovsky as emblematic opposites, the ironic modernist versus the naive metaphysician, both share an uncommon seriousness, an extraordinary refusal to compromise, and a passionate need always to explore. Godard's longer career has left us many more artifacts of exploration, but Tarkovsky's seven films all answer repeated viewing. Each time we see *Solaris*, for example, we are shown again what cinematic seeing looks like and feels like. Are there other film theorists whose programs and descriptions carry such memorable conviction?

> *"I am not Rheya."*
> *"Then who are you?"*
> *"Rheya. . . . But I know that I am not the woman you once loved."*
> *"Yes, but that was a long time ago. That past does not exist,*
> *but you do, here and now. Don't you see?"*
>
> —STANISLAW LEM, *Solaris*

Andrei Tarkovsky's *Solaris* provides a detailed and complex model for cinematic illusion. *Solaris* is not explicitly about cinematic illusionism, as are films like Buster Keaton's *Sherlock, Jr.* (1924) or Woody Allen's *Purple Rose of Cairo* (1985), but it is a film implicitly about film. Interpretation makes the implicit explicit, and convinces because it *works*, not because it is accurate. Freudian readings or Marxist readings of literature and art are not correct, but they are often productive. Because they seem to do interpretive work, we learn more about a particular work of art and art in general by deploying Freudian or Marxist categories. Instead of turning to Freud or Lacan, I will draw on Tarkovsky's *Solaris* for some interpretive categories and ideas for this introductory chapter and the remainder of the book.

Solaris (1972) is Tarkovsky's third feature film, following *Ivan's Childhood* (1962) and *Andrei Rublev* (1969). The science fiction world of *Solaris* allows Tarkovsky to pursue what he called "poetic cinema," a cinema that proceeds by intuition and association in contrast to cause-and-effect narrative.[22] The premise of the film is that, under the influence of the planet Solaris, the dreams of astronauts in a space station come into the reality of waking life. *Solaris* centers on the consciousness of the astronaut Kris, who meets once again his long dead wife, Hari. For Kris, the appearance of his resurrected wife is at once a beautiful dream and a horrific agony. His agony is that he knows, every moment, that she is a figment of his imagination. They embrace, even make love, but she is not real. *Solaris* is a ghost story, but with a peculiar sort of ghost. What Kris sees is exactly his wife, but the figure before him was never his wife. The relationship between Kris and his dead, perfectly real wife I take to be the archetypal relationship of audience and screen at the cinema. There is photographic reality, sensual and emotional immersion, but also a concurrent knowledge that the reality is all along an artifice, a constructed hallucination.

To use *Solaris* as a model for cinematic hallucination, I do not necessarily need to show that Tarkovsky intended such a reading, yet there are indications that he might go along. Tarkovsky is often characterized as a cinematic naif, the antithesis of self-conscious, self-reflexive, and sophisticated Godard. We imagine Tarkovsky strolling through the woods, talking about immortality and God. We read his lyrical and ecstatic prose, and he comes to appear indeed as someone who wants only to get transcendental beauty and emotion on camera, without any thought of the camera itself.

Yet I would argue that Tarkovsky is a deeply self-conscious director, consistently and overtly aware of expressing himself through the medium of film. Although Tarkovsky rejects the technological realism of Kubrick's *2001: A Space Odyssey* (1968) in *Solaris*, the sci-fi framework still allows Tarkovsky to represent an ongoing consciousness of technology and communication. Television monitors, video players, audiotape recorders, and photographs play important visual and narrative roles in *Solaris*. Tarkovsky does not use the science-fictional bric-a-brac to think about the future of manned space flight, but he does arguably use it to think about cinematic illusion. That this impossible love takes place in a spaceship full of television monitors and video recorders helps us see that Kris's love for Hari is like our impossible desire for cinema. What we desire is contact and communication, but both the monitors and Hari ironically emphasize our solitude. We would recognize our solitude less, perhaps, if we were simply alone.

In his book *The Cinema of Andrei Tarkovsky*, Mark Le Fanu reads *Solaris* as a "film-within-[a]-film" that emphasizes the permanence of memory.

> From the early sequence where the youthful Burton looks back at his older ruined self from the widescreen wall monitor; to the middle scene in which the video of the dead Gibaryan addresses Kelvin "from the far side of the grave"; to the central and profoundly moving sequence where Kelvin's own "home video" shows Hari the image of herself as she was on earth near the snow-covered dacha — everything combines to demonstrate that memory need *not* be extinction; and that on the contrary we live in significance to the extent that we are prepared to embrace the shadows of our loss.
>
> But isn't this also, really, the metaphysics of film itself? Derrida calls cinema the "science of ghosts." Those actors on screen (the big screen, not just the screen-within-a-screen), aren't they *also* present to us and absent at the same time? And isn't this in fact what makes the cinema often so poignant? Its present tense is so often also a past tense.[23]

As I will argue below, one of Tarkovsky's most important contributions is a re-evaluation of this present absence, of this poignancy. For Le Fanu, Tarkovsky's cinematic self-consciousness is not so much self-reflexivity, a meditation on cinema, as it is a "meditation on immortality."[24] In this view, *Solaris* is about love, memory, and death, and it uses cinema to get there.

But I would balance Le Fanu's examples of perfect photographic memory with the equally numerous examples of Lethean forgetfulness. These are images that empty out their presence. Hari, for instance, is an amnesiac. She is often confused as to who she is and where she came from. We ourselves are never sure what happened to the couple in the past. We know that Hari committed suicide, but we are not sure what kind of lives these characters lived before that. Indeed, from this evidence, we might well conclude that film has access only to brief moments in the past, but not to anything substantial in the end. Yes, Hari is "immortal," continually reviving herself, yet she revives with only blurred memories. In a later chapter, I will discuss the idealizing of cinematic memory through digital technology. But Tarkovsky's *Solaris* does not make these idealized gestures. In one of Soderbergh's most substantial annotations of Tarkovsky, his Kris says, "I was haunted by the idea that I remembered her wrong." This addition is very much in line with the spirit of Tarkovsky's earlier version.

And Hari is more than a beautiful amnesiac, for she is not even a woman at all. She is one of the most complicated aliens in all of science fiction. Neither a bug-eyed monster nor a human-like cyborg, Hari is neither machine nor human being. Tarkovsky's *Solaris* makes her scientific status purposefully uncertain. Her presence raises all of the same philosophical questions about identity and consciousness as those that loom around the cyborgs in Ridley Scott's *Blade Runner* (1982). But the problems surrounding her go deeper than those attached to robots and artificial intelligence. For her identity and her otherness are radically unclear. She has some of the same characteristics as a machine, since she is almost impossible to kill (she drinks liquid oxygen and survives). She exhibits superhuman strength when she tears right through a door of the spaceship. And the other crew members all treat her as a thing, indifferently. They call her "a mechanical reproduction, a copy." She is a machine on the edge of the human—"I am becoming a human being," she says—yet she is more like a ghost or a dream. Like cinema itself, she is a copy, a reproduction, an alien, a ghost.

It might be argued that the Solaris effect is the essence of self-conscious film. Film self-consciousness is signaled not only through self-reflexive postmodernism, but also through the insistent foregrounding of ghosts. I would encourage the reader to think back on how frequently films narrate analogies to this problematic of screen existence. This book is not a history of European film, nor does its survey of American film stand or fall on its theory, but I will remind the reader from time to time of other films that work through this same disorienting ontology. This is why thematic studies of cinematic ghosts and monsters are so important, and why the genres of horror and science fiction are so central to our understanding of film. In contemporary American film, recent works by M. Night Shyamalan, especially *The Sixth Sense* (1999) and *Signs* (2002), are not just ghost movies, but are also about the ghostliness of film representation. It is no coincidence that the great movie lover and independent director Jim Jarmusch recently made films called *Dead Man* (1995) and *Ghost Dog: The Way of the Samurai* (1999), films which are not only about death, but about the liminal, spectral nature of movies as well. Films as different as *Ghost World* (Zwigoff, 2000), *The Man Who Wasn't There* (Coen brothers, 2001), and *The Blackout* (Ferrara, 1997) all enact commentaries around the idea of the film screen as an imaginary signifier. Hal Hartley's *No Such Thing* (2001) ends the moment that his monster (borrowed from Cocteau) dies.

World cinema can often be read similarly through this kind of self-conscious elaboration of presence and absence. Akira Kurosawa's repeated theme, that the world is illusion, overlaps with an idea that the screen is there and not there.[25] Surely the impression of *Rashomon* (1950) or *Throne of Blood* (1957) is one of life as a temporary ghostliness. The ghostliness of life becomes partly an existential, philosophical claim, but is also a commentary on the condition of film. When, at the end of Antonioni's *Blow-Up* (1966), the photographer vanishes amidst a vast lawn of green, we realize once and for all that we have been watching a powerful dialogue between something and nothing. The genius of Kiyoshi Kurosawa's *Cure* (1997) is found in its creation of a villain who is purely zero, an embodied absence. François Ozon's *Under the Sand* (2000) is another Solaris film, in which a woman (Charlotte Rampling), after the loss of her husband, lives her life in desperate fantasy. Hitchcock's *Vertigo* (1958) is yet another telling of *Solaris, avant la lettre*, and we will come across it more than once in the pages that follow.

The tone of *Solaris* is particularly significant. *Solaris* ought to be a tragedy, a dramatic retelling of the story of Orpheus and Eurydice. But even Cocteau's genre-disrupting *Orpheus* (1949) has more straightforward dramatic and tragic signals than *Solaris*. Le Fanu finds that the most substantial difference between Lem's novel and the film is that Tarkovsky foregrounds "human sorrow, which has only a minor place in the book."[26] But where do we see such sorrow in the film? In moments like this: "What profound melancholy and suffering is implied in [Hari's] inexpressive subtle gaze."[27] Although this is a dramatic situation, to say the least, Tarkovsky has deliberately avoided theatrical forms of drama. "Inexpressiveness," indeed, becomes a keynote.

Think how passively these characters respond to their remarkable circumstances. For a long time Kris is too stunned by Hari's return to register what is going on, and Hari is likewise quietly confused. Kris appears to be "emotionally dead" for most of the film, which is not a mistake on Tarkovsky's part, but a deliberate avoidance of dramatic tragedy.[28] Electronic music surges in and out, underscoring the hauntedness of things, but not the particular crises. The plot crises (when Kris sends Hari off on a rocket ship; when she commits suicide) are thus evened out and neutralized. The felt torture and despair of the ship's inhabitants is pressed out and flattened by the inexorable weight of time.

What *Solaris* gives us as a model is a different way of understanding and feeling the relationship of cinematic absence and presence. Instead of psychoanalytic identification, *Solaris* emphasizes existential solitude. Instead of tragic loss, or Deleuzean affirmation, *Solaris* emphasizes ongoingness and waiting.

In any case, my mission is accomplished. What next? Return to earth? Gradually everything will return to normal. New interests, new friends. But I won't be able to concentrate on them fully. Never. Have I the right to refuse even the remotest possibility of contact with this giant with which my race has tried to establish understanding for dozens of years? Or to stay here? . . . On the station, among the things and objects we both have touched? Which still remember our presence? To what end? In the hope that she'll return? But I do not have that hope. I must wait.[29]

Time is neither idealized nor demonized. The divisions in time caused by death or catastrophe are divisions that we cause in ourselves in the present. The ghosts in *Solaris* are of the dreamers' own making, a product of both love and betrayal. Cinematic ghosts do not haunt us because they are dead, but because we have betrayed them by outliving them.

Tarkovsky's *Solaris* models not only our perception of the cinematic object but also the status of the cinematic object as art. Besides being cinematically self-conscious in general, conscious of their identity as products of camera and photography, Tarkovsky's works are aesthetically self-conscious, conscious of their place in a field of artistic objects. Paintings occur in many of Tarkovsky's works, and Tarkovsky's characteristic long take seems to call attention to itself as a species of painting.[30] The long takes, the artworks, and the classical music may strike the viewer as signs of pretension—look, my film too is an artwork! Yet when paintings in museums and studio galleries incorporate other paintings, this is simply called self-reflexivity, and is recognized as an appropriate option for art. Surely film, too, can provide its own preliminary cultural annotations. When Kubrick uses classical music, he does not claim for his own films the cultural status of a waltz by Johann Strauss or a sarabande by Handel. Similarly, a painting "quoted" by Tarkovsky does complicated work. Tarkovsky never simply confirms the "timeless" nature of a masterpiece in his terrifically time-conscious cinema.[31]

Tarkovsky sets his film down amid art most deliberately in a late sequence. The three male astronauts and Hari gather together in the ship's library. Almost exaggeratedly, the library contains all kinds of representative artifacts from earth's culture. The room is cluttered with shelves of books, a bust of Homer, a small Venus de Milo, framed photographs, a stained glass window, African masks, and a violin on the wall. A beautiful chandelier hangs from the ceiling, and the room is filled with lit candles. The characters philosophize over a copy of *Don Quixote*. Most strikingly, a series of Brueghel paintings stands in the background, a miniature gallery. The whole room is clearly representative, not real, and frames the dialogue as surely as a frame around a picture. We are going to talk about art and culture in here, the movie says, in this room that goes out of its way to look timeless and even anachronistic (what are those candles doing here?).

And it is during this sequence, and in these confines, that Hari cries out that she is becoming human. It is here that the men call her a "matrix," a "copy," and a "mechanical reproduction." When Sartorius accuses her in these words, the Venus de Milo stands out in the background. Hari's identity does not just waver between human and inhuman, between reality and hallucination, but between art and technology. How should we categorize her existence? What should we call her artifice? Is she like a painting? Is a movie like a painting? Is a painting like a person? She weeps in despair and Kris tries to console her. The other two astronauts leave. Kris walks Sartorius back to his room.

When Kris comes back to the library, he finds Hari sitting at the table, absorbed in thought. Tragedy has dissipated to meditation. She is smoking a cigarette, turned away, and the smoke rises out of the top of her head. We turn around to look at the front of her, at her absorbed eyes, and then the film cuts to a close-up of Brueghel's *Hunters in the Snow*. We are plunged into a long sequence in which the camera pans all over the picture, as if to mimic Hari's eyes. A few sounds re-create images from the painting (dogs barking, bells ringing), but weird electronic music is foregrounded in the sound track. Through the music, the painting becomes haunted, ghostly. The visual idea is devastating in itself, as Hari, the mechanical reproduction, broods over a copy of Brueghel's painting. The ghost is haunted by a picture. If Tarkovsky here aligns his film with art, then, movie with painting, he draws a parallel between the ability of each picture to haunt us with its images. Art in this instance is surely not about masterpieces, but about ghosts.

In their commentary on *Solaris*, Tarkovsky scholars Vida Johnson and Graham Petrie idealize the artworks.[32] The spaceship has undergone a loss of gravity at this moment in the film, and Kris and Hari now levitate in each other's arms. Johnson and Petrie say that the couple is "at last content"; they float in front of the paintings and are happy. Johnson and Petrie say that Tarkovsky's "nostalgia for the earth" explains why Brueghel's paintings so appeal to him at this moment. Yet this description will not do. Hari and Kris are not expressing contentedness; they actually look rather blank. They are never able to sink into their contentedness, for the unreality of their situation is always all too apparent. The levitation is beautiful but temporary. Their time together is really one manner of disorientation after another. And the paintings around them are strangely lit; they seem to have been reproduced on glass, and to be backlit. This scene does not imply the "naturalness" and "timelessness" of art, but instead the ghostly artifice of art. And then the next sequence begins with the revelation that Hari has drunk liquid oxygen, further eroding any idealistic reading of the levitation. Altogether, we see Hari standing before a replica of the Venus de Milo and meditating on a copy of Brueghel. She floats before the painting and then tries to kill herself. In this sequence, neither the copies nor the suicide provides an idealizing framework for art.

Tarkovsky not only situates film's relationship to art, but also works through film's relationship to nature. In Chapter Three I will examine how recent independent American film expresses an overt or secret yearning for nature as an alternative to special-effects Hollywood, or as a ground to a decentered virtual reality. But I will also express serious doubts about this return to nature. After all, the medium itself is immersed in technology and artifice. Tarkovsky, of course, has been similarly and severely criticized for his naive invocations of the natural world. Fredric Jameson has probably stated the case most succinctly:

> The deepest contradiction in Tarkovsky is then that offered by the highest technology of the photographic apparatus itself. No reflexivity acknowledges this second hidden presence, thus threatening to transform Tarkovskian nature-mysticism into the sheerest ideology.[33]

But Tarkovsky's representation of the natural world is as self-consciously contextualized and as subtle as his references to art. *Solaris* is a complex discussion of art, nature, and film, in comparison to which contemporary American films often appear naive and unselfcritical.

The first section of *Solaris* takes place in a rustic setting, a clear contrast to the space laboratory to come. But the apparent contrast of natural earth to outer space is also complicated at once, since the waving, watery images with which the film begins recall ahead of time the swirling waters of the planet Solaris. Nature and imagination, or earth and outer space, are therefore not opposites, but clearly related pairs. As we will see, many American films, such as π and *Minority Report* (Spielberg, 2002), undermine themselves by celebrating a feature-length rush of artifice and then returning to nature in conclusion. By contrast, *Solaris* ends by ambiguously blending together the planet Earth and the planet Solaris, as the camera rises up spectacularly to reveal the family's country house now settled into the middle of a churning Solarian sea.

The natural world is framed self-consciously throughout this first section of the film. The very first image shows us a leaf floating right to left across water, water that reflects and shimmers. There are already layers to the water, and no clearly idyllic associations. Soon we meet Kris, in a pan from his feet to his head; he holds some sort of metal case in his hand, a tool or even a camera. Nature is displayed in fragments in these opening sections; space is dislocated, and we see Kris in clearly different landscapes. A horse runs back and forth, but in no coherent spatial relationship to Kris. There is, however, a clear sense of editorial arrangement, selection, and framing, with the consequence that nature seems parceled out. Hence we do not have to wait until the scenes set in the science-fictional spaceship to see machinery present in the world. Man has already imposed his technological eye on the landscape.

When the visitors arrive at the house, the boundaries of nature and culture are once again emphasized and confused. The open door makes the interior of the house seem continuous with the exterior, as if the house is quite happily missing a wall. Yet inside we find a birdcage, wooden beams showing the grain, an arrangement of flowers—all signs, in other words, of man's conquest over nature. A bearded bust of Plato or Homer continues this theme, as does a framed picture of a balloon (perhaps a reference to Tarkovsky's previous film, *Andrei Rublev*). Immediately the talk is about the space station, and after a short rain shower, they start watching television. The landscape is beautiful, it seems, and the house idyllic perfection. But neither landscape nor house is presented in simple terms. Kris's father says, "It's so pleasant here. This house reminds me of my grandfather's house. I really liked it. So we decided to build one just like it." Even the house, so simple seeming, is built out of desire—a copy, a duplication. As a beloved copy, this house is the very first exhibition of the Solaris effect.

The Solaris effect stands in between psychoanalysis and Baudrillard. In Baudrillard, contemporary culture can no longer be analyzed by psychology or sociology, because the alienation of subject and object has given way to the smooth screen of the network. For Baudrillard, "in our virtual world, the question of the Real, of the referent, of the subject and its object, can no longer be posed."[34] In my own thinking, Baudrillard's description of the simulacrum, the pure simulation with no relation to reality, applies to most Hollywood films. By comparison, the Solaris effect will be evidenced in these pages by films that split through the simulacrum by referencing the real.

Reality can break into a fiction film through a documentary effect, as it does so often in Godard. Reality also gathers around certain accidental features, such as the prosthetic hands of Harold Russell in *The Best Years of Our Lives* (1946).[35] In Tarkovsky's *Solaris*, one might attribute a hovering reality effect to the long sequence in the first third, in which we ride in an automobile through tunnels and across highways. As in Godard's *Alphaville* (1965), we are simply supposed to pretend that this obviously contemporary world belongs to the future. This lack of pretense ensures that reality will remain an ongoing question. Above all, however, it is self-reflexivity that makes manifest the materiality of film, by breaking through the simulacrum. The Solaris effect keeps open the question of the real, and makes work with subject and object continue to remain useful.

The Solaris Effect is a selective survey of contemporary American film. What follows will generally emphasize independent film at the expense of Hollywood film.[36] There were hundreds of U.S. films released in the 1990s, of course, but I will talk substantially about only sixty or so. But within the limits of this survey I hope to address some of the most important debates that have sprung up around contemporary American film. In some ways, this book is old-fashioned and humanistic. It does not go into much detail about the economics or sociology of moviemaking and moviegoing. Despite my sometimes severe judgments, this book also celebrates a substantial cross-section of recent U.S. films. It does not take the approach of "The End of Cinema" at the end of the twentieth century.[37] And while *The Solaris Effect* also offers an ontology of film, it is one less apparently complicated than those deriving from Lacan or Merleau-Ponty.[38] I use the word "reality" from time to time, for example, in a rather innocent sense. Nonetheless, my hope is that, by the end of the book, my use of Tarkovsky's *Solaris* will have borne fruit, and that its conclusion can stand as a contribution to the debate on contemporary film aesthetics and value.

The Solaris Effect continues in the next chapter with a look at the career of Steven Soderbergh, often regarded as the most independently minded director in Hollywood. Soderbergh began his career with a landmark of cinematic self-reflexivity, *sex, lies, and videotape* (1989), and every subsequent film has been, among other things, a meditation on the surface of the screen. Just as Soderbergh goes back and forth between independent filmmaking and Hollywood, shuttling from no-budget movies like *Schizopolis* (1996) to glamorous star vehicles like *Out of Sight* (1998), Soderbergh's films circle back and forth between reality and artifice, refusing both Hollywood's simulacrum and the naturalism of John Sayles. Although critics and Soderbergh himself always emphasize how different Soderbergh's films are, one from another, all of Soderbergh's films work through the absent presence of cinema; they are always, with different emphases and tonalities, performing the Solaris effect. Thus Soderbergh's career has been aimed towards a remake of Tarkovsky's *Solaris* since the very beginning.

Following the chapter on Soderbergh, the next six chapters will take different approaches to contemporary American film and the Solaris effect. Chapter Three will look at films by Robert Redford, in addition to films shown at Robert Redford's Sundance Festival. Redford's films, such as *A River Runs through It* (1992) and *The Legend of Bagger Vance* (2000) are transparent paeans to nature, in line with the overt environmentalism of the Sundance community. But even very urban entries in the Sundance Festival, such as Darren Aronofsky's π (1998) and Marc Levin's *Slam* (1998), often reject artifice and attempt to ground themselves in nature. Chapter Four studies the dream aesthetic of David Lynch, by emphasizing the constructedness of Lynch's dreams. Lynch's films emerge self-consciously as dream theater, with red curtains over the portals amid the trees. All of Lynch's films also give us the opportunity to study the intense, impossible love of film known as cinephilia, so central to the Solaris effect. Here we will compare the ramifications of the Solaris effect, where Kris dreams back his alien beloved, to various examples of critical cinephilia offered by the great French film magazine *Cahiers du cinéma.*

In Chapter Five I will focus primarily on Steven Spielberg's *A.I. Artificial Intelligence,* reading it both as a poignant performance of the Solaris effect and as a self-reflexive commentary on digital cinema. Digital technology changed cinema forever in the 1990s—or did it? Against certain theorists who maintain that digital cinema is absolutely postphotographic cinema, I argue that the Solaris effect still holds, whether we are looking at computer-generated imagery (CGI) or 35 mm film. Chapter Six directly examines artists and art by describing films that are explicitly about artists and their paintings. Directors such as Robert Altman and Stanley Kubrick practice an aesthetics of meaninglessness, in which cinematic art is that which has not more meaning, but less. This meaninglessness often sits on the edge of an abyss of horror, which leads to a discussion of art in the contemporary serial-killer film. Chapter Seven consists of a broad survey of directors who work explicitly under the banner of artifice, directors like Gus Van Sant, Harmony Korine, and Todd Haynes. These directors are contrasted to those who want, in the name of nature, to opt out of the artificial. In my argument, the pretension to naturalism makes no more sense than Hollywood's pretension to global conquest.

My final chapter will most polemically argue against this pretension to naturalism. In the age of empire, American film must identify itself as ephemeral or collaborate with the globe-trotting artifacts of imperialism. Hollywood films, like cartoons, radiate omnipotence, whereas many independent films ground themselves in the immortal truths of nature. But contemporary American films must align themselves with the humility and ghostliness of the Solaris effect, or else contribute to the American effect, the McDonaldization, or the Matrixization, of everything. In my description, many American films do embrace the Solaris effect, offering themselves, in many different ways, as examples of cinematic transience.

Tarkovsky's *Solaris* is the perfect encyclopedia for the study of contemporary American film. Like Spielberg's *A.I.* and Aronofsky's *π,* it is a science-fiction film. Like Lynch's *Twin Peaks: Fire Walk With Me* and *Lost Highway,* it is a horror film. *Solaris* analyses the visual representation of the natural world, like Todd Haynes's *Safe* and Van Sant's *Gerry. Solaris* examines the role of painting in relation to cinematic art, like Altman's *Vincent and Theo* and Scorsese's *Age of Innocence*. Above all, *Solaris* tells the tale of impossible love that is at center of all cinema, the love of that which is both present and absent, alien and human. I argue that American film must either retell this ghost story or else tell dangerous stories of immortality. Tarkovsky is a serious director, often maligned for poisoning film with his metaphysics and his ethics. Movies ought to be fun! But when film, and the capital that follows film, is so obviously a part of U.S. cultural imperialism, an ethical response to U.S. film seems called for. So Tarkovsky points us also in the direction of an ethical response by reminding us that if movies can be so important, then they need to be judged carefully and critically.

Steven Soderbergh's Tinted World 2

....

Soderbergh, Oliver Stone, and the Transformation of the Screen

Fredric Jameson's denunciation of Tarkovsky in *The Geopolitical Aesthetic* comes in the middle of a chapter-length celebration of Alexander Sokurov's *Days of Eclipse* (1988).[1] Here Jameson is especially taken with Sokurov's yellow filter, which denaturalizes color and tonality. "The filter," he writes, "desaturates images in such a way as to mute the autonomy of multiple colors in *Days of Eclipse*" (100). Jameson is so convinced by his description of Tarkovsky's cinematic naiveté that he completely forgets what the movies actually look like. Tarkovsky's "grandiose mysticism depended very much on a kind of naturalization of the coloring" (97). Thus Tarkovsky's visual "splendor," which radiates primal "*naturality*" (97, Jameson's coinage), stands in complete contrast to the tinted world of Sokurov.

> Meanwhile a genuine range of color emerges in Sokurov's outdoor shots, as though sharpened by the filter and as it were miniaturized by it. The yellow remains, but a wondrously delicate combination of hues becomes visible through it like a garden or carpet; a true invention of saffron pastels, as though saturation of an extremely low level heightened the intensity and revitalized the visual organs, making the viewer capable of minute perception quite impossible in the grander official full-color achievements of high Hollywood or Tarkovsky, for example. (101)

Jameson has gone crazy here for two reasons, I think. First, the stereotype of Tarkovsky as the naive nature mystic does take some work to overcome, and even Tarkovsky scholars could do more to break down the cliches. Second, since there is not an easily accessible history of filters in cinema, one would not have to write things like "About the filters, something more needs to be said, for this seems to be a Soviet innovation." (97)

Given that Sokurov considers himself a disciple of Tarkovsky, it ought to be rather surprising to conclude that the two directors are at polar extremes from each other. Sokurov's single-shot feature-length *Russian Ark* (2002) is a purposefully logical elaboration of Tarkovsky's longer and longer shots. And, indeed, the desaturated palette of *Days of Eclipse* descends directly from Tarkovsky's *Stalker* (1979). *Stalker*'s monochrome sepia sections alternate with sections in color, but even the color sections are scarcely naturalistic. *Stalker* is Tarkovsky's most visually extreme film, yet still typical of his work with desaturated color. "As usual," write Johnson and Petrie of *Stalker,* "Tarkovsky works with a very restricted color scheme."[2] Cinematographer Sven Nykvist calls the color of Tarkovsky's last film, *The Sacrifice,* "monocolor," an effect he achieved in a postproduction laboratory.[3] Considering that *Ivan's Childhood* and *Andrei Rublev* are in black and white, it could hardly be said that Tarkovsky *typically* naturalizes color.[4]

Films have often manipulated color through filters, set design, lighting, or tinting. Yet American films in the 1990s saw more rapid shifts in color design than ever before. Digital editing allows for easy manipulation of the color scheme, and almost every MTV video at the turn of the twenty-first century looked quite denaturalized. But it is Steven Soderbergh who has most deliberately sought to retool the visual potentiality of American film. Soderbergh thinks more readily of 1960s directors such as Godard and Richard Lester rather than Tarkovsky. Both Godard and Lester used extravagant filters on occasion (*Pierrot le fou, The Red Sitting Room*) as they sought for visual correlatives to their radicalizing visions. In films such as *Les Carabiniers* and *Alphaville,* Godard manipulated various kinds of film stock to achieve a visual texture that is a central aspect of Godardian self-reflexivity. Likewise, Soderbergh's importance as an American film director in the 1990s stemmed not only from an ethic of independence and originality, but also from his experiments in visual texture. Nearly all of Spike Lee's films after *Clockers* (1995), for example, manipulate film through a method taken straight from Soderbergh. Now every MTV video looks like *Clockers,* but the impulse in the 1990s to color, to tint, and to denaturalize came above all from Soderbergh.

To tint the screen may stand as simply one more way to make the picture interesting, no more or less significant than an interesting framing, an odd face, or a glowing lamp in the background. But in Soderbergh the tinted screen has everything to do with his repeated performances of the Solaris effect. Photographers and painters draw our attention to the surface of photographs and paintings in order to remind us of the medium. When our vision is mediated, not transparent, we are made aware of the artifact, of its construction. With the tinted screen and with other similarly self-reflexive gestures, Soderbergh repeatedly makes us aware of the cinematic medium. His films perform the Solaris effect not only by exhibiting themselves self-reflexively as constructed artifacts, but also by simultaneously performing their transience, their disappearance. Soderbergh's tinted world and the Solaris effect go together, hand in hand.

Soderbergh made a sudden appearance on the stage of world cinema when his first film won the Palme d'Or at Cannes in 1989. Although *sex, lies, and videotape* is not tinted, it does relentlessly dramatize the condition of film watching. This is not just a film that foregrounds sexuality—like the landmarks *Carnal Knowledge* (Nichols, 1971) and *Last Tango in Paris* (Bertolucci, 1972)—but it is also a film that foregrounds the relationship of sexuality and film. *Sex, lies, and videotape* is a contemporary elaboration of the powerfully erotic monologues in Bergman's *Persona* (1966) and Godard's *Weekend* (1967). When the woman in an early scene of *Weekend* sits on a desk and recounts a convention-strewn pornographic fantasy for her male listener, Godard is showing, with disturbing directness, the way that eroticism is inflected through cultural media. When Alma (Bibi Andersson) tells Elisabet (Liv Ullmann) about her youthful orgy in *Persona*, sexuality only seems to emerge naturally and spontaneously. But after all, this speech is part of Alma's feature-length monologue to a silent actress, and takes place in a film that occasionally starts to burn away. Eroticism seems as if it ought to stand as a central truth of the human condition, as nature's clearest directive, but these overwhelmingly erotic monologues appear in films that are self-reflexive constructions from beginning to end. The mediated, constructed expression of sexuality that Godard and Bergman work through in their different but related ways becomes the denaturalizing impetus that drives *sex, lies, and videotape*.

The film begins in the precincts of marital infidelity, but then moves into much less familiar territory. We soon find that the visiting friend, Graham (James Spader), masturbates to a collection of video interviews with women. Initially, of course, John (Peter Gallagher) and Ann (Andie MacDowell) take this behavior as the height of perversion, but the film clearly wants us not to judge Graham any more harshly than the "normal" married couple. On the contrary, the middle-class lifestyle inhabited by the lawyer John and his frigid wife Ann is seen to be empty, meaningless. Although Graham is rather pathetic, the movie still takes the masturbating, video-watching loner for its hero, in contrast to the cynical lawyer. Graham's house is completely empty except for pictures on the wall, a big television, and videotapes. In other words, Graham leads all too literally the mediated life of the cinephile.

Soderbergh dramatizes cinematic experience most powerfully when John breaks into Graham's house to watch the tape that Ann has just recorded. John locks Graham outside his own apartment, then cues up the tape. As he does this, *sex, lies* cuts back to the moment when Graham and Ann were actually recording the tape. During this whole flashback, then, we watch with the consciousness that Graham is watching this same scene *as a tape.* The recorded nature of film is underlined in this way, with the same emphasis as a monochrome filter. To further the effect, ghostly electronic music plays throughout this section, as if this scene were literally haunted. But the music is not scary because the characters are talking about sex; it is scary because they are inhabiting another world—a world on videotape. Even though the film switches from the flickering videotape that John watches to the clear 35 mm film that we watch, the haunted music works exactly like an orange filter, to denaturalize the scene and our seeing. The entire sequence is tinted with our consciousness that John is watching it with us as a tape. Through this tape recording of sexual confession, the emotional paradox of cinematic presence and absence could not be embodied more determinedly.

For surely this is already Solaris—Graham is aroused by recorded women, not real women. Graham is impotent around actual women, but aroused by the same women on tape. He notes, too, that pornography doesn't work, only his own tapes. Such a plot is emblematic in the extreme, frankly unbelievable, and verges on the science fictional. As in *Solaris,* the ghostly music then reads the science fiction over into something like horror. But this is also the condition of the movie watcher, of the cinephile, who invests himself in recordings of reality rather than reality. As in Tarkovsky, the scenario is almost impossible to believe and yet terrifically powerful. As in Tarkovsky, the model for film watching is also anything but idealistic. Kris's love for his alien, dead wife and Graham's recordings of lying, confessing women are each equally painful to contemplate. The relentless awareness of the surface of the screen is simultaneously compelling and distracting, erotic and nightmarish.

Soderbergh's implicit description of the Solaris effect in *sex, lies, and videotape* is demanding and even excruciating, yet his movie concludes with a stun-

The Solaris Effect

ning evasion. After consistently living on the tortured surface of the screen for the entire film, *sex, lies* attempts to return to grounded reality at the end. After the confrontation with John, Graham comes back inside, breaks up all of his tapes, smashes his camera, and throws everything out the door in a box. Heavy-handedly, this box is labeled "Jim Beam." We are obliged to deduce that Graham is kicking his video habit. At the very end of the film, we see him outside the house, sitting on the steps, having now apparently triumphed over his interiorized former life. Above all, he sits next to Ann, suggesting that he has successfully entered the "real world" of heterosexuality. In a remarkable evasion, *sex, lies, and videotape* thus concludes by, in effect, untinting itself, in a gesture that Soderbergh would never repeat.

Without exception, and with many misgivings, critics noted the complete stylistic shift from *sex, lies, and videotape* to *Kafka* (1991). But *Kafka* is a stronger restatement of the themes of *sex, lies*—and this time there will be no escape. Whereas Graham could just throw his tapes out the door in a whiskey box, Kafka (Jeremy Irons) is trapped permanently in a labyrinthine nightmare. Kafka is not just trapped among literary and existential themes, but among the visual bric-a-brac of movies. *Kafka* is a cinephilic nightmare, but, above all, a brilliantly *flat* cinematic nightmare. As everyone noted, the film is immersed in other films, in the canted cameras and shiny streets of *The Third Man* (accentuated by a zithery harp on the sound track), along with the crazy sets of German expressionism and 1930s Hollywood monster movies. But in the recapitulation of these films, *Kafka* determinedly rejects the baroque (there is only one canted camera for every twenty in *The Third Man*). Critics mistakenly compared *Kafka*'s weirdness to that of David Lynch, while yearning for the excesses of Terry Gilliam's *Brazil* (another dystopia) and of David Cronenberg's *Naked Lunch* (another nightmare with a writer at the center).[5] But *Kafka* purposefully refuses the wide-angle lenses of Gilliam and the ecstatic grotesque of Cronenberg. Such dynamic excesses would be at odds with its desiccated subject. Like the atmospheric images and music in *sex, lies, and videotape*, *Kafka* underscores the emptiness at the heart of cinephilia.

Kafka is also Soderbergh's first authentic "machine." Later on, *Ocean's Eleven* (2001) will give the undeniable appearance of a cinematic machine, yet *Kafka*, with its smooth and relentless gathering of images, may already be characterized as "la machine Soderbergh."[6] Soderbergh's cinephilia is dry, cold, even boring ("For sheer banality the ending takes some beating");[7] there is none of Tim Burton's camp, Peter Greenaway's glitter, or Lynch's exuberance. *Cahiers du cinéma* described the protagonist as "phlegmatically played by the always perfect Jeremy Irons," and *Film Comment* called Irons's underplaying as "phoning it in."[8] In this manner of genre revisionism, Soderbergh shows more than a few affinities with Kubrick, who likes to take horror movies (*The Shining*), war movies (*Full Metal Jacket*), and sex movies (*Eyes Wide Shut*) and make them less scary, less exciting, and less sexy than we might have expected. Just as Kubrick's *2001* is a sci-fi movie with about five minutes of action, *Kafka* is a "noir thriller" with only a few moments of excitement and thrills. *Kafka* collects eccentric styles with what ought to be cinephilic affection, but the overwhelming impression is one of coldness and emptiness.

As the 1990s moved along, Soderbergh, his interviewers, and his critics began to cultivate a narrative of Soderbergh-as-chameleon. Instead of a *Cahiers du cinéma*–style auteur, Soderbergh came to be understood as a director who changed his approach according to each new work at hand. In his interviews Soderbergh invariably repeated the idea that he was not a director who looked to impose his own style on given material, but rather one who hoped instead to find an appropriate style for each project.[9] The model for this career becomes a director like John Huston—toward whom *Cahiers* was always very ambivalent—not Fellini or Antonioni. Soderbergh's third film, *King of the Hill* (1993), so very different in look and tonality from the very adult conversations of *sex, lies, and videotape* as well as the expressionistic angst of *Kafka*, seems to embody our first strong indication that no clear style or theme will attend on Soderbergh's filmmaking, that the adjective "Soderberghian" will never be as meaningful as "Lynchian," "Scorsesian," or "Kubrickian."

Yet *King of the Hill* creates another visually detailed world of fantasy. The teen hero of the film, Aaron Kurlander (Jesse Bradford), surrounds himself with lies as a defense against the felt shame of his family's poverty. Almost everything that he tells the other people around him is fabricated to one extent or another. Aaron's dire circumstances make him much more sympathetic than either John or Graham in *sex, lies, and videotape*, but he is equally disconnected from the social world around him. His fantasies culminate in a scene in which he is so hungry that he eats pictures of food cut out of magazines. He collapses into hallucinations and dreams.

King of the Hill also begins a trend in Soderbergh's filmmaking toward strong tinting or filtering. Ostentatious, extreme filters are at the visual core of films like *The Underneath* and *Traffic*, in which the filters serve to dislocate reality and to remind us of the surface of the screen. Typically, Soderbergh shoots on location (Baton Rouge for *sex, lies, and videotape*; St. Louis for *King of the Hill*; six cities for *Traffic*) and uses naturalistic acting and dialogue. Yet the filtering works at odds with the naturalism by visually insisting that the film is remembering or re-creating these scenes. This paradoxical combination of on-location realism and ostentatious artifice is reminiscent of Godard.[10] Although historically detailed, *King of the Hill* never pretends to be a realistic representation of the Depression. Instead, the film is shot in warm nostalgic colors—brown, yellow, amber—that look forward to the similarly manipulated visuals of the home sequences in Spielberg's *Saving Private Ryan*. Nearly all of Soderbergh's films after this will call attention to themselves as processed visual artifacts, whether through palpable filtering and digital manipulation in the larger films, or by playing with the idea of video texture in smaller-scale films such as *Full Frontal*. *Kafka* turns from black and white to color in its tour through cinematic memory, while *King of the Hill* selects its colors very subjectively, "tainted with nostalgia."[11]

Michael Wilmington's best film list for 1994 included three films that famously experimented with visual texture: Krzysztof Kieslowski's *Three Colors* (*Red* appeared in 1994, and Wilmington chose the trilogy altogether as his best film), Robert Zemeckis's *Forrest Gump*, and Oliver Stone's *Natural Born Killers*.[12] Taken with the digital triumph of Spielberg's *Jurassic Park* in 1993, these films signaled a newfound desire to manipulate the screen with abandon. The real world of Bazin's photographic image seemed, once and for all, to be going up in digital smoke. In Chapter Five I will discuss the advent of digital filmmaking and reflect on how that technology influences the Solaris effect. For now, I will pause for a moment to compare Soderbergh's work with film texture to that of Oliver Stone. For it was Stone who, at the time, seemed much more obviously to be testing out what the American movie screen would contain.

Oliver Stone sees himself as an entirely self-conscious filmmaker, and often refers to himself as a film "deconstructionist." The question asked in his historical films *JFK* (1991) and *Nixon* (1996) is, he says, "What is the past?"

> We as dramatists are undertaking a deconstruction of history, questioning some of the given realities. [Mine is] an ambivalent shifting style that makes people aware that they are watching a movie and that reality itself is in question.[13]

In *JFK*, Stone switches back and forth so rapidly from documentary footage to re-created counterfeit documentary that it can be hard to tell which is which. *Natural Born Killers* (1994) constantly changes film stock—16 mm black and white, 35 mm black and white, 35 mm color, 8 mm color—while driving the killers in front of crazy back projections, and even showing a rapidly cut history of the twentieth century through Mickey and Mallory's motel room window. Home movies (8 mm) are often used to evoke "the real," to create a documentary effect, and in Chapter Seven I will discuss a number of contemporary directors who follow the practice of Derek Jarman in this respect. But none of the film stocks in *Natural Born Killers* seem to occupy anything close to reality. On the contrary, switching from one stock to another seems to be merely one more special effect that embodies the film's impatience with holding still. Switching film stocks in *Natural Born Killers* has little to do with cinematic reality, but much to do with cinematic speed; it is the logical extension of the documentary texture in *JFK*, and shows where Stone's emphasis truly lies.

Speed is the main lesson that Stone seems to have learned from Godard's *Breathless.* "The movie that most influenced me as a filmmaker, to *be* a filmmaker, was Godard's *Breathless*, because it was fast, anarchic," said Stone in an interview. "I'm into anarchy."[14] But *Breathless* brilliantly juxtaposes cinematic genre conventions with neorealistic documentary. There are the many famous jump cuts, but there are also scenes, such as those in the travel agency and in the newspaper office, entirely made out of patient, circular tracking shots. "Anarchy" is about the least subtle way to describe what happens cinematically in *Breathless*. Although Stone invokes Godard from time to time in interviews, and his self-reflexive political films make him seem like a contemporary American Godard, his films leave an extremely different impression. "Movies have always existed to me as illusion," says Stone, "I've always accepted them as such."[15] But Godard's films cycle between reality and illusion. Stone's films do not test out the loop between artifice and reality that constitutes the Solaris effect.

An extended MTV video, *Natural Born Killers* does not touch down for a moment in the real world. Like Darren Aronofsky's *Requiem For a Dream*, it moralizes about the American nightmare while using the excitement of that nightmare to propel its own roller coaster. *JFK*, too, does not so much question reality—by which Stone means questioning accepted academic historical explanations—as provide its own alternative reality. Stone felt obliged to construct a coherent plot for both *JFK* and *Nixon*, even though life and history were thereby left behind. "You cannot string together a movie from a series of random, interesting facts. You have to have a pattern, a theme."[16] Hence, despite the myriad gestures of self-reflexivity and the manifest political urgency in Stone's films, his work is still governed by a very conventional sense of narrative and character. Stone may look experimental compared with

Zemeckis, but his cinema has nothing to do with Godard's.[17] He gives the American mainstream audience what it wants regarding plot, character, violence, and speed. In its ponderous slowness and weird casting (British actor Anthony Hopkins as the American president), *Nixon* is probably Stone's most challenging film. But the legacy of *JFK* and *Natural Born Killers* is to be found in video games.

Thus I will make the somewhat odd historical claim that Soderbergh's *The Underneath* (1995) is a more significant contribution to the visual development of American film than Stone's *Natural Born Killers*. And even though it has been relatively invisible to film critics, *The Underneath* is also a central film in the development of Soderbergh's career. The greenish tinting is extraordinarily present; this is not a shy nostalgic yellow or sepia. The radical tinting of *The Underneath* is in part an attempt to find a color equivalent to the chiaroscuro of 1950s film noir. Lars von Trier sought a similar effect in *The Element of Crime* (1984) when he doused his postmodern noir in a magnificently orange palette. *The Element of Crime* is orange noir from beginning to end, but Soderbergh's *Underneath* is green noir only in the robbery sections. In this shaping, *The Underneath* follows the atmospheric logic of film noir. Slavoj Zizek notes that the big robbery in caper films "as a rule is presented as a fantasmatic scene: all of a sudden, everyday 'reality' is suspended, we seem to enter another, ethereal dimension."[18] And Zizek continues, "We cannot conceive of both domains [the traumatic and the everyday] as belonging to the same reality."[19] *The Underneath* seems to have separated out by color the intensity of the bank robbery from the relative clarity of ordinary life.

Yet we saw flickering video merge with ghostly 35 mm in *sex, lies, and videotape*, and the color scheme of *The Underneath* is more complicated than the description above will allow. For one thing, the film begins immediately in a heavy green filter, which means that our footing is unstable from the start. What is going on? Are we looking at the characters through night-vision goggles?[20] "Normal" has yet to be established, and it will take awhile to figure out what the rules are. But then Soderbergh also puts a sculpture of colored glass squares in the family's "everyday" house. The camera will sometimes shoot through these squares, which thus themselves become color filters, coloring the "normal" world as much as the green filtering does the "traumatic." When we cut from the second green section back to home, there is essentially no transition: there is a lotto sign at a gas station in the green world, then the same lotto sign reproduced in a newspaper at home; we cut from green Michael on bank-robbery day to Michael shot through the exact same green at home. Throughout the film we find preternatural numbers of green windows—on the armored truck and in the office.

So there is no enormous difference between the layers of time after all; everything is haunted, brooding. And soon parts of the "ordinary" world start to get shot through blue filters. When the final crisscross takes place, in a cabin out in the woods, there are two emblematic lamps, one with a green shade, one with a blue. Every light in the film, this lamp seems to say, comes with its own color filter. The significance of these filters derives from a conception of cinema that has to do with absence and emptiness, in distinct contrast to the special-effects velocity that attends on Oliver Stone's film textures.

The Underneath also signals the beginning of Soderbergh's strong impulse to do remakes, a tendency that will continue through his version of *Solaris*. *Ocean's Eleven* comes very loosely out of the 1960 Rat Pack movie of the same name, and *Traffic* follows on a six-part BBC television miniseries. *Kafka* and *Schizopolis* are not remakes, but are intentionally immersed in palpable styles, following *The Third Man* and the comedies of Richard Lester, respectively. The Hollywood remake is usually aligned with the desire to exploit success: if it made money once, do it again. But for Soderbergh the remake is another way to indicate the absent presence of films. A remake is automatically haunted by the past; a remake empties out authorial originality. *The Underneath* is a remake of Robert Siodmak's *Criss Cross* (1949), starring Burt Lancaster, Yvonne de Carlo, and Dan Duryea. As will be the case with Soderbergh's *Solaris*, the credits for *The Underneath* say only that the film came from the novel (by Stanislaw Lem for *Solaris*, by Don Tracy for *Criss Cross*), even though whole scenes in Soderbergh are very similar to scenes in Siodmak (and later on, Tarkovsky). There are numerous alterations and updates, but also a clear sense that we are moving through very similar terrain.

Soderbergh doubles the theme of repetition that already attends on a remake by choosing remakes that focus on an ex-wife. The *Solaris* return of Hari is foreshadowed in *The Underneath*, in which Steven and Rachel may get back together, and also in *Ocean's Eleven*, in which George Clooney's character regains the affections of his ex-wife (Julia Roberts). In *The Underneath*, Steven needs to save Rachel from her "bad" husband, Tommy, while Clooney in *Ocean's Eleven* needs to save Julia Roberts from bad husband Andy Garcia. The motif of the ex-wife is not just a detail personal to Soderbergh (although it is that, since his ex-wife plays his character's wife in *Schizopolis*). But more than this, the plot involving the return of an ex-wife has itself become a crucial film genre, and not just in the classic screwball comedies that Stanley Cavell treats in *Pursuits of Happiness: The Hollywood Comedy of Remarriage.*[21] The re-marriage plot in Soderbergh brings with it the Solaris effect, the present desire and the broken love of the cinephile. In Bazinian terms, the photograph or the film captures the past, and the remarriage plot seeks to recapture the past as well. Soderbergh's remakes, which are built out of remarriage plots, thus double and treble a Solaris emphasis on film's haunted desire.

The crisscrossing of time zones and the endless betrayal of one character after another in *The Underneath* desubstantializes both time and space on the screen. Cliff Martinez once again supplies ghostly electronic music, which contrasts with the more upbeat rock-and-roll sound tracks of many thrillers. "You're not very present tense," says Rachel to compulsive gambler Michael, and that is surely the sense of the film. People are there on the screen, but they aren't there; "I feel you're somewhere else," she says. In Rachel's concluding speech, she tells Michael that he should never have come back and that she will now leave too. "There is something very powerful about being absent," she tells him. From title to plot to music, Soderbergh's *Underneath* reminds us everywhere of the absent presence of film.

"The underneath," most literally, says that beneath everything is Michael's earlier betrayal of Rachel. That is the bottom line: a betrayal in the past. So ghosts are everywhere. *The Underneath* is haunted by these ghosts of the past, and also cinephilic ghosts. In a late scene Michael becomes anxious that the vengeful gangster will try to kill him in his hospital bed, so he calls the nurse. This scene quotes Siodmak's film almost verbatim. But Soderbergh doubles the cinephilic haunting by casting Shelley Duvall as the nurse. Cinephilic rec-ognition entirely shatters the suspense of the scene. For the sake of suspense, Soderbergh should have put no one in particular there, and important parts in the rest of the film are played by unheralded actors. Yet here is Shelley Du-vall in a cameo, reminding us in general of the past (she is noticeably elderly) and of particular movies like Robert Altman's *Three Women* (1977), in which she plays a nurse. Is this a thriller or a ghost story? The present-tense thriller is continually betrayed by ghosts from the past.

Disappearing and Reappearing: From *Schizopolis* to *K Street*

Soderbergh's career began in glory but quickly ran aground. The heights of *sex, lies, and videotape,* which made Soderbergh instantly famous, were matched by the depths of *The Underneath,* which vanished quickly into oblivion. In *Getting Away with It: Or, the Further Adventures of the Luckiest Bastard You Ever Saw,*

Soderbergh details this strange moment in his life when he was directing a Spalding Gray monologue for film (*Gray's Anatomy*, 1995), working on various scripts, and producing Greg Mottola's *Daytrippers* (1996).[22] At this juncture, Soderbergh's career looked particularly amorphous. *Getting Away with It* consists not only of journal entries, but also of extended interviews with the British director Richard Lester. In films like *A Hard Day's Night* (1964) and *The Knack . . . and How to Get It* (1965), Lester made extraordinarily lively contributions to the 1960s British film scene. Soderbergh found career-renewing inspiration in the spontaneity and bravery of Lester's comedies, and he immediately set to work on *Schizopolis*. Two years later, one director after another bowed out of a major Hollywood project, and Soderbergh found himself signed onto *Out of Sight*. He would then continue to go back and forth between big films and small films up to the time he remade *Solaris*.

Schizopolis (1997) is a low-budget experimental comedy that weirds around for a while and then suddenly turns into *Solaris*. Emblazoned with "independence" at every turn, *Schizopolis* stars Soderbergh himself, features no other recognizable actors, and contains only location shots—there are no built sets and no indication of any budget whatsoever. If *Kafka* is a flattened-out version of *The Third Man*, *Schizopolis* is a flattened-out version of a Richard Lester comedy. The film plays self-consciously with the idea that this is Soderbergh's "most personal film"; not long after the opening, Soderbergh's character masturbates hurriedly in an office bathroom. The sequences wander back and forth between an office conspiracy, a terminally boring marriage, and a man who is decked out in a jumpsuit and goggles and goes around attacking people. The jumpsuited man has clearly descended from a meandering sixties farce. The scenes that show the grinding routine of middle-class marriage look forward to the more gruesome depictions by Todd Solondz; both Soderbergh and Solondz associate Muzak with the mind-numbing world of the middle class. And a comparison with Solondz shows how Soderbergh chooses against the baroque, against extremes. Whereas Solondz dares us to laugh at child rape (*Happiness*, 1998) or anal rape (*Storytelling*, 2002), Soderbergh's comedy willfully inhabits a low key. It satirizes the middle class, but not by going over the top. The satire of Solondz is absolutely vicious; we sense a wellspring of savage anger beneath each of his films. The satire of Soderbergh seems, by contrast, mostly silly and ultimately empty. But once again this is an effective, powerful emptiness that speaks to the condition of film.

The Solaris effect is confirmed when *Schizopolis*, almost anagrammatically, swaps around a couple of its plots and leaves us suddenly in the middle of

Solaris. Soderbergh is an office drudge at the beginning of the movie, haplessly writing a speech for a New Age philosopher named Azimuth Schwitters. Schwitters looks rather like Soderbergh, but not as much as Soderbergh himself does. Halfway through the film Soderbergh appears in a new character as a dentist. Now, the bored wife of Soderbergh-the-office-drudge leaves him for Soderbergh-the-dentist. "I'm having an affair with my wife," says the dentist. After a while the two Soderberghs become differentiated linguistically; one speaks Japanese, and the other Italian. One of Soderbergh's comic points is that no matter what either of them says, it is certainly so unremarkable that they may as well be speaking other languages. Soon the wife is offended by the dentist ("you worm!") and meets yet another Soderbergh, this one dubbed in French.

In this version of *Solaris*, the wife (played by Soderbergh's ex-wife, Betsy Brantley) meets the same man everywhere while trying to escape the previous incarnation. This confined repetition is felt as dull torture, not romantic torment, but it does show us that Soderbergh, like Tarkovsky, is using the same language of fantasy and love's betrayal to frame cinematic self-consciousness. That the various Soderberghs, for example, are dubbed in Japanese, Italian, and French is a purely cinematic joke. For these are the languages of classic art film, and the dubbing is something a cinephile can only loathe. *Schizopolis* is partly a social satire on middle-class conventions, but it is more clearly a personal characterization of cinematic elements. The love affairs of the Soderberghs not only show us the interchangeable tedium of middle-class affairs, but also stand as a *Solaris*-style allegory on the condition of filmmaking. Tarkovsky's tragic *Solaris* sees film as profound and profoundly evanescent, whereas Soderbergh's comic *Schizopolis* emphasizes the onanistic, confined emptiness of film. Yet these films are not as distant from each other as they may appear.

The Hollywood films in this section of Soderbergh's career are not so thematically obsessive, yet some of the signature Solaris motifs continue to appear. Soderbergh's first big commercial hit, *Out of Sight* (1998), enacts an Elmore Leonard version of the Solaris plot. Jack Foley (George Clooney) is a career bank robber and Karen Sisco (Jennifer Lopez) is an FBI agent, so this love is doomed from the start. *Ocean's Eleven* (2001) is another Soderbergh film that belongs to Stanley Cavell's "Hollywood comedies of remarriage." Like Cary Grant in *The Philadelphia Story* and *His Girl Friday,* George Clooney aims to win his wife back from a dour, overly serious husband. *Erin Brockovich* (2000) brilliantly juxtaposes the situated realism of a working-class environment with the self-conscious deployment of Julia Roberts as a star. Her outfit throughout the film — push-up bra, miniskirt, spike heels — is an outrage to the film's low-key realism, even if it is in fact somewhat accurate.[23] Even though Soderbergh has hired himself out for all of these large-budget films, the Solaris motifs remain in evidence, though muted. It should not come as a surprise that the more control Soderbergh has over the picture, the more we will sense Solaris.

The Limey (1999) is Soderbergh's most beautiful Solaris thriller. Dave Wilson (Terence Stamp), a hardened criminal, seeks revenge for what he assumes is his daughter's murder. But he really does not know what happened to her, except that she died in a car accident during a relationship with Terry Valentine (Peter Fonda). Wilson's voice-over, "Tell me about Jenny," begins the movie while the screen is still black. The movie is cut to emphasize Wilson's interiority; it is a father's imagination that has sent him on this mission.[24] Thus the film inserts flashbacks of his young daughter on the beach, but also cuts the narrative out of order, continuing, for example, to find Wilson on a plane or in a hotel room when he has long since left these places. Most remarkably, Soderbergh often cuts the dialogue between two characters into several different locations. The dialogue makes perfect sense, but the background swaps out with each new speaker. It may be that three different conversations have been spliced together, which is odd enough, but the effect is quite surrealistic, and the dialogues seem to occur in a purely imaginative sphere. The frequent use of asynchronous sound (we hear dialogue but nobody on the screen is talking), fantasy flash-forwards (Wilson imagines shooting Valentine several times), and these dislocating edits desubstantialize the thriller, turning Terence Stamp's character into an angry ghost.

The Limey is, indeed, another cinephilic ghost story. As in Kafka, however, nostalgic cinephilia is also fiercely complicated and critiqued. Terence Stamp's character flashes back to his youth from time to time, and the past is visualized with clips from Stamp's movie Poor Cow (Loach, 1967). The music in The Limey is all '60s and '70s rock, even though the locations are all contemporary. Terence Stamp the actor is haunted by his status as a 1960s British movie idol, and this haunting is doubled by casting Peter Fonda as his nemesis. Valentine (Fonda), a music producer, talks about his days on a motorcycle and the golden days of the 1960s. A cinephile's slugfest takes place at the end, then, when Stamp, the star of '60s films such as Pasolini's Teorema (1968) and Fonda, the star of Dennis Hopper's Easy Rider (1969), wrestle together on the beach. But here The Limey also proposes a striking contrast between the seething, vengeful anger of Stamp's Dave Wilson and the ironies that mitigate our cinephilic nostalgia. That is, Wilson's mourning for his daughter is pitched much more emotionally than the film's mourning for the 1960s. At one point, for example, Fonda's character deidealizes the decade by saying that the 1960s were only 1966 and part of 1967. And the period music is relatively conventional, even boring. Cinematic nostalgia is thereby distanced. Even as cinephilia approaches, it is pushed away.

Traffic (2000) is another Soderberghian dream vision, which this time desubstantializes the war on drugs. *Sight and Sound* criticized Soderbergh for refusing to enter into the subjective experience of drug taking (unlike Tarantino, Aronofsky, and P. T. Anderson) and for sticking to a "naturalistic" point of view.[25] But when one section is tinted yellow and one section is blue, the film's aesthetics can scarcely be described as naturalistic. The realistic components (jittery handheld camera, on-location detail, various sorts of jargon) are immersed in radical tinting and, once again, atmospheric music. The movie thus dreams itself into an artificially constructed space. Narrative ellipses are rendered through overquick scenes and jump cuts; the music covers up the most theatrical events (an execution, a car bomb) and holds the disparate plots together with a drifting, electronic hum. *Traffic* moves along with the dislocated continuity of a dream, realistic in many respects, but distant from that reality as well. The effect is very similar to Ridley Scott's *Black Hawk Down* (2001), which is realistic in its narrative and detail, but so vehemently tinted and recolored that every visual reminds us that the film images are re-creating an event. The blue and yellow filters of *Traffic* similarly remind us that this is a filmed reality.

Soderbergh jokingly calls *Traffic* a "Hollywood Dogma film," which does not make too much sense taken literally, but more generally does account well for the paradoxical nature of the movie.[26] A main point of Dogma in its original formulation is to remove special effects—so there are no tinted Dogma movies! Contrary to the dictates of Dogma, Soderbergh's image is thoroughly manipulated: the yellow filters in Mexico are combined with a shutter speed that makes the images almost stroboscopic.[27] What is more, the filters are deployed with a formalism that completely contradicts any documentary-style realism. Although the blue filter may or may not accompany the action in Ohio and Washington, the yellow filter always washes out any scene in Mexico. In one instance, Michael Douglas looks across the border; Mexico is shot yellow from his point of view, but the reverse shot at him is transparent. The way reality cycles back through the most blatant deployment of artifice makes *Traffic* closer to some aspects of Godard than Dogma. But it *is* a

Hollywood Dogma film—or at least a Hollywood independent film—insofar as it works with Hollywood actors in a way that is rarely ever seen. As Patrice Blouin points out in *Cahiers du cinéma*, both the stars and the unknowns in *Traffic* receive the same cinematic treatment.[28] Michael Douglas has only a few moments of standard Hollywood-style heroism (when he drags his daughter's boyfriend out of class, for example, the film alludes to Douglas's psychotic vendetta in *Falling Down* [Schumacher, 1993]). But his character's final gesture is simply to abandon his office as national drug czar, a gesture that is almost incomprehensible on Hollywood's terms.

Full Frontal (2002) immediately followed *Ocean's Eleven*, an experimental small-scale pendant to the big-budget studio thriller. The title has no particular relation to the film, but may rather be taken as a sign that this is Soderbergh's most personal film after *Schizopolis*, with nothing hidden from view. Everything is there, open to exposure, including a philosophy of film. *Full Frontal* was ripped apart by reviewers, who wanted more *Out of Sight* and no more *Schizopolis*. But *Full Frontal* is another captivating experiment, and it helps us understand how Soderbergh thinks of the nature and possibility of film. In its deliberate cinematic self-consciousness, it is as important for a consideration of his career as Lynch's *Mulholland Drive* and Altman's *The Player* are for an understanding of theirs.

Like Altman and Lynch, Soderbergh cuts back and forth between a movie (here called *Rendezvous*) and several layers of reality. A film like *The French Lieutenant's Woman* (Reisz, 1981) uses this structure most clearly, in which the richness of Victorian romance contrasts with the relative wreck of modern relationships. We figure out where Altman's *The Player* is only at the very end, as a kind of punch line. Both Soderbergh and Lynch layer film and reality much more complicatedly than Altman and Reisz; Lynch in *Mulholland Drive* declines to give any explanation as to what's what, and the DVD commentary for *Full Frontal* reveals that Soderbergh and his screenwriter, Coleman Hough, do not even agree between themselves where the layers of reality are. *Mulholland Drive* and *Full Frontal* both contrast the idealizations of Hollywood with the ugly relations of everyday life. But neither director allows independent film an easy victory over Hollywood in this contrast. For all of their satire on Hollywood, both *Mulholland Drive* and *Full Frontal* are much more deeply about the nature of film in general.

Full Frontal contrasts a parody movie called *Rendezvous*—complete with fake opening credits—to a real-world set of characters who lead far less attractive lives. Soderbergh describes *Rendezvous* as a "meet-cute romantic comedy," and he shoots that movie in 35 mm. By contrast, the more realistic layers of the world are shot in digital video and look like home movies—grainy, badly lit, shot with a handheld camera, erratically edited. But *Full Frontal* ends by finally backing out of an airplane set with "real" characters in it, to underscore that they too are just characters in a movie. This is not a surprise ending, as in Altman, but rather the final punctuation of a thematic emphasis—that all the stories are filmed constructions.[29] Blue is no more "real" than yellow in *Traffic*, and digital video is not more real than 35 mm in *Full Frontal*.

As in Tarkovsky's *Solaris*, human relationships model the cinematic experience. Everyone in *Full Frontal* has what Soderbergh calls "connection issues." Technology and bureaucracy are visually present throughout as we move through a world of offices, cell phones, television monitors, and references to the Internet. Many dialogue scenes play as interviews, a favorite form for Soderbergh. The interview has an important place in film history, not only in documentary film, but also in films that purposely relate themselves to such traditions, such as Fellini's *Intervista* (1987). In films like *Masculine-Feminine* (1966) and *Two or Three Things I Know about Her* (1967), Godard specializes in dialogue scenes that are actually interviews. Many of the dialogues in *Full Frontal* emphasize unequal power, and the interview format shows us who is in charge. There are literal interviews in the human-resources office, where Lee (Catherine Keener) tortures her prospects with absurd questions and requests. Carl (David Hyde Pierce) is fired because he can't tell his boss the right answer to the question, "How do you drink your beer?" *The Sound and the Führer* is the experimental play-within-the-movie, sending up Hitler in a much drier version of Mel Brooks's *Producers*, but the actor who plays Hitler is a little dictator himself, and bosses around the play's director. There is real emotion in some scenes, and between certain characters, but there is also palpable distance, isolation, and unequal power. These relationships, both romantic and alienated, fulsome and empty, mirror the power of cinema over us, its transient but fierce tyranny.

Soderbergh's *Solaris* (2002) did not conclude his interest in working through Solaris themes and ideas. *K Street* (2003), a ten-episode television series for HBO, summarizes practically every aspect of his career and nearly every ramification of the Solaris effect. *K Street* finds its occasion in a representation of the Washington, D.C. lobbyist scene during the summer and fall of 2002. *K Street* goes back and forth between documentary and fiction by juxtaposing mostly unknown actors with recognizable senators and congressmen from Capitol Hill. There is little plot, music is rarely heard on the sound track, and the dialogue appears improvised (no scriptwriter is credited). Yet Soderbergh also foregrounds fiction and narration from time to time by introducing flamboyant flashbacks ("Flashback #2" says a title card, with determined awkwardness, to begin episode nine). To emphasize the fictional side of things, a main character in episodes four and nine is Elliott Gould, now a completely recognizable movie star. The two central characters of the series are James Carville and Mary Matalin, who are "themselves," and who seem to be going about their daily routines, but are also well known from their appearances on CNN. Carville looks most of the time just as he did in *The War Room* (Hegedus and Pennebaker, 1993), a documentary about the Clinton candidacy. Is Carville a real person or an actor on television? The discussions of oil, the Middle East, power, and influence make television shows like *The West Wing*, with their prepackaged debates, look like cartoons. Yet clearly *K Street* is not a documentary and proceeds to self-consciously show its artifice at every turn. Soderbergh signals the movement between fiction and documentary in the very first shot: we look through a handheld camera (realism) while the screen is ostentatiously tinted brown (artifice).

The movement between realism and artifice is grounded in the particularities of the situation. Washington, D.C. itself seems to constantly turn between reality and fabrication, and the lobbyists do their best to spin reality this way and that. But Soderbergh describes the condition of the image once more through couples—this time through two couples. As in Soderbergh's *Solaris*, the wreck of "now" is juxtaposed with a potentially happier "then." In the present, Maggie has broken up with her girlfriend, Gail, and Tommy's marriage to Sara is falling apart. The Solaris effect compares the tenuous nature of screen existence with the instability of love. *K Street* tells the story not only of the lobbying firm, but also of these two fragile couples. At the very end of the series, it looks as if the two women might be getting back together. But Tommy's a goner. A lobbyist with his head in CNN all day, Tommy is lost in a world of images. Tommy's wife has recently found porno tapes that she told him to get rid of, and he visits prostitutes late at night. He sleeps with a woman in a red dress, Anna, who commits suicide in their hotel room. Afterward we see her haunt him as a ghost. In the very last image of "today" in episode ten, we see a red shape come between Tommy and ourselves, as if the ghost, the woman in red, has gained such substance. We know that she cannot be real, but there she is. The red ghost of Anna stands in for the now red planet of Solaris.

The publicity company is owned by the mysterious Berkowitz (Gould), who is said to watch *Mildred Pierce* (Curtiz, 1945) all day long. At the very end of the series Berkowitz finally emerges from his apartment; the man who meets him at the station holds a sign that says "M. Pierce." That the owner of this business is obsessed by old movies turns yet another loop in the endless cycle between reality and image. That the most recognizable film star in the television series plays a character who hides in an apartment all day also multiplies these themes. But above all, *Mildred Pierce* stands as another ur-*Solaris* film, in which Mildred Pierce (Joan Crawford) begins the film next to the body of her second husband and ends the film standing next to her first husband. Instead of Stanley Cavell's comedy of remarriage, *Mildred Pierce* is a melodramatic film noir of remarriage, in which we see Mildred (once the chronology is straightened out) go from the first husband to the second husband, then back to the first. Most of the film is told in two extended flashbacks, so time is always split between past and present, and we are never sure if Mildred is telling the police the truth. The absent Gould runs his company while watching this classic movie of divorce and remarriage over and over. Apparently it is not only Gould's character who is obsessed with this plot, but Soderbergh as well.

Soderbergh's *Solaris* and the Empty Image

The credits of Soderbergh's *Solaris* say that the movie is "based on the book by Stanislaw Lem." In interviews Soderbergh has repeatedly said that he adapted the movie from Lem's novel and certainly not from Tarkovsky's film: one does not remake a cinematic masterpiece. Since we know how fast and loose Tarkovsky played with his source material—to Lem's profound annoyance —it would seem quite reasonable to make a *Solaris* that followed the novel more closely. Yet we should observe straightaway that Soderbergh's interview remarks concerning Tarkovsky are disingenuous and that the official script credit verges on deceit. For Soderbergh's *Solaris is* a remake of Tarkovsky's film, and a much more interesting film if read that way. The screenplay credit that appears on the DVD is more honest. It says "based on the novel by Stanislaw Lem and the script by Fridrikh Gorenshtein and Andrei Tarkovsky."

In some respects Soderbergh's *Solaris* is almost as hyperdeliberate in its quotations of Tarkovsky as Gus Van Sant's *Psycho* (1998) is in its quotations of Hitchcock. Soderbergh's film begins with rain, and it continues to rain for the whole opening sequence. A movie that is called *Solaris* and that starts with rain has rain from Tarkovsky, not Lem. It rains on and off in the opening section of Tarkovsky's *Solaris*, and through so many of Tarkovsky's films that rain amounts to a visual signature.[30] Numerous visual elements of Tarkovsky's film were transposed to Soderbergh's, not the least of which is George Clooney's large round rugged head topped with short black hair, a head that bears a strong resemblance to that of Donatas Banionis, the original Kris. And Natascha McElhone is also not so far away from Natalya Bondarchuk, considering all the other casting possibilities.

Entire sequences in Soderbergh are directly borrowed from Tarkovsky. At one point late in both films, for example, the camera pans around the room to find one Hari after another. The most Tarkovskian element in Soderbergh's remake is actually not even in Tarkovsky's film. Tarkovsky, who was the son of the poet Arseny Tarkovsky and who so often spoke of cinematic poetry in his essays, famously included poems in many of his films — in *Stalker, The Mirror,* and *Nostalghia.*[31] In a poignant addition, Soderbergh repeatedly makes use of a Dylan Thomas poem ("And death shall have no dominion"), and takes the time at one point to have it read it all the way through. This poem, along with all the other visual recollections, signals a total immersion in Tarkovsky. Soderbergh's *Solaris* is as much a cinematic replicant as Hari.

Yet even as Soderbergh has drastically shortened his film relative to Tarkovsky's, he has also clarified and refined many elements of the earlier film. For one, Soderbergh's spaceship is about the most artificial spaceship ever conceived. There is nothing in it. Tarkovsky's spaceship was cluttered with earthly artifacts: paintings, notebooks, potted plants. But Soderbergh's ship does not even pretend to be lived in. The walls are smooth, shiny metallic grey, interrupted only by mounted television monitors. There are very few personal effects visible, which we see even inside the equally shiny spaceship of Kubrick's *2001*. The brand names placed all over the interiors and airports of *2001* and *Minority Report* are conspicuously absent. The shiny blankness emphasizes all the more what a dream screen Soderbergh's spaceship is, that the film's fantasies are not just romantic but cinematic. Soderbergh vacuums out Tarkovsky's spaceship to make the cinematic subtext even more apparent.

The imagelessness associated with Soderbergh's spaceship is commented on explicitly at several points in the film. In an early scene, the psychologist, Kris, leads a grief counseling group; one of the participants shares a sense of being inundated by images: "I see the TV, and see the Internet, and I see those T-shirts, and I feel nothing. The more I see the images, the less I feel, the less I believe that it's real." This description helps us understand why Kris has arranged his own life as he has. Here is how Rheya (Hari) remembers his apartment: "It's dark, very, very dark. And there are no paintings on the wall. No pictures anywhere. No pictures on the fridge, even . . . which I always thought was a bit strange."

Before he meets Rheya, Kris has tried to arrange a world without imagery, without illusion. Yet in the final sequence, which takes place we know not where (it looks like earth, but he seemed to plummet into Solaris on the spaceship just moments before), he has a photograph of Rheya stuck on the fridge. The image, and the film, may not be true, but it is necessary, or inescapable. Godard's films always analyze images and imagery, whatever else they may be doing.[32] Soderbergh's *Solaris*, too, in its own way, self-consciously enacts a discussion about the status of images.

Soderbergh adds a couple of important plot elements to Tarkovsky's version, one of which comes from Lem and one which is of his own devising. In Soderbergh, as in Lem, Kris is visited on the spaceship by Gibarian, the astronaut who committed suicide. In Soderbergh, as in Lem, we cannot be sure whether this Gibarian is merely dreamed by Kris or if he is a full-fledged "visitor," a ghost just like Rheya, courtesy of Solaris. In Lem and Soderbergh, this is the scene that precedes Rheya's attempt to commit suicide by drinking liquid oxygen. Whereas Tarkovsky plots the suicide attempt after the levitation in the library, Soderbergh sets down one suicide after another, Gibarian next to Rheya. During his ghostly visit, Gibarian tells Kris that his suicide might have been a mistake, but then Rheya, who has already killed herself in human form, tries to kill herself again. The juxtaposition of Gibarian with Rheya in Soderbergh emphasizes questions of inevitability and predetermination. Were their suicides inevitable? Can time be redeemed? And the juxtaposition also emphasizes the isolated, even suicidal feel of Soderbergh's film. Whereas Tarkovsky's Kris returns to his father and mother, who are at least as important as Hari by the end, Soderbergh's Kris is notably isolated, alone in his imageless apartment. There are no parents in Soderbergh's version. And when Soderbergh's Kris returns to Earth, it looks for all the world like a suicide. At the end Kris refuses to go into the shuttle with Dr. Helen Gordon (Viola Davis), choosing instead to stay on the space station with Snow (Jeremy Davies) while the station falls into Solaris in a shower of lights. Kris has been overwhelmed with guilt following Rheya's suicide on Earth, but instead of saving her life in her next life, he ends up choosing a form of suicide himself. He cannot change the narrative of suicide, it seems, although he may change its interpretation.

Soderbergh's crew also stands as a substantial revision of Tarkovsky's, and in these changes Lem is not a precedent. In Tarkovsky and Lem the alien nature of Hari-Rheya is highlighted through her contrast with the male astronauts. She is Other as alien, but also as woman. When the astronauts gather together to discuss her fate in Tarkovsky, it is a male conclave deciding the fate of an isolated supernatural woman, and not so very far away from Dreyer's Joan of Arc. Soderbergh, however, significantly alters the composition of the crew. First, he makes Dr. Snauth, a white male, into Dr. Gordon, a black woman. In such a small crew, this casting of the new Dr. Gordon is not a gesture of tokenism, as it seems to be for a character like *Star Trek*'s Uhuru. On the contrary, this recasting powerfully complicates the crew's relationship to the alien, and Dr. Gordon herself comments self-consciously on her social status.

What is more, Snow himself will, at the end, turn out to be another alien simulacrum, just like Rheya. In one sense this looks merely to be a plot twist: surprise! The body of the real Snow is stowed away in the freezer. But the switch leaves a more lasting impression, is more than mere peripety. The large-scale effect is to reduce the sense that humans are radically distinct from aliens or that we outnumber them. On Soderbergh's ship there are two humans and two aliens. Both Tarkovsky and Soderbergh end up at a desired home by using Solaris to dream that home, but Soderbergh's seems much more otherwordly. Soderbergh's reunion in Kris's shining kitchen seems more intergalactically cold and abstract than the dreamt details of Tarkovsky's dacha. With Rheya's picture taped to the refrigerator door, Soderbergh's *Solaris* seems most evidently to evidence the epigraph by Godard with which we began. "The image, sir, alone capable of denying nothingness, is also the gaze of nothingness on us."

Just as in *The Underneath,* in which Soderbergh added a remembered background plot to Siodmak's *Criss Cross,* his *Solaris* expands on Tarkovsky by visualizing concretely the remembered past. Whereas Tarkovsky keeps the past relationship of Kris and Hari completely vague, Soderbergh flashes back frequently to earlier times when they were together. Yet in both *The Underneath* and *Solaris,* Soderbergh shows us a very rocky relationship in the couple's past. Even though the first meeting of Kris and Rheya is a storybook idyll, soon they are on edge with each other, and then arguing furiously. In one respect the flashbacks serve to clarify character and plot: in both *The Underneath* and *Solaris* we can see where the romance came from, as well as the conflict and suicide. But the memories also serve, paradoxically, to make memory less concrete. When Soderbergh described *The Limey* as "*Get Carter* plus Resnais," he implied that the memories were subjective and even contradictory, as in *Last Year at Marienbad.*[33] So that the scenes elaborated by memory in *Solaris* both explicate and destabilize character. Rheya is completely split apart by memory: "I have a memory of this, but I don't remember being there." As a simulacrum, she was there in memory, but never there in reality. "I'm not the person I remember," she says. She has been selected by Kris's memory, as she objects to him on several occasions. "My memory is under your control," she says. What Kris remembers are the milestones: first meeting, marriage proposal, making love, quarreling, her suicide. But she says that she is suicidal only because he remembers her that way. This is why Kris says, "I was haunted by the fact that I may have remembered her wrong." And this is the ghost's objection, too.

In *Solaris* both Earth and spaceship are tinted worlds. Scenes on Earth are strongly tinted brown, whether in the past or the present. The color may allude to the extraordinary brown in which Hari first appears in Tarkovsky's *Solaris*, one of the most beautiful entrances in all of film. Or it may simply stand as an earth color, an aspect of nature, in a world where otherwise only the rain seems earthly. Because everything on the ship is either silver or gray, the spaceship is, in effect, tinted, in a vastly reduced palette. The grey insists that this space station is a dream space, between night and day. *Solaris* goes back and forth between the brown world and the gray world, between past and present, Earth and space station, yet both worlds are equally dark, and a bright color scarcely ever breaks through. In the end, neither world is more real or more natural than the other. Both worlds restrict our seeing by limiting the color. Both worlds are places where images either run rampant or are strikingly absent.

Faces peer out of the emptiness in Soderbergh's *Solaris*, like images of reality surrounded by artifice. James Cameron notes on the DVD commentary track how early on the uniforms blend in with the ship, which gives the impression of a movie made out of talking heads. Later on, bodies are more frequently exposed, most notably George Clooney's, whose twice-naked rear end serves as the film's obligatory cleavage. Otherwise what is most strikingly present are the faces, along with Jeremy Davies's wandering, Dennis Hopper–like hands. The face becomes the image that can defy time; the face becomes the photograph on the refrigerator. When Rheya returns from the dead at the end, she looks directly into the camera, with the austere frontality we associate with Pasolini or the illusion-breaking gaze in Godard.[34] The couple's final embrace dissolves into the seething planet of Solaris, just as the human faces on the spaceship are immersed in metal walls and shiny suits. The face is more than a face in Soderbergh's *Solaris:* it becomes an image that looks back at you, with all of an image's promise, and all of an image's emptiness.

Soderbergh's worlds are tinted, constructed, desubstantialized, denaturalized. His films look very different from one another, yet they all circle around these same themes of emergence and disappearance. But many films have no interest in denaturalizing themselves; on the contrary, they want to take the beauty and authority of nature for themselves. And then there are films that only pretend to fling themselves into a tinted, artificial world, when what they really want is clear, transparent nature after all. In the next chapter we will journey to Sundance, Utah, where western scenery provides a spectacular background for America's most famous film festival.

Aronofsky, Sundance, and the Return to Nature 3

··

The Solaris effect circulates through reality and artifice, between the non-reality of the simulacrum and the groundedness of experiential nature. The Solaris effect results in paradoxes of presence and absence; it emphasizes contradictions, hovering between life and death, fullness and nothingness. But many American films want only to come down on the side of nature in order to escape the contradictions of the cinematic condition. But in America there is no escape, and certainly not into the woods. Nature cannot conceal technology. And naturalism cannot conceal cultural imperialism.

Cyberpunk π and the Computer's Joy

The last sequence of Darren Aronofsky's π (1998) returns us to nature—to calm, to normalcy, to at least a smile, even if not to actual happiness. Until this quiet conclusion, the film has writhed about in a hip-hop techno-frenzy while the mathematical genius, Max Cohen, tries to write a computer program that will predict the behavior of the stock market. According to Cohen's logic, and his manic hope, the stock market should behave like an organism. If humans can use mathematics to describe the orbits of planets and other natural phenomena, then perhaps they can also use mathematical calculations to forecast the more complicated events that arise from human society. Why not? This is surely a credible sci-fi premise, and the ultimate impossibility of success forms the basis of a tragic plot. Max Cohen's mad quest to crush what is beyond nature into the realms of nature can lead only to failure. In the penultimate sequence, Max turns his tools against himself and plunges a drill into his own shaved skull.

Yet after ninety minutes of desperate rush, the final sequence of π reveals this apparent suicide to be another one of Cohen's hallucinations (which always follow his terrible headaches), and we are left to unwind for a few moments, before the end credits, in a tree-lined park. A little girl brings Max a leaf. "Pretty, huh?" she says. It turns out that Max can no longer multiply large numbers in his head. All is calm, and he smiles for the very first time in the movie.

The whole film works against nature, outside of nature, despite nature. It is all computer, electronic beat, stimulants, and transgressive genius. At the end, however, π lets nature back in, in its own version of a happy ending, everything back to normal. Unlike the films of David Lynch, π has a ground, a reference against which we can gauge normalcy and sanity. The film clearly concludes that the obsessive hyperactivity that constitutes the compulsive excitement of the film—it is a "thriller"—is ultimately inhuman.

"Nature" is a rather vague, albeit traditional, category, but of utmost critical concern for many of the most interesting American films at the end of the twentieth century. What does American film look like in the decade of the Internet? How are its vast landscapes—its purple mountains and western deserts—represented in a "virtual" decade in which everyone seemed glued to cable television or a video game? Do American films of the 1990s merely collapse into the simulacra of Baudrillard? How is art seen in relation to nature? In his recent biopic of Jackson Pollock, how does director Ed Harris contextualize the abstract expressionist's famous remark "I am nature?" What does Steven Spielberg imply in *A.I: Artificial Intelligence* when the carnival barker speaks out vehemently against "artifice"? How does a film festival like Sundance support independent film when all of its side concerns are enthusiastically environmental and it is guided by "The Natural" himself, Robert Redford?

The Solaris Effect charts the course of art and artifice in recent American film. As we now extend this description, we shall focus on nature—art's traditional contrary.[1] Although these films appeared in a decade of virtual reality—during the rise of digital technology, during what may turn out to be one of the most radical metamorphoses of information culture in world history—there is a notable nostalgia for nature in 1990s American film. Even science fiction, which apparently revels in technology, often wishes that "nature" would be people's true home or the source of their ultimate values. Spielberg's *Minority Report* (2002), like π, stuns with technological spectacle and wit, but then relaxes into a natural landscape at the end. In such films, technology supplies the discordant melody, narrative progression, and the ideas, but nature provides the tonic and the resolution, and thus allows the door to swing open so that the audience can return home.

This chapter will look at Darren Aronofsky's first two films, π and *Requiem for a Dream*, with the goal of showing a hidden link between their techno-frenzied tragedies and the naturalistic reveries of Robert Redford. I will also make a brief excursion through some recent Sundance award winners, suggesting, perhaps provocatively, that these films often are, in their attitude toward nature, closer to Redford's overt environmentalism than they are to technological experimentalism.

Aronofsky's *Guerilla Diaries* for π shows quite unembarrassedly to what extent his film is aimed right at the Sundance Film Festival (parenthetical page references are to π *Screenplay and the Guerilla Diaries*).[2] The very first entry for the diaries, on January 31, 1996, reads: "Just got back from Sundance and I'm feeling amazingly restored. I badly want to believe that if you make *your own* film, and you make it well, it will get recognized. It may not be Sundance Competition — or even Sundance Midnight — but the film will find its audience" (3). And then the very last entry in Aronofsky's *Diaries* is given — tactfully — as an Editor's Note:

> π had its world premiere at the Eccles Theater in Park City, Utah, on January 18, 1998. The Sundance audience welcomed it with a standing ovation. Two days later *Variety*'s front page read "π = $1,000,000." The film was bought by Artisan Entertainment for worldwide distribution. At the awards ceremony, Darren Aronofsky was presented with the prize for Best Director. (59)

The Sundance festival frames this diary perfectly, purposefully, and is clearly the origin and end of Aronofsky's cinematic quest. Sundance both legitimates the director's artistic labors, and, not at all incidentally, provides the arena for a lucrative deal. The film crew, actors, and even the crew's families worked like maniacs on π through long hours and cold nights, no money in sight. But the payoff was Sundance, and that made it all worthwhile.

> My reply: "Sundance . . . Competition."
> My parents — who had no idea what either of those words meant six months ago — are ecstatic and screaming. My dad starts pulling out his hair. No one can believe it. (55)

That the obsessiveness of the film's hero paralleled the obsessiveness of the film crew was not lost on Aronofsky. Several times he points out that the urgency and intensity of the filmmaking worked to augment the performances. Just as Max Cohen (Sean Gullette) is chased through the streets by industrial thugs, Aronofsky shot his movie "hardcore guerrilla style" (40). At the end, "I talked about the way we just fought and I thanked everyone and once again I almost cried. . . . It was a great, hard, vicious journey" (41). In life, as in the film, the journey was partly intellectual and aesthetic, no doubt, but it was also a quest for money. Max Cohen lives in a world of abstractions, spirals, and mathematical proofs, but his goal is to crack the stock market. In his turn, Aronofsky clearly thought of his cinema as aligned with "art": "I need to choose a DP for artistic merit" (14), and he talked a man into working for him by arguing that "music videos are parasitic television commercials" (15). But Aronofsky was also interested in his movie as a saleable product. Thus the selling point of the title:

> The second brainstorm was the title of the film. I want to call the movie
> π. When the idea came to me it made so much sense. Plus it's a great
> marketing angle. I can see it now: πs everywhere—stenciled on buildings
> and streets corners, billboards, napkins, match books, beer coasters. (8)

Max Cohen's obsessive techno-quest makes for an exciting cyberpunk thriller, yet it is also not too difficult to read his narrative as a kind of parable or allegory for the obsessions of the indie filmmaker on his "hard, vicious" way to fame and fortune (with a little help from his machinery).

What film genres are conducive to both art and profit? Thierry Jousse suggests that horror is the last truly "resistant" genre in American film, one allowing creativity to go hand in hand with audience appeal.[3] In many respects, π qualifies quite handily as a horror film: black-and-white photography, a transparently low budget, and a hero-scientist who violates nature's laws.[4] But Aronofsky prefers to name the genre of his film a little differently; he calls it "cyberpunk."

> We want to make a film for $20,000. That's how much we figure we
> can raise for sure. At Sundance we saw *Tokyo Fist*, by cyberpunk master
> Shinya Tsukamoto. I admire his passion and fierce fucking originality. I
> want to bring cyberpunk to America. Cronenberg did it in Canada but no

one has pulled it off in the States, especially not in NYC, where the ideas fit the environment perfectly. (3)

"Cyberpunk" was originally a literary term associated with a 1980s science-fiction movement spearheaded by William Gibson in novels like *Neuromancer* (1984), *Count Zero* (1986), and *Mona Lisa Overdrive* (1988).[5] The classic cyberpunk film is usually taken to be Ridley Scott's *Blade Runner* (1982). The transformation of nature, especially the human body, into mechanical artifice is recurrent in cyberpunk literature and film, and even though *Scanners* (1981) and *Videodrome* (1983) do not seem quite so cyberpunk, the notion of bodies radically altered by technology is certainly a central theme in all of Cronenberg. Cyberpunk in the work of Tsukamoto is also characterized by the radical and mechanical alteration of human bodies. In *Tetsuo II: Body Hammer* (1997), the characters repeatedly undergo monstrous physical alterations, as guns and armor punch out from the inside of constantly fighting bodies. Cyberpunk imagines a future society in which nature will all but vanish and human bodies will be transformed by technology and capital into something barely distinguishable from machines.

Aronofsky scarcely had the budget to produce the atmospherics of *Blade Runner*. For urban detail he relied on the New York City streets as they were. At one point on the DVD commentary he complains that Mayor Giuliani cleaned up the streets so much that New York has lost its visual "edge." Elsewhere on the commentary he admits to being embarrassed by the tiny superchip that the industrial thugs deliver to Max Cohen. It looks silly and meager, but it was the best the budget allowed. Instead of special effects or many elaborately dressed sets, the cyberpunk atmosphere had to come from the electronic music, the weird contrasts of the black-and-white photography, and the anarchic mangle of computer parts that makes up Euclid, Max's computer. Indeed, cyberpunk artifacts are typically characterized by a layered, archaeological collage. In direct contrast to the look of Kubrick's *2001*, in which everything is clean, shiny, and new, the cyberpunk future is a helter-skelter layering of modern and old technology. Aronofsky intentionally builds up Max's computer from an early Apple monitor, and the tubes and ducts hanging off of it (drawn, as Aronofsky says, from Terry Gilliam's *Brazil*) add to the improvised, cobbled together look. In cyberpunk literature, the human body is usually as cobbled together as these machines.

Yet except for Euclid, Aronofsky's film basically seems set in a contemporary New York City. The science-fictional or cyberpunk aspects are emphasized only thematically and occasionally. It is not the audience's constant concern to know that this place is *not* our world or that this story takes place in a near future. On the contrary, time and space are simply assumed to be the present. Although the script was in its earlier stages entitled *Chip in the Head,* and although Max drills into his own head at the end, there is no indication that Max's obsessive pathology is caused by anything but his mad will-to-discover, augmented by an around-the-clock cocktail of uppers and painkillers. In other words, the usual cyberpunk blending of man and technology is not present in π. π is cyberpunk in its visual landscape of man plus computer set amid gritty urban intensity. Man and computer, however, never blend.

Instead of a plot in which man becomes machine — a "six-million-dollar man" or yet another android — the machine itself is shown to change into a kind of organic object. The film visualizes this transformation with some care. As noted above, Max Cohen's mad project is to treat the stock market as a natural entity. Early in the film Aronofsky emphasizes the transition from nature to culture by slowly dissolving from tree branches in the sky to a close-up of a crawling stock ticker. Max's point of view is implied in the dissolve, but the plot of the film confirms the near relationship of the natural world to cultural artifacts.

The treatment of the computer clarifies this near relationship of the natural and the constructed. In a later sequence, Max has the stock ticker running across the top of Euclid; he hits RETURN for some results. Meanwhile, he can hear, as the script has it, "Devi and her boyfriend making love" next door (88). We hear the sexual moans for a while, and then the electricity in the room goes off; the lights black out. The computer has crashed, and when Max puts on gloves and a mask to figure out what went wrong, he finds that a "strange, gooey, gel-like substance covers the board" (89). Like the little splatterings in Todd Solondz's *Happiness,* this goo is surely the result of an orgasm, a kind of come. We hear sexual sounds, the computer spits out a result, and then it gives up in exhaustion. Max throws away the resulting number as an error, but we learn later that the result was true. At the climax of the calculations, then, the machine suddenly orgasms, and so becomes a "natural" artifact.

The scene is repeated in the film thirty minutes later when Max has the computer programmed to analyze numbers based on Hebrew letters in the Bible. The plot has changed from an attempt to predict the stock market to an attempt to crack the numerological code of the Torah. The sex sounds return and now escalate to a pitch that the script describes very well: "His neighbors are cumming and their cries of joy are twisted and agonizing" (124). Again Max finds goop on the computer, although not quite so much in the film as in the script: "Max looks at Euclid. The screen is blank. He looks at the mainframe. It is covered with the filo substance" (126). The DVD commentaries by Aronofsky and Gullette do not make too much of the goo; Gullette says, reading thematically, that "Max has tried to banish all organic life from his apartment" and failed. The film does take rather a long pause now to watch Max put the goop under a microscope. But he discovers that the cells are formed in spirals, and so he redesigns Euclid and the program to account for the golden spiral that appears in all things.

Like most DVD commentaries, the one recorded by Gullette and Aronofsky tends to focus on anecdotal and technical aspects of the filmmaking, and the director and lead actor quite reasonably do not wish to deprive viewers of their own interpretations. But it does not seem to be a personal or oblique interpretation of the sound track, narrative drive, or visual evidence before us to conclude that Max's computer has achieved a human-like orgasm at the moment of success. Hence the cyberpunk transformation in π occurs not in the human, but in the machine.

The payoff of Max's mad quest is figured here not only through what in other circumstances would be called a money shot, but also as religious transcendence. Max is trailed by a group of mystical Hasidic Jews as well as the industrial thugs. The thugs believe that Max's program will tell them how to forecast the stock market; the Hasidim believe that the number Max has found will lead them to "the true name of God." In this later stage, with his program reconfigured, Max is taken into a "blinding white void" (150). This space is not the n-dimensional hyperspace of a film like *The Matrix* (1999) where Laurence Fishburne and Keanu Reaves discuss the reality of our "real world."[6] Instead this is clearly a spiritual place, like Heaven:

Blinding White Void
    —where Max looks around starry-eyed. The pain is gone. Everything is new to Max—even his hands. The stress releases from his brow and his shoulders sag.
    Max continues to recite the number. His voice becomes tender and peaceful. As he starts to become part of the void, his voice turns into a whisper and his eyes start to close. (150)

Even though π takes us into a world that seems framed by technological bric-a-brac and confusion, the narrative uses clearly naturalistic—and relatedly—supernaturalistic markers to annotate its trajectory. At the moment of solution and dissolution, when the computer crashes and a result appears, the machine becomes orgasmic. Later, this state of exalted understanding is figured visually not only as sexual, but as spiritually transcendent. Far from the usual deterritorializations of cyberpunk, then, Max Cohen crosses briefly through a rather clearly marked heavenly elsewhere. Unlike the mayhem in David Lynch, where the demonic otherworld is absolutely unassimilable and truly chaotic, π marks its cyberpunk rush through metaphors from nature and religion with surprising neatness. π must strike one, therefore, as remarkably conservative in its cyberpunk ideology, since nature continues to have the final word, and since nature continues to function as a ground of reference throughout the electronic rush of everything.

Cyberpunk, self-conscious, potentially postmodern π would not seem likely to mistake the artifice of filmmaking for the natural world. As we noted earlier, this is Tarkovsky's error, according to Jameson:

> The deepest contradiction in Tarkovsky is then that offered by the highest technology of the photographic apparatus itself. No reflexivity acknowledges this second hidden presence, thus threatening to transform Tarkovskian nature-mysticism into the sheerest ideology.[7]

We would not expect to characterize Aronofsky's hyperactive urban nightmare in similar terms. Yet the cinematic impulse to embody "nature-mysticism" is a deep one, especially in 1990s American film. The description above shows that Aronofsky's π uses both "nature" and "spirit" as foundational points of reference. We will see that these grounding assumptions are related to other kinds of hypotheses about the hierarchies of genres and of the arts, for critical consequences follow on these categories of "nature" and "spirit." One may well assume next, for instance, that cinematic art is to some degree inherently superior to television art. If one thinks in hierarchies and foundations, then it makes sense to see a continuity between an aesthetic grounded in nature and a proud claim of cinematic superiority. David Lynch will severely question the aesthetic hierarchy of film over television, but scattered comments by Aronofsky in the *Diaries* seem, instead, to reinforce the ranked distinction. We will return to this idea in the last section of this chapter, when we return to Aronofsky and his television-bashing *Requiem for a*

Dream. But for now we will take our discussion of nature and spirit into the capital of cinematic spirit, the Sundance Film Festival.

Sundance, Redford, and the Spirit of Nature

Sundance, the Oz of π, that ardently desired showground for independent film, is overseen, if by anyone, by Robert Redford. According to Kenneth Turan of the *Los Angeles Times*:

> Involved in the festival, almost from the beginning, was local resident Robert Redford, who had purchased land in the Wasatch Mountains as far back as 1969. Redford, related by marriage to Sterling Van Wagenen, the festival's first director, was chairman of the board of directors and the key figure in eventually having his cultural-minded, multidisciplinary arts organization, the Sundance Institute, take on the festival in 1985, and eventually change the name in 1991.[8]

When attempting to sum up Sundance from the top down, journalists and interviewers go to Redford. Redford sees his work as art that celebrates and protects "freedom." When he received the Honorary Academy Award in 2001 he said:

> There are really two areas: my own work which is the most important to me, and the work of putting something back in our industry, an industry that is and has been good to me. Sundance, of course, is the manifestation of that desire and the result of a grand collaboration with a far-reaching group of artists, of colleagues. I'm grateful to those of you who have believed and who have participated.[9]

Yet Redford is quite aware that his festival for independence and creativity has become a weeklong bidding war. "You have a stock-trader mentality, where you get guys running out onto the floor bidding after a 15-minute viewing," said Redford at the festival in 1998.[10] It is easy to see the relevance of this stock-trading description to Aronofsky's Sundance allegory in π. Although Redford's Hollywood celebrity has helped bring the festival to international prominence, it has also brought the industrial money and ways of thinking that could potentially sap the independence of independent film. As Turan writes, "Ever since Redford's Sundance Institute had taken over the festival, the putative specter of the evil empire of Hollywood and the movie establishment has hung over the event."[11] In interviews and press statements, Redford is quite critical of the homogeneity of, and gratuitous violence in, independent films; he repeatedly gives the impression of fighting for authentic originality while letting the deals and distributions happen as they will.

Redford's own movies and Sundance Festival movies look very different, one from the other, it is true, but I want to suggest in this section that there may be underlying similarities worth attending to. Redford's movies and the Sundance Institute come to us in western wear, with mountains in the background, speaking to us of the virtues of nature. Sundance films—dramatic features, documentaries, and shorts—come from all over the world, and are judged by imported judges, who probably arrive from an urban metropolis, not a ranch in Utah. Yet even a cyberpunk thriller such as Aronofsky's π, which takes place in a grey city and in a room occupied only by a computer, may still be significantly framed by "nature" and "spirit." π is not as transparent as the Sundance catalogue, but I want to call attention to a common underlying ideology that has formed around ideas about nature.

The Sundance Institute, with Robert Redford as president, is part of a "Sundance Family," and is joined in that community by the Sundance Film Festival, Sundance Village ("a year-round mountain community for art and nature that fosters artistic pursuits and recreational activity while preserving the naturally beautiful and unique environment of Sundance"), the Sundance Catalog Company ("Sundance Catalog celebrates art, craft, and design, showcasing the work of artists and artisans from around the world and offering customers hand-crafted, unique, and functional art"), Sundance Farms, and the North Fork Preservation Alliance ("a not-for-profit organization developed to preserve and protect the open spaces and wildlands of Provo's North Fork Canyon").[12] The Sundance family of organizations foregrounds environmental concerns and supports artistic pursuits that seem related to those concerns. A problematic relationship of environmental activism to leisure capital, and of politics to money, is not difficult to detect in the Sundance Catalog promotional descriptions, yet this is a relationship found often at the heart of the Sundance Film Festival as well.

The ideology of the Sundance Catalog is transparent. It gestures seductively toward high-end purchasers through the language of "homemade," "organic," "international," and "handcrafted." The catalog features "artists" and "artisans" from around the world. You buy "art," but art that is "functional," not pretentious or merely decorative. The catalog clearly wants to claim the glamorous

The Solaris Effect

freedom of the Sundance Film Festival for its own offerings in jewelry, men's and women's clothing, home decor, and gifts. Yet the items for sale have nothing to do with movies; they are "independent," presumably, in their "uniqueness," their originality, their "art." As much as the merchandise sold by L. L. Bean or Martha Stewart, Sundance clothing intends to cultivate a lifestyle, in this case one that exhibits a concern for the environment and also shows its good taste in art.

I readily admit, once again, that the political pretense and class sophistry of the Sundance Catalog is completely on the surface. But I will linger over this discussion for a few more moments, since I think that even a Sundance advertisement has something to tell us about a Sundance film. The catalog features a number of artists and artisans; here follows the description of Roxanne Spring, who specializes in lighting:

Roxanne Spring brings studies in sculpture and video art at the SF Art Institute, extensive worldwide travel, and a love of gardening to light in Kindabugsya hand blown glass lampshades. Roxanne was inspired to start Kindabugsya in 1991 after walking by a glass shop in Berkeley[,] California. The molten pot of glass that several young people were forming into goblets, cups and other vessels amazed her. Inspired by the hot glass vessels she realized that when lit the colors stay alive! She then commissioned several lamps for her home, and voila! Guests began asking for similar works for their homes, bistros, beauty salons, eyeglass shops— you name it. Spring began working with several amazing glass blowers to create the organic, colorful lighting that makes for spectacular interior effects. The last decade has been marked by the public's increased awareness of hand blown glass. Here on the west coast, we are lucky to have a wealth of great glass schools and talented individuals. Kindabugsya Lamps are hand-crafted individually by a two-person team. There are many complicated techniques that are integral to the design. Each piece is finished "hot," which is the way of traditional, rather than industrial glassblowers. Kindabugsya lamps can be found lighting up many different kinds of rooms throughout the US and beyond. The Luster lamps (shown by Sundance) are inspired by the fantastic and intriguing Japanese ceramic lusterware of the early 1900s. The forms are at once contemporary industrial and organically derived. The sheen comes from a glass powder that has a high percentage of silver nitrate. The silver comes to the surface because of a reduction process that occurs at about 2000 degrees. These original and colorful lampshades are great as solo light sculptures, assorted groups, and wonderful serial lighting for kitchen bars, or other linear applications.[13]

The audience for this description obviously consists of upmarket businesses and wealthy homeowners. Roxanne is a sculptor, not just a craftsperson, and this is art flavored by San Francisco and Japan. The buzzwords are blatant and even contradictory: this glasswork is "traditional, rather than industrial," yet the forms are "at once contemporary industrial" and "organically derived." We are indeed lucky to have a "wealth of great glass schools," because we must be looking for something on which to spend our superfluous wealth. To be precise, we will need $525 for the "tall cherry cylinder," at the lower end of the price range, and $580 for the "sky blue vertical light," at the upper end. But after all, they are organic *and* they are art. To sample an argument that I will expand on later, this is not so much environmental art, art made organically as an homage to nature, using traditional techniques. Rather, this is art that fears displaying itself as artifice and so needs to refer to nature. In the way that a Victorian gentleman quoted Virgil as a sign of cultural prestige, this Sundance catalog quotes nature also as a sign of prestige.

Now surely Redford's film projects make a different impression than the Sundance Catalog copy. Although his picture is sometimes on the cover of the Sundance Catalog, a mere photo no more makes a statement, one might say, than the face of his partner, "Butch Cassidy," does on the bottle of Newman's Own salad dressing. Redford's movie *Quiz Show* is certainly not an advertisement for sportswear. Redford entirely convinces when he says that "the films that I've made in my career that I had any control over were really independent films made within the studio system. I was fortunate to be financed by the studios, but I was left alone to make the films I wanted to make."[14] The films that he directs are clearly distinct from the Hollywood pictures that he stars in otherwise, such as *Sneakers* (1992), *Indecent Proposal* (1993), *Up Close and Personal* (1996), *The Last Castle* (2001), and *Spy Game* (2001). Yet what are the assumptions behind Redford's recent films? How do films brought about by his Wildwood Productions work through and represent Nature?

Robert Redford directed three films in the 1990s, *A River Runs through It* (1992), *Quiz Show* (1994), *The Horse Whisperer* (1998), and one after, *The Legend of Bagger Vance* (2000). Natural surroundings play a strong role in three of these films, *A River Runs through It, The Horse Whisperer,* and *The Legend of Bagger Vance;* a Sundance sensibility is strongly felt in them.[15] In these films, there are numerous beautiful landscapes, photogenic mountains, splendid sunsets. These films intend audience members to renew their relationship to the natural world. A resourceful director, Redford has definite ideas and feelings about nature and he wishes to put them on-screen. But only *A River Runs through It* renders the natural world with any kind of multiformity.

Redford's most recent effort, *The Legend of Bagger Vance,* tells its story with a simplicity that approaches simplemindedness. This is the story of a southern golfer, Rannulph Junuh (Matt Damon), who is pitted against the golf legends Bobby Jones and Walter Hagen in an almost movie-length golf tournament. Junuh has lost his golf stroke because of horrific experiences in the First World War, and he needs to regain his old form. Fortunately, a black caddy (Will Smith) appears and coaches Junuh back to himself; then the caddy mysteriously departs, strolling quietly along a sunset beach in the final sequence. Smith as the golf guru continually reminds Junuh to become one with nature: "See the place where the tides, and the seasons, and the turning of the earth, all come together, and everything that is becomes one, and you got to seek that place with all your soul." Smith gives a dignified performance as a good-humored Obi-Wan Kenobi, even though his advice is nearly always risible cliche ("There's only one shot that is in perfect harmony with the field, the authentic shot . . . that shot is going to choose him . . . there's a perfect shot out there looking to find us"). When these transcendental moments come upon Junuh, the screen confirms his sublime focus through visionary special effects, and when he sinks a putt in the crucial last round, religious music even annotates the experience further ("It's a miracle," says a boy, for anyone who might be wholly insensible).

Redford admits that *The Legend of Bagger Vance* is not a golf movie ("I'm not interested in a film about golf, but I am interested in golf as a metaphor"), but a "classic" narrative that takes its "Herculean" hero from "darkness" to "wisdom."[16] *The Legend of Bagger Vance* embodies a Sundance sensibility at its bluntest and happiest, as nature and spirit descend upon the hero to help him play championship golf. And since it is a "legend," Redford sets his story in a 1920s South populated with named historical characters but without a hint of racial turmoil. Redford's earlier *Quiz Show* looked at such a game, and such a winner, with a good deal more scrutiny.

Redford's *Horse Whisperer* also narrates a Sundance legend, a dramatized idealization of nature and spirit. A high-strung New York editor, Annie MacLean (Kristin Scott Thomas), drives her daughter's horse, Pilgrim, out to the famed horse whisperer, Tom Booker (Redford), who lives on a ranch in Montana. In the ghostly slow-motion sequence that begins the film, the horse slips in the snow, badly hurting both Annie's daughter, Grace (Scarlett Johansson), and also the horse itself. All of Annie's workers want to put the horse down. But the horse whisperer manages to save the horse and also to heal the relationship between mother and daughter. The control-freak editor from the city must learn the ways of the country, its silences, its intuitions. Annie keeps jabbering away—and in a British accent, signaling cultural pretension—while Redford goes on about his business, in touch with his feelings, at one with nature. Helicopter shots show us expanses of the ranch and the beautiful mountains beyond; triumphant music annotates the countryside and idealizes those moments of ranch labor that we are allowed to see. Cowboys sing around the campfire, and an occasional posthole gets sunk, but whereas Annie's magazine is clearly current and fashionable, there are few signs that Booker's ranch is set in a contemporary world. There are air-gun inoculations that were not part of Howard Hawks's *Red River* (1948), and Redford does his account books for a moment, but otherwise this Montana and this western seem entirely nostalgic. Hollywood prestige and plot seem to demand that Redford and Thomas fall in love with each other, even though this seems completely beside the point. So while Redford's character may be intuitive and capable of finding peace ("sometimes, not all the time"), Redford himself is also a movie star, and so requires homage by both the camera and this completely unavailable woman, Annie MacLean. Awkwardly, Booker's powerful feelings do not seem to register in any way the existence of her husband, Robert (Sam Neill). With these blunt gestures, *The Horse Whisperer* shouts out nature and spirit quite as loudly as *The Legend of Bagger Vance*.

Redford's earlier "Maclean" movie, *A River Runs through It*, is probably his most convincing Sundance film. Lessons about life and life's graces are taught both by the Reverend Maclean (Tom Skerritt) and the timelessly flowing river. *A River Runs through It* encourages us to live for those transcendental moments when we are completely in touch with nature. Although art is scarcely mentioned in *The Legend of Bagger Vance* or *The Horse Whisperer* (Tom Booker listens to Dvořák concertos, thus modifying his otherwise potentially stereotyped cowboy), one of the Reverend Maclean's two sons, Norman (Craig Sheffer), grows up to be an English professor at the University of Chicago, and it is he who tells the story (in a voice-over by the otherwise absent Redford). Norman loves poetry, especially Wordsworth's, and knows early on that he wants to be a writer. But ironically it is his "wild" brother Paul (Brad Pitt) who becomes the truest work of art. When Paul catches a huge fish at the end of the film and is pulled down the river over rapids and rocks, the voice-over says:

> My brother stood before us, not on a bank of the big Blackfoot River, but suspended above the earth, free from all its laws, like a work of art. And I knew, just as surely, and just as clearly, that life is not a work of art, and that the moment could not last.

Norman is orderly and cultured, whereas Paul gambles and drinks and whores. But Paul's graceful and tumultuous fly-fishing approach "art," even if only for a moment.

The nostalgic treatment of the past that Redford so loves, and that forms such a significant part of his acting career (*Butch Cassidy and the Sundance Kid*, *The Sting*, *The Great Gatsby*), is strongly felt in *A River Runs through It*. At the same time, however, the film also tries much more seriously than either *The Horse Whisperer* or *The Legend of Bagger Vance* to measure the darkness of nature's power and wildness.

With no majestic mountains to be seen and no horses running free, Redford's *Quiz Show* seems the least like a Sundance film. Yet just as in *All the President's Men* (1976), in which Redford's Bob Woodward exposed political corruption in the highest offices, thus protecting American democracy, *Quiz Show* retells one of the greatest scandals in the American culture industry, the fixing of the game show *Twenty-One* in the 1950s. *Quiz Show* does not, this time, speak didactically on behalf of nature, but now didactically on behalf of class struggle. Television loves the wealthy, handsome son of Columbia professor Mark Van Doren (Paul Scofield), hence the producers run Herbie Stempel (John Turturro) off the air and away from the game show. "The great white hope," Charles Van Doren (Ralph Fiennes), ought to be America's model, not this "annoying Jewish guy." *Quiz Show* does not demonize Charlie Van Doren or make it too easy to sympathize with Stempel (who is rather pathological and kooky), but the exposé which supplies the energy of the film is one in which the equality of classes and of ethnicities stands as a democratic ideal.

Quiz Show not only attacks ethnic prejudice in the culture industry, it attacks television. As the government investigator (Rob Morrow) says in conclusion: "I thought we were gonna get television. The truth is, television is going to get us." The implicit idea is that film is smart enough and interesting enough to avoid the banalities of television, and Aronofsky's *Requiem for a Dream* makes a similar claim. *Quiz Show* is in fact a very clever project, and therefore less obviously hypocritical than other films that set themselves apart from television.[17] But I would suggest that to assume a cultural hierarchy of film over television is not just a mistaken idealization, but an assumption related to the idealization of nature and spirit in the Sundance codes.

Quiz Show makes its hierarchical case by casting Rob Morrow in the role of the government investigator and Martin Scorsese in the role of the chief television producer. This was Morrow's first film role after his critically acclaimed series *Northern Exposure* (1990–1995), and Morrow brings a kind of Sundance authenticity to the part. In *Northern Exposure*, Morrow's character began as a skeptical doctor from the city, but one who listened so well and so often to the ways of nature that he eventually moved to even wilder climes. Redford's *Quiz Show* takes Morrow up into the land of film and asks him to speak with a Kennedy accent. The accent is important because the whole film is about ethnicity and privilege. The Harvard education provides Morrow's character with the opportunity to talk to "Charlie" Van Doren as a social equal. But the accent is rather ridiculous, too, especially with *Northern Exposure* in our ears. What *Quiz Show* does is to boldly reoutfit the television star with a new voice, have him run an investigation of television's greed and prejudice, and then sit him down at the table with Martin Scorsese, a hero of American independent film, but now the villain of the piece. The image of Rob Morrow attacking television, while Scorsese defends it, makes for a splendidly paradoxical visual debate. The result is not so much that Scorsese gives the viewpoint of the television producer moral weight through his presence, but rather that he gives the debate with Morrow, and thus the whole film, cinematic weight. Morrow needs Scorsese's baptism, but the film does not see what extraordinary contradictions arise in this scene. Morrow brings a Sundance heroism to the table, but he is still a television star, and the film is deeply vexed about television.

For *Quiz Show* not only questions the idolization of the brilliant white youth, Charles Van Doren, it questions the power of television. Montages show us that absolutely everyone watches television, wholly captivated, even nuns. Yet even as *Quiz Show* wants to expose the fraudulence of Charles Van Doren as the "great white hope," the film does not attack the cultural prestige of his father, Mark. The Columbia professor is everywhere represented as a model of the cultured intellectual, quoting Shakespeare, writing and teaching, trying to be a good father. The quiz show itself is a cultural travesty, since it uses quotations only on behalf of an empty game, in a disguised form of a lottery. The television producers initially motivate Charles to play the fixed game by saying that he will inspire young people all over America to read and learn. But Professor Mark Van Doren sees right through such claims; he sees that the show, when played honestly, is all gimmick and has nothing to do with the intellect. *Quiz Show* ultimately takes the professor's side by implying that culture and art are good, and pretense and dishonesty are bad. The result is that *Quiz Show* attacks class hierarchy while agreeing with cultural hierarchy—the hierarchy of film over television. We are meant to see ferocious irony in the scene in which Charlie gives his dad a television set for his birthday. What a nightmare gift that is, we are to think. And there will be an exactly parallel scene in *Requiem for a Dream*, in which Harry gives his mother a new television set. In each case we are invited to thank the movie for showing us what a disaster television really is.

So far Robert Redford's films have not excited much critical enthusiasm in magazines like *Film Comment* or *Sight and Sound*, nor are they likely to in the future. There will not be a *Cahiers du cinéma* volume on Redford to match the one on that other actor turned director, Clint Eastwood. But Redford's films are worth our critical attention for now, insofar as they exhibit a return to nature in a clear and even institutionalized form. The contradictions and consequences of Redford's turn to nature come before us relatively undisguised.

In the next section of this chapter, I will discuss several films that actually took part in the Sundance Film Festival. Such a brief description of Sundance films can be, at most, only suggestive rather than definitive. There are over one hundred films shown at Sundance each year, and I will discuss here only five. My purpose is simply to continue this book-length discussion of art and artifice in American contemporary film by working through some important recent examples. Although the showing of documentaries is crucial to the overall output and impression of the Sundance Film Festival, for the purposes of this description I will focus on five films that won the Grand Jury Prize in the category for feature-length dramas. These films are *Welcome to the Dollhouse* (1996), *Slam* (1998), which won the year that Aronofsky took the directing prize for *π*, *Three Seasons* (1999), and the cowinners for 2000, *You Can Count on Me* and *Girlfight*. Since Todd Solondz's *Welcome to the Dollhouse* is, for purposes of this discussion, the most interesting of these films, I will reserve that discussion for last.

Three Seasons is an American movie shot entirely in Ho Chi Minh City, and so looks more like a film by Anh Hung Tran (*The Scent of Green Papaya*, 1993) than one by Richard Linklater. Indeed, Anh Hung Tran's second feature, *Cyclo* (1995), centers on a cyclo driver in Ho Chi Minh City, while one of the three stories in *Three Seasons* also takes a bicycle cabbie as its protagonist. Harvey Keitel, the executive producer of *Three Seasons*, provides the American element for this otherwise foreign film, although his acting role is relatively small. As in Theo Angelopolous's *Ulysses' Gaze* (1995), although on a smaller, less angst-filled scale, Keitel plays the questing hero in foreign lands, allowing the American audience its connection with the surroundings. But the "white" element of Ho Chi Minh City is otherwise criticized in the film, since the Vietnamese characters—prostitute, street child, cyclo driver—all labor endlessly in the shadow of a modern luxury hotel. While the film moves through the alleys and backstreets of the city, Western progress and capital does not seem to have made its way very far down the economic ladder.

The film reveals its nostalgia for an older Vietnam most clearly in the story of the old poet and the girl, Kien An (Ngoc Hiep Nguyen), who picks and sells white lotuses. She inspires the old man to write poetry again, and at the end she dreams of the floating marketplace of the old man's youth. One day she cannot sell any of her flowers, because people want to buy only plastic lotus flowers. Yet social criticism in the film is often subtle rather than blunt. The old man stops writing poetry because of the onset of leprosy, not from any Western influence or invasion. Yet however subtle in places, the criticism of modern society is perfectly clear elsewhere, and a sense of melancholy and nostalgia is strongly felt.

The desire to return to nature is most evident in the story about the cyclo driver, Hai (Don Duong). As he drives her back from the hotel each night, Hai falls in love with a prostitute, Lan (Diep Bui). The romantic plot thus saves the woman not only from degradation, but more importantly, it seems, from artifice. She wants only to get out of the city; she is willing to marry anyone rich in order to achieve this. Although her clothes, looks, and manner make her seem way out of Hai's league, he sees by the look of her lowly apartment that they have much in common. By winning a cyclo race, in a very low-key victory, Hai comes into enough money to pay for a night with her in the hotel. But he does not make love to her; he just wants to watch her sleep, peacefully, in the air-conditioned room. He does not ask for sex, but he does ask that she change into traditional clothes, saying, "I want you to put them on without your makeup." This is the trajectory of the story—that he can save her not only from prostitution, but also from her fantasies about wealth and luxury culture. At the end of the film, as leaves fall all around them, he says, "You don't have to pretend anymore."

This return to nature is paralleled by a return to Vietnamese written art.

After the death of the old poet, Kien An receives his sheaf of poems. Written culture is passed on, into the future, even as she dreams herself—the film turns sepia—into the past. Similarly, even as the red leaves fall around the happy cyclo driver and his beloved, he gives her a book, and we can see clearly that it has a Vietnamese title. We have seen Hai reading the book at intervals throughout the film, and this gift signals the cultural transition of the woman from luxury-hotel prostitute back to her Vietnamese identity. The book is passed from hand to hand as naturally as love, as naturally as the leaves fall. True cultural artifacts are a part of nature. Implicitly, the film itself comes to us as an art that claims to be nature. The bar in the film around which much of the action takes place is called The Apocalypse Now Bar and Grill. *Three Seasons* returns us to the ongoing, cyclic world of nature, at every remove from Francis Ford Coppola's tarted-up neon landscape, his Vietnamese Whore of Babylon at the end of time.[18]

Kenneth Lonergan's *You Can Count On Me* was very well received beyond Sundance, and critics observed that material that could have turned into a TV movie of the week became in Lonergan's hands an extremely well-made, well-acted, sophisticated film. Martin Scorsese is one of the executive producers, and Barbara De Fina, who produces all of Scorsese's pictures, is one of the producers of *You Can Count On Me*. Since the release of Scorsese's first feature film, *Mean Streets* (1973), which starred Harvey Keitel, both Keitel and Scorsese have often been associated with independent and independent-minded film. Just as Keitel not only starred in *Three Seasons* but also produced it, it was not surprising to find both Scorsese and De Fina associated with *You Can Count On Me*. There are not gangsters here, however, as there might be in Scorsese, although Lonergan later helped create the dialogue for Scorsese's *Gangs of New York* (2002). Instead we find just consistently good writing, a wide range of tonality, some rather surprising plot points, and an inconclusive ending that stands out against the strong impulse of Hollywood film to affirm, moralize, and sum up. At the end, the main characters seem not to have resolved their problems to any degree, nor even to have changed very much.

You Can Count On Me is structured as a good sibling–bad sibling family drama, a set-up that puts it in the company of hundreds of other films, Hollywood and otherwise. Sammy (Laura Linney) has stayed in her hometown, raising her son and working at a bank job, while her brother, Terry (Mark Ruffalo), is a wanderer, moving from town to town, even spending some time in jail. American film often analyses the "wild," and what happens to the wild character has much to do with the categories of nature and culture. The natural beauty of the landscape in Terrence Malick's *Badlands* (1973) is connected with the wild, socially unfit character of Kit (Martin Sheen). Sean Penn's *Indian Runner* (1991) contrasts the "natural," "native" restlessness of the bad brother, Frank (Viggo Mortensen), with the conventionality of good brother Joe (David Morse), who has become a cop. In *You Can Count On Me*, Terry is rebellious, but not a murderer; he smokes pot and swears a good deal. Terry's much less diabolical behavior intends to mark the film as realistic, in contrast to all the more pretentious, quasi-allegorical gestures of directors like Malick and Penn. Lonergan, it appears, is not interested in statements about nature, or in the extremes of human experience, but wants to study character, using a drama in which the people behave credibly rather than hysterically.

The brother's return to the family does not necessarily make him less wild. On the contrary, he continues to perform socially unacceptable actions (such as introducing Sammy's son to her nasty ex-husband), to the point that she has to ask him to leave. But the brother's wildness does help the sister's own wildness emerge, and she passionately experiments during his visit. Even before he arrives we have seen that she can stand up for herself, as when she confronts the new bank manager (Matthew Broderick) about his superfinicky attitude toward her schedule. But even as she warns her brother about his wayward behavior, she suddenly starts an affair with her boss, whom we know to be already married to a very visibly pregnant wife. Since the brother has taken over many of her parenting roles, it seems that Sammy is now able to experiment with a more romantic sensibility.

By the end, we have perhaps some sense that she has achieved a degree of self-understanding or independence. But there is no thematic speech to indicate that. This inconclusive conclusion intends to give the impression that "things just happen," just as in life. But another, more annoying way to say this is that the film fears showing us the constructedness of things—of plot, of character. These characters do not make anything of themselves; they do not make anything, period. The brother plays a good game of pool; the sister seems profoundly competent at the office, even if she is always running late. We might congratulate the film for its realism, although of a type that is a thousand miles from Cassavetes, or we might more simply say: this movie lives in fear of art.

One way to underline this latter point would be to compare Linney's acting in this film to that of Holly Hunter generally. Laura Linney is an established Hollywood and Broadway actress, but in this film she looks remarkably like Hunter. The kind of tragicomic situations she finds herself in—the tomboy feminism (her name is Sammy), the impression of both confusion and strength—all recall a range of Hunter's performances. Of course, Hunter is physically a more extreme screen presence: she is both notably diminutive and also speaks with a thick southern accent, which many films need to resolve, explain, transform, or erase; this was done most radically in Jane Campion's *Piano* (1993), in which Hunter plays a mute. Hunter's performances thus typically live on the edge of caricature and exaggeration. We see such exaggeration not just in *Raising Arizona* (1987), a film by the masters of the cartoon, the Coen brothers, but also in Hunter's performance as a Spielbergian tomboy in *Always* (Spielberg, 1989), as a heart-struck Bostonian (with the world's strangest accent) in Lasse Hallström's melodrama, *Once Around* (1991), and even as a depressed divorcée in the dreamily surreal girl-power movie *Living Out Loud* (LaGravenese, 1998). The Hunter movie that most resembles *You Can Count On Me* is *Miss Firecracker* (Schlamme, 1988)—both films were originally plays—in which the return of the bad brother (Tim Robbins) changes the household of the two sisters, played by Hunter and Mary Steenburgen. In all of these films the artifice and constructedness of Hunter's performance are palpable, and her exaggerations show an openness to represent her characters as something beyond "the real." These performances do not make the movies art, of course, but they do indicate an openness to an aesthetics that is not necessarily limited to naturalism.

You Can Count On Me was cowinner of the 2000 Sundance Grand Jury Prize with *Girlfight*, directed by Karyn Kusama. John Sayles is one of the executive producers of *Girlfight*, and he has a cameo as a high school teacher. Whereas *You Can Count On Me* seems to retreat from exaggeration in all cases, *Girlfight* welcomes self-conscious creativity. *Girlfight* is a boxing movie, and boxing is a craft, a technique, a learned art. A sign in the gym says "Champions are made not born." The movie in some respects does seem to be all realism: these are clearly either inexperienced actors or nonactors; all the sets look like what they are supposed to be; much of the film is shot on location. Gavin Smith writes that the film is "grounded in a precise, unemphatic naturalism" with a "completely authoritative sense of the boxing and working-class milieu."[19] Kusama's DVD commentary continually talks about the "authentic" look that she strove for in the locations and the acting; she uses real boxers, for example, and real referees. In the only mention of another director on her commentary, Kusama notes her admiration for the early films of Michael Ritchie, those in which he employed a documentary style. She refers here to Ritchie's first two critically acclaimed movies, *Downhill Racer* (1969) and *The Candidate* (1972), both of which starred Robert Redford.

Kusama is much more willing to align herself with realism than with art, but the film is as expressively stylized as it is "real." For she not only scouts locations for an authentic look, but as she points out on the DVD commentary track, she chooses the sets for color. The urban landscape in the film is made out of bright primary colors; this is not just an actual New York City high school, it is a school with angry red lockers and even a very red principal's office. From the first image, of Diana Guzman (Michelle Rodriguez) glowering directly at us before a field of red, character after character is placed in an interior with red, blue, or green walls. The walls are almost all "there"— found, not repainted for the film—but the accumulation of color is almost as hyperreal and coincidental as anything in Kieslowski's *Three Colors.* Instead of a dark, dirty, or even gritty urban landscape, these city scenes are filled with bright color and framed by a painter's eye. Diana's apartment is painted strikingly in colorful stripes, like an interior by Gregg Araki or Pedro Almodóvar, and the gym where Diana practices looks like a gallery installation more than a gym. In her DVD commentary, Kusama notes how she put fluorescent lights vertically on the sides of the green columns in the warehouse that serves as the set for the gym. Yet unless this is a fashion show, the lights look completely impractical, and the cross of lights above the ring looks equally unlikely.

Kusama wants us to see how Diana's dreams and her imagination take form in her training body. Diana's imagination is otherwise not emphasized very much (there is one scene in which she daydreams), and we know that she is not a closet intellectual ("Why is the history of the world so fucking boring?" she asks her friend). But *Girlfight* as a whole moves toward her interiority, her passion, although these are embodied in a public place. Eventually, through an entirely melodramatic plot, she must box against her beloved, girl against boy. The power of such a narrative has nothing to do with realism; this is sheerly operatic romanticism, with a consciousness of contemporary gender politics all around. As Kusama observes, the filming of the successive boxing sequences becomes less and less realistic, and the final bout is not about boxing at all, but is entirely focused on Diana's interior world. On the DVD commentary, Kusama says that she attempted to shoot this final match "surrealistically," and the editing, music, and camera angles all substantiate this intent.

The sequence and logic here drift close to the world of Derek Jarman's *An-*

gelic Conversation (1985), in which the two male lovers first fight, then make love. The characters in *Girlfight* are not in any way potential artists. We see that Diana's brother has a talent for drawing, but this aspect of a character is not developed, as it will be in Terry Zwigoff's *Ghost World* (2001). No one writes poetry. Kusama herself is much more comfortable talking about authenticity than art, as are the film's critics. But *Girlfight* is as expressionistic in plot and mise-en-scène as it is realistic. As so often happens in American film, the "authentic" seems to need no argument on its behalf, whereas the aesthetic or artificial ("I like the greens here") is mentioned almost apologetically.

Slam (Marc Levin, 1997) won the Grand Jury Prize at Sundance the same year that Aronofsky won the director's prize for π. Most reviewers agreed that these were the two most exciting, original, and "edgy" (to use the ultimate indie word of praise) films at the festival. *Slam* as a title is a pun, signifying both the Washington, D.C. jails, which seem to swallow up the entire population of the city's young black males, and also slam poetry, the phenomenon of spoken-word poetry. Now, at last, this would seem to be a film that foregrounds *art*. Yet once again, this art happens only by making itself as much like nature as possible. In this case, cinema verité does seem like the right description for *Slam*. Marc Levin honed his filmmaking skills by making documentaries such as *Gang War: Bangin' in Little Rock* (1994) for HBO. The set for the jail scenes is the D.C. jail, and there are no blue walls or stained-glass windows around to make the place seem pretty. There is, without a doubt, an air of authenticity about the characters, setting, dialogue, and plot of *Slam*.

Yet this is a world filled with poetry, music, and rhythm. Ray Joshua (Saul Williams) is a poet whose rhymes are so powerful that two opposing prison gangs come to an astonished halt in the courtyard and decide to leave him alone. Joshua's poems are compelling, overwhelming; he is a visionary genius. But the film pushes beyond the conventional image of the solitary poet and toward the idea that there is a poem inside of everyone. When Ray gets stuck in prison in the beginning, he trades rhymes with a nearby inmate who has already started a rap. When one of the gangs has a meeting, a prisoner keeps time all the while on the bottom of a table. At a reading group in the prison, inmates stand up to read their poetry. Slam poets Beau Sia and Bonz Malone are cast as characters in the film. Their characters do not read poems behind a podium, but their dialogue has a style nonetheless, a rhythm. By casting numerous poets in the film, and by showing musical speech in every corner, *Slam* means to show that the poet Ray does not have a monopoly on poetry. Poetry is a natural impulse, and everyone has a need to listen, and also to express.[20]

Slam poetry in general is an antiacademic movement that follows in the older traditions of Beat poetry and the newer traditions of rap. It intends to bring poetry back to the people; it is antielitist, democratic. It has important things to say about social reality, in contrast to the ivory-tower mannerisms of literary magazines. Slam poetry thus embodies another "back to nature" aesthetic: it uses the word "art" sparingly, and "artifice" only as a putdown. *Slam* realistically shows us Ray writing down his poems, thinking long and hard about them, so that we will not imagine that his poetry is sheer improvisation. But the slam aesthetic is ultimately not very much interested in craft, preferring the stronger virtues of performance, passion, and power.

The slogan for the movie poster is "Words make sense of a world that won't." The *Slam* book cover reproduces reviews that have cooperatively followed that slogan: "a visceral look at art's redemptive powers" (*Premiere*); "[*Slam*] delivers the message: art redeems life." This completely classical sense that art transforms life is a pleasant motto, but is this really how *Slam* works? In this film there are many "poetic," rhythmical, musical responses to the sufferings and confusions in these lives, but is anyone "saved" by the poetry? The world all around is still oppressive and violent. At the end of the film Ray stands in front of the Washington Monument, and at that giant memorial obelisk the film leaves us in indecision and ambiguity. Will he go back to jail? We can see the bar of the grille on the monument behind him. The Washington Monument seems to imply confusion, or worse, incarceration. The antimonumental slam poems embody momentary truths and flights of verbal brilliance, but then these poems, however "real," are gone. Contrary to the slogans, the film is wise enough not to idealize the salvific power of poetry. If anything, the movie tries to save poetry as an idea, but without claiming that such poetry will then save us.

Todd Solondz's first feature film, *Welcome to the Dollhouse*, cultivates an aesthetics of irony and cruelty that will be developed in the director's later works.[21] One can read the film simply as a realistic slice of adolescent nightmare—how incredibly, unbearably mean teenagers are to each other. And the film works very well as that, as the exact opposite of a nostalgia movie, which forces viewers to remember all the things otherwise best left forgotten. But there is an aesthetic principle at the center of this depiction of suburban high school life, and it is, indeed, "Welcome to the Dollhouse." The dolls are the beautiful ideal, and the idealization of the beautiful absolutely wrecks everything. In interviews, Solondz shows no interest whatsoever in articulating a political stance, but *Welcome to the Dollhouse* is, in its own way, a version of

Toni Morrison's novel *The Bluest Eye*, in which we see how even the persecuted internalize a devastating ideology of beauty. There is no rape in *Welcome to the Dollhouse*, as there is in *The Bluest Eye*, although Dawn is repeatedly threatened with "rape" by a tough boy who seems to like her. In Solondz, the brutal threats of rape emerge as elements of the only language suitable for addressing such an "ugly" girl.

Dawn (Heather Matarazzo), the main character, is tormented by society's worship of cool, of beauty, and has to share a room with her adorable little sister ("You're so lucky," she says to her while she sleeps). All the cruelty, rudeness, and rejection that she receives, she then passes on to others. She knocks a ball away from little children, says mean things to her little sister, and rejects the only other friend she has. She spends most of her time swooning over the coolest, handsomest boy at school, utterly mesmerized as he slurps soda pop and chomps fish sticks in front of her. There is a realism to the sets (the shlocky carpets and wall hangings of the middle class in the 1980s) and to the nonidealized approach to plot and character.

But the sheer relentlessness and extremes of cruelty push the film away from a realistic narrative, in which one thing happens after another, and toward a self-conscious narrative that selects only the cruelest moments of a life. One girl forces Dawn to "take a shit" whiles she watches. Dawn is dressed in only the most ridiculous pajamas and T-shirts. Again, we can say that this *is* the cruelty of teenagers or that this is real life. But our final impression is that, in fact, this is the cruelty of the movie, whose constructed narrative tortures Dawn from beginning to end. The film never shows her in any kind of heroic light (she submits, pathetically, to be raped) and never offers any kind of poetic justice (we see a dream of hers in which everyone likes her for a moment, but that quickly vanishes). Solondz is not really interested in documentary reality, but in the effect his film has on his audience. John Waters once said of his "theater of trash" that if someone in the audience has thrown up, then he has made an effective film. With his savage irony and scarcely watchable scenes, Solondz intends to make his audience cringe, with a self-consciousness that will become even more apparent in later films such as *Happiness* and *Storytelling*.

Solondz's aesthetics of cruelty ferociously undoes what passes for aesthetics in Hollywood. In a later film, *Storytelling* (2001), Solondz goes out of his way to attack *American Beauty* (Mendes, 1999). Mendes's film was widely received as a brilliant satire on middle-class society. But Solondz's satire exposes and eviscerates the Hollywood sensibility of *American Beauty* by zeroing in on its naive aesthetics. In *American Beauty*, we are supposed to understand that the strange camera-wielding teenager, Ricky Fitts (Wes Bentley), has a true heart and a correspondingly authentic eye, that he sees through the superficial hypocrisies of middle-class suburbia. In one sequence Ricky watches a paper bag float about on the sidewalk—ah, even that paper bag is beautiful. By contrast, in *Storytelling*, Solondz's parallel artist, nicknamed "American Scooby," watches a straw wrapper float around, and it is very clear that this character is a stupid, affectless, Gen-Xer, not a closet visionary. Solondz attacks not only the middle class, then, but also idealized and sentimentalized forms of aesthetics. This severity of approach makes Solondz at times seem closer to elements of contemporary American art than to most contemporary film.[22] Solondz is one of the relatively few independent directors of recent years whose aesthetics does not seem to yearn either for Hollywood's vapid simulacrum, on the one hand, or nature's consoling embrace, on the other.

Aronofsky's Requiem for the Artificial

Aronofsky's second film, *Requiem for a Dream*, repeats in many ways the frenzied, tragic trajectory of π. Where π's Max Cohen followed his mathematical obsession into insanity and self-destruction, *Requiem* now shows us the decline and fall of four individuals, Sara (Ellen Burstyn), Harry (Jared Leto), Marion (Jennifer Connelly), and Tyrone (Marlon Wayans). Sara gets hooked on diet pills, and her son, Harry, his girlfriend, Marion, and his buddy Tyrone are all junkies. Whereas the end of π leaves Max Cohen outside, smiling, looking up at the trees, the protagonists of *Requiem* all collapse in a gory heap: Tyrone ends up in prison; Harry is stuck in a hospital, his arm amputated; Marion maintains her drug habit by prostituting herself; and Sara is in a psych ward after undergoing electroshock therapy. As in π, the frenzied excitement of *Requiem for a Dream* is that of the world going to hell in a handbasket. The movie is made out of hyperactivity and hallucination, both of which are finally judged to be absolutely *wrong*.

The moralism of *Requiem* is, if anything, clearer than that in π. One probably cannot generalize too much from a geeky, asocial computer genius who writes a one-of-a-kind stock market program and whose work cannot be duplicated by anyone else in the world. Max Cohen's ambitions are "unnatural," as we have discussed, by the film's own definitions, but the cyberpunk film can have no further moral than "Scientist, don't go too far!"—a traditional moral that has been offered already by Mary Shelley's *Frankenstein*. *Requiem for a Dream*, however, clearly does make a generalizable antidrug statement.

The attractive young people almost kill themselves through drugs, and Sara's relationship to her television eventually sends her off the deep end. Sara's television seems always tuned to a hyperenergetic self-help program, and her tragic decline is caused, more or less, by her obsession with television and its idols. She wants to win, she wants to be on television, but then she needs to look good enough to appear on television.

Like the Sundance winners *Three Seasons* and *Welcome to the Dollhouse*, *Requiem* criticizes the mass-cultural worship of celebrity and beauty. But *Requiem* clearly wants to differentiate between its own hyperactive manner of proceeding and the screaming and yelling coming out of the tube. That television watching is as addictive as drug taking was probably a more novel thought in 1978, when Hubert Selby, Jr.'s novel *Requiem for a Dream*, originally appeared.[23] But the film takes a more problematic stance when it regards television as categorically inferior to film. According to *Requiem for a Dream*, film is open, sophisticated, even artistic, while television is loud-mouthed, repetitious, even dangerous. Once again this hierarchy of film over television depends on our believing in a more basic axiom, that nature is more truthful than artifice.

In interviews, Aronofsky said that what he wanted to get across most in the film was the *pain* of these characters. He saw Selby as centrally concerned with violence and pain, and he wanted the audience to feel the suffering of his addicted characters. But Aronofsky also wanted us to see that the "world of the film [is] much more like a dreamland."[24] Thus he set *Requiem* in Coney Island, tinted the screen, shot through filters, used split screens to show multiple subjectivities, and added pulsing, atmospheric electronic music. As in π, there are numerous hallucinations, almost all of which are nightmares. Even the pleasant dreams, such as when Harry imagines Marion by the ocean, burst apart to prove once again the agony of illusion. The substantial artifice of the film, in sum, is given over to distortion and insanity. There seems to be no way for Aronofsky to imagine artifice in a positive way. Even though Aronofsky speaks of art and artists relatively more often, I would say, than other young directors, there is a strong idea that nature still grounds art, in contrast to the illusions and hallucinations of artifice.

In Selby's novel, Marion is a painter, and her dream is to open a store that sells clothing based on her sketches. Marion is terrifically cultured, and her mind is filled with ideas about Italian museums, Renaissance music, and light: "All that summer and fall she painted, mornings, afternoons, evenings, then walked around the streets that were still echoing the music of the masters, and every stone and every pebble seemed to have a life and reason of its own."[25] Selby's novel is made out of interior monologues, and a film is necessarily more visual, more exteriorized. A film can never hope to reproduce every element of a 275-page book. But for whatever reason, Aronofsky's *Requiem* has almost entirely given up on the idea that Marion is an artist. She is surrounded by her pictures when we last see her in the film, but otherwise the painting, which is so important to the book, vanishes almost entirely. One is tempted to see more than just narrative economy here. For the film seems rather confused about how to deal with Marion's creativity and her art.

And Aronofsky himself seems confused about what the dream actually is in *Requiem for a Dream*. In Selby's novel, clearly the idea is that we are sad that the dream of the store, of Marion's paintings, has been lost; hence our requiem. But Aronofsky says that the dream is addiction itself:

It's an addiction to a dream of yourself: wanting to be skinny or healthy. And it's an addiction that's extremely dangerous, because we can believe in the dream to such an extent that we don't live the present, we don't change our lives now, and that can lead to a collapse, as in the book. Then there's another message about the myth of the American Dream, which is what makes Selby such an archetypal American writer—because all of his material is about that myth. Selby says that the educational system in America tells us that we are all born jerk-offs, and that the goal is to make us rich jerk-offs. Selby talks about "unlearning the lies." These are all the lies we're given, which are basically an opiate; the opiate of the masses, the American Dream.[26]

In Selby the dream seems not to be ironic; we mourn that an authentic dream has been set to one side. By contrast, in Aronofsky's reading the dream is addiction and the American dream; the movie, in its powerful representation, ends those dreams. But then why would anyone sing a requiem? For we would be glad to have such dreams exposed and exploded. The confusion about where the dream is or what Aronofsky's relationship is to the American dream is further confirmed when we note the setting of the interview with Aronofsky that introduces the *Requiem* script. It is set at the "Cannes Film Festival, 18 May 2000." Just as π was framed by Sundance, *Requiem* begins at Cannes. "This is art," says Cannes, confirming a cinematic dream, but an art grounded, according to Aronofsky, in reality.

The Solaris Effect

Aronofsky ends his interview by equating most people with the addicts in his story because they will not face reality:

The bottom line is this: perhaps the most disturbing shot is the needle in the hole, in the open wound. There was a lot of debate about that between the studio and me, as you can imagine. For me, that image completely sums up what the movie is about; which is how far we will go to deny our existence in the present, and live in the fantasy of a dream. How far we will go to hold onto that dream, to fill that hole inside of us, with any addiction, rather than face the reality that is happening now. There's no possible way I would ever remove that shot, because as soon as you start pulling those punches, then why the hell are you making this movie?[27]

In this interview set at the Cannes Film Festival, Aronofsky heroically faces down the studio in the name of art's freedom and in the name of reality. At the end of the film, he visually underlines this point by having each of his protagonists end up in fetal positions.

And then Harry starts to cry. As we float up high above his we watch him curl up into a ball.
[Marion] pulls out a large bag of dope and stares at it. Happily, she fondles the bag. Then, she hugs it tight against her bosom. Slowly, she curls up into a fetal position, content.
Then, Tyrone and his bed dissolve into the past. Young Tyrone rests in his mom's generous arms.[28]

And Sara dreams of her young self hugging Harry on television ("I love you too, Ma."). The screenplay again underscores the priorities:

A smile fills Sara's beautiful face. Happiness. Total and complete love. Except for the truth, the nagging reality. It means tears for Sara and her sparkling eyes well up with fantastic, warm tears.[29]

Unlike the beautiful, impossible dream of Tarkovsky's *Solaris*—deluded and lovely at the same time—Aronofsky's dream is only satirical, signaling weakness, in crying need of reality's "truth." The brief review of *Requiem for a Dream* in *Cahiers du cinéma* sums it up well. Of the end of the film, the reviewer writes: "It is a horrific catharsis, a tottering monument and frankly touching, dedicated to the damned of all sorts, of whom Aronofsky makes himself the proudly naive singer ('*le chantre fièrement naïf*')." In its "artifices and holograms," *Requiem,* as the *Cahiers* review says, "*est bien contemporain de 'Matrix,'*" yet there is a strong sense that while Aronofsky may well be the master of his art, he is not yet master of its artifice.[30]

This discussion of Aronofsky's films and the Sundance films can only be, at most, suggestive of a certain tendency in independent film.[31] My claim in this chapter is, to some extent, a relatively obvious one: that a primary aesthetic for contemporary filmmakers revolves around nature and realism. This is an obvious claim insofar as film has always been the least modern of the twentieth-century arts, and in that film's interest in narrative, representation, and character has more often been linked to the Victorian novel than to twentieth-century developments in music or painting.

Yet my claim is not so obvious in this respect, namely, that American independent film often finds a need to counter the artifices of Hollywood film by the substantiality of realism. As Hollywood film becomes more and more star-driven, money-driven, glossy, and repetitive, it is Hollywood that comes to seem the domain of the artificial. John Cassavetes, the father of much of today's independent film, countered Hollywood gloss and shapeliness with rough-edged documentary-style movies. Hollywood film in the 1990s was more dependent than ever on special effects, computer-generated imagery, titanic budgets, and budget-bending stars, so it is not surprising that many independent films tended to decry artifice and turned to the traditions of neo-realism in Rossellini, the loosely formed narratives of the French New Wave, and the seemingly spontaneous and always explosive performances in Cassavetes. In the decade of Spielberg and Lucas, independent cinema more often aimed for realism than not. Smaller films need not carry the country or the world, so regional films tended to aim toward realistic depictions of a specific locale, and African American film and related multicultural cinema also tended to be urban in setting and realistic in method.

But realism in contemporary American film almost always implodes. To make an American fiction film in the 1990s meant pretending that one's camera and one's fiction were not radically reorganizing reality in the process of filmmaking. One of my recurrent polemical arguments is that the choice is not between Hollywood artifice and smaller-scale naturalism, but rather between transparent Hollywood and self-reflexive independence. As we will see in Chapter Seven, American films that choose an aesthetics of naturalism are almost unwatchably contradictory. The most successful filmmakers of the 1990s therefore did not avoid the artificial—they plunged into it, self-consciously and self-reflexively. Thus whereas Larry Clark, the director of *Kids* (1995), takes a more-realistic-than-Hollywood approach, his scriptwriter, Harmony Korine, joyfully immerses himself in trickery and artifice in *Gummo* (1997) and *Julien Donkey-Boy* (1999). Todd Haynes, in his DVD commentary for *Safe* (1995), says that "it is a very good thing when nature looks as artificial as possible." Gregg Araki's *Totally F***ed Up* (1993) explicitly invokes Godardian methods of self-conscious labeling and satire. Gus Van Sant and Jon Jost combine realistic treatment of character with the wildest surrealism. "Death to realism!" shout the supporters of the video game eXistenZ in Cronenberg's 1999 film of that name. Although Aronofsky compared his cyberpunk π to Cronenberg, Aronofsky sent up a requiem where Cronenberg sent up cheers. In the next chapter, we will look at the work of David Lynch, perhaps the most important American director who cries out on behalf of cinematic artifice.

Mulholland Drive, Cahiers du cinéma, and the Horror of Cinephilia

4

....

David Lynch's *Mulholland Drive* (2001) was accounted a masterpiece by critics in America and Great Britain. *Film Comment* and *Sight and Sound* both put *Mulholland Drive* on their covers. In *Sight and Sound,* Kim Newman called *Mulholland Drive* "emotionally overwhelming," and in the year-end polls, the *Village Voice, Film Comment,* and the New York Film Critics all ranked *Mulholland Drive* as the best movie of 2001. Such an outpouring of praise approached the limits of unanimity, a surprising response given the weirdness of the film and the awkward circumstances of its origins as a television pilot. To some extent, Lynch had prepared the ground for critical approval with *The Straight Story* (1999), but that film was, indeed, oddly "straight," seemingly uncharacteristic of Lynch. Since *Blue Velvet* (1986), Lynch's films had not met with much critical approval in the United States. The first sentence of Roger Ebert's review of *Mulholland Drive* (which he gave four stars, his highest rating) might be taken as a summary of much U.S. critical opinion: "David Lynch has been working toward *Mulholland Drive* all of his career, and now that he's arrived there I forgive him *Wild at Heart* and even *Lost Highway.*"[1] Although *Mulholland Drive* easily topped the *Village Voice* list for 2001, Lynch's films from the 1990s are still buried at the very bottom of the *Voice*'s list of the decade's best movies. *Wild at Heart* is ranked #210, *Lost Highway* #223, and *The Straight Story* comes in at #236.

If we move now to France, we find that *Mulholland Drive* also tops the 2001 *Cahiers du cinéma* poll. But for the *Cahiers* critics, Lynch had already charted many times before. *The Straight Story* was #8 on the *Cahiers* poll for 1999, and

Lost Highway, which Roger Ebert felt needed his forgiveness, was #3 in 1997. In the overall decade poll, in which *Cahiers du cinéma* ranked the best films of the 1990s, Lynch's *Twin Peaks: Fire Walk with Me* was ranked #4. *Wild at Heart* did not make a *Cahiers* top ten list, although it did win the Palme d'Or at Cannes. *Twin Peaks: Fire Walk with Me* was ignored almost entirely by *Cahiers* at the time of its release, but by the end of the decade Lynch had been accepted into the *Cahiers* pantheon to the extent of a retrospective canonization. Thus when *Mulholland Drive* was ranked #1 by *Cahiers du cinéma* in 2001, it was not an abrupt success after a series of botched experiments, but instead one more top ten film—indeed, the fourth in four tries—an achievement that reconfirmed Lynch's status as a master auteur.

What do the French see in Lynch? Their taste for Jerry Lewis springs too readily to mind, and they have been extremely patient with Woody Allen over the years. Are all the French crazy? For while it is the case that *Twin Peaks: Fire Walk* was ranked #4 by *Cahiers* for their best films of the 1990s, it is also true that Brian De Palma's *Carlito's Way* (1993) was ranked #1. And two of Clint Eastwood's movies were in the top ten (*The Bridges of Madison County, Unforgiven*), all in a decade-long list of *world* cinema. What gives—beyond a provocative, intellectual anti-intellectualism?

In this chapter I will characterize the dream aesthetic of David Lynch by developing insights and approaches from *Cahiers du cinéma*. While *Cahiers* does not have the kind of influence it had in the 1950s and '60s, it is still one of the most interesting film periodicals in the world. Its reviewers demand art and arresting aesthetics from films, yet they constantly redefine where that art may be found. Masterpiece theater has never impressed them. By looking at Lynch's films through a lens framed by *Cahiers*, we can understand what it might mean to regard Lynch's films as art and where, more generally cinematic art might be found.

My first chapter insisted on the idea that to talk about the art of film is inseparable from talking about the nature of cinematic illusion. *Solaris*, Tarkovsky's ghostly love story, provides a powerful model for thinking about cinematic illusion. Cinephilia, the love of cinema, is yet another love story, and both Lynch and *Cahiers du cinéma* are passionate lovers of the dream screen. How is the Solaris effect related to cinephilia? What kinds of love stories are these? In this chapter I will compare the haunted cinephilia of *Mulholland Drive* to the critical cinephilia of *Cahiers du cinéma*. The first section of this chapter will serve as an introduction to the approach of 1990s *Cahiers* by using its treatment of Brian De Palma as an exemplary focus.

Cahiers du cinéma in the 1950s was written by critics who would later go on to become some of the most important directors of the New Wave, and indeed, of world cinema. At *Cahiers*, Francois Truffaut, Jean-Luc Godard, Jacques Rivette, Eric Rohmer, and Claude Chabrol all contributed to one of the most fertile explosions in the history of writing about film. In the late 1960s and early '70s, *Cahiers* became a much more theoretical and political magazine, and some of the most significant Marxist critiques of film were written then.[2] *Cahiers* nowadays is more obviously devotional than fiercely political, but the magazine has certainly not left behind its attention to the politics of imagery.

The American pantheon now consists of directors like Lynch, Scorsese, De Palma, Tim Burton, Clint Eastwood, Jim Jarmusch, and Abel Ferrara. The enthusiasm of *Cahiers* manifests itself in articles, top ten lists, the magazine's film of the month, and a line of books published by *Cahiers* on various directors. Most U.S. critics would agree on the importance of Scorsese and Coppola, but might express surprise at the attention given to Eastwood and Burton. *Cahiers* loved not only Eastwood's *Unforgiven*, but also *The Bridges of Madison County* and *A Perfect World*. Burton possesses an individual style, no doubt, but *Cahiers* celebrates his genius much more often than do critics in the United States or the United Kingdom. And practically no one else paid Brian De Palma any serious attention in the 1990s. Yet De Palma's *Mission: Impossible*, of all things, was ranked #8 by *Cahiers* in 1996. And, to state the miraculous once again, *Cahiers* voted De Palma's *Carlito's Way* the best film of the 1990s. Selecting directors for the pantheon is clearly a decision that goes beyond intellectual assent and becomes essentially an act of devotion.

In *A Cinema of Loneliness: [Arthur] Penn, Stone, Kubrick, Scorsese, Spielberg, Altman*, one of the finest critical studies of contemporary American film, Robert Kolker barely mentions De Palma. And when he does, it is only to set him forcefully to one side: "Brian De Palma has made a career of the most superficial imitations of the most superficial aspects of Hitchcock's style, worked through a misogyny and violence that manifest a contempt for the audience exploited by his films—though in *Scarface* (1983) and *The Untouchables* (1987) he has shown a talent for a somewhat more grandiloquent allusiveness."[3] A more generous reading will at least admit that De Palma's films of the seventies (*Obsession, Carrie, The Fury*) were important contributions to American cinema at that time. But few American critics take De Palma's later work very seriously. In one of the rare recent defenses of De Palma in an American film magazine, Armond White characterizes De Palma as having "the worst press a major American film-maker has ever received."[4] But except for this piece by

White, *Film Comment* almost entirely ignored De Palma in the 1990s. Indeed, beyond a trouncing of *Mission: Impossible* by Howard Hampton ("De Palma palms off drab, bloodless efficiency as entertainment"), *Film Comment* went on about its business by pretending that De Palma no longer existed.[5]

By contrast, during the same period *Cahiers du cinéma* ran special extended sections for *Carlito's Way, Mission: Impossible,* and *Mission to Mars.* This admiration for De Palma goes back at least twenty years. For its "Made in the USA" double issue (334/335, April 1982), *Cahiers* interviewed De Palma, along with Scorsese and Peter Bogdanovich. In the amazing Isabelle Huppert issue of *Cahiers* (477, March 1994), Huppert interviews De Palma and talks at length about *Carlito's Way. Cahiers* criticism is enthusiastic: it is a magazine for cinephiles by cinephiles. And they love cinephilic directors. At the heart of *Cahiers'* enthusiasm for Tim Burton's *Ed Wood,* for instance, is the fact that the movie is sheer cinephilia.[6] A constant American reference for *Cahiers* is Martin Scorsese, who has shared his own love of film in documentaries such as *A Personal Journey with Martin Scorsese through American Film* (1995) and *My Voyage to Italy* (2001). In issue 500 of *Cahiers du cinéma,* which is dedicated to Scorsese, the director of *Taxi Driver* and *Raging Bull* makes it clear that De Palma ought to be regarded as a peer of himself, Spielberg, and George Lucas.[7]

The stark difference between American and French criticism of De Palma can be seen in the treatments of his *Mission to Mars* (2000). In the United States, the movie failed at the box office rather miserably, and American critics were very unkind. Despite some attractive visuals, Roger Ebert found the dialogue stereotyped and the "meditative tone" unearned, and so could not recommend the film.[8] But *Cahiers* presented *Mission to Mars* by way of a review, an extended critical analysis, a career overview, and a long interview with De Palma. Its assumption was that anything that De Palma does is of significance for the history of cinema. To *Cahiers* it seems transparently obvious that *Mission to Mars* merits our fullest intellectual and emotional attention. *Cahiers* would eventually rank *Mission to Mars* #4 in its list of the best films of 2000.[9]

The interview with De Palma underlines some of the repeated *Cahiers* emphases. The interviewer notes that characters in *Mission to Mars* interact like those in Howard Hawks's films, as professionals in dangerous situations.[10] Hawks is one of the key auteurs in the *Cahiers* pantheon, and De Palma himself compares Hawks's use of Cary Grant to his own use of Tom Cruise, Nicolas Cage, and Sean Penn. De Palma gives the perfect *Cahiers* interview, really, since he is happy to range over his entire career and to bring into the discussion movies both classic and contemporary. After mentioning Howard Hawks, the interviewer asks De Palma whether he referred to John Ford's Monument Valley in his visual depiction of Mars. De Palma goes on to compare his film to Kubrick's *2001*; whereas *2001* is rather cold, elegant, abstract, and mysterious, he says, *Mission to Mars* is simpler and more human.[11] De Palma begins the interview by noting his film's realism, which marks an approach common to both *Mission to Mars* and *2001*. The spacecraft in Kubrick and in De Palma look like authentic NASA-issue vehicles. But the *Cahiers* interviewer is more interested in the way that De Palma deploys illusion, spectacle, and dream. *Mission to Mars* begins with a rocket launch that turns out only to be some fireworks, just as *Carlito's Way*, on a larger scale, is structured as a dream, a flashback. De Palma says that his films critique the American dream (*"Le rêve américain est un enfer!"* [The American dream is a hell!]), but he notes that what one demands of cinema is in fact a dream.[12] De Palma appears more interested in justifying his films through realism than the interviewer, but they both clearly enjoy their odyssey through the movies.

An accompanying article on De Palma also treats *Mission to Mars* as obviously worthy of intellectual discussion. "Mission to Venus" by Stéphane Delorme begins with the idea of simulation in *Mission to Mars*. Whereas De Palma has often been regarded as a director of appearances (*"un cinéaste du faux-semblant"*), he is now, according to Delorme, to be regarded as a Godardian educator who teaches about lying images.[13] How shall we read De Palma, asks the reviewer, as being concerned with lying images or *absent* images? Delorme argues that the whole film is about absence: the absence of a chromosome, the absence of a length of cable that would save Blake's life, the absence of women. A rare moment of fullness (*"l'un de ses rares moments de plénitude"*) occurs when Blake and Terry dance together weightlessly. Delorme compares this scene to the famous circular traveling shot in *Vertigo*, although a comparison to the floating scenes in Tarkovsky would not be far afield either. In the way that we have deployed *Solaris* as an exemplary myth, Delorme uses the couple's love story as a model for cinematic presence. In Tarkovsky's *Solaris*, an astronaut finds his lost wife in outer space. In *Mission to Mars*, an astronaut goes into outer space with his wife, and there they are lost to each other forever. The absence and presence of the cinematic image is worked through self-reflexively in each marriage plot.

The writers for *Cahiers du cinéma* are always interested in these models of love, even as they display their own ebullient love of cinema. Their ingenious interpretations and excessive enthusiasm stand at the heart of *Cahiers'* journalistic identity and signify, altogether, a wildly passionate cinephilia. So playfully intellectual in approach and encyclopedic in knowledge, *Cahiers* loves cinema too much, beyond all reason. In his career overview of De Palma, "L'intouchable," Emmanuel Burdeau calls *Mission: Impossible "sans doute le plus grand film américain des années 90*" (without doubt the greatest American film of the '90s).[14] This is cinephilia, surely, at the edge of insanity, but *Cahiers* has always been out of its head. Delorme's article, cited above, is a little more circumspect. He criticizes the ridiculousness of De Palma's alien, as well as the film's conclusion, suggesting that the end of *Mission to Mars* is unfortunately closer to the "naive ideology" of James Cameron's *Abyss* than that of Kubrick's *2001*. Yet, what of that, thinks Delorme—the death scene of Blake is powerful, and the four astronauts spacewalking together is "*le plus beau du film*" (the most beautiful scene of the film). When Terry has to leave her husband behind in space, writes Delorme, this can only remind us of Orpheus and Eurydice. And at this moment, he continues, "Can we any longer reduce De Palma to a formalist virtuoso?" Although the word "art" is never mentioned, Delorme's outcries of cinephilia imply that De Palma has revealed himself, in these instances, as a true artist of the cinema.

An issue of *Cahiers* sets films down into a heterogeneous collection of visual imagery. Included in the same issue (546) as the sixteen-page dossier on De Palma (whose name appears on the cover with those of Buñuel and Oshima) are articles on the videogame Pokemon, the documentarian Frederick Wiseman (*Belfast, Maine*), Chris Marker's documentary on Tarkovsky, the pornographic films of John Root, and the experimental films of Len Lye, in addition to a long collection of essays on Buñuel and an article on film distribution. *Cahiers* frequently discusses Internet sites, art installations, computer games, and American television series. Film is loved, but not overessentialized. *Cahiers* frequently follows a Godardian emphasis by speaking about the image. Instead of analyzing cinematic "art," one analyzes visual imagery, an apparently more concrete artifact. Directors are praised not so much for beautiful images (although such praise is often present), as for the knowing deployment of images. Hence how very often the articles find themselves in the vicinity of the Solaris effect, weighing the presence and absence of imagery. This is just where Emmanuel Burdeau concludes, as well, in his essay on the body in De Palma:

> The great directors (of contemporary American film), De Palma and Ferrara, are starting to leap over beyond the common point of distinction between the cinema of the body, warm, concrete, open to the uncontrol-

lable rush of desire, and the cinema of images, cold, abstract, produced by intelligence and destined to be privileged by it.[15]

"*S'efface comme par enchantement*" concludes the paragraph; the distinction is "erased as if by magic." In De Palma and Ferrara, according to Burdeau, the image is both enchanting and distanced, warm and cold at once.

If De Palma was one of the favorite *Cahiers* auteurs of the 1970s, then David Lynch was one of its favorites of the 1990s. Its devotion materialized most concretely in the *Cahiers du cinéma* series of film books. It published bilingual scripts of both *Lost Highway* and *The Straight Story;* a set of interviews with Lynch by Chris Rodley (originally published in England by Faber and Faber); a translated set of essays on film noir by Barry Gifford, who worked closely with Lynch on *Wild at Heart* and *Lost Highway;* and a study of Lynch for its series on auteurs. In this series, only Cassavetes, Eastwood, Coppola, and Kenneth Anger are American, and they appear alongside the likes of Oshima, Bresson, Chabrol, Tati, Tarkovsky, Fassbinder, Pialat, Paradjanov, Buñuel, and Ozu. The *Cahiers* volume on Lynch was written by Michel Chion, who is especially known for his books on voice and sound in cinema.[16]

David Lynch by Michel Chion is especially prescient, for it appeared in 1992, long before the films that would "confirm" Lynch's reputation—*Lost Highway, The Straight Story,* and *Mulholland Drive* (page references to the book will appear in parentheses).[17] The most recent Lynch films that Chion had seen at that time, *Wild at Heart* and *Twin Peaks: Fire Walk with Me,* had struck most critics as remarkably uneven or simply as disasters. *Wild at Heart* had won the Palme d'Or at Cannes, but the decision had been controversial in France, and almost incomprehensible elsewhere. Thus Chion treats Lynch not as a canonical figure like Bresson or Ozu, but rather as an ongoing experimentalist, a "creative artist" who continually adds to what the cinema can offer (xii). Chion sees *Blue Velvet* as Lynch's "classic" film, but he also regards *Twin Peaks: Fire Walk with Me* as a "glorious failure" that "expanded and extended the cinema . . . through the daring narrative structure" (155). And he calls *Wild at Heart* "the most beautiful love ballad which the cinema has ever whispered into the night" (140). For Chion, Lynch is "*the* romantic film-maker of our time" (158), and Chion's perspicacious ear is open to that romantic voice.

Chion's "romantic" Lynch seeks to overturn a "postmodern" Lynch. He wants to emphasize the vitalism of Lynch's films, not their cleverness and irony. When Lynch provides his own list of favorite movies—Fellini's *8 1/2,* Wilder's *Sunset Boulevard,* Kubrick's *Lolita*—Chion takes that list as an indication of passionate affiliation, not as a set of signs to be referenced and collaged. "Too much has been made of the quotes and allusions in *Twin Peaks*," writes Chion (113). The television series succeeded not through "calculating cynicism," but through "comic fantasy and emotional ardour" (114). Lynch's romanticism is complicated and wide-ranging, "morbid and tearful, fond of the trivial and the shockingly strange" (159). But however complicated, this romanticism, for Chion, is *not* self-reflexive:

> Lynch, moreover, is a romantic film-maker in a period of film history where cinema itself is romantic, that is to say, impure, hybrid and re-invigorated, renewing its alliance with its popular base. Lynch's sense of curiosity makes him discover cinema with every step he takes, but he externalizes this discovery, that is, he places cinema in the service of a narrative while seeking to renovate its forms. In other words, his films do not mistake themselves for their subject. (159)

Chion's cinephilia attaches itself to Lynchian romanticism so as to specifically avoid Lynch's potential for cinematic self-reflexivity. This cinephilia exists as an either-or: either the enthusiasm of 1950s *Cahiers* or the ideological critique of 1970s *Cahiers*. But much of the best work in *Cahiers* manages to account for both passion and self-reflexivity, and Lynch's potential for critique and self-description should not be erased by pleasure. In this chapter, I will read *Twin Peaks: Fire Walk with Me* and *Mulholland Drive* as parables of cinephilia, which insist that the love of cinema is always tied to cinematic self-reflexivity. I will argue, furthermore, that although *Cahiers du cinéma* investigated cinephilia as often, as variously, and as closely as any institution in the critical world, it still never followed cinematic pleasures as far down darkened corridors as did David Lynch's films, in which cinephilia is always revealed to be horrific. Lynch's dream screen is always a nightmare.

Twin Peaks: Fire Walk with Me: On the Constructedness of Dreams

Twin Peaks: Fire Walk with Me stands as the most remarkable instance of *Cahiers* rehabilitation and cinephilia. Even *Cahiers* did not love Lynch enough in 1992. After Lynch's *Wild at Heart* took the Palme d'Or at Cannes in 1990, *Twin Peaks: Fire Walk with Me* was booed loudly at Cannes in 1992, and went on to receive poor reviews in every quarter. At the time, *Cahiers* gave the film a single page of notice, and Antoine de Baecque's review was far from positive. De Baecque deplored the unnuanced Manicheanism of the film, the cliche of the monstrous father, and the relentless torturing of the viewer throughout the film.[18] That *Cahiers* even reviewed the film was, relative to the rest of the critical press, an act of generosity. But by the end of the 1990s, Lynch had become one of the most highly favored auteurs at *Cahiers*, and *Twin Peaks* ended up tying for fourth among the best films of the entire decade.[19] In the December 2001 collection of DVD reviews, which were chosen to spotlight the usual darlings (including Jarmusch's *Dead Man* and De Palma's *Carlito's Way*), *Twin Peaks: Fire Walk* is now suitable for selection. In the American press, *Mulholland Drive* does not cause anyone to love *Twin Peaks: Fire Walk* more, or at all, but in the collective mind of *Cahiers du cinéma*, a devotion to *Lost Highway* and *The Straight Story* should make us revisit *Twin Peaks: Fire Walk*, and revisit it with affection. Chion's praise for *Fire Walk* in his book on David Lynch is probably the most generous critique that anyone offered at the time, and by the end of the decade *Cahiers* as a whole had caught up with one of its most interesting writers.

Before turning to *Mulholland Drive*, then, I want to provide a detailed reading of *Twin Peaks: Fire Walk with Me*. Like many of Lynch's films, *Twin Peaks* makes most sense taken as a dream. Most interpreters will speak of Lynchian "dream logic," and Lynch himself often speaks of film as a dream. When he goes to watch other films, he says, he wants to be taken into a dream.[20] What I want to emphasize in this section is, above all, the constructedness of the Lynchian dream. Recent criticism, following Chion, perhaps, too often tries to save Lynch from the alleged superficiality of his postmodernism by emphasizing the vitality or the deeper reality of his dreamscapes. But the Lynchian dream is self-consciously artificial, a construction. As Lynch says in an interview: "When you sleep, you don't control your dream. I like to dive into a dream world that I've made, a world I chose and that I have complete control over."[21] Let us emphasize not only the dream, then, but also the thoroughgoing artifice of that dream.

To read a film as a dream is often to naturalize and humanize the film. To read the film as related to the figures of Freud or Lacan is to say that the logic of the film follows the logic of the psychoanalyzed human mind. But Lynch's dreams are machines rather than organisms. I want to underscore the brilliant machinery of Lynch, his artifice, rather than his romanticism, humanism, or the truths of his unconscious. The cinematic unconscious is structured like cinematic language. Hence, when cinema dreams of cinema, we ought not to bend film dreams into human dreams unaware. Our final interpretive moral will thus be a stern warning against interpretive anthropomorphism. The So-laris effect is modelled by the dynamic relationship between two people, Kris and Hari, except Hari is not human, but an alien confabulation.

We should, then, immediately confront the important argument made by Martha Nochimson in *The Passion of David Lynch: Wild at Heart in Hollywood*. Like Chion, Nochimson reads Lynch as a romantic; hence, the fires in *Fire Walk* burn with intuitive, primal desire. In her reading, Lynch reopens the images and cliches of Hollywood film, and such openings lead to a liberation from Hollywood's structures of confinement. Lynch eschews "transparent" reality, wherein "an image is realistic because it resembles our idea of reality," and instead leads the audience toward a deeper, subconscious reality.[22]

> His methods, derived from painters who impressed him as a young stu-dent, give him the insight to represent both the mirror-image ideals of the filmic image and the wild energies that disturb it. In this balance, we find that he taps into the vitality of Hollywood *and* is often a corrective to the lies and repressions involved in Hollywood's pretense of a rationalist form of realism.[23]

Nochimson celebrates Lynch's irrationalist dream aesthetic as a new "real-ism," as a truer realism than the transparent realism of Hollywood. The fluid, mobile world of Lynch is "real," while Hollywood is "pretense," "lies," and "re-pression." This argument quite properly describes Lynch as the opposite of classical transparency, but it falls back, nonetheless, on "realism" as a founda-tion of aesthetic virtue. The conclusion to her chapter on *Twin Peaks: Fire Walk with Me* states, consistently, "As long as our ordinary 'social realities' threaten to immure us within artificial limits, the winds will rise again and with it *this kind of fire*, particularly in the forest of Holly-wood(s)."[24] Romantically, social realities are seen as conventions from which we can liberate ourselves. In this view, Lynch becomes an enemy of the walls and restrictions of artifice.

Nochimson wants to reclaim Lynch from merely "cool," superficial post-modernism. Instead of postmodern skepticism and nihilism, she finds in Lynch optimism and even joy. Her description of Lynch's aesthetics recalls the writings of Tarkovsky. Tarkovsky also argued for poetic film, film that in its seemingly random associations and connections pointed toward truth in a way that ordinary narrative film could not.[25] And like all good professors of poetry, Nochimson wants to remind us that metaphor and imagination have a reality, too. But by describing Lynch's dreams as forms of "higher reality," Nochimson loses the sense of how constructed these dreams are. Provocatively, she wants to read narrative disorientation as freedom—a very compelling way to read the apparently aimless horror of a film like *Twin Peaks: Fire Walk with Me*. But her "freedom" is too idealized; it makes film into a dream too easily, too transparently. If Lynch's films do not transparently repeat a real world, then neither do they transparently represent a dream world.

In his review essay on Lynch's later film *Lost Highway*, Frédéric Strauss places the dream film in a more artificial context. The powerful dream ("sweet, bad, and wet") reminds Strauss of something "between a moving sculpture-machine by Jean Tinguely and the pure form of a stone totem by Henry Moore; something between an etching by Escher in its depths and the surfaces of a Polaroid saturated with colors."[26] Even as Strauss underlines the dream logic of the film, he also stresses the film as a thing, as an object. *Lost Highway* is a "pure vision," but one that provokes us like a "ready-made" by Marcel Duchamp. For Strauss, the key emblem from the film is the image of dead Andy with his head cut into a table (Strauss underlines: "*une table design*").[27] In other words, think of the head not as a repository of swirling interiority, but rather as part of the design, part of the sculpture.

In his romantic interpretation, Michel Chion notes the ongoing presence of mechanical humming in *Twin Peaks: Fire Walk*:

It is one of those machine sounds with an implacable regularity which are omnipresent in Lynch's work. Their meaning is neither erotic nor sexual as such, nor can they be reduced to some primary function. They are life itself, vital power, absurd and ever-present.[28]

Yet why should the mechanical noises signify "life itself"? Why should the artificial imply the organic? Do not the omnipresent machines in Lynch point to constructedness rather than vitality? As a title, *Twin Peaks* speaks more clearly about twins and repetitions than it does about peaks and other natural landmarks. There is an enormous difference between the haunted woods of *Twin Peaks*, which dissolve into red curtains, and the wise woods of *Northern Exposure*, where nature contains truths, not red rooms. The phrase "fire walk" in the subtitle implies the constructedness of social ritual rather than the sudden irruption of nature, and the repetition of this phrase throughout the television series underlined this sense of chanted magic.

Many other aspects of *Twin Peaks: Fire Walk*, taken together, denaturalize its dream narrative and foreground our sense that this dream is being built. The use of celebrity actors in stunningly brief cameos, for example, can only emphasize the staginess of the film. The sudden appearance and disappearance of David Bowie is the opposite of a neorealistic event. One of the detectives at the beginning is played by Chris Isaak, a pop star who in 1992 was at the height of his fame. The presence of Bowie and Isaak can only disrupt any tendency to drift into a flow of unconscious imagery. On the contrary, their presence heightens the sense that this is show business, that the dream is staged. If Hitchcock's cameos tell us, with mild amusement, that this is only a movie, then Lynch's more extended appearance at the beginning of *Fire Walk* must further strengthen our sense that this dream is a self-conscious construction.

Lynchian weirdness appears theatrically, not naturalistically. Lynch's own performance as a deaf man who talks too loud is transparently a role. At the airport, the FBI agents are treated to a bizarre dance by Lil, who gestures and spins around. With red hair and a red dress, Lil is a prototype of theatrical artificiality.[29] Later on, the boy who brings Laura Palmer the painting wears a mask, another plain indication that this is dream theater. Dialogue and acting are anything but naturalistic. When Special Agent Desmond wants to see the local sheriff, the deputy and his secretary smirk and laugh to themselves too overtly, too loudly, more like cartoons than people. Or consider the old lady who comes into Teresa Banks's trailer. She is a forerunner of the monstrous homeless man behind the dumpster in *Mulholland Drive*. This woman is completely silent and essentially painted brown. If she is supposed to look dirty, then the makeup is a disaster. What her brief appearance does make manifest is once again the overtly staged quality of the strange.

The first time we meet the inhabitants of the other world, we do so by dissolving through a man in a mask. This whole scene is superimposed over a blurry television screen, a move that thereby aligns the other world with television projections. "We live inside a dream," a voice says clearly. Meanwhile the little man in the red suit runs his hand over a table: "This is a Formica table. Green is its color." A bearded man flaps his hand before a door-sized frame of aluminum foil, and a mouth says, "Electricity." The images feel randomly assembled, but they are clearly linked by themes of theatricality and artifice. The scene concludes by showing us the curtains and tiles of the red room while the boy lifts his mask on and off. Altogether, this is Lynchian dream theater par excellence, and completely self-conscious. The whole first part of the film, with its painted homeless woman, flapping Lil, performing Lynch, and disappearing Bowie, is built out of one theatricalized dream gesture after another.

Since Lynch's films emphasize fluidity and mobility, it is easy to under-emphasize their artifice. They seem to flow like water or air. Paintings in the films dissolve and shift, and photographs, like Cocteau's mirrors, open out into other worlds. One of the photographs in Laura's room is of a door, which eventually opens into another reality. *Twin Peaks: Fire Walk* seems to re-describe three-dimensional space by piercing it through with demonic spirits and *n*-dimensional chambers. The frames of paintings and pictures seem un-able to contain the dynamic energies of Lynchian intuitive flow. Walls fall away, and space seems boundaryless, unbounded.

But Lynch's wandering dream films are not swirling pools of water; they are carefully constructed labyrinths. A labyrinth may be extraordinarily com-plex, but it is still the work of a Daedalus, a master artificer. At the end of the *Twin Peaks* television series, Agent Cooper runs back and forth between two red-curtained rooms, stuck in a miniature maze. Although it ought to stand as some sort of transcendental resting place, the red room functions to deflect closure from every direction, and we see Laura screaming like a demon at the end. This is almost certainly not the way we want to leave her. Boundaries collapse at the end, and even the final edge of the series is immensely con-fused. The image before us is a labyrinth, not an ocean. Recall that even the ocean world of Tarkovsky's *Solaris* is controlled by an alien entity and is itself essentially a dream machine.

Indeed, *Twin Peaks: Fire Walk with Me* comes into existence as another ver-sion of *Solaris*. In the television series that preceded the film, Laura Palmer is dead, and our only access to her is through photographs and video clips. In the television series, we see the actress who plays Laura (Sheryl Lee) only a very few times in the same space as the other characters. In the fourth episode, for example, she shows up as Madeleine, a relative of Laura's; here she is simply Laura with different hair, in a momentary allusion to Hitchcock's *Vertigo*. We also see Laura in the red room dreamed by Agent Cooper, although there she speaks electronically monsterized red-roomese, just like the little man in the red suit. At one point (in episode two) the little man asks Cooper, "Doesn't she look just like Laura Palmer?" Which means that even when we see Laura freed from her photograph, as Madeleine or in the red room, it is still never quite she. The central premise of *Twin Peaks* is that Laura Palmer has been brutally murdered and that therefore all the stories, memories, and visions of Laura serve only to remind us of her absence. Most of the television episodes conclude by rolling the credits over her smiling photograph.

Twin Peaks: Fire Walk is a labyrinthine *Solaris* that complicates the binary structures of presence and absence. The love that ties together Kris and Hari in *Solaris* circulates now through all the characters in *Fire Walk*. Laura herself has two boyfriends, is raped by her father, is possessed by the demon Bob, and has an extradimensional relationship with Agent Cooper. A wedding ring is offered to her by the little man. Instead of a Hari who embodies the love and life-memories of Kris, everyone in *Fire Walk* is Kris in a community of shared memories and dreams. Laura Palmer is not a private dream, but a communal projection. At the end of Soderbergh's *Solaris*, there is a picture of Rheya taped to Kris's refrigerator; by contrast, there is a metaphorical picture of Laura Palmer on everyone's fridge in *Twin Peaks*. Laura Palmer is an archetypal image, an image among images, the prom queen in a trophy case. There is never a real woman in that photograph of Laura Palmer, but instead a collage of projected dreams.

When the film *Twin Peaks: Fire Walk* comes into the world as a prequel to the television series, it breathes life into Laura Palmer, but as a woman who is headed straight for death. For a fan of the television series, the body in the plastic bag at the beginning of the film is going to be read as Laura Palmer's, so the movie captions the body "Teresa Banks." For someone who is not a fan of the television series, so many figures have appeared and disappeared by the time Laura finally shows up, halfway through the film, that she cannot seem too confidently substantial. Either way, when Laura now appears in the film, she emerges into a theatricalized ghost world. Her section of *Twin Peaks* does not seem so obviously stagy as the first part of the film, but it will only be a matter of time before the curtains part for her, too. Laura's character will eventually become as theatricalized and artificial as the dream world we have already seen.

We are invited to see Laura initially as a photograph, an idealized image, a prom queen, but her character is soon revealed to be fantastically mobile. Laura's character is spectacularly inconsistent, moving from rage to tenderness to exuberance in a few seconds. Sheryl Lee's performance is reminiscent of Christopher Walken's in Abel Ferrara's *King of New York* (1991), in which Walken's face shows amusement, then ferocity, then calm, all in the space of a few moments, thereby outwardly embodying the paradoxes of his socially charitable mob kingpin. When Bobby accosts Laura after she misses their date, she insults him rudely ("I was standing right behind you but you're too dumb to notice"), smiles jokingly at Dinah ("If he turned around he might get dizzy"), absolutely lets him have it ("Get lost, Bobby!"), then appeases him with a seductive smile ("C'mon, c'mon, smile"). Her boyfriends all want her and her good looks for themselves, but she is uncontrollable and unfathomable—tender, ferocious, fearful, and composed by turns. This multiplication of tonality and mood characterizes Laura's performance throughout, and reaches its most visible extreme when her face turns painted white and her teeth turn colorized yellow in a fit of demonic rage.

When Laura's demonic possession is visualized by simply recoloring her face on the screen, we realize that the nightmarish dream theater has once and for all stepped up into her world, has made its entrance. The masks and curtains of the first part of the film have descended. Before she turns into a mask herself, Laura now utters the film's title as a bit of satanic ventriloquism: "Fire walk with me." And then her face is suddenly painted white, her lips red, her teeth yellow. *Fire Walk with Me* thus indicates that it is not only a nightmare of love, but also a nightmare of artifice.[30]

Mulholland Drive and the Nightmare of Cinephilia

Cinephilia reproduces its own romanticism. Love wants to find that love again and again. Chion, like Nochimson, wants to defend Lynch from superficial postmodernism. Thus Lynch, in Chion's reading, becomes the "romantic filmmaker of our times."

> He is a film-maker who enables us to breathe the night air and feel the force of the wind, who touches directly on the mythic and the archaic. He celebrates the beauty and immenseness of the world in all its disparity, its tonal breaks, its sublime as well as its derisory aspects. He speaks to us about ourselves in our totality, including the utter dereliction of human experience, and as the world we live in tends ever towards greater abstraction and repetition, he renews man's connection with both his or her deepest emotions and the infinite universe.[31]

The endless signifying of postmodernism becomes the experimental vitality of romanticism. This cinephilia foregrounds human desire in its reading of film. And it celebrates and affirms that desire, however complex and tumultuous. Although without method, cinephilia is grounded in positivism and ultimately in humanism. The spectator's love of cinema is attended by an assumption that desiring, well-rounded subjects exist and fall in love, and that such love is a complicated good.

In this section I will read *Mulholland Drive* as a critique of cinephilia on its own terms. It is one thing to criticize *Cahiers* criticism simply on the level of its subjectivity. If one takes a critical approach that requires more logic, more method, and more science, then cinephilia can be dispensed with as appreciation, as mere impressionism. It is easy to argue that academic literary criticism should not be written in the mode of Walter Pater, Oscar Wilde, or their latter-day descendants, Harold Bloom and Geoffrey Hartman. Similarly, it can be argued, and has been argued, that film criticism needs to avoid cult and enthusiasm, steering instead towards an ideal of Arnoldian disinterestedness.[32] Yet much recent thinking in the humanities deplores the traditional hierarchy of reason over emotion and celebrates the particularized truths of subjectivity. A cinephilic approach may thus seem like a very appropriate way to write about film, the most important art form of the twentieth century. The emotion of cinephilia signifies that the writer has not yet adopted the role of museum curator, guiding the reader around the nineteenth-century precincts of Keats or Balzac, and is instead commenting on a living art, one that is a necessary part of our lives, of our culture. In the argument below, therefore, cinephilia is not mistaken because it is full of emotion, but because it has not become fully aware of its assumptions. *Mulholland Drive* is an embodied representation of cinephilia that provides a critical alternative to romantic cinephilia.

In his review of *Mulholland Drive* for *Cahiers du cinéma*, Thierry Jousse describes the "ambient" postmodernism of Lynch's latest film. All the postmodern citations, imitations, parodies, and mannerisms aim, he writes, ultimately toward a depiction of love:

> But all of this dream-like construction, all of its play of traces, all of this incredible accumulation of multiple strata, all the figurative sedimentation, is nothing if *Mulholland Drive* is not above all, and before everything, a powerful reflection on the doings of Hollywood . . . and above all [it is] the magnificent story of love between two women, of a lyricism practically without equal in contemporary cinema.[33]

Here cinephilia murmurs its ecstasy for lyrical love, but also for critical cinema. Lynch's film is more than a sedimented accumulation of cinematic memory, more than a postmodern list of deformed conventions. For in *Mulholland Drive*, according to Jousse, the conventions add up to a substantial critique of Hollywood—all the better for cinema! And at the center of the film is a profoundly lyrical love. *Mulholland Drive* gives us love, layers upon layers of film memory, and a critique of Hollywood. What more could any cinephile want?

Yet as Jousse points out, this love is complex, to say the least: "Like *Twin Peaks*—a film which is at first a story about incest, and *Lost Highway*, which is about a marriage crisis, *Mulholland Drive* is the story of an impossible love (*'l'histoire d'un amour impossible'*), ambivalent, vital, yet mortal at the same time."[34] As Jousse describes the structure of the love story, it develops gradually and euphorically until the nocturnal declaration (*"le sublime* I'm in love with you"), then descends into shadow, nightmare, and morbidity. Jousse concludes his essay, "L'amour à mort," by speculating on the role of Lynch in all of this. But we might extend his description by using *Mulholland Drive* to underscore the morbidity, or impossibility, of cinephilia itself. *Twin Peaks: Fire Walk with Me, Lost Highway*, and *Mulholland Drive* are movie-haunted, but each love story is also a catastrophic nightmare. Cinephilia, read through Lynch's films, has much more to do with solitude and nightmare than with community and ecstatic dream. Surely the Rita whom Diane loves does not exist. Rita is, in other words, exactly as real as the film we watch and fall in love with.

The film finds its sublime model for cinephilia at the Club Silencio. After making love and then awakening from sleep at two in the morning, Rita (Laura Harring) and Diane (Naomi Watts) take a cab to a strange theater. In several languages (*"no hay banda," "il n'y a pas d'orchestre"*), the demonic host (Geno Silva) warns the audience that there is no band, that all the music is tape-recorded. "It is all an illusion," he says. Sitting in the theater, Rita and Diane reenact the stages of their love. First, all is ghastly, terrifying, mysterious; then the song begins, and they cry together to the beautiful music. Love emerges out of fear, in the larger plot and in this sequence. The song is transcendentally lovely—Roy Orbison's "Crying" rendered in Spanish—but we know that it is not real. We have been told repeatedly that the euphoria of the song, of the beautiful singer, is all an illusion. Yet the two women are carried away nonetheless. Just as the dreams of *Twin Peaks: Fire Walk* were always marked as theatrical, so too is this beautiful song marked over and over as artifice, from the curtains to the singer's makeup (she has a teardrop painted on) to the completely straightforward warnings. Yet the lovers fall into the beautiful illusion, forgetting that it is an illusion, or remembering, which itself heightens the pathos of love. She sings about love, "I cry for you," and they cry, in love with the song, and with each other. The singer faints dead away, falling to the stage, but the song keeps going. We know it is a dream, but it is a beautiful dream. Let us keep dreaming.

The sequence can be read as an idealized performance of cinephilia, in which we recognize the artifice of film yet long for its emotions nonetheless, falling further into love. But everything after that scene emphasizes the solitary nightmare of love. What follows shows how conventional and horrific Diane's fantasy is. When we see Diane masturbating on the couch, in absolute frustration, this is about as close to reality as we will ever get.

There are various ways to make sense of the various obscurities of the dream narrative. In my understanding of *Mulholland Drive*, Rita does not exist at all.[35] What has happened, in my view, is that Betty has broken up with the unnamed woman in apartment 12. The last section of the movie starts when a bedraggled Diane wakes up (the cowboy says, "Time to wake up, pretty girl"), and the woman from 12 is at the door, coming to collect her last few things. Diane's fantasy thus turns this woman into Rita, a transformation that we see clearly a few moments later. When Diane turns around in the kitchen, now looking suddenly well groomed, Rita is there too, an obvious hallucination. Diane, in other words, tells herself the story of her breakup with the unnamed woman, and her account takes the form of a Hollywood movie in which she is an aspiring actress and Rita/Camilla is a gorgeous starlet who is stolen away from her by a famous director. The movie plot provides her hurt feelings with an explanation for the breakup (only something as powerful as the movie industry — a glamorous director — could have drawn her away from me) and also a model for her emotions, for how she should feel about her broken love.

At one point in this final section Diane climbs on top of a naked Rita, who looks like a *Penthouse* centerfold. Airbrushed and completely made-up, her appearance is extremely improbable, but a powerful part of Diane's dreamt narrative. Rita first says, "You drive me wild," but then says, "We shouldn't do this anymore." It is unlikely that anyone is going to announce the imminent breakup of a relationship while lying naked, supine, and looking as captivating as possible. Yet this is exactly the breakup scene in Diane's mind: love is represented as heightened sexual desirability, just as in the movies. What Diane really has, however, is nothing: frustration, masturbation, solitude. These tears now represent sheer depression, not love, and Diane apparently kills herself at the end of the film.

Mulholland Drive asks us to redescribe cinephilia as something much more like masturbation and loneliness. Instead of a cinephilia that brings the lover of movies into a community of lovers, into a fellowship with movie history and appreciation, this model of cinephilia emphasizes the despairing solitude at the heart of cinematic love. *Mulholland Drive* provides not only a self-righteous and ferocious critique of Hollywood, in which the producers of movies are seen as no less than organized crime figures, but also the opposite, a critique of cinephilia. If anything, the latter critique is the more substantial. Although the critics all focused on the "Hollywood nightmare" of *Mulholland Drive*, the nightmare is truly the nightmare of cinephilia, the despairing intensity with which the cinephile loves the cinema, even unto death.

The plot of *Mulholland Drive* makes Rita the perfect empty vessel for Diane's fantasies. The amnesiac plot is itself a species of film genre (from *Random Harvest* [LeRoy, 1942] to *Amateur* [Hartley, 1994] and *Memento* [Nolan, 2000]), but we can understand this element as the logical consequence of Diane's cinematic desires. For in her amnesia, Rita becomes pure exterior, pure glamour and mystery, the ideal Hollywood star. She becomes Rita only by looking up at a poster of Rita Hayworth, and beyond that she has virtually no character. In the wake created by Rita's amnesia, Diane can then create herself as a powerful detective, a supertalented actress, and a beautiful lover, all in one. But Rita is a blank cover girl, and Diane has invested herself in emptiness. The scene in Club Silencio shows that Lynch is not criticizing us for investing ourselves in Hollywood. Although Diane is in love with glamorous emptiness, her love is not undermined at the easy level of cultural critique. On the contrary, cinematic love is seen as being resplendently seductive, sophisticated, and penetratingly deep in our consciousness. It is not a matter of simply turning the channel or of recognizing the superficiality and greed of Hollywood. For this cinematic love is as authentic, as physical, and as deep as any love, although it is ultimately a love painted over an abyss.

In *Mulholland Drive* the seductive love of cinema is inextricably aligned with possession. Rita is a blank to be filled in by Diane's fantasies, but Diane is equally a blank, one to be filled in by idealizing enthusiasms and the ghosts of disaster. When Diane auditions for her part she is completely taken over by a sexual power, and she suddenly performs the dialogue as a soft-core porn scene. When the women audition for Adam Kesher (Justin Theroux), they do not speak dialogue, but instead lip-sync oldies, thus demonstrating their ability to speak in tongues. At the Club Silencio, where the disjunction between voice and body is made most clearly, Betty shakes violently in her seat, her body possessed by some horrific energy. Demonic possession is more explicit in *Twin Peaks: Fire Walk*, but present nonetheless through every dream and description of identity in *Mulholland Drive*. To fall in love is to lose oneself, to forget oneself, to lose possession of oneself. To fall out of love is to lose possession of one's most precious self. Falling in and falling out of love are equally characterized by amnesia and ghostly hauntings.

Mulholland Drive also makes a frequent thematic pun on possession (by demons) and possession (of things). Adam takes his fury out on the mob producers by smashing their car in the parking lot, and when he catches his wife in bed with another man, he does not speak a word but instead pours paint all over her jewelry. The final sequence of the film is a theatricalized exercise in material dispossession, as Diane is forced to watch Rita give herself to Adam in marriage and, even worse, accept a long kiss from another woman (the other Camilla Rhodes). This analysis of love, cinematic and material, is as thorough, even if not as explicitly critical, as any in a film by Godard. Although often documentary in approach, Godard's early films regularly feature beautiful women in the role of an actress or a prostitute. In films like *Vivre sa vie*, Godard reflects deliberately on the cinematic possession of beautiful women. Like Godard's films, Lynch's studies of beautiful women in *Twin Peaks: Fire Walk* and *Mulholland Drive* have more than a little to teach the students of imagery and materiality at *Cahiers du cinéma*.

Thierry Jousse, who describes the ambient dream of *Mulholland Drive* so well, may be taken as representative of a *Cahiers du cinéma* critic in the 1990s. The elegant essays collected in *Pendant les travaux, le cinéma reste ouvert* (*During its labors, cinema stays open*, 2003) move easily throughout the world of film in the 1990s, from a series of entries on Godard, to sections on French and European film, to Asian film and also American. He writes about key auteurs (Eastwood, Antonioni, Oshima, Suzuki) and theorists (Guy Debord), about cable television and the spectacle of 9/11. He effortlessly connects films from many times and places in lyrical descriptions that do not hesitate to excoriate the banal. His reviews of American film line up like the *Cahiers* pantheon itself: *Raising Cain* by De Palma, the Coen brothers' *Barton Fink*, Van Sant's *My Own Private Idaho*, Kubrick's *Eyes Wide Shut*, Lynch's *Lost Highway* and *Mulholland Drive*. Jim Jarmusch's *Dead Man* is "*un des grands films de ces dernières années*" (one of the great films of recent years).[36] This is criticism that is both cinephilic and critical, but not relentlessly critical, nor methodically self-critical. These essays are certainly aware of the political and economic landscape in which cinema occurs, but they do not emphasize political critique the way *Cahiers* did in the 1970s and '80s. The essays aim to be perfectly weighed descriptions, and in this goal they nearly always succeed.

In "Les dandys du câble," an essay focused particularly on cinephilia and later collected in *Critique et Cinephilia*, Jousse compares the structures of contemporary cinephilia to those of decades past.[37] First there is cinema alone, then cinema next to television, and now cinema in the context of cable television. Whereas 1960s cinephilia was hierarchical and vertical, contemporary cinephilia is nonhierarchical, horizontal, "rhizomatic." Whereas before there were clear lines to be drawn from Griffith and Lumière to Godard and Fuller, there are now no more masterpieces or obvious points of reference. Television or film? The loss of referents destroys a rationalized organization of memory and amounts to a programming of amnesia.[38] Yet Jousse concludes by describing a return to the old manner of cinephilia, which was characterized by a certain clandestine viewing and the collecting sensibility of a dandy. Now the dandy collects DVDs.

Surely *Mulholland Drive*'s analysis of cinephilia exists in exactly this critical space where television collides with film and where an onslaught of images creates, in effect, amnesia. But whereas Jousse finds contemporary cinephilia either opening out or circling back on itself, Lynch shows a response to these images that results in nothing less than horror. Cinephilia anatomized shows us more than a clandestine dandy with his DVD collection, according to Lynch. Going much further and more fiercely, we descend from a clandestine apartment full of possessions into an unforgiving nightmare in which we are haunted and possessed.

The *Cahiers du cinéma* critic who most consistently analyzed the detail and consequences of his own cinephilia was Serge Daney. Daney wrote for *Cahiers* from 1970 to 1982, when he quit his position as chief editor at *Cahiers* to write for the daily newspaper *Libération. Cahiers du cinéma* has since published the essays he wrote while working at *Cahiers* (collected as *La Rampe*) as well as those from *Libération* (*Ciné Journal I, Ciné Journal II*).[39] In the beginning, Daney's essays appeared alongside those of Jean-Pierre Oudart and Jean-Luis Comolli in the highly theoretical pages of post-1969 *Cahiers*. But his essays became progressively less doctrinaire and less abstract than those of his Lacan- and Marx-wielding colleagues. Daney stayed closer to Godard than Oudart, in that he combined political awareness and critical scrupulosity with an ongoing affection for cinema and the history of cinema.[40] He is clearly a pivotal figure in the history of *Cahiers du cinéma*, looking back toward Bazin and Godard while also looking forward to the recovery of cinephilia in its contemporary writers such as Charles Tesson and Jean-Michel Frodon.[41] Daney's four brief theoretical essays, "La fonction critique" (1974), form the centerpiece of the aforementioned *Cahiers* anthology *Critique et cinéphilie*.[42] Essay by essay, this anthology traces the tension between cinephilia and critical reflection over forty years at *Cahiers du cinéma*.

Many of the essays written for *Cahiers* during the 1970s and 1980s tend either to generalize all of film into one overarching ideological effect or to split films into, on the one hand, the ideologically suspect, and on the other, the politically correct. Daney's "La fonction critique" is linked to the first impulse when it generalizes about the critical abilities of cinema: "One image cannot critique another" and "The film, like a dream, does not know negation."[43] Who speaks for the film? What does the film say? What is the relationship between the political discourse of the film critic and the political discourse of a film? These four essays focus primarily on a number of overtly political films and intend to show that there are critical and political readings of film that go beyond the expressed politics of the film. In the midst of a deluge of political filmmaking and political criticism, Daney wishes to self-consciously reflect on what a political reading of film might be. The overt Lacanian and Marxist valuations of most of his colleagues are conspicuously absent from this essay. Later on, his essays will become even more personal and searching, and even less methodical. Psychoanalytic attention to the unconscious and Marxist attention to private ownership and capitalism clearly have important things to say about film as a possession—in both senses. But Daney prefers a more personal approach to his descriptions, even though psychology and political economy are usually not far from the discussion.

Daney's later reviews typically move from metaphor to metaphor, proceeding by association rather than linear argument. He is suspicious of films that impose narrative and is dismissive of conclusions that are overly clear, that lack ambiguity. His essays contain perfect descriptions of faces, images, or scenes, but they proceed sideways, in a series of surprising statements. The essays purposely reject academic learnedness and controversy, coming instead to resemble the films that he admires. The essays constantly shift point of view, from paragraph to paragraph; they are organized by metaphor and metonymy. Daney is happy to ask questions that lead to no conclusions. A sense of groundedness comes through in a relatively consistent set of aesthetic and political concerns—the process of spectatorial identification, the significance of "America," the nature of cinematic "registration" and Bazinian realism, the status of the "human." To provide context, certain directors repeatedly appear: Ford, Lang, Welles, Mizoguchi, Rossellini, Godard. But this sense of groundedness or centeredness is offset by a constant sense of movement or floating as the questions work to dislocate rather than confirm and the metonymical shape of the essays push the reader away from certainty and a solid conclusion. These are film reviews, then, that are in many respects cinematic. They not only contain the intellect and emotion of a film by Tarkovsky or Lang, they cut from one thing to another, as in Fellini or Godard.

Daney's most explicit and searching analyses of cinephilia and film criticism occur in one of the most beautiful journals ever published, *L'exercice a été profitable, Monsieur* (1993; page references to the book appear in parentheses).[44] This book consists of unpublished writing by Daney from 1988 to 1991 (he died in 1992). The book is necessarily composed of fragments, but larger themes and ideas arise. These themes turn out to have a special pertinence not only to Lynch but also to the Solaris effect in general. Since the journal goes out to 1991, it even includes a few pages of comments on Lynch's *Twin Peaks* television series. Daney is "positively intrigued" by the program, writing:

> I watch, almost by accident, with S.P. an episode of *Twin Peaks* on the television. I had already seen one and was positively intrigued. Same sentiment yesterday. Same pleasure at leaving behind "the chains" of film, one time in a vague connection with the plot and one time in the passage, always stimulating, of one scene to another. Well, one says, this is *of* cinema, which is to say that here it articulates constantly another way. (332–333; my translation)

Over the years, Daney becomes more and more fascinated by the relationship of television and cinema, a relationship that is also clearly at the center of Lynch. And Daney is always interested in the movement from one sequence or scene to another, both in film and in writing about film.

Although he frequently refers to his Bazinian desire for the real (*"mon Bazinism"*), Daney is more powerfully compelled by films that dream, that take place at night, that are full of clouds. He is strongly drawn to Buñuel and Raul Ruiz; he loves the "floating clouds" of Japanese director Mikio Naruse; his favorite film by Tarkovsky is *Stalker.*[45] A film that he frequently refers to as having an overwhelming impact on his childhood cinephilia is Charles Laughton's *Night of the Hunter.* He cites Jean Douchet's description of film spectatorship as a *"rêverie intime"* (20), and writes that "the darkened theater is a place where one dreams, innocently" (24). He wonders what happens to the "dream body" of film (181).

Daney is drawn to Buñuel, Ruiz, and Fellini not out of any mysticism or mannerism, but because the dream cinema will not hold still, because such cinema is fluid, always moving. One of Daney's favorite metaphors for cinema is that of the voyage: *"Voir des films, voyager, c'est la même chose"* (To see films, to travel, it's the same thing; 23). These voyages are not escapes from the world, however, or voyages for their own sake. Just like Daney's own voyages, cinematic voyages are anything but random, for his voyages are always pilgrimages. He goes to Sweden to find and interview Bergman, to India to find Ray, to Moscow to contemplate the relics of Eisenstein, to Cairo to visit Youssef Chahine.[46] Cinematic movement is thus not experienced for its own sake, but in its relationship to desire and love.

Daney loves films with multiple points of view. In his journal he distinguishes between "obsessional" films with one point of view (Antonioni), a double point of view (*Jaws*, in which we identify both with the shark and the child's leg), and "*le plus grand*," the cinema of n points of view (197). Lynch's *Mulholland Drive* is partly obsessional, in the singular cataclysmic dream of Diane, but ought more properly to be described as n-dimensional, since no single scheme can make sense of everything. Lynch uses handheld point-of-view cameras throughout *Mulholland Drive* to make us identify with the suspense of a character in his or her particular space—what is around that corner? But he also often disconnects the camera from any particular point of view, thereby ungrounding a single or even a human perspective. When the two men talk in the Winkie's restaurant about a frightening dream, the camera floats up and down behind them. Sometimes the camera going around a corner is exactly Diane, but sometimes she is somewhere else, so it is just the camera. The camera sometimes passes into a character for a psychological effect, but when we go into the Club Silencio, we ride along with a camera tied to the front end of a car. The whole screen lurches up and down before we suddenly speed toward the entrance. There is nobody in that invisible car except us, and we are riding on the bumper. The camera is thus too fast and too low, just as the video footage in *Lost Highway* is terrifying partly because it is shot by someone who is invading the house, but also because it is shot by someone ten feet off the ground. The multiple perspectives do not allow meanings to coalesce, and they significantly trouble our sense of the individual and the human.

There is a continuing thread in *L'exercice a été profitable, Monsieur* that complicates the status of the human in cinema. Daney writes alongside the death of man in Foucault, and he is clearly up-to-date in his reading of Lacan, Deleuze, and the Italian philosopher Giorgio Agamben. Daney praises films for their humanity or their sense of the human, but it is usually in a complicated context. In the same way, then, that he describes *Stalker* as a "realist film," which ought to surprise us, given its imaginary circumstances, he praises Hitchcock's *Vertigo* as a "human" film ("*Le cinéma est un art très humain*" [Cinema is a very human art]), but only after comparing James Stewart to a "robot" and calling Kim Novak a "*fantasme*" of the man.[47]

L'exercice contains numerous passages that critique the impulse to treat the cinematic screen as a human being. In one such passage, "Pelliculomorphism," he tests out the metaphor of film as a person (97). He mocks the anthropomorphism of Annaud's *The Bear* (151) and meditates on his own desire to anthropomorphize (130). "The image is not liable to anthropomorphism," he writes (40), suspicious of those who treat images as persons. "*L'humain mais comment?*" (Human, but how? [40]). What happens to the human when recorded on film? Daney equally distrusts academic distance and the nearness of humanizing identification. His sideways metaphorical approach to film reproduces this play of emotional distance from the cinema and our nearness to it.

Because Daney continually tests the metaphorical relationship between cinema and the human, his characterizations of cinephilia will necessarily be complex. In *L'exercice* he writes about cinephilic alienation (97), his condition of "*biocinéphilie*" (104), and the melancholy of cinephilia (323). He makes notes on a "theory of kidnapping" to account for the rapture, the possession of cinema (60). He writes down a list of his favorite movies, and then a longer list with different categories ("A masterwork for others, and finally for me, too"; "Sublime or important, at one time, for 'us' " [86]). The self that loves films is as mobile as the films it loves, and so moves in and out of contexts and quotation marks. And so this typical paragraph of self-analysis:

> My object of predilection—linkages ["*les enchaînements*"]). Always—in music, films, trips, in a day. Style (fortune, grace) is in the art of passing from one stage to another (*stades, stases*) in the Zeligian conscience of being (the self) and not being (the same). All the cinema that touches me is that where the necessity of linkage is made the object of true work. (61; my translation)

The Zeligian consciousness is named after the chameleon hero of the Woody Allen film, and it names a moving and open spectatorial consciousness. This amorphous consciousness is brought to the consciousness of love when connection itself is made a central issue.

One of Daney's key puns sounds together "*cinéphile*" (movie lover) and "*ciné-*

fils" (movie-son), sonically associating the love of film with cinematic affiliation. Of his personal life, for example, Daney writes that he was born within
the history of cinema, as a child of cinema, with a love of cinema:

> *Ciné-phile, ciné-fils, né quelque part dans une histoire du cinéma, entre deux*
> *pages du Sadoul, entre deux guerres ou entre deux films du guerre.*[48]
> [Movie-lover, movie-son, born somewhere in the history of film, between
> two pages of Sadoul, between two wars, or between two war films.] (my
> translation)

The two war films are Rossellini's *Open City* (1945) and Resnais's *Hiroshima,
Mon Amour* (1959), and the memory of war always shadows the love of film.
In Daney's narrative of film history, modern film arose as a direct response to
World War II. Modern cinema makes war against the illusionism and indus-
trialism of Hollywood, and was born, not by chance ("*pas par hasard*"), in the
Europe traumatized and ruined by the World War II. What haunts all the inno-
vations of the modernists, who reject propaganda in the name of truth, are the
Nazi death camps and Hiroshima. Modern cinema's relation to World War II
is evidenced most clearly in Resnais (*Night and Fog, Hiroshima, Mon Amour*),
but Daney finds such a presence also in the work of Bresson, Tati, and Welles.
Modern cinema for Daney is always haunted by the horror of war.

Thus Daney always reflects on cinephilia and complicates it, although he
never goes so far as to align cinephilia with horror. When he describes the
"*filiation*" (*ciné-phile, ciné-fils*) between Wim Wenders and Nicholas Ray in *Light-
ning over Water* (1980), Daney employs the metaphor of vampirism:

> The actors are privileged figures: they are essential to the dialogue be-
> tween directors. Because of this, the cinema is not able to exist as a simple
> succession of styles or schools and the phenomena of filiation are carried
> out across nostalgic images, even across old bodies themselves. This his-
> tory is not ever told because is it always intimate, erotic, made out of
> piety and rivalry, of vampirism and respect. (my translation)[49]

The deidealization of love, of eroticism, of cinephilia is recurrent, but Daney's
writing is too heterogeneous and nomadic (to use Deleuze's word) to lend
itself readily to motifs.[50]

In their metaphorical and metonymic ways, both Lynch and Daney relentlessly analyze the problematics of image, sequence, and cinephilia. In *Twin*

Peaks: Fire Walk, *Lost Highway*, and *Mulholland Drive*, Lynch is more likely to associate cinephilia directly with horror, but Daney's vision is not much less frightening. Both focus on the play of cinematic absence and presence, distance and nearness, memory and amnesia, amid a culture of proliferating images. Love of film pulses always through these images, but for Lynch and Daney it is always a difficult, even impossible, love. Both Lynch and Daney want not only to deidealize cinematic love, but also to question the very nature of the human-to-cinema relation. The cinema is and is not human. In the notes collected in *L'exercice a été profitable, Monsieur*, Daney likes to try out theories ("*théorie du kidnapping*") or what he calls effects ("*L'effet-JLG*" [i.e., the Jean-Luc Godard effect; 252]).[51] David Lynch names the nightmarish fluctuation of the Hollywood image "Mulholland Drive." I follow with Tarkovsky's ghost story, naming it the Solaris effect. These are all similar stories about memory and amnesia, the human and the inhuman. They are horror stories, and they are also love stories.

Spielberg's *A.I.:* Animation, Time, and Digital Culture 5

....

We do not take part in the lives of the people we see on screen;
we take part in the lives of their images.

—Chris Marker

Advances in digital technology gave a whole new look to American film in the 1990s. Science fiction special effects became more remarkable and more detailed. Films like *Terminator 2: Judgment Day* (1991), *Jurassic Park* (1993), and *The Matrix* (1999) each ushered in a new set of visual effects. Digital technology improved to the point that a viewer might rightly have suspected nearly every frame of every studio film, whether sci-fi or not, could have been digitally manipulated. All kinds of films have always contained special effects, from the glass shots of silent films to the back projections in 1950s taxicab windows. *Citizen Kane* (1941) is heightened drama, not science fiction, yet it contains special-effects process shots in almost every sequence. But never had the screen seemed so potentially malleable or manipulable as it did in the 1990s. Dialogue has been "looped" (rerecorded in postproduction) for many years, so dialogue can be changed after the fact. And if there is money, scenes can be reshot. But never has film seemed so entirely alterable in postproduction. Now people can be added or subtracted at will, most famously perhaps in *Forrest Gump* (1994) and in the orgy sequence of Kubrick's *Eyes Wide Shut* (1999). Hence the "photographic" nature of film seems to have been entirely transfigured by digital technology.

What would André Bazin say about the ontology of digitally processed film? Although no one thinks anymore that the neorealism practiced by

Rossellini and de Sica was entirely without artifice, the films so celebrated by Bazin, such as *Paisan* (1946) and *Umberto D* (1952), seem to be made out of entirely different materials than those used in *Minority Report* (2002) and *Star Wars: Episode I—The Phantom Menace* (1999). The nature of the photography seems to have changed the nature of the cinematic object. Remember Bazin's famous argument about realism and editing: If you show the lion in the same frame as the gladiator, the scene seems real; but if you cut back and forth between the lion and the gladiator, the audience grimaces at the fakery.[1] Then what would Bazin make of the dinosaurs in *Jurassic Park?* For every frame of computer-generated film is potentially cut into already. None of the human actors ever exists in the same real-world space as the dinosaurs.

Does digital technology rephrase the Solaris effect once more, or offer something else? If photography offers up an achingly impossible real, as embodied by Hari in Tarkovsky's *Solaris*, what kind of reality does digital cinema resurrect, when there is no more impossible? Does digital cinema take place on Solaris, or do we land on a different planet entirely?

Throughout this book I have claimed that films have always self-consciously commented on their own phantasmal sense of reality, and in this chapter I will argue that the most interesting films produced with the latest technology have also commented on their own digital artifices. The main cinematic text in this chapter will be Spielberg's *A.I.* (2001), which replays once again the hallucinations and despair of the *Solaris* plot. *A.I.* is a self-conscious reflection on the way that its fairy-tale love story is told through digital artifice and traditional animation. Along the way, we will encircle *A.I.* with some of the more significant examples of 1990s science fiction and animation. Some works are completely and overtly self-conscious about their animated form, like Richard Linklater's *Waking Life* (2001), but even films that seem mostly to be about plot, speed, and spectacle still sometimes comment on their status as digital artifacts.

Lev Manovich, Raymond Bellour, and Technological Fetishism

In 2002 Spielberg and Universal released the twentieth-anniversary edition of *E.T. the Extra-Terrestrial*. Spielberg made many small changes for the new edition. He changed "terrorist" to "hippie." He caused a spoken "shit" to lose its final *t*, and thus presumably its vulgarity. With computer-generated imagery (CGI), he changed guns to walkie-talkies. Spielberg thus cleaned up his fairy tale. Scholars probably will not create a variorum edition of these different versions of Spielberg's text, and the different editions of contemporary American films ("director's cut," DVD versions) tend not to cause as many problems as the various editions of old books or music scores. But Spielberg made another alteration, which might well be characterized as substantial; namely, he turned the 1982 puppet E.T. into an almost entirely CGI E.T. The point of this change was to upgrade the quality of the special effects to that expected by today's audiences. The CGI makeover provides "better" special effects, and so the new E.T. is more realistic.

Yet what is the cinematic status of this new E.T.? To use Bazin's word, what was the ontology of E.T. in 2002? The doll looked a bit awkward at times, but at least it was *there* in 1982, in the same frame with Drew Barrymore, whereas the CGI creature is not there — it is an animation. As recent theorists of new media have noted, CGI space is no longer "indexical" of any given reality. According to many writers, CGI makes cinema into a new medium, with new properties and emphases.[2] The 2002 *E.T.* looks like the same story as the 1982 *E.T.*, with the same plot and dialogue (the new edition adds a bathroom scene), but the upgraded special effects have potentially changed the nature of the artifact.

Yet how much has changed? The realism of these improved special effects is open to question. The CGI E.T. is less fakey than the puppet, but in either case we all know that E.T. is a fake. In one case we suspend our disbelief (or not) before a puppet; in the other, we suspend our disbelief before a CGI animation. If we were interrupting ourselves in the earlier version by saying, "That's a puppet," surely we don't interrupt ourselves any the less now. The dinosaurs in *Jurassic Park* are very realistic, but very few in the audience will believe for a moment that they are real. Clearly, we must think to ourselves, live actors have been combined on the screen with animated dinosaurs. Yes, the dinosaurs have never been so skillfully animated, but we do not believe in them any more than the ones in the silent film, *The Lost World* (1925, with a preface by Conan Doyle in person). Most audience members will agree that there is a difference between good special effects and bad special effects, but do good special effects make a science-fiction film more realistic? Whether the spaceship is a model hanging on a string (à la Ed Wood) or a brilliantly detailed Death Star (courtesy of Industrial Light and Magic), the only difference is technique, not reality. We admire (or not) the craftsmanship of a good spaceship, but it is still a fake either way, all made up. And it is not only before science-fiction films that we, as Coleridge put it, willingly suspend disbelief. I will argue for the idea that digital cinema may not, in the end, change the ontological nature of the cinematic experience any more than earlier technological innovations, such as the incursion of sound, the widening of the screen by CinemaScope, or advances in color.

In their textbook *Studying Contemporary American Film: A Guide to Movie Analysis* (2002), Thomas Elsaesser and Warren Buckland teach their students the wrong thing about digital cinema (page references to the book appear in parentheses).[3] In their chapter "Realism in the Photographic and Digital Image," they idealize the digital animation in Spielberg's *Jurassic Park* and *The Lost World* (1997). They bring forward an important term created by cognitivist Richard Allen—"sensory deception"—in which "we see something that does not exist, but this doesn't necessarily lead us to believe that it does exist" (210). Sensory deception is an updated and particularized form of Coleridge's suspension of disbelief. I would argue that sensory deception attends on *both* the puppet E.T. and the CGI E.T., but Elsaesser and Buckland assert that there is significantly less disbelief when there are better special effects. "Digital compositing equipment does not have the technical limitations inherent in optical printers, and so it can create a seamless blend of live action and animation, leading to the deception that the composited events do occupy the same diegesis" (211). Yet our knowledge that these very well animated but impossible dinosaurs are indeed digital composites surely interrupts the "seamlessness" of this characterization.

Instead of pursuing the ideas of Richard Allen, Elsaesser and Buckland then turn to the notion of "suture" in Stephen Heath. They summarize Heath's position as follows.

> The result of this imaginary positioning is that the spectator perceives the space of the image as unified and harmonious. For Heath, this position of imaginary plenitude and spatial unity constitutes the cinema's impression of reality. . . . Inevitably, the symbolic dimension of the image becomes apparent to the spectator when this illusion of all-seeingness is broken—most notably, when attention is drawn to off-screen space. The spectator's perception of spatial unity and harmony in the image is similarly broken. . . . According to this theory, realism is nothing more than an effect of the successful positioning of the spectator into an imaginary relation to the image, a position which creates a sense that the film's space and diegesis is unified and harmonious. (202)

Elsaesser and Buckland argue that digital animation provides better suturing. The inherent limitations in the previous technology "break [the spectator's] imaginary relationship to the image." But today's digital technology, they write, has "utterly transformed the spectator's relationship to the cinema" (218). And they conclude the chapter by quoting a senior official at Industrial Light and Magic: "The viewers will see something they have never seen before: dinosaurs that looks as if they are actually in the shot. This is not the usual effects trickery, this is another level of experience" (218).

Yet clearly this is too easy. If we are going to hazard a description of an audience member's subjectivity, it needs to be more complicated than a matter of good special effects versus bad special effects. The "sutured" mind cannot be so one-dimensional. Because of this logic, Elsaesser and Buckland are obliged to argue that suturing in Spielberg's later dinosaur film, *The Lost World,* is better than that in *Jurassic Park* because the special effects are more advanced: "In *The Lost World,* the interactions and camera movements have been improved considerably" (216). But are not some members of the audience now going to become unsutured by the fact that *The Lost World* is a much stupider movie than *Jurassic Park?* Suturing was a term originally taken from Lacan by Jean-Pierre Oudart to characterize the transparency of classic Hollywood film.[4] One is thrown out of such suturing by something like modernist narrative, but not by bad special effects. Otherwise, classic Hollywood film would itself turn opaque at rather frequent intervals. This simplified version of Oudart and Heath— watching in some kind of organic, harmonious haze, only to be occasionally unsutured by a bad special effect—just seems like a model of spectatorship not worth pursuing. Can I not become unsutured by my admiration (good special effects) as easily as by my skepticism (bad special effects)? It would seem that all of my internal commentary (good lighting, bad lighting, good acting, bad acting) would be equally disruptive.

Another idealization of technological change occurs in one of the most important and influential recent works on digital media, Lev Manovich's *Language of New Media* (2001; page references to the book will appear in parentheses).[5] The new media are computer-driven technologies that do things that traditional, projected cinema cannot do, and the conclusion is that computers allow us to see "the world and the human being anew, in ways that were not available to 'a man with a movie camera'" (333). According to Manovich, new technology leads directly to new perceptions. But the direct link that Manovich posits between technology and expression needs to be complicated. New media, according to Manovich, decenters cinema, which now appears as only one form of expression among many. Yet cinema nonetheless dominates his book, and the culminating chapter is called "What Is Cinema?" The book's conclusion is that the new media substantially alter our conception of what cinema is or can be. But Manovich's flawed descriptions of both traditional cinema and new media suggest that his account is not to be trusted. Manovich needs cinema because it actually has a history and because it actually exists. As we shall see, the same cannot be said for digital media.

First, Manovich's description of traditional cinema is sometimes quite odd. Take, for example, his description of the role of rear projection in creating "the illusion of a coherent space" (146).

> In general, Hollywood cinema has always been careful to hide the artificial nature of its space, but there is one exception: the rear-screen projection shots introduced in the 1930s. A typical shot shows actors sitting inside a stationary vehicle; a film of a moving landscape is projected on the screen behind the car's windows. The artificiality of rear-screen projection shots stands in striking contrast to the smooth fabric of Hollywood cinematic style in general. (147)

This is a particularly strange moment, but typical of an analysis that depends, like the argument by Elsaesser and Buckland cited above, on pitting good special effects against bad special effects. No other film historian, as far as I am aware, thinks that Hollywood tried to reduce artifice everywhere except in the case of rear-screen projection. By our contemporary standards, some back-screen projections are quite noticeable, but certainly not all of them. In their histories of 1930s Hollywood film technology, Bordwell and Thompson fail to note the low quality of rear-projection systems even as technology was improving.[6] But of course rear-screen projections in classic Hollywood film were no more systematically artificial than any other special effects—matte shots, miniatures, or other kinds of optical printing.

Manovich's misappropriation of Bordwell and Thompson here and elsewhere is tantamount, in fact, to a misreading of the goals of traditional cinema. For example, Manovich cites a passage from Bordwell, Staiger, and Thompson's *Classical Hollywood Cinema:*

> "Showmanship," realism, invisibility: such canons guided the SMPE [Society of Motion Picture Engineers] members toward understanding the acceptable and unacceptable choices in technical innovations, and these too became teleological. In another industry, the engineer's goal might be an unbreakable glass or a lighter alloy. In the film industry, the goals were

not only increased efficiency, economy, and flexibility but also spectacle, concealment of artifice, and what Goldsmith [the 1934 president of smpe] called "the production of an acceptance [sic] semblance of reality."[7]

Here Manovich says that Bordwell and Thompson "are satisfied with Goldsmith's definition of realism as 'the production of an acceptable semblance of reality.'" But in fact the authors go on to qualify what this phrase means for their own analyses.

We can see from observations like Goldsmith's that this too was rationally adopted as an engineering aim—but wholly within the framework of *Hollywood's conception* of "realism." Otterson's remark about invisibility makes it clear that any absolute phenomenal realism is qualified by aesthetic criteria. "The Cinema" is not "evolving" towards a "total realism." Rather, institutions, such as the smpe, chose in a specific historical context to modify an already-defined aesthetic system according to an ideology of progress. (emphasis in the original)[8]

As Bordwell, Staiger, and Thompson make clear, Hollywood's conceptions of realism and invisibility need to be carefully understood when describing "traditional" cinematic illusionism. Self-reflexivity in classical Hollywood film is usually not in the mode of Godardian modernism (although sometimes it is), but neither is Hollywood artifice entirely invisible—on the contrary!

As Bordwell explains in the first chapter of *Classical Hollywood Cinema*, the two categories of "showmanship" and "invisibility" can often tend toward a contradiction.[9] Bordwell provides many examples of traditional Hollywood films that exhibit "flagrant theatrical virtuosity" and spectacle, and emphasize artificiality (21). Bordwell himself tries too hard to render these moments "invisible" once again by saying that the films employ "artistic motivation" (21). In other words, spectacle or virtuosity is not unmotivated or random in Hollywood film, since it is motivated by the conventions of spectacle and virtuosity. And so Bordwell returns cinematic artifice to the well-behaved domain of invisibility. But today one might be likely to emphasize much more strongly the potential contradictions between showmanship and invisibility.

Neither *Classical Hollywood Film* nor Manovich dwell at any length on the notion of the "star," yet this is one of the most overt ways that traditional Hollywood cinema bares its artifice. The appearance of Cary Grant or Bette Davis in a 1930s film warps reality as much as a dinosaur in *Jurassic Park*. Jimmy

Stewart and E.T. may each be considered as fictions that are composited into otherwise seemingly real space. By following lines of argument such as these, Manovich could have complicated our sense of classic Hollywood cinema. But doing so would eliminate our sense that the arrival of the new media stands for something truly new.

If his treatment of traditional cinema is problematic, Manovich's outline of digital cinema is equally open to debate. *The Language of New Media* shows the difficulty of writing a history of cinema in the absence of masterpieces, or without any distinction between high and low culture. As Robert Stam writes in his essay "Post-Cinema: Digital and Theory and New Media,"

> Implicit in the notion of visual culture as developed by such figures as W. J. T. Mitchell, Irit Rogoff, Nick Mirzoeff, Anne Friedberg, and Jonathan Crary, is a rejection of the aestheticism of conventional art history, with the emphasis on masterpieces and geniuses, and its consequent failure to place art in relation to other practices and institutions.[10]

The Language of New Media for the most part consists of sets of descriptions—descriptions of aesthetics. As Manovich tells us, his book's title could just as well have been *The Aesthetics of New Media*, but he decided against using the word "aesthetics" because "*aesthetics* implies a set of oppositions that I would like to avoid—between art and mass culture, the beautiful and the ugly, the valuable and the unimportant" (12). And the effect of *The Language of New Media* is, indeed, often to provide continuity between video game, CD-ROM, video clip, and cinema, so that the opposition between "art and mass culture" seems to collapse, now no more than an old-fashioned, mistaken distinction.

Yet to write history, or even to make an argument, one needs to foreground important things. Otherwise, how will one sort out these descriptions? In actuality, Manovich argues repeatedly in terms of "importance"; certain elements of technology are important, others are not. As an interpreter, he will tell us what is "crucial," "fundamental," or "major." He continually refers to cinema, for instance, because it is "the major cultural form of the twentieth century" (86). Sometimes he chooses his examples because they are popular. This is why he discusses the computer games *Doom* and *Myst*, whose popularity became a "phenomenon," defining "the new field and its limits" (244). Sometimes his examples are "landmark achievements," such as *Jurassic Park*, which is a "triumph of computer simulation" (201). Thus even though Manovich does not want to foreground an aesthetics that distinguishes between "valuable and unimportant," between "art and mass culture," he repeatedly makes choices about what is important, about what is exemplary.

Manovich is thus inevitably led to ask whether works are "successful." He writes of "strong aesthetic systems," which are built by both individual artists and commercial culture (63). He asks of a film, "Was this attempt successful?" (240). He stops in his tracks to wonder:

> This may explain the popularity of this particular temporal dynamics in interactive media, but it does not address another question—does it work aesthetically? Can Brecht and Hollywood be married? Is it possible to create a new temporal aesthetics, even a language, based on cyclical shifts between perception and action? In my view, the most successful example of such an aesthetics already in existence is a military simulator, the only mature form of interactive narrative. It perfectly blends perception and action, cinematic realism and computer menus. (209–210)

"Maturity" here becomes an interesting aesthetic category. One suspects that Manovich does not ask about aesthetic success more often because his examples of new media technology are not very often "mature." The newness of the new media guarantees evolutionary immaturity.

One of the major problems with Manovich's writings about "new" digital cinema, then, is that there are no examples. There is a problem when you try to say something about digital cinema and all you have are *Jurassic Park* and *Star Wars: Episode I—The Phantom Menace*. The movies are very good at special effects, but they are not very good movies. The film that Manovich keeps going back to again and again is Dziga Vertov's *Man with a Movie Camera* (1929), which he calls an "avant-garde masterpiece" in the first sentence of his book. I do not notice that Manovich uses the word "masterpiece" ever again, but it might be a good word to add to the tool kit. *The Man with a Movie Camera* serves as an exemplary film for Manovich; he uses it in his "Prologue: Vertov's Dataset" to introduce many of the basic ideas of the book. According to Manovich, Vertov films reality in a way that looks forward to digital composition: "As theorized by Vertov, film can overcome its indexical nature through montage, by presenting a viewer with objects that never existed in reality" (xviii).

But besides Vertov's film, there are no other masterpieces. There are certainly no digital masterpieces. Rather pathetically, only Peter Greenaway is allowed to join Vertov in the pantheon of digital visionaries: "Along with Greenaway, Dziga Vertov can be thought of as a major 'database' filmmaker of the twentieth century" (xxiv). If Manovich's history of digital cinema can only bring us Vertov and Greenaway, then this is an impoverished history indeed.

Manovich later notes that "Peter Greenaway, one of the few prominent film directors concerned with expanding cinema's language, once complained that 'the linear pursuit—one story at a time told chronologically—is the standard format of cinema'" (237). Here Manovich happily invokes his one-member canon—but "prominent" to whom? Critics and cinephiles think that all sorts of directors are "prominent." Is Godard a nonprominent director trying out new things, or a prominent director not interested in new kinds of cinema?[11] Perhaps only Greenaway is doing what Manovich wants cinema to be doing, which might suggest that Manovich is looking at the wrong things. Greenaway's quoted sentiment above could come from any hundreds of non-Hollywood directors who simply want to avoid linear narrative. Above all, if Greenaway is the only living filmmaker who seems like a success, then Manovich has written a history of cinema without any examples. This may even be a history without a subject. His severe contrast between traditional cinema and digital cinema thus seems less than credible.

What the immature history of digital cinema needs is a masterpiece. Not a masterpiece of influence so much as a masterpiece of critical self-reflexivity. Manovich's examples either occur before the digital (Vertov, Greenaway) or give little indication that they are self-aware. *Jurassic Park*, for example, is a "triumph" of digital technology that also happens to tell the story of science and technology failing disastrously. There is apparently a total discrepancy between the critical descriptions in *The Language of New Media* and the self-conscious descriptions in the films themselves. Because of the expectations of its audience, a Hollywood blockbuster is unlikely to display the same sort of critical self-awareness as a contemporary painting or video installation. Yet it might be argued that an art object without any self-awareness does not exist, especially in contemporary America. This argument will be presented more fully in the final chapter, when I discuss the idea of American cinema as an art. For now, I will simply nominate *A.I.* as the most interestingly self-aware Hollywood film that has been made during the digital regime.[12]

A related analysis of technological development can be found in the work of Raymond Bellour. Bellour has been writing about film since the 1960s, so his descriptions of classic film tend to be much more convincing than those of Manovich. But there is in Bellour a similar tendency to find that different technologies make for substantially different effects. Much of Bellour's recent work describes gallery installations by artists such as Bill Viola, Gary Hill,

Thierry Kuntzel, and Douglas Gordon. For Bellour, an installation's apparatus (or *dispositif*, in his preferred terminology) significantly alters the meaning of its content. Thus, a film projected as film—in a darkened theater, on a screen—is not the same film when projected into the air or into a closet. When Douglas Gordon's *30 Seconds Text* (1996) shows you a paragraph about a guillotine coming down and then ceases projection, it does something, according to Bellour, that no film can do. Since a film continues to show moving images, it can never represent death the way that this installation can, when it simply ceases to project anything at all.[13]

But if Bellour overessentializes media and technology, at least it is because he is immersed in the history of aesthetics. Godard and Chris Marker are two of Bellour's cinematic heroes, and they supply Bellour with numerous very good inspirations. Certainly Bellour's heroes themselves essentialize when they make distinctions between cinema, television, and video. In 1985, for example, Godard spoke of a war between cinema and digital, in which cinema remains "the only possibility of observing suffering" in the face of digital attempts to dissolve such observations.[14] Marker, in his turn, often likes to quote Godard's distinction between cinema and television: cinema is that toward which we lift up our eyes. But Godard is no Bazinian idealist of reality, and *In Praise of Love* (2001) shows Godard more than willing to paint digitally, just as he had earlier often exploited varying textures in film. Surely Godard's work in video (*Numéro Deux*, 1975) complicates rather than insists on a difference between television and cinema. What Bellour's immersion in a history of cinema does gain from Godard and Marker is a way of interpreting cinema metaphorically. Bellour reads images, films, and installations as a series of meditations on death and on the death of film, and in this way his analyses often parallel the questions and concerns that we have raised around the Solaris effect.

One of Bellour's most important analyses of digital technology may be found in his essay "Le Livre, Aller, Retour (Apologie de Chris Marker)," which describes Marker's CD-ROM *Immemory*.[15] In contrast to Manovich, who limits his descriptions to the formal interfacings of games like *Myst*, Bellour interprets not only the interactive technology of *Immemory*, but also its content and effect.[16] Hence, Bellour compares the effect of this CD-ROM to that of other CD-ROMS and to the effects of autobiographical films and texts. The technological format in this instance does not overdetermine meaning, and the way memory comes through in the CD-ROM is comparable to the presentation of memory in films and photography. Bellour not only describes the various menus and zones on the CD-ROM (the word "zone" comes from Tarkovsky's *Stalker*), but also reads imagery and memory metaphorically. For my purposes, however, he does this exactly backwards.

Bellour contrasts Godard's cinematic memory to Marker's: "There are two ways to treat this nostalgia. The Marker way, and the Godard way."[17] According to Bellour, a cinematic image in Godard is an "icon" that registers belief and resurrects reality. By contrast, there is no such transcendence in Marker; there is no such faith in images. For Godard there is a "tragic quality of the image" due to the centrality of cinema. But for Marker the image implies further images:

> The privilege of cinema [in Godard] thus stems from projection, which it alone of all the arts has received in heritage, along with the possibility to project and reproject all the images of the world.... Hence the tragic quality of the image, a tragedy of cinema which becomes its guarantor. This tragedy is what Marker has always sought not to ignore but to accommodate, within a vision of culture that cannot have cinema as its focal point, because in truth there is none, and cinema circulates in an infinitely wider history, even if it carries out an incomparable reprise of that history.... If the image of cinema is to remain this image of childhood [in Marker], larger than life and projected, no doubt it must also allow one to imagine truly new configurations beyond itself.[18]

At the end of this passage, Bellour equates childhood with the imagining of new configurations, hence the autobiographical images on Marker's CD-ROM.

Instead, I would parallel the exactitude of childhood memory with digital technology. Earlier, Bellour speaks of the "uncertain memory of childhood," but childhood memory in Marker is not uncertain.[19] Adult memory may be confused and tortured, as in Hitchcock's *Vertigo*. But childhood memory is exact, and this is the whole premise of Marker's *La Jetée*. I would say that the reason *Immemory* makes sense on CD-ROM is that it embodies the connection between a technology that passes quickly from one image to the next in an autobiography peopled by images from childhood. All through *Immemory* the photographs and film clips carry with them this childhood desire and this fixation on images:

> This is the image that taught a child of seven how a face filling the screen was suddenly the most precious thing in the world, something that

haunted you ceaselessly, that slipped into every nook and instant of your life, until pronouncing its name and describing its traits became the most necessary and delicious occupation imaginable . . . in a word, that image that taught you how to love.

Both childhood memory and digital technology tends toward the iconic. But Godard's films never show us anything like the layers of time and memory in Resnais or Marker.

We can substantiate this description by recalling Marker's *One Day in the Life of Andrei Arsenevitch* (2000), in which, although Marker shows much less self-consciousness about technology, he demonstrates a parallel self-consciousness about memory. *One Day in the Life of Andrei Arsenevitch* surveys Tarkovsky's seven films alongside footage of Tarkovsky on his deathbed. The technological self-consciousness of the film is completely minimal; the technical effects, such as the superimposition of one film over another, are primitive. Marker works with three main sets of footage: Tarkovsky's films themselves, a documentary on the making of *The Sacrifice*, and Marker's own video of Tarkovsky's bedside. The main impression of Marker's film derives, then, from the editing. Editing here explicitly stands in for acts of memory as scenes in real life remind Marker of scenes in Tarkovsky's films. Tarkovsky's films thus seem to have a strength and permanence, and the mind readily gathers them together. Here are the scenes of levitation; here are the scenes of conflagration. There is no problem recollecting images or quoting images in *One Day in the Life*. On the contrary, images rise up perfectly to rhyme with one another and with the dying life before us. Why is this? How do cinematic images acquire the presence of religious icons, in contrast to the ghostly affect of old photographs?

In part, the permanence of memory derives from the fact that *One Day in the Life* comes into the world as an act of devotion. Tarkovsky's images thus acquire an iconic permanence for Marker, but it does not follow that all film images will. In this film, Marker aligns Tarkovsky with the Innocent in *Boris Godunov*, and calls *Andrei Rublev* the "only true film of our time." Marker makes Tarkovsky himself into a cinematic icon, not through the glamour of a Hollywood film, but through the love of a disciple. Marker loves Tarkovsky, yet not as a lover, but with the love of a child. The final sentence of *One Day in the Life* seems like a strange poem, but makes sudden sense in the context of Marker's other work. "Tarkovsky is the only filmmaker," says Marker, "whose entire work lies between two children and two trees." Here Marker indicates—

with a perfect memory—where *Ivan's Childhood* begins and where *The Sacrifice* ends. The intense, perfect memories of some of Tarkovsky's films are often like the images associated with childhood memories. Above all, they resemble the childhood memory in *La Jetée*. Thus, even though part of Marker's hagiographical approach to Tarkovsky omits much overt technological self-consciousness, is there not an implicit parallel being drawn between the intensity of childhood memory and the perfection of digital memory in 2000?

The significance of the child is underscored if we recall Marker's masterpiece, *La Jetée*. This is "the story of a man marked by an image of childhood." In a postapocalyptic world, the protagonist is chosen to take part in time travel precisely because of this childhood image, this childhood memory. Because of this intense capacity for memory, the logic goes, he will be able to hold himself together as he travels through time. And the image that holds him together through the dislocations of time travel is that of a woman's face. While he travels through time, his experiences expand on this image, and he meets the woman regularly, soon to fall in love with her. She calls him "her ghost," and their most glorious day is spent in a museum. Their love is ephemeral, ghostly, and Marker's movie consists entirely of slides, still photographs. The movie is all stills, except for one surpassing moment, when the woman suddenly opens her eyes, now not in a slide, but in a one-second movie. Which all the more serves to emphasize the impossibility of this love. *La Jetée* complicates the Solaris effect—the impossible desire for the loved one—by speaking at the same time not only of the man's love for the woman, but also of the child's intense memory of the image.

La Jetée is entirely explicit about its photographic medium and its meditation on images. Photography and images are self-consciously thought through in a narrative embodied by both adult love and childhood memory. Just as Tarkovsky thinks about art and cinema through the figures of Kris and Hari, Marker thinks through photographic experience by working with the time traveller. The intensity of love is associated with the adult, but the intensity of memory is associated with the child. With digital technology, cinema memory becomes perfectible. "Nothing is forgotten, nothing is erased," writes Manovich. "Just as we use computers to accumulate endless texts, messages, notes, and data . . . 'spatial montage' accumulates events and images as it progresses through its narrative. In contrast to cinema's screen, which primarily functioned as a record of perception, the computer screen functions as a record of memory."[20] In Spielberg's *A.I.* this perfect digital memory will once again be associated with a child.

Cartoonism and Devotion: Kevin Smith,
Quentin Tarantino, and Walt Disney

Cartoons are juvenile power trips, figurations of immortality, whether addressed to children or grown men. In *The Dangerous Lives of Altar Boys* (Care, 2002), a teenager's comic books come alive for extended sequences, a show of creative power in an otherwise confusing world. In Jim Jarmusch's *Ghost Dog: The Way of the Samurai* (1999), the mafia gangsters all sit around and watch violent cartoons; their ridiculous, exaggerated, homicidal lives seem to follow a cartoon code. When Monty Python's animator, Terry Gilliam, remakes Marker's *La Jetée* as *Twelve Monkeys* (1995), he shows the "crazy" people in the mental institution watching cartoons. Gilliam also makes sure that we see the heroic characters of Bruce Willis and Madeline Stowe fall asleep while watching cartoons on television. Gilliam likes the romantic vision available to apparently crazy people, as evidenced in both *The Fisher King* (1991) and his broken-off film about Don Quixote.[21] Gilliam sees animation as creative, vitalistic, and emotional. His fish-eye lenses, fantastic sets, and caricatured acting all contribute to a cartoon-like sensibility in his live-action movies. In *Twelve Monkeys*, Gilliam takes the plot of *La Jetée* and changes it from a meditation on photography into a cartoon.

Spielberg's *A.I.* is a retelling of *Pinocchio*, a story we are far more likely to know from the 1940 Disney animation than from the Italian novel by Carlo Collodi. *Pinocchio* is itself a tale of animation, in which inanimate puppets come to life. In this section I will argue that *A.I.* uses animation in complex and self-conscious ways. *A.I.* does not just allude nostalgically to the history of animation (by way of Disney's *Pinocchio*) or use CGI as a species of animation (although it does do this), but it also reflects on the contemporary state of digital animation as a species of cinema. I will also argue that animation's omnipotence, or what I will call "cartoonism," may be projected by both live-action and animated film. Hence both newly composed digital cinema or old-fashioned analog cinema may equally render up the precarious existence of the Solaris effect.

Animated film has always lived in a strange conceptual place. Since there is no animated *Citizen Kane* or *Breathless*—no obviously influential masterpiece—animation is not often treated in most theoretical works on cinema. Although Deleuze in his two volumes on cinema talks about the silliest musicals and a range of experimental film, there is not one word about animation. Animation is not photographed, so the impulse toward uninflected Bazinian reality is never there. Animation is often aimed at children, and not too serious when aimed at adults, which once again allows us to ignore it. But as Spielberg knows more than anyone, some of our most deeply held cinematic images come from animation because they are images from childhood. Thus, even though film theory often sets animation to one side, our memories do not.

The recent deluge of writing on virtual reality and digital media also tends to ignore animation. Animation is an "old" technology, while digital is brand-new. Yet films like *Toy Story* (1995, the first entirely computer-animated film) and *Shrek* (2001) should make us realize that morphing and other digital effects are kinds of animation. As an encyclopedia of special effects, *A.I.* helps us reflect on the relationship of animation to CGI, of old to new technology. Some sequences in the film, such as the gathering of robots at the stadium, are constructed out of indistinguishable layers of makeup, animation, and CGI. In scenes like these, the CGI technology has no desire to call attention to itself; on the contrary, it wants to disappear, like a happy illusion. A lot of contemporary animation hopes that we won't notice—as when the live-action hero in Sam Raimi's *Spiderman* (2002) turns into a cartoon in order to fly around between buildings—and some animation in *A.I.* is certainly in this serviceable, "invisible" mode.

Yet in several places *A.I.* self-consciously attaches itself to the history of cinematic animation. The first instance occurs in the darkened chambers of Dr. Know. The robot child, David, comes here in search of the Blue Fairy, who, he thinks, will make him a real boy. Dr. Know is a powerful Wizard of Oz–type character and could be visualized in any number of ways. He could be seen as a sage wizard from *The Lord of the Rings*, or as another robot on the verge of becoming human. Instead, Dr. Know turns out to be a rather classically animated character, voiced by Robin Williams, who at his best is his own kind of cartoon.

Dr. Know makes his pronouncements from inside a small-scale movie house. In the projection room there are two space-age viewing chairs and a screen covered by theater curtains. Although he is a high-tech computerized fortune-teller, Dr. Know reveals his answers from within an old-fashioned movie screen. When the curtains part, explosions and astronomical images come right out of the screen and spin into three-dimensional space. Dr. Know thus makes his appearance as an animated hologram that can jump right off the screen (there are point-of-view shots in which we look through his glasses from behind him). Futuristically, he is three-dimensional, but is still drawn like a classic Disney character. Dr. Know is a comic Einstein, but also another funny old mustache-wagging guy like Cookie in *Atlantis: The Lost Empire* (2001). He is deliberately drawn in-between the persistently flat characters of Disney's non-Pixar offerings (*Pocahantas, Tarzan*) and the three-dimensional computer-generated toys, ants, and ogres of the Pixar division. Dr. Know is a theatrically framed cartoon that possesses the power of infinite knowledge.

The visual style in which this animated Einstein appears also prepares us for his answer — namely, the animated Blue Fairy. Dr. Know shows David animated characters from the Pinocchio story, and they look like up-to-date holographic figures from the Disney movie. This is the moment when the Blue Fairy flies out of Dr. Know's futuristic theater and into David's memory banks. *A.I.* purposefully uses its own animation to comment on the role of technology and animation in film. The film self-consciously splits Dr. Know and the Blue Fairy into two camps. Dr. Know is simply a good special effect attached to a powerful computer. But the Blue Fairy is more than a special effect, since she is processed as an archetypal image. Using our own memories as confirmation, the Blue Fairy is downloaded as a deep memory into David, the robot child.

David confirms the profundity of this image when he finds the Blue Fairy buried underneath the sea. In the future world of *A.I.*, the oceans have risen, drowning many of the world's great cities. David takes his amphibicopter under the water and quickly runs into the watery grave of Coney Island. With the ship's lights playing over the old wires and beams of the debris-covered landscape, David seems to be on another search for the *Titanic*. The descent into the water is metaphorical and archeological, a descent into the past. But whereas the *Titanic* is an image of elitism and power, Coney Island is an idiomatic reservoir of classless entertainment and fun (see Harold Lloyd's beautifully detailed excursion to Coney Island in *Speedy* [1928]). And in its archetypal significance, Coney Island also stands for a region of memory, of intense feeling. David throws his lights upon the open page of a giant book, "once upon a time." Then he drives the amphibicopter through the Pinocchio exhibit, thereby repeating the "ride" that was, but with an emotion far beyond that of mere amusement. David drives the ship over stairs and up to the wooden statue of the Blue Fairy.

We might feel that Spielberg has played a trick on us by making the object of David's quest a movie. Viewers of *Raiders of the Lost Ark* (1981) might well have suspected that Spielberg tricked them there, insofar as the Holy Grail turned out to be nothing more than a movie after all, nothing sacred, just a collection of spectacular visual effects. *Close Encounters of the Third Kind* (1977) might be characterized the same way, since we learn nothing about the visiting aliens, but instead are treated to a very nice light-and-sound program. *Raiders of the Lost Ark* makes a holy quest into an amusement park ride, but David's quest for the Blue Fairy makes an amusement park ride over into a holy quest by claiming that a movie may stand as a divine memory. And in contrast to *Raiders* and *Close Encounters*, the substitution of movie for icon in *A.I.* seems earned, insofar as cinephilia, the love of movies, is now made so rigorously problematic. To celebrate the animated *Pinocchio* may seem like Spielbergian self-satisfaction, since in fifty years a yet-to-be-born Kubrick will have his robot boy search for the now classic E.T. But it isn't, because there will be no satisfaction. Because the image of the Blue Fairy is profoundly deep, but also profoundly empty.

For David, the Blue Fairy is an image, and rather exactly an icon, and he now prays to her: "Please, please, make me into a real live boy." An artificially intelligent robot prays to sculpted wood for reality and life. Surely this is another poignant rendering of the Solaris effect. Some movies may be dismissed as entertainment, yet even these films may contain images that we carry around with us, that we work through with intense desire. If Cavell has shown even remotely that *Bringing Up Baby* and *It Happened One Night* are cinematic reflections on the possibility of happiness in marriage, then *A.I.* may well be considered a cinematic reenactment of remembered film images. David has a child's innocence and devotion together with a computer's diligence. And so he prays to the wooden Blue Fairy for two thousand years.

> He prayed until all the sea anemones had shriveled and died. He prayed as the ocean froze and ice encased the caged amphibicopter and the Blue Fairy too, locking them together, where he could still make her out, a blue shape in ice, always there, always smiling, always awaiting him. Eventually he never moved at all. But his eyes always stayed open, staring ahead forever all through the darkness of each night and the next day and the next day . . .

As the camera pulls away from the wreck, many viewers have the delicious and terrible sense that the film will end right there. For what can this empty blue ghost do? There is the familiar Solaris disjunction between the powerful Blue Fairy in David's mind and the wooden Blue Fairy before him in the water. But like Tarkovsky's *Solaris*, the movie continues on, not to overcome this disjunction, but to render it even more exquisitely.

A.I. captures the agony of cinematic devotion to imagery, something that most animated films necessarily eschew. Disney movies can become quite scary, but they do not brood elegiacally. Almost all the heroes of Disney films need to figure out who they are, and so go searching for their identity. But the infinite possibilities of an animated world almost guarantee success. When Hercules finds a temple and kneels to pray, his giant father, Zeus, is there smiling upon him in a jiffy (*Hercules*, 1997). Animation acts out faith itself in *The Prince of Egypt* (1998) when the magic of cartoons assures us that the Red Sea will part and that the prince's singing people will be saved ("There can be miracles, when you believe, / Who know what miracles you can achieve"). *The Lion King* (1994) imagines an animal world characterized by a "circle of life." When the elder king, Mufasa, dies, he still watches his son, Simba, from the clouds above. The shaman, Rafiki, anoints Simba at birth and returns to guide him when Simba is ready to take his rightful place as the Lion King. Circularity and repetition shape this world, not disjunction and dislocation.

In contrast to what happens in Walt Disney movies, David's prayers in *A.I.* are given a far-from-perfect answer by the superadvanced robots of the future. The robots wire themselves into his memory banks and download David's long-sought desire. They stage his desire visually by creating a live encounter between David and the Blue Fairy. The Blue Fairy is not only a deeply held image from David's memory, but now also a visual mediator between the computer-robots and the boy robot. On the one hand, she is merely an anthropomorphic computer monitor, an amiable interface like Dr. Know. Yet on the other hand, she is the center of the boy robot's mythological universe. She embodies a deeply sunk memory, yet she is not as powerful as David hopes. She tells David that although she can do anything that is possible, she cannot make him a boy. As a powerful but purposefully artificial image, she appears as another embodiment of the Solaris effect. Whereas animation may often be said to idealize the presence of cinematic imagery, *A.I.* uses several different kinds of animation to underline elegiac themes of memory and desire.

It was Eisenstein who most influentially associated animation with creative omnipotence. In 1932 he remarked that Disney's work was characterized by "plasmaticness," which has to do with the "poly-formic capabilities of the object."[22] The flexibility, the squashability, of Disney's animated characters was terrifically exciting to Eisenstein, who thrilled at the vibrating lines of Disney's images:

> In animation especially, the satisfaction depends not simply on the
> ability to represent other impossible worlds, but rather to remind us that

the skill and virtuosity involved in form is supreme and fundamental in achieving this world. In this way, it is true that animation is often at its best when we marvel not only at the subject matter, so to speak, but at its means of achievement. We are conscious of technique here in the way that we are often not in narrative film.

So, if in animation we witness the omnipotence of thought, we also witness necessarily the means of achieving that omnipotence and to that extent animation separates itself from other kinds of cinema. In animation, at its best, we thrill to the means of representation and not only the representation.[23]

In a commentary on this passage, Michael O'Pray emphasizes the control, the "skill and virtuosity" of animation, although I would foreground the ideas of omnipotence that surround the "plasmatic." Above all, O'Pray reminds us that animation conceived in this way contrasts to a cinema associated with the "fragility of the image."[24] If Eisensteinian animation is characterized by omnipotence, the Solarian cinema is characterized by fragility and fracture.

This discussion of animation requires us to take one further step, a step that is not taken often enough. That is, we need to consider that it is not just animation that possesses these plastic, squashable properties, but many photographed films as well. Many contemporary American films can be described in some of the same terms as animated films. Frank Tashlin, a figurative grandfather of the Farrelly brothers, began his career in animation, and the "live-action features he directed [afterward] tend to be very 'cartoony' in nature."[25] Contemporary American films are inundated with cartoonism—live-action films made from cartoons (*Scooby Doo, The Flintstones*), comic books (*Batman, Spiderman*), and video games (*Mortal Kombat, Lara Croft: Tomb Raider*). Morphing technology means that live-action characters are potentially as flexible and plastic as cartoons, an effect we see in science fiction (*The Abyss, Terminator 2*) as well as comedy (*The Nutty Professor, Shallow Hal*). Actors like Jim Carrey and Robin Williams appear again and again in live-action films that border on cartoons, and directors like Tim Burton and Joel Coen specialize in caricature and exaggeration.

Cartoonism is rampant in contemporary American film. Cartoonism represents the powerful assumption that cinema is not a ghost, is not ephemeral. Unlike the turn to nature, which grounds cinematic authority in realism, cartoonism grounds cinematic authority in creative artifice.

What are some of the key attributes of cartoonism? Cartoonism gives the impression of infinite repeatability. Cartoons tend to be serial, not singular. The cartoon world is cornucopian, overflowing, not empty. Video games are packed with scene after scene of violence and death, but the most important rule is that you can start over. In the *Vertigo* section of *Immemory,* Chris Marker quotes Scottie (James Stewart): "You're my second chance." And then he writes:

> Replay—
> What else is offered us by video games, which say so much more about our unconscious than the complete works of Lacan.

Whereas an improved version of a computer program is called an "upgrade," an improved video game is a new "episode"; the player looks forward not only to better graphics, but also to a new plot. Proliferating sequels are even more the rule in video games than in American film, and top twenty charts show many games dated and numbered: *Unreal Tournament 2003, Hitman 2, No One Lives Forever 2, Sim City 4, Unreal II: The Awakening, Madden* NFL *2003, Need for Speed: Pursuit 2, MechWarrior 4: Mercenaries, RollerCoaster Tycoon 2, Master of Orion 3.*[26] Computer-gaming worlds proliferate and multiply. These are dangerous worlds, whether they are "action and adventure," "first-person shooters," "strategy and simulation," "platform and puzzle," or "beat-'em ups."[27] Yet however dangerous, violent, and realistic, video games embody resurrection rather than finality.

One of the most deliberate overlaps between cartoons and film occurs in the work of Kevin Smith. Most of his movies contain substantial references to comic books, and he has written graphic novels for both DC (*Green Arrow*) and Marvel (*Daredevil*). To expand on this description of cinematic cartoonism, I will look at Smith's *Green Arrow* comic book for a moment before turning to his films. Comic books, like video games, take place in a world of seriality and proliferation. Violence and death occur at regular intervals, but the main heroes verge on the immortal. Mrs. Fantastic is now something like seventy years old, but in the June 2003 issue, she is a new mother, and decked out in a fashionable midriff-revealing top. Comic books are full of rubbery shape-shifters (like Mr. Fantastic); this is a plastic world of infinite energy and life.

In Smith's graphic novel *Quiver,* the Green Arrow appears suddenly as a blank figure in the world; he can't account for the last ten years of his life. He is a "walking anachronism," a "hollow man." "You're not the archer," says one of the bad guys, "just his quiver."[28] Eventually, it will turn out that the Green Arrow did in fact die ten years ago, but the hero's soul magically sent the body back to earth. In the end, the two divided halves of Green Arrow have a long chat in heaven, and they decide to get back together for a plot-fulfilling reconciliation. Fullness and vitality thus overcome ghostliness and melancholy. Smith's smart-ass jokes and references to film (he alludes to *Citizen Kane* on the first page of the comic book and *Casablanca* on the last) effect a degree of self-consciousness—I am inhabiting this costumed contraption, here I am! But continuity rather than deconstruction seems the overall effect of the internal jokes and the self-parody. When characters make fun of one other's hyperbolic behavior or ridiculous costumes, it only shows how long-lasting the characters are, that they can stand up to anything.

Just so, Smith's films also create a serialized universe in which movies are not unique, unrepeatable experiences, but instead are purposefully self-reproducing, just like comic books. *Jay and Silent Bob Strike Back* (2001) borrows the typical language of sequel (*Star Wars: Episode V—The Empire Strikes Back*) to frame a film that refers to all of Smith's previous work (*Clerks* [1994], *Mallrats* [1995], *Chasing Amy* [1997], and *Dogma* [1999]). Jay and Silent Bob are the "real life" models for the comic book *Bluntman and Chronic*, and they themselves are barely distinguishable from comic book characters. In *Jay and Silent Bob Strike Back*, the two grungy heroes meet up with four beautiful jewel thieves, women who are as stereotyped in their Hollywood good looks and manner as can possibly be imagined. In an early sketch, Jay and Bob are picked up by a van filled with characters from *Scooby Doo*. At the end they dress up as costumed superheroes and battle Mark Hamill with light sabers. Pop culture is here to be toyed with endlessly, and there is no touch of mortality on Silent Bob.

Chasing Amy (1997) is certainly Smith's most interesting depiction of cinematic cartoonism. Whereas *Jay and Silent Bob Strike Back* does not try very hard to confound the fictional and the real (a visit to the set of Gus Van Sant's *Good Will Hunting* simply becomes another sketch), *Chasing Amy* takes some rather dramatic, serious issues and runs them into comic books. Comic-book artist Holden (Ben Affleck) falls in love with another comic-book author, Alyssa Jones (Joey Lauren Adams), although she is a lesbian. Their romance is played dramatically, as if it took place in what we understand to be the real world. Difficult "adult" topics of sexuality and sexual orientation are discussed in great detail, and the candid, open quality of the dialogue can only recall Soderbergh's *sex, lies, and videotape*.

Yet the seriousness and the drama of the romance are continually subverted by the cartoon mise-en-scène. Holden and his best friend, Banky, argue tooth and nail in front of comic book posters on the wall. When Holden and Alyssa have their fallout at a hockey game, a fan sitting next to Holden deflates the tragic atmosphere by saying, "Even I knew what you were getting at," like a kibitzer out of *Seinfeld*. Above all, in his hour of need Holden goes to talk to Jay and Silent Bob about his difficulties. The author thus shares his troubles with what are, in essence, his comic book creations. With the romantic lead and the stoner brothers essentially composited together from different conceptual universes, the scene is almost as much a combination of live action and animation as the Toons in Robert Zemeckis's *Who Framed Roger Rabbit* (1988).

But then Silent Bob suddenly breaks his silence—breaking out of character—and goes into his own version of a Sam Shepard monologue. Bob tells a story that is, by coincidence, the exact duplication of Holden's, about how he drove the perfect woman away because of her previous sexual experiences. It was not disgust but fear, he says, fear that he lacked experience, that he wouldn't be able to measure up. And ever since, he has been "chasing Amy." The speech is eloquent, and psychologically rather convincing as an interpretation of the men's behavior. But it is also completely ridiculous in that it so perfectly duplicates Holden's situation and comes from the stoner mute. The most interesting way to read this scene is to see a blurring of boundaries between "real" Ben Affleck and "cartoon" Jay and Silent Bob, and a mixing of the rules of art film, romantic comedy, and comic books.

But in the end, surely, the cartoon swallows them all. Marvel comics, just like Smith's *Dogma*, often deal with adult issues, but plastic cartoonism is the bottom line in either case. After watching *Jay and Silent Bob Strike Back*, critics complained of Smith's refusal to grow up, but that is a stance he has self-consciously adopted. His small independent films are no less childlike, or adolescent, than the cartoons of Hollywood. Whereas Holden in *Chasing Amy* is anxious that he does not have enough experience, Kevin Smith celebrates his lack of cinematic experience by looking at the world as if it were a cartoon. His famously unmoving camera signals a lack of pretense that does not evade pretending. Smith wants to pretend that this is not a movie in order to assure us that the movie will never end.

Quentin Tarantino's films represent perhaps the most interesting use of comic books and cartoonism in contemporary American film. The self-conscious use of comic books is evident in *Reservoir Dogs* (1992), in which Mr. Orange (Tim Roth) has posters of the Silver Surfer and the Kamikaze Cowboy on his wall, as well as in *Kill Bill, Volume 1* (2003), which turns into ten minutes of Japanese anime at one point.[29] Tarantino works explicitly with the link between childhood and animation in *Kill Bill*, since the anime cartoon sequence comes into the otherwise live-action film as a flashback to O-Ren Ishii's childhood. The anime sequence is a blood-spattered gorefest, which is certainly a familiar mode of Japanese anime, but here annotated by dramatic Sergio Leone–style music. The exuberance created by the juxtaposition of Leone music with martial-arts plotlines here and elsewhere is reminiscent of the grotesque thrills in Bill Plympton's animated films (e.g., *I Married a Strange Person* [1997]), which are funny and wild, not morbid, despite all the blood. In Sergio Leone, a childhood tragedy often determines the heroic, vengeful future of a life (as in *Once Upon a Time in the West* [1968]), and Leone's existential westerns are surely wide-screen cartoons. The bride (Uma Thurman) in *Kill Bill* kills at least a hundred people on her vengeful path, yet the fountains of blood and the sundry decapitations are never remotely realistic, but are always ensphered in an impossible fantasy world.[30]

Compared to *Kill Bill*, which is all cartoon, Tarantino's *Pulp Fiction* (1994) much more determinedly arranges a collision between comic books and the real world. In some respects, *Pulp Fiction* is just a comic book in which Mr. Wolf (Harvey Keitel) cleans up an impossible mess with nearly superhuman composure, and with its stories all taken from rehashed B-movie plots, such as the one about the boxer who refuses to fix his fight. At one point, a young man fires six bullets at bad guys Vincent (John Travolta) and Jules (Samuel Jackson), and all of the bullets miss. This is a supernatural event from the same impossible page as the rain of frogs in *Magnolia*, and the Bible-quoting Jules takes it, indeed, for a miracle. The rearranged circular narrative, in which Vincent is killed in the middle but still alive at the end, also gives the impression of immortality. These resurrected plots just keep going and going. Unlike the melancholy flashback that comes at the end of Atom Egoyan's *Sweet Hereafter* and allows us to compare the healthy girl we see before us with the real, broken self we know her to be, at the end of *Pulp Fiction* the living Vincent must strike us instead as merely amusing, decked out in ridiculous clothes, moving on to his next stupid job.

Yet the comic book elements of *Pulp Fiction* keep colliding with more realistic events. When Vince and Jules, in their matching suits and anachronistic hairstyles, go over to muscle around some college students, the scene plays as if a comic book world has come crunching up against a real one. Tarantino's character, Jimmie, also seems to dwell on a more realistic planet than his visitors, Mr. Wolf, Vincent, and Jules. And the torture scene, in which Butch (Bruce Willis) and Marsellus Wallace (Ving Rhames) are captured by rednecks, recalls the film-long bleeding to death of Mr. Orange in *Reservoir Dogs;* now this is not comic book violence.[31] Indeed, with its handheld camera and occasional cinema verité look, *Reservoir Dogs* stages the cartoon-versus-realism conflict most purposefully of all.[32] Judging by *Kill Bill: Volume 1,* this is a conflict that Tarantino has become less and less interested in. There are more children in *Kill Bill: Volume 1* than we have ever seen before in Tarantino, and also more cartoons.

Tarantino named his production company A Band Apart, after Godard's *Bande à part* (1964; English title, *Band of Outsiders*). In 1992 Tarantino called Godard's film "one of the greatest films in the world," insofar as it "reinvents an entire genre from the inside out."[33] Tarantino's films are all genre revisions, and as exuberant and liberating in some respects as the French New Wave. But Godard's cinematic revisionism is much more severe than Tarantino's. The heist plot in *Bande à part* has vanished almost to nothing; Tarantino still likes to tell stories. Godard is both more artificial and more realistic than Tarantino can imagine. In Godard's film, characters break into a dance routine for five minutes or so — the *Magnolia* effect once again — and even then the music cuts in and out quasi-randomly. Although *Bande à part* is one of Godard's lightest movies, even so it contains a good deal of political commentary and cinematic experimentation. Yes, there are cartoons in Godard, but also novels, poems, and paintings. At one point the three main characters go charging through the Louvre, which is great fun, but also serious.

By contrast, Tarantino seems stuck in Cap'n Crunch; his pop references do not collide with philosophy, or seemingly even with thinking. Tarantino only feels the liberating aspects of Godard, and he never refers to any Godard after *Pierrot le fou.*[34] But even before *Weekend* (1967) and *Ici et ailleurs* (1976), Godard's cinematic romanticism went hand in hand with cinematic critique and political severity. Godard does not play with movies just to play, but to criticize the money and class privileges that attend on Western filmmaking. Tarantino absolves himself of any political responsibility by calling himself an artist; he wants only to make films that are exuberant and thrilling. Thus whereas *Pulp Fiction* concludes in the full space of the infinite present, *Bande à part* makes almost exactly the same closing gesture, but with a much stronger sense of irony and mortality (which comes through the tone of the voice-over and the photography as much as the words): "My story ends here like in a pulp novel at that superb moment when nothing weakens, nothing wears away.

An upcoming film will reveal in CinemaScope and Technicolor the tropical adventures of Odile and Franz."

A.I. and the Dislocations of Time

Unlike Tarantino's *Pulp Fiction* or, for that matter, Spielberg's *Jurassic Park*, *A.I.* is a serious meditation on both digital cinema and animated cinema. Characters such as the Blue Fairy and Dr. Know are linked to the history of film, and their special effects are deployed critically and self-consciously. The Blue Fairy embodies the intense power of childhood memories and also the equally powerful grasp of digital computing. But *A.I.* qualifies the reach of both child and computer by pasting them into a Solaris narrative of impossible love. The love of Hari and Kris on the spaceship hovering over Solaris is an impossible love. The love of David and his mother in *A.I.*'s house at the end of time is equally an impossibility.

Cartoonism, as I have described it, is not limited to animation. And the reverse is true, too, which is to say that there may well be animated films that look more like Solaris, in the terms I have set out, than like cartoons. Most importantly, cartoonism in this discussion goes beyond the impression of omnipotence and spatial plasticity because, above all, cartoonism has to do with a claim of perfect memory. Not only is there omnipotence in space, but there is also omnipotence in time. The Solaris effect underscores time's passing, the irretrievability of the past. Solaris cinema sees a dislocation between past and present, between the "now" of the film and the "now" of our viewing. Tarkovsky's *Solaris* shows the irreconcilable nature of past and present, the irreducible pastness of Hari alongside her simulacrum in the present. By contrast, cartoonism idealizes both creativity and technology—I can make anything I want happen—to deny time and the human experience of time.

In *Sculpting in Time*, Tarkovsky compares the project of cinema to that of Proust (page references to the book are in parentheses). "Proust also spoke of raising a 'vast edifice of memories,' and that seems to me to be what cinema is called to do" (59). But Tarkovsky's memories are moral, not accidental: "Time cannot vanish without trace, for it is a subjective, spiritual category—and the time we have lived settles in our soul as an experience placed within time" (58). The past exists in the present as a layering of cause and effect to be discovered by the "human conscience." When Tarkovsky says that "memory is a spiritual concept," he denaturalizes the flow of time by placing the mediation of human conscience between past and present. One cannot listen to everything in the past equally; one only hears selections.

> Why do people go to the cinema? . . . The search for entertainment? The need for a kind of drug? All over the world there are, indeed, entertainment firms and organizations which exploit cinema and television and spectacles of many other kinds. Our starting-point, however, should not be there, but in the essential principles of cinema, which have to do with the human need to master and know the world. I think that what a person normally goes to the cinema for is *time*, for time lost or spent or not yet had. He goes there for living experience; for cinema, like no other art, widens, enhances and concentrates a person's experience—and not only enhances it but makes it longer, significantly longer. (63)

Cinema may relate to the human need for mastery, but the experience of time in *Solaris* is not mastery.

Although we persist in thinking of Tarkovsky as a theoretical naif, Deleuze's conception of the time-image in *Cinema 2* seems much more idealistic than Tarkovsky's. For Deleuze sees the time-image as embodying an inextricable continuity between past and present:

> First, there is no present which is not haunted by a past and a future, by a past which is not reducible to a former present, and by a future which does not consist of a present to come. Simple succession affects the presents which pass, but each present coexists with a past and a future without which it would not itself pass on. It is characteristic of cinema to seize this past and this future that coexist with the present image.[35]

The stroboscopic separation of past and present is crucial to Tarkovsky, but alien to Deleuze. As Alain Badiou characterizes Deleuze's Platonism:

> Were the past only an aftermath of the present, it would not be creation or power, but irremediable absence; it would be the production of the nothing of the present-that-passes. Being would then have to be said, at the same point, in two different senses: according to its mobile-being and according to its absence. There would be a *nostalgic* division of Being. Nothing is more foreign to Deleuze (or to Bergson) than nostalgia.[36]

Just as Deleuze refuses to read the cinematic screen as loss, he refuses also to read the past as lost, as nostalgically divided from the present. This latter refusal is brilliantly counterintuitive, but also sublimely utopian, and it amounts to a digital memory, or cartoonism, in short. The time-image in Deleuze does not have the capacity either to select or to forget. Human time in *A.I.* is characterized by elegy and melancholy. Nature is ongoing, in waves or frozen ice, and so are the machines. Only humans fade to nothing. The storyteller (Ben Kingsley), who provides the voice-over at the beginning and at the end, speaks in a softly mournful voice. The film begins with ocean waves rolling, and the voice-over will later come in to tell us that David has frozen in the ice and that humans have long since died. The storyteller must therefore be a robot like David, who possesses the artificial intelligence of human emotion. David's inventor (William Hurt) has brought David into the world to replace the loss of his own son. At one point we pan across the inventor's family photographs, coming to rest finally on a portrait of David, which is captioned "In loving memory of David." David the robot exists as a living tombstone for the real David, as an eternal sign of human loss.

David's mother, Monica, also sees David as an equally elegiac replacement as she mourns the probable death of her terminally ill son, Martin. Science eventually manages to cure Martin, but there will be no cure for time. The substitute artificial child outlives them all. The whole film is based on these temporal disjunctions—of past and present, of gain and loss—that can never be harmoniously reconciled. The conclusion, in which the robot "becomes a boy" in the presence of his long-dead mother, is the final aching impossibility. The teddy bear marching across the bed is a cloyingly Spielbergian touch, but even that cuteness cannot mask the powerful impression of evanescence at the end. Surely this is the fairy tale version of Tarkovsky's *Solaris*.

The final day that David spends with his mother is a day that never happened. He wants his mother back again, but this is an impossible day, a made-up memory. What we have seen of their actual past is a series of rather awkward incidents: Monica putting David in a closet to get him out of the way, or his weirding her out by making himself part of the telephone circuit and voicing (like a ventriloquist) the caller at the other end. Quietly spooky music plays under most of these early scenes. When David's human brother arrives, they immediately become competitive. David gets into one scrape after another, "breaking" himself by eating spinach (which is only for "rabbits, people, and Popeye"), and finally almost drowning his brother because of an apparent design flaw.

But at the end of the film, David's love for his mother seems to erase all that went before in order to imagine a final, perfect day. At the end, there is, of course, no brother. David's love is not for the family, but only for mom. Devotional memory is selective memory. Even Monica's husband is gone, completely beside the point. David imprints on Monica and immediately calls her Mommy, but he never gets beyond calling his father Henry. So David's house at the end of time is populated by carefully selected ghosts. Now their relationship is not awkward or pressured at all; everything is fun and wonderful. David does not have a birthday; he can't, since he is a machine. But on this impossible day he celebrates his birthday. The whole time spent is a beautiful, impossible dream, and then it is over, like film itself.

All of Spielberg's films of the 1990s foreground memory, but only *A.I.* represents a dislocation between past and present. The other films are, in the way they handle time, cartoons. *Jurassic Park, Schindler's List, Amistad,* and *Saving Private Ryan* all circle around "film's loving memory," and the "redemptive power of cinema."[37] These films all idealize the continuity between past and present. The historical films, *Schindler's List* and *Saving Private Ryan,* offer cinema as a salvific witness. All of the films implicitly claim for themselves an omnipotent vision, a perfect memory. We can see this most clearly by turning briefly to one of Spielberg's history films, *Amistad* (1997).

Amistad intends to tell a story that is not ordinarily told, in film or otherwise. John Quincy Adams (Anthony Hopkins) tells the Supreme Court that if this African man, Cinque (Djimon Hounsou) were white, then epic poems would be written about his heroism, but since he is black, no one will sing his song. *Amistad* wants to be that song, which tells the dreadful history of the slave ship *Amistad.* Spielberg's film thus brings itself before us as a memorial witness to atrocity and horror, as did Spielberg's earlier film, *Schindler's List* (1993). Both films depict shocking scenes of cruelty and suffering: massacres by the Nazis, on the one hand, beatings and murders performed by the slave owners, on the other. Both films also manage to end happily, since small groups of Jews and African slaves survive their terrors and are set free. Spielberg chose relatively upbeat plots in which to remember these terrible histories, and in both cases he was roundly criticized for his irrepressible optimism. One should emphasize that it is, above all, the assumption of irrepressible memory that makes these exhibitions possible.

Compare John Quincy Adams's speech, for example, to the last words of Gigolo Joe (Jude Law) in *A.I.* As he is caught up by a helicopter, Gigolo Joe cries, "I am. I was." Time is provokingly rent apart in such a formulation, and this temporal fracture is felt everywhere in *A.I. Amistad*'s John Quincy Adams, however, concludes his eleven-minute speech to the Supreme Court by appealing to tradition and the Founding Fathers. He observes that Cinque has been empowered and consoled through this trial by his ancestors, and he argues that we Americans ought to invoke our ancestors as well. He points to a framed Declaration of Independence, and touches the busts of the great statesmen from America's heroic past. "Madison, Hamilton, George Washington," he intones. "Who we are is who we were," he says in conclusion, and that sense of continuity from past to present accurately sums up the sense of memory and history in *Amistad*.

Adams is introduced to us as a dozing amnesiac who cannot stay awake and cannot pay attention to anything when he is not asleep. But by the end he is a clear-eyed luminary who says everything that we would like to say ourselves. Whereas the scenes on the *Amistad* are treated with gruesome realism, Adams is treated hagiographically, surrounded by a glowing halo. In the middle sequences he is always shown in a greenhouse, cultivating and studying nature. Adams argues before the Supreme Court that slavery is not natural, that freedom is natural, and the film wants us to associate Adams's uncompromised politics with nature itself. A quietly patriotic melody always attends Adams; the tune will later develop into a main theme for *Saving Private Ryan*.

Just as *Saving Private Ryan* bathed the homeland scenes in nostalgic oranges and browns, Adams descends to us from Capra's *Mr. Smith Goes to Washington*, from a history without criticism. This is history as propaganda, as spin-doctoring, as flag-waving hagiography. To obtain a saint, realism must be forgotten. But the film nowhere admits to selectivity, omission, or forgetting, since it implies that the scenes of horror and the scenes of propaganda are all equally true. Spielberg's anachronisms (all the lawyers yell Yes! like Marv Albert, in celebration of the final victory) are not self-reflexive admissions that historical memory is complex, contested, and shadowy, but rather signs that my history can do whatever it wants to, thank you very much.

Before we return to *A.I.*, we can usefully compare the treatment of memory and history in *Amistad* to the way they appear in Julie Dash's film of 1991, *Daughters of the Dust*. Dash's film depicts the Gullah people of South Carolina at the beginning of the twentieth century. The Gullahs were descendants of slaves, but since they lived on sea islands off the coast, they managed to retain many aspects of West African culture. A title card at the beginning says: "The Gullah community recalled, remembered, and recollected much of what their ancestors brought with them from Africa." The African ancestors are just as important to *Daughters of the Dust* as they are to *Amistad,* but each film represents memory and the past very differently. Memory is all-important in *Daughters,* but the incantation of synonyms (recalled, remembered, recollected) suggests that memory will be wider and more elaborate than we might otherwise have expected. The situation that frames the film—a plot is barely evident—is that most of the community will soon be moving permanently to the mainland. The past is of paramount importance to this community, but is also open to debate. Over the course of the film there are many subtle discussions about past and future, tradition and innovation, involving everyone from the oldest ancestors to a child who is about to be born. As Dash says, the dust *is* the past—these women are daughters of the past.[38] Yet these daughters spend the time of the film looking at their mothers, and at their pasts, in different ways. One woman critiques tradition by arguing that "old people think they have all the answers."

Daughters of the Dust works out an extended parallel between cultural memory and cinematic memory. Both kinds of memory shift back and forth between ghostly intuition and factual precision. *Daughters of the Dust* gives the impression of realism and accuracy through the varieties of character on the island and especially through the use of different spoken dialects, which are often not readily understood. Yet the characters also spend most of the day wandering around on a beach; we do not spend much time in their houses or learning how they live day to day. The linguistic realism combined with the idyllic landscape and the holiday atmosphere makes for an effect at once both historical and surreal. Memory can be detailed, as when stories of slave traders are told, but memories can also arrive in fits and starts ("They come to you when you least expect it").

Dash self-consciously includes many of the optical toys of the day—a kaleidoscope, a slide viewer, and, of course, a camera. At one point, a slide on the viewing machine turns (before our eyes) into footage from a silent newsreel. The cameraman goes around trying to capture this historical moment: "Look! Look up! Remember Ibo Landing! Hold!" But in another scene the spirit of the daughter to be born glides through the cameraman's vision, but not the camera's. In other words, Dash characterizes Gullah memory and cinematic history by invoking elements of both ghostliness and accuracy. The photographer takes his pictures, accompanied by a puff of smoke, and many of the images in the film look like still photographs. Yet there are also substantial differences between cultural memory and photography. The ghost child that flits in and out of the photograph suggests the inaccessibility of cultural memory through technology. The ghostliness of cinema is different from the ancestral ghosts. In *Daughters of the Dust*, cinematic memory is humbled before cultural memory.

In contrast, then, to *Amistad*, *A.I.* formulates a repeated dislocation of past and present. The theme of the whole film could, indeed, be glossed by Gigolo Joe's final words: "I am. I was." As Joe is pulled upward by the police, toward certain expiration, his final words describe a discontinuous identity in time, an absence of gradations between past and present. His identity as a sex robot orients him to the surface, to the present. When David and Gigolo Joe go to Rouge City, Joe has to be reminded to stay with his mission; he is distracted by women and wants to score another trick. When David talks about the Blue Fairy in the forest, Joe can only sexualize her, and proceeds to vocalize the orgasmic moans that he will get out of her if they ever meet. Joe embodies a robot mentality as a present tense in a sea of eternity.

In his turn, David has no birthday and does not remember being built. "I don't remember," he tells his human brother. "What is the first thing you can remember?" asks Martin. "A bird, a bird with big wings," he says, and he draws the company logo. Later he will stare at the winged fairy for two thousand years. Whereas Gigolo Joe is a sex robot, built to please women, David is a boy robot, built to love, with "a love that will never end." David's eternal present is shown in one of his writings: "Dear Mommy, I love you and Henry and the sun is shining." The present tense eternity of robot time will never mesh with human time. On a day-to-day scale, he does not sleep and he does not eat (when he does, egged on by his brother, he breaks). On an epoch-to-epoch scale, the robots will outlive the humans. Since he does not want to be alone, David asks his mother how long he will live. "Is fifty years a long time?" he asks his mother. She replies that it is "ages," but Teddy says, "I don't think so." When David is discovered in his frozen hovercraft, there are no humans left in the world. David was one of the first robots, say the super-robots, who "knew living people."

Although robot time-consciousness occurs in an intense present, it also partakes of human change and mortality: "I am. I was." Except for David, the robots gathered at the flesh fair do not express human terror at their coming annihilation, but they are not happy about it either. They tell their captors that they are still useful, even though they are older robots. "Seventy-five years ago, I was *Time*'s Mecha of the Year," says one, with dignity. They are stoical, but they prefer existence to nonexistence, otherwise they would not have run away in the first place. Joe removes a tracking device from himself, disobeying orders, to "stay alive." Even though they are programmed to live in an intense present, they are conscious of the possibility of nonexistence and death. Yet it is also this possibility of change that gives David hope, a hope that the future will be different from the present, that he will become a boy. "I forgive you all your past misdeeds," says the Blue Fairy in the Pinocchio book; "In the future you will always be happy." Change is possible in robot time, but radically disjunct. The present is discontinuous with both the past ("I am. I was.") and the future. When David finally returns home to his mother, all the humans on earth have been dead for thousands of years.

Self-reflexivity is discovered by interpretation. One does not have to argue too vehemently to find *Tristram Shandy* or Godard very often self-reflexive, but no abstract painting by Rothko or de Kooning is self-reflexive on its own. An interpreter must argue to what degree a Rothko painting is about its own medium, to what degree it is self-conscious or self-critical, and of what. In such an interpretation, authorial intention is equally open to discussion. Eisenstein's *Ivan the Terrible* does not necessarily do everything that Eisenstein says it does. That *A.I.* has something interesting to say about its own technology is what we have to show, then, and this is not dependent on what Spielberg, or even Kubrick, thinks it does.

But one might add to this argument by citing Dennis Muren, visual effects supervisor for Industrial Light and Magic. On one of the DVD extras, he describes the shape of *A.I.* as moving from a contemporary environment in David's home, to the strikingly futuristic look of Rouge City, to the "most synthetic" world of two thousand years in the future. "The movie's about AI," says Muren, "but by the end of the film we're essentially making it, and AI actually becomes how we're making the movie. We're starting out contemporary, and ending up totally artificially in the future." As Muren observes, the last section of the movie takes place in a striking overlap between form and content. Here the movie is almost entirely computer generated, and in the story only computers have survived. The overlap seems suggestively self-reflexive, and therefore readable, but we still need to decide what the film might be saying when it self-consciously refers to itself.

In a recent article, Mark Williams, calls *A.I.* and *FairyTale: A True Story* (Sturridge, 1997) "reflexive" films about "digital anxiety" (page references to the article are in parentheses).[39] "The startling frankness of the concluding sequence" and the "literalization of the post-human" (robots only) are only two of the ways that [*A.I.*] registers the difficult relationship of subjectivity to digital technology (170, 171). Williams usefully describes the trajectory of David's subjectivity, with an emphasis on key stages. After the flesh fair, where "artificiality" is summarily demolished, and the journey to Rouge City ("characterized by blatant sexual figurations"), David encounters another version of himself, and he "demolishes the robot in a manner not dissimilar to that seen at the Flesh Fair" (169). After seeing box upon box of mass-produced Davids, he "sits dejectedly at the edge of the building, and soon simply falls off into the depths below" (169). Williams summarizes the anxiety around the final scene, then, as a culmination of these encounters with sexuality and death:

> This quality and capacity for transience, and more specifically for mortality, is the final aspect of subjectivity that David accesses. Again this is rendered in decidedly gendered and Oedipal terms, as David is afforded one day to spend with his "mother" (based on a regenerated DNA sample), at the end of which she, and apparently he, will drift off to sleep and death. The tone established for this conclusion is quietly powerful, and disturbing in its elegance and beauty. Sleep, with which David had no previous acquaintance, is designated as the place where dreams are born—and by relation, creativity and art. Yet the scene renders this via a decidedly precise form of classical Oedipal "perversion," as David lies contentedly in bed with his mother—or, more specifically, her corpse. (170)

This reading not only provides a good description of the ambivalent tonality of the end, but the sexual focus also helps us account for the subplot of Gigolo Joe in the development of David's narrative.

Let us examine the role of sexuality in *A.I.* a bit further, then, to augment this psychoanalytically framed account. Gigolo Joe and David make for one of cinema's oddest couples, and many critics diagnosed the incongruity as originating in the Kubrick-Spielberg tension. There is a striking jump in tone at the end of the first third of the film: we cut from the melodramatic scene of David left behind in the forest, crying for his mommy, to a bedroom scene in the city, where Joe is talking a woman into having sex for the first time with a robot. But David's domestic world has never been very cute; he is a spooky robot kid always attended by ominous music. His world is seemingly protected and secure, but, ironically, he breaks when trying to keep himself safe: "Keep me safe!" he says to his human brother while dragging him down into the swimming pool. *A.I.* makes a journey through archetypal images of innocence and experience, in which Rouge City is the real world, the fallen world of adult sexuality. But the innocent world of David's home is already complicated, shadowy, premonitory. And if the innocent world of domesticity is ambiguous in the first third of the movie, it is ambiguous ten times over when David returns to it at the end.

This way of looking at Rouge City as an adult world makes sense if we read *A.I.* as a human narrative, as David's bildungsroman. *A.I.* becomes Spielberg's *Book of Thel;* in both cases the protagonists move out into a world of sexuality, but then flee that world, returning from whence they came. But as a reflexive narrative, *A.I.* is also about technology. How should we read the sex robot, Gigolo Joe, self-reflexively? In part, Gigolo Joe is there to define the artificial intelligence of David. David is a robot built to love. We are to contrast the complexity of David's emotional project with the more utilitarian motivation of Joe. Visually, Joe looks more like a robot than David: he is shiny and metallic, and he moves more abruptly. By contrast, David looks exactly like the child he wants to be, and as the movie goes along, the robotic quality of his gestures becomes more and more reduced.

The sexiness of robots, in any case, might well make more sense to us than their tenderness. Cyberspace is much more likely to be described as erotic than loving.[40] The Internet revolution has famously brought with it an avalanche of easily accessible pornography, and the net cowboys in William Gibson's novels jack in for ecstatic pleasure. Gigolo Joe is high-tech, sleek, and powerful. He is not a "cold" machine, like *Star Trek*'s Data; on the contrary, he is cool, confident, graceful, knowledgeable. His advanced technology, his artificial intelligence ("I know what women want") makes him an extra-advanced sex toy.

But *A.I.* needs both sex robot Gigolo Joe and love robot David, just as Chris Marker's *La Jetée* needed both the child's intense memory and the adult's romantic love. David is a child, with a child's love, but a child who is set free in a nighttime world of sexuality and fear. The child's vision and the adult's vision are always disjunct, but always linked, like the two sides of the women's faces in Bergman's *Persona*. Both Joe and David are linked intimately to humanity, but also, in the end, alienated from humanity as well. Whereas in *Solaris* the human wants to join the alien, in *A.I.* the robot wants to join the human. In *Solaris* the films spirals down to the dream of home on Earth, and *A.I.*, too, rounds to a close in another nostalgic fantasy of home. In either case the screen fills with impossible dreams, even as the film performs its own death and concludes. Just as when the film spins around in the projector and the lights switch off in *Persona*, there is nothing left but projection at the end of *Solaris* and *A.I.* The world has become a screen, and then there is darkness.

When David is given the last day with his mother, he knows where this last day comes from. He knows it derives from his memory, that his mother has been dead for two thousand years. He knows, in other words, that this world is a digital reality. Is this artificial reality really so different from the artifice of photographed reality? Does our position as spectators change ontologically before the digital screen? Surely the result is more dialectical: that it is partly about the technology of the screen, but partly about our relationship to it. Many theories of digital cinema are purely materialistic: technology changes, so our relationship to the screen changes. But the unappeasable desire for the image can take place as powerfully in a photographic regime as in a digital regime.

Cinema against Art: Artists and Paintings in Contemporary American Film 6

....

American film directors like to say no to art. But the no means different things and comes from different places. There is the unthinking no and the thinking no, the negation spoken by the know-nothings, and the negation of the know-everythings. To directors who align themselves with producers, cinema is not an art, because if cinema is a business, then art spells only commercial disaster. If we must tell the story of an artist, then we will make that artist into every other kind of conventional hero and leave the art behind. Art will appear as intuition and genius, since that way we will not have to talk about it. But there is also the negation of art by directors who very happily call themselves artists. This kind of negative aesthetics does not say no to art because it fears pretentiousness or elitism, but because it wants us to realize that cinematic art—"the seventh art"—is not arty, from an art gallery, like the other arts. Film art is a different kind of art.

Contemporary art continually rearranges its own meanings and semiotics. Contemporary art is in large part a training ground that instructs us to read art differently. Robert Rauschenberg's "combines" refuse to settle down into a discrete genre (painting or collage); most disturbingly, the combines refuse anything like a stable meaning.[1] Contemporary sculpture, as Rosalind Krauss observes, is often predicated on negativity and absence: "not-landscape" and "not-architecture."[2] Although such strategies are relatively familiar in modern art, we do not usually consider that a contemporary film might take part in these ongoing reframings and negations. Unless of course it is Godard, who continually says no to everything. From the film director in *Passion* (1982), who is never satisfied with the lighting, to the tyrannical director in *For Ever Mozart* (1996), who repeatedly tells everyone no! Godard self-consciously enacts an ongoing cinema of negation. *In Praise of Love* (2001) is explicitly anti-Spielberg and anti-*Matrix*.

But contemporary American film often emerges with its own freight of negative aesthetics. In this chapter I will use paintings and painters to focus on this recurrent negation of art in American film. To linger over paintings is often to self-consciously reflect on the signifying power of representation. To tell the story of a painter allows one to think through the differences between the arts of space (painting, photography) and the arts of time (music, cinema). There are instructive overlaps between the intuitive aesthetics proposed by Ed Harris's *Pollock* and Robert Altman's *Vincent and Theo*. The overlaps appear not only because these films focus on art and artists, but because both movies are also, in various ways, saying no to art.

Throwing Art into the Ocean from *Pollock* to *Basquiat*

Pollock (Ed Harris, 2000) is a perfect example of an American film that takes an artist for its hero yet nonetheless refuses to talk about art. If Jackson Pollock himself was close-mouthed about art, it does not necessarily follow that the movie needs to be as well. But *Pollock* tells a story of the abstract expressionist's career in the most recognizable plot, with the most conventional visuals. Pollock (Harris) just stares down cultured dinner conversation; the language of art criticism spoken by both Lee Krasner (Marcia Gay Harden) and Clement Greenberg (Jeffrey Tambor) is "blah blah blah" for Pollock. "I am nature," says Pollock, and the movie sides with him, preferring his know-nothing anti-intellectualism to their art talk. Pollock's great discoveries take place in a cold barn in the countryside, and we see him look into a swirling stream and walk next to the ocean. We are to see his drip paintings as manifestations of the natural. The paintings' fluidity is like the stream, and he makes his paintbrush into a "stick." His explanations intend to stifle thought. "It's like looking at a bed of flowers," says Pollock. "You don't tear your hair out over the meaning." When an interviewer asks him, "How do you know when you're finished painting?" he replies, "How do you know when you're finished making love?" He picks up a dog lying in the middle of the road and takes it to the vet, saying, "Please save this beautiful dog."

The movie does not overidealize the artist's primitivism, since it leads to a drunken decline and a fatal car accident. But *Pollock* avoids at all costs a sense of the artificial in art. Jackson Pollock pisses in the fireplace, sleeps with whatever women he wants, drinks all the time, and paints. Meanwhile he reflects on life and art not at all. The *Life* photographer has to ask him to slow down so that it will look like he is thinking.

In Hollywood films, art nearly always descends from the sky, and thus resists any possible intellectual discussion. From the standpoint of aesthetic ideology, *Great Expectations* (Alfonso Cuarón, 1998) emerges from the same set of taciturn principles as Ed Harris's *Pollock*. Whereas Dickens's *Great Expectations* is the central Victorian analysis of the gentleman, Cuarón's contemporary retelling makes Pip (now called Finn, played by Ethan Hawke) into an artist. The alteration implies that although a "gentleman" is no longer a relevant category or goal, an "artist" is, and Finn takes the New York art world by storm. But as in *Pollock*, this art is completely naturalized, and all aspects of artistic development are explained through nature. Although *Great Expectations* reverses the geographical structure of *Pollock*—Finn grows up on the seashore in Florida, then moves to New York City—it says exactly the same thing about the role of nature. Art comes from nature and is not antithetical to nature. The film begins by showing us Finn sitting in his boat, sketching. His sketches are representational simplifications (Klee seems to be the model) of fish, cats, stars, and birds.

Unlike *Pollock*, which is a tragedy of self-absorption, *Great Expectations* is a romance. Whereas Pollock is a socially inept, selfish bastard, Finn paints out of love ("Everything I do is for you"). In either case, however, art emerges from the natural world and unsophisticated society. In either film, we are not so much concerned with aesthetics (artistic talent is a "gift" for Finn) as with success. The New York critics authenticate the art with their language and their money, but each movie wants us to sympathize with the passionate, intuitive, and even naive character of its hero, who stands in contrast to the art-gallery sophisticates.

These idealizations and naturalizations culminate when Finn paints a final, verbal picture for us at the end of the film. Here Finn and Estella hold hands next to a glittering ocean, and time itself melts away. Although she is married, with a child, and has often treated him cruelly, we are supposed to grant that this is a beautiful picture nonetheless: "And the rest of it, it didn't matter. It was past. It was as if it had never been. There was just my memory of it." Time here is not dislocated, as in the Solaris effect, into past and future, but rather the past itself is whisked away into a void. This art flees from thought and insists that we call artifice love. Finn's imagination allows him to overthrow reality, history, and narrative in the name of a romantic moment.

There is an exactly parallel appearance of art in James Cameron's *Titanic*

(1997), which appeared the year before *Great Expectations*. The frozen moment is literalized pathetically in *Titanic*, as Jack Dawson (Leonardo DiCaprio) slowly freezes to death after the great ship's collapse. *Titanic* gives us plenty of chances to see the romantic freeze-frame coming. For although it is a tumultuous action adventure for the last hour, the film begins with still photographs, and it will end with them. The story begins when a contemporary salvage expedition finds a drawing of a nude woman in the *Titanic*'s safe (although the crew was hoping, of course, for treasure). The film concludes with the aged Rose, who survives the disaster, surrounded by photographs of her young self.

Rose's story turns out to be the story of an artist, Jack Dawson, and their brief but powerful love. "I don't have even have a picture of him," she says, but her boundless love has stored Jack permanently in her memory. The old Rose is like a sane Miss Havisham who has lived with the experience of her love for all these years. After such a love, and such a disaster, time has virtually stopped, and at the very end she dreams herself back into the world of the yet-floating ship with Jack. The last photograph on her nightstand, over which the camera lingers, shows the young Rose on a horse in front of a roller coaster. This photograph embodies perfectly the tension in *Titanic* itself, which, as a film, is a spectacular, dynamic, amusement-park ride, but which promotes at the same time a frozen dream of romantic eternity. "I'll never let go," say Rose (Kate Winslet), as they hold hands in the icy water. The ocean of time into which the *Titanic* sinks is, once again, not the swirling, time-swamped waters of Solaris.

Jack, like Finn in *Great Expectations*, is a lower-class artist who works from intuition, not education. Rose thinks his work is very good, although the film makes no effort to distinguish his drawings stylistically. But we are supposed to credit Rose as an authority on art, since we see her praise the work of Picasso over the objections of her terrifically dull fiancé. *Titanic* the movie makes an amusing, even if not necessarily intentional, joke in this scene between Rose and her betrothed when it shows us recognizable paintings by Picasso, Degas, and Monet. These paintings in Rose's cabin are about to sink to the bottom of the sea, yet somehow they also wind up in various museums![3] The movie wants us to see how imperceptive Rose's prospective husband is, and so hangs these pictures to make certain that we will agree with her taste. Then, once her authority is established, we are supposed to grant Dawson's completely ordinary drawings some sort of aesthetic merit.

Titanic thus uses art to signify passion and perception, even if in the most calculatedly contradictory ways. In his book-length reading of *Titanic*, for example, David Lubin shows how nature is taken for the authentic power in this world, despite the fact that the world in the movie is conjured out of CGI.[4] The overlapping of theme and imagery in *Great Expectations* and *Titanic* emphasizes these contradictions of nature and art. Both films provide images of young romantic love, naked women in pictures, aging women in romantic stasis, and nature conquering civilization (the mansion equivalent to Dickens's Satis House in Cuarón's film of *Great Expectations* is overrun by trees and birds, the roof open to the sky). That is, one frozen moment after another, yet with the underlining foundation of the natural. Art is apparently central to the structure of both films, yet everywhere it is masked, even overwhelmed, by romantic ideology.

Compare the imagery and aesthetics of *Pollock*, *Great Expectations*, and *Titanic* to a film made by the painter Julian Schnabel. Like *Pollock*, Schnabel's biopic *Basquiat* (1996) contrasts the relatively inarticulate bohemian artist to the smooth-talking New York City gallery owners and critics. In the first sequence after the titles, we see Basquiat (Jeffrey Wright) get out of a cardboard box where he has been sleeping in a park. Like *Pollock* and *Titanic*, the movie could easily deploy the categories of nature and class to support a narrative of artistic origin and success. As Andy Warhol tells Basquiat, "You're a natural." But an interviewer (Christopher Walken) points out that Basquiat was, in actuality, raised middle-class, so if he lives in a cardboard box, it amounts to adopting a role. Even from the very beginning, we see that Schnabel's *Basquiat* will not revert to nature in order to explain artistic success. During the title sequence, we see the young Basquiat walking through a museum with his mother. They stand in front of Picasso's *Guernica*. His mother looks down on him, and a bright magical crown appears on his head. Her child is a prince. In this way, *Basquiat* does not attempt to ground the artist's talent or success in nature. His art simply appears, although we cannot say exactly why.

The narrative of *Basquiat* signals artistic success in complicated ways. When Jackson Pollock first creates his recognizable drip paintings, the sound track of *Pollock* annotates his achievement with triumphant music, and Lee Krasner is immediately there to say, "You've cracked it wide open." Pollock's gallery successes and critical acclaim are transparently underlined in Ed Harris's film. By contrast, the success of Basquiat is more ambiguously marked. He starts to have some money; he starts hanging around with Warhol; agents start to compete for his attention. But there is no particular moment of triumph. The movie leaves us, indeed, with questions as to whether Basquiat's art is objectively important or whether his fame is linked to his exploitation as a black artist. As a character, Basquiat drifts into his art, seemingly just as interested in music, drugs, and women, and the movie drifts, too, not needing to overemphasize antithetical anger or career success.

Basquiat, as a film, does not borrow its form from its subject. Basquiat began as a graffiti artist, but the film does not attempt to reproduce the visual style or verbal sloganeering of urban graffiti. Derek Jarman's *Jubilee* (1978), painted from stem to stern in graffiti, and Jarman's video for the Smiths' "The Queen Is Dead" (1986) are more deliberate attempts to translate the spirit of graffiti art into film. By contrast, *Basquiat* is filmed for the most part rather straightforwardly, giving us in each sequence a clear sense of three-dimensional space, and in realistic rather than noticeably artificial colors. The implication of the mise-en-scène is that artists live in a real world, but one in which particular scenes and an overall narrative are not so easily evaluated. *Basquiat*'s relatively conventional visual appearance is partly attributable to its sheer number of stars (David Bowie, Gary Oldman, Dennis Hopper, Willem Dafoe), who are not going to show up in some distorted thesis about representation.[5] But the visuals also reflect an implicit distance from Basquiat himself, who seems stoned most of the time. How easy it would be to make Basquiat into Caligari!

Yet it would be wrong to characterize the film as realistic, since it frequently calls attention to itself as an artificial construct. At one point Basquiat wakes up next to his girlfriend and decides to paint over some of her paintings; he also paints her dress. Why does he do this? The scene is intercut with a silent-movie fantasy in which a stork eventually eats a talking frog (the frog helplessly slides down into the long beak). There is no clear relationship between the domestic conflict (why is he painting her dress?) and the interpolated film. The interpolated film (*Frogland*) is a kind of travesty of nature, while Basquiat, in his turn, paints a dress, but what we register in the crosscutting is a lack of connection. Unlike Eisenstein's relatively overt symbolism, such as the mechanical peacock in *October,* the intercut film in *Basquiat* comes in to underscore artifice, but not an artifice that implies depth or makes more sense. Here art does not signify death, nature, love, or truth—as it does in *Pollock, Great Expectations,* or *Titanic.*

This is an art that refuses to signify, and we will see that this is a main aspect of the negative aesthetics orchestrated by both Kubrick and Altman. *Basquiat* does not use self-conscious devices like these filmic interpolations all the time, but they occur with enough frequency to unsettle. Music, for instance, is used for relatively complex annotation; when Basquiat is beaten up, there is an opera aria on the sound track, and the effect is not the simple, though powerful, irony of Muzak in Todd Solondz. At another point the camera blurs against a fence, and we think we are going into Basquiat's dreamy subjectivity, whereupon he rides his bike into his own apparent point of view, a favorite denaturalizing device of Martin Scorsese.

Basquiat's imagination is visualized in several instances by showing a surfer riding the waves over tall buildings. A basic way of understanding this image is that, as an artist, he sees things in the city that are not there. But this is a more particularized fantasy. The surfboarder seems specifically to connote an idea of escape. Basquiat wants to get out of the city and go off to an island. He says several times that he needs to leave New York ("Let's go to Hawaii"). At the end of the film we see him pretend to surf, standing up, arms outraised, in an army jeep. Basquiat's very last words in the film are "Let's go to Ireland. We'll stop at every bar." So the surfboard indicates a kind of visionary idyll, a desire for nature and for home (his father is from Haiti), in contrast to the alienations of urban life. At one point the surfer falls into the ocean, however, which suggests that Basquiat knows that his dream will never come true. Altogether, the ocean in *Basquiat* is both peaceful (*Great Expectations*) and powerful (*Titanic*), and the floating surfer in the artist's daydream potentially encompasses both of these attributes.

The most self-conscious and interesting working out of Basquiat's oceanic figure comes in a sequence at the end of the film. Andy Warhol has died, and we see Basquiat watching home movies of Warhol, crying and remembering his friend. Warhol is played in the film by David Bowie, but the home movies intercut Bowie's Warhol with the real Andy Warhol. The very first sequence of home-movie footage shows us the ocean, and then Warhol on the beach with his camera. The footage showing the real Warhol comes from *Scenes from the Life of Andy Warhol* (Jonas Mekas, 1990). Mekas himself shoots in a shaky, stroboscopic manner (leaving out frames) to intentionally denaturalize his subject. Mekas's film includes many different scenes of Warhol — with the Velvet Underground, working in the Factory, partying with Allen Ginsberg — but Schnabel has started *his* Warhol home movie with the ocean, and Warhol on the beach. Which is the real Andy Warhol? this footage asks. Which Andy Warhol made the Brillo boxes and all those Marilyns? And which is the real ocean? Is it always out there, somewhere else? Are we not already there? Are we not drowning already?

Just before the section in which Basquiat looks at the Warhol home movies comes another vision of that surfer, with crashing, grating sounds on the sound track. Something is wrong. Meanwhile, Basquiat writes "TITA" on a round oval. Later we see him walking down the street in clogs. Suddenly we realize that on the back of each shoe Basquiat has written "Titanic." So the ocean is already here, but it is not the real ocean. And Basquiat goes down with his ship.

Traditionally, art ought to mean something. Art objects ought to be more significant than other objects. Artists ought to be more interesting than other people. In *Pollock* and *Great Expectations*, art means brutal honesty or romantically creative dishonesty. In *Titanic*, art sets a standard for emotional sensibility. In *Basquiat*, art does not necessarily mean anything at all, nor is art necessarily more important than anything else. Indeed, contemporary art has often followed Duchamp and Warhol by questioning cultural hierarchies and the uniqueness of art objects. Of all these films, Julian Schnabel's most strongly resembles the way contemporary artists treat their own artworks. But the desire to reduce and rearrange emphasis and meaning also has an important place in the history of cinema. In the next sections we will see how Stanley Kubrick and Robert Altman meditate on the significance of art. Does art signify? Is art more important than other things? We will see how often these art directors vacuum out the significance of art in order to redefine what art is or where it can be found.

Along these lines, I will conclude this first section with a glance toward one of the most poignant of all the recent Solaris films, Jonathan Nossiter's *Signs and Wonders* (2000). In *Signs and Wonders*, a husband (Stellan Skarsgaard) looks obsessively for signs: for signs that he should stay in his marriage or that he should leave his wife (Charlotte Rampling) for another woman. The husband's search for meaning is seen as absolutely pathological, since the wife that he dreams is there is simply not there any more. Set in Greece, *Signs and Wonders* radically interrogates the traditional sense that meaning coheres around us, in either the world of love or the world of art.

And observe that this narrative film, *Signs and Wonders*, has developed straight out of Nossiter's documentary from the same year, *Losing the Thread* (*Perdere il filo*, 2000). What *Losing the Thread* had already concluded about art, *Signs and Wonders* goes on to conclude about love. *Losing the Thread* is a documentary portrait of an Italian artist, Lorenzo Pezzatini. The subtitle of the documentary is "an attempted film," and Nossiter goes so far as to appear at the beginning to say that the days of shooting have gone down as a "peculiar failure." He says that he has failed to "connect to anybody or to anything," and that Lorenzo lives in a fantasy world "and has no connection to anything."

Before the film has even got underway, Nossiter calls his own project "a total fiasco." But the fiasco is only with respect to a search for meaning.

Pezzatini's particular artistic obsession is called the "*filo*," a thread. Every painting, mural, sculpture, piece of furniture, and performance is centered on this multicolored thread. It looks, of course, to be an emblem of sheer continuity. The thread must be that which connects, which links one thing to another. But as we hear Pezzatini talk, as we watch him wheel his metal cart of thread into the center of Florence, we feel only discontinuity, the absence of connection. Nossiter, the director, does not efface himself in this documentary; on the contrary, he is always there to foreground this lack of connection. The paintings and sculptures of thread ought to mean something, connect to something, but they do not. There is nothing to say about them. There is love; there is no love. There is cinematic presence; there is not cinematic presence. There is meaning; there is no meaning. The husband in *Signs and Wonders* is looking through the world in the way that we watch a film. He sits right next to Tarkovsky's Kris, Lynch's Diane, and Spielberg's David in an auditorium of presence and absence. The cinematic artwork that wards off art necessarily surrounds itself with the bright, tentative artifices of the Solaris effect.

Cinema as Negation: Kracauer, Rossellini,
and Stanley Kubrick's *Eyes Wide Shut*

Siegfried Kracauer's *Theory of Film: The Redemption of Physical Reality* (1960) was recently reprinted in 1997 with an introduction by Miriam Bratu Hansen (page references to the book are in parentheses).[6] Kracauer's penchant for realism and reality may seem antiquated among today's digital technologies, since, as Hansen says, "traditional models of representation have given way to the reign of simulation" (viii). Although Kracauer has been attacked and virtually refuted as a proponent of "naive realism," Hansen wants to emphasize the complexities and useful inconsistencies of Kracauer's thought. She wants to redeem Kracauer from critical obsolescence by emphasizing his historical importance: "What *Theory of Film* can offer us today is not a theory of film in general, but a theory of a particular type of film experience, and of cinema as the aesthetic matrix of a particular historical experience" (x). Yet Kracauer's work is important for reasons that go beyond historical particularity. In this section I will argue that Kracauer's general theory still has a peculiar relevance to contemporary film, and specifically to Stanley Kubrick's last film, *Eyes Wide Shut* (1999). Kracauer's theory is, above all, concerned with what is proper to the cinema as an art form, and *Eyes Wide Shut* may be said to embody another discussion of this question. Although Kracauer's theory seems in many respects archaic, a product of the 1950s with an outmoded emphasis on realism, we might also emphasize a continuity with film at the end of the twentieth century, despite many apparent differences.

In *A Cinema of Loneliness*, Robert Kolker observes that Kubrick's films often incorporate paintings (154–155). There are strikingly placed paintings in *Paths of Glory, Lolita, A Clockwork Orange, Barry Lyndon,* and *2001*. In Kolker's view, the paintings tend to represent a "civilized artifice" in contrast to the violences of the world; in *Lolita,* Humbert Humbert shoots Quilty through a reproduction of Gainsborough's *Blue Boy.* "In all instances," writes Kolker, "Kubrick uses paintings for ironic juxtaposition" (155). And he continues, "The contemporary paintings that hang in the rooms of *Eyes Wide Shut* act as decorations, expressing taste divorced from feeling—much like the characters themselves" (155). Kolker uses the paintings in Kubrick to discuss both theme (civilization versus barbarism) and style (the static antinarrative tendency). We can also use paintings in Kubrick to discuss the way he presents his own films as art.

What is most remarkable about the paintings in *Eyes Wide Shut* is their refusal to signify anything. With one notable exception, the staging never calls particular attention to the paintings. Paintings are, indeed, everywhere, in nearly every upper-class space. Not only is the Harfords' apartment covered with paintings, but so are Ziegler's house, Marion's apartment (where her father died), and the mansion where the masked orgy is held. Frederic Raphael, who wrote the script with Kubrick, wanted to give Alice Harford (Nicole Kidman) some kind of job. In the source story, Arthur Schnitzler's *Traumnovelle* (1926), the wife has no profession, but in *Eyes Wide Shut* she has become the former owner of an art gallery.[7] Art, therefore, is foregrounded visually, and also in the process of adaptation, but then rendered entirely without emphasis. The paintings do not signify anything more than social class; wealthy people have paintings, whereas the student-prostitute Domino does not. But the film does not frame its scenes or figures to animate the paintings into significance, ironic or otherwise. On the contrary, the paintings seem to disperse their signification into so many fragments of light—no more important, ultimately, than the ubiquitous Christmas trees and lights.

Michel Chion's brilliant book-length reading of *Eyes Wide Shut* underlines this absence of signification.[8] In essence, Chion argues that the widely felt tedium of the film is in fact the point. Instead of castigating the film's *longueurs*, we should celebrate the film as a new way of seeing.

These phrases ["Hello, how are you?" "Thank you"], heard throughout the film, are not platitudes to tell us that the characters are flat, but real phrases, as they are spoken in reality. Kubrick's singularity is that he films both phrases of this kind that have no obvious importance and phrases regarded as important (Alice's story) with such great care, and has his actors speak them with such precision. He brings the same meticulousness to bear on filming the act of opening a door and, a few seconds later, of passing a hand across a dead man's face. By always paying the same degree of attention to the act of listening and looking, no matter what it is that we see or hear, Kubrick gives us a different perspective on existence. The film does not impose on us a hierarchy of what is important and what is not. (25)

Chion does not mention the paintings, but his description applies with special force there as well. Art is exactly that which ought to appear with significance, as more significant than the surroundings, as radiating suggestion and symbol. Yet the paintings in *Eyes Wide Shut* are no more important than the objects. And the objects themselves are rendered only as objects. Chion's description of *Eyes Wide Shut* intends to make comprehensible the pallid lack of emphasis in the film—so fatal for the film's detractors—by praising it for exactly those elements. With the passion characteristic of *Cahiers du cinéma*, he writes, "Yet *Eyes Wide Shut* remains a film that had never been made before and is unlike any other, including the previous films of Stanley Kubrick" (37).

This way of talking about *Eyes Wide Shut*, about its absence of signification, is exactly the right idea. Yet *Eyes Wide Shut* is by no means a unique manifestation of this aesthetic. Even Kubrick's penultimate film, *Full Metal Jacket* (1987), exhibits many of the same characteristics. The parroting that Chion notes in *Eyes Wide Shut*, in which characters respond by repeating previous dialogue (Ziegler: "I had you followed." Bill: "You had me followed?"), occurs also in *Full Metal Jacket*.[9] The flattening of dialogue in *Full Metal Jacket*, as in *Eyes Wide Shut*, marks an impulse to refuse witty and dramatic speech. After Lee Ermey's astonishing humiliations and putdowns in the first section of *Full Metal Jacket*, the second half of the film seems comparatively formless, episodic, dull. Almost every review found the first forty minutes entertaining and creative, but the second half boring. Obviously Kubrick has nothing to say about the Vietnam War, according to the reviews, and is lost outside the intense focus of the marines' barracks.

But the second half of *Full Metal Jacket* is in fact a clear predecessor to *Eyes*

Wide Shut in its negative aesthetics. *Full Metal Jacket* refuses to give us the war movie we want or expect, and the action sequences are determinedly dull. Just so, audiences expected eroticism and sex in *Eyes Wide Shut*, but Kubrick everywhere frustrates those expectations. Both films occupy a clear thematic and generic space (war film, erotic film), but then occupy that space with a profoundly negative aesthetics. These films refuse theatrical emphasis, symbolic signification, and generic cooperation. In its aesthetic negativity, the second half of *Full Metal Jacket* looks directly toward the complete dampening of affect in *Eyes Wide Shut*.

Eyes Wide Shut is not only a movie like *Full Metal Jacket*, but also, more importantly, a movie like those favored in Kracauer's *Theory of Film*. The main impetus of Kracauer's book is to celebrate the "truly cinematic" aspects of film. Such an impulse—to ward off the literary and the theatrical—may seem unduly prescriptive, but is in fact an idea that contemporary critics and directors still find themselves thinking through with regularity. Almost all major film critics at some point write about the relationship of theatre to cinema as well as about the nature of literary adaptation. These discussions are not so much exercises in critical purification or Aristotelian rule making as they are discussions of what makes film an art. The most general reason to compare films to plays or novels is to remind ourselves that if film is an art, it is not an art like literature or theatre. What is effective or artistic or beautiful in a novel or a painting is not necessarily so in a film. Kracauer's *Theory of Film* may seem offputtingly Olympian and regulatory in its judgments (this is a true film, this is not), but it is scarcely a treatise whose importance is entirely historical. To talk about film as an art today is inevitably to move through critical territory that Kracauer has already scouted out.

Kracauer contrasts the realism of photography to the artifice of painting. Compared to paintings, photographs are only randomly meaningful.[10] Film, for Kracauer, is essentially a photographic medium, and it is used more properly when artifice does not stand in the way of the world of objects. The world of objects that speaks through film consists for the most part of natural objects and scenes from lower-class urban life. Kracauer repeatedly mentions films that register the "moving wind in the trees" and those that reproduce the movement of "the streets." Hence Kracauer usually approves of Italian neorealism, and de Sica's *Umberto D* (1952), for example, is regularly praised. Kracauer's avowed social realism may seem distinctly at odds with Kubrick, but *Theory of Film* has, in actuality, much in common with the negative aesthetics of *Eyes Wide Shut*.

Eyes Wide Shut manages to turn a psychological story from the time of Freud's Vienna into a series of visuals and exteriors. Film is about surfaces, not psychology, according to Kracauer: "Films cling to the surface of things. They seem to be the more cinematic the less they focus directly on inward life, ideology, and spiritual concerns."[11] Kubrick's film follows in that emphasis. "*Eyes Wide Shut*," writes Chion, "is a film that talks about life; a film that describes everyday life through a couple that have procreated and perpetuated life, and as such it has no precise meaning."[12] An actor for Kracauer is an object among objects, sometimes no more important than the furniture, and Kubrick uses Tom Cruise in an unglamorous way. Nicole Kidman does indeed sparkle and charm, but just as Lee Ermey vanished from *Full Metal Jacket*, so too does Alice disappear almost entirely from *Eyes Wide Shut* (an absence lamented in almost every review). After which we are left with watching Tom Cruise, not known for his registrations of psychology and interiority, and now entirely deprived of any "action."

Kubrick reorients our sense of cinematic form, acting, theater, scene structure, and plot in ways that often overlap with the descriptions in Kracauer's *Theory of Film*. Kubrick has made a film that is not overdetermined by punctuated scenes, theatrical acting, and notions of psychology. This art is one that goes out of its way *not* to signify. What Kracauer calls the "formative" — the artificial elements of film that obstruct our vision of physical reality — is also what Kubrick tries to avoid. Reality has its own significance for Kracauer; what film should avoid is occluding that significance with its own artifices. Kubrick's negative aesthetics in *Full Metal Jacket* and *Eyes Wide Shut* thus resonates in many places with Kracauer's pronouncements in *Theory of Film*.

Yet even as we emphasize the similarities, we must note that Kubrick's aesthetics seems in many ways at odds with Kracauer's formulations. Notoriously, Kubrick does not photograph reality; he builds sets. Vietnam in *Full Metal Jacket* was somewhere down the road in England, and the New York City in *Eyes Wide Shut* was born on a London soundstage. The social realism that characterizes Kracauer's work is seemingly light years away from *Eyes Wide Shut*, which looks much more like Woody Allen's New York than Spike Lee's. Kracauer condemns staginess and theatricality (*The Cabinet of Dr. Caligari* is a recurrent example of the anticinematic); the cinema prefers "nature in the raw." But there is no "nature" in *Eyes Wide Shut*; instead, it is a world of glowing lights, elaborate sets, and masks. Instead of Kracauer's idea that cinema needs to stay out of the way of reality, Kubrick, more paradoxically, makes a cinema that stays out of the way of its own artifices. *Eyes Wide Shut* partakes of

Kracauer's dislike of overly "formative" acting, narrative, and mise-en-scène, yet it does not believe in nature or in physical reality. This film is thus both an artificial creation, in no way "real" or natural, and one that refuses to organize itself as significant, meaningful, or formed in aesthetically recognizable ways. It is art—a creation, a similitude, a story—but an art attended with a remarkably negative set of aesthetics.

Kracauer conceives of film as a celebration of the indexical and as a refusal of the iconic. Cinema starts with the material world and registers that reality on film. Actors, music, and narrative that supply heightened meaning are all problematic. To this conception, Kubrick adds one more step. He refuses *both* the indexical and the iconic. Kubrick rejects the iconic meanings that are traditionally attendant upon art, literature, and theatre. But he also rejects the indexical; cinema has no material foundation or starting point in the world.

Eyes Wide Shut thus implicitly expands and reverses Kracauer's aesthetic. It expands on Kracauer by tacitly observing that social realism is itself a "formative" occlusion. But it reverses Kracauer by emptying out the category of nature. Kracauer's aesthetic applies most clearly to Rossellini's neorealistic films, *Open City* (1945), *Paisan* (1946), and *Germany Year Zero* (1948), but Rossellini himself moved beyond that. Kracauer never mentions, for instance, *Voyage to Italy* (1953), even though it falls well within the chronological range of his study. In Kracauer, Rossellini is associated with the use of nonactors, but in *Stromboli* (1950), *Europa '51* (1952), and *Voyage to Italy,* Rossellini uses Ingrid Bergman and other internationally recognizable stars. The historical obsolescence of Kracauer's work is perhaps most strongly felt here, in his inability to account for the development of directors like Rossellini and Visconti.

One might, in fact, read *Eyes Wide Shut* as a feature-length allusion to Rossellini's *Voyage to Italy.* Each narrative centers on a marriage in crisis. Although concentrating on the couple at the start, each film comes to focus on one figure, Katherine (Ingrid Bergman) and William Harford (Tom Cruise). (The British title of Rossellini's film, *The Lonely Woman,* carries the emphasis.) Each film uses its Hollywood stars in unexpected, deliberately unglamorous ways. The ordinariness of the character's life is then doubly underlined by our mistaken expectations. Each film is portentously slow and repetitious. Italy speaks to Katherine with a voice of vitality at every stop. She is affected most strongly at the museum, overcome by the naked power of the ancient sculptures. Sexuality speaks to Harford at almost every stop; he is affected most strongly at the orgy, struck by the masked naked figures who stand circled in some sort of ritual. Psychology and explanation are at a minimum in either case. The private marital crisis collides with and is transfigured by a deeper, more mysterious force. The sculptures in Rossellini's museum are tremendously sexual, but also art; the ritual in Kubrick's mansion is both sacred and highly sexual as well.

Without acceding to anything more than this archetypal logic, the plots in either case resolve the broken marriage by the end. Katherine and Harford pass through these stages of spectacle and sexual emotion to return to their marriages. Both endings are reconciling, although tentative. Both endings occur in public—in a street festival and in a toy store—indicating the overcoming of personal crisis. Rossellini's *Voyage to Italy* is much more difficult to grasp interpretively than *Open City*, an earlier work, because it does not possess the social realism or messages of that film. Rossellini had moved well beyond *Open City*, and *Voyage to Italy* became one of the most influential films of the rest of the century.

Aligned with this attempt to refuse conventional artistic signification, most of the paintings in *Eyes Wide Shut* indicate absolutely nothing to us. It would be quite easy, and quite traditional, for the paintings to comment, to annotate visually what is going on. "Often, paintings and posters *attack* the characters," writes Raymond Durgnat. "A laughing clown points his finger mercilessly at Anny Ondra in Hitchcock's *Blackmail*, as, knife in hand, she edges back from the corpse."[13] Yet Kubrick signifies his lack of signification by a palpable absence of annotating pictures except in one very clear instance. During the party at the beginning of the film, as Alice is courted by Sandor Szavost (Sky Dumont), William Harford is called away from two flirtatious models. Upstairs he finds Victor Ziegler (Sydney Pollack) in a huge bathroom, attending a comatose naked woman.

The naked woman is collapsed in a chair, and above her is a more-than-life-size painting of a naked woman. The parallel is exact: both women are basically lying down and, very strikingly, both are lying amid a field of red. Clearly we are to see a parallel—that Ziegler collects both paintings and prostitutes. Naked bodies in paintings are deemed acceptable, but in real life they are rather surprising and perhaps scandalous. Kubrick renders the woman's naked body in his film as completely unerotic; although she is perfectly formed, she has also overdosed on drugs. We are meant to judge Ziegler harshly, since the camera gets to the room before Harford, and we see Ziegler hastily zipping up his pants. The doubling of painting and woman thus results in editorializing and social comment, linking art collecting to prostitution. But there is also a more metaphysical comment, since the unerotic naked body is not far away from a dead body. This woman who almost dies, lying beneath the painting, may well be the same woman Harford sees later in the morgue. This significant painting brings with it a welter of editorial commentary, then, but the main theme that it brings is the alignment of art with death and horror. Most of the paintings in *Eyes Wide Shut* are meaningless. What the remaining painting means is death.

Eyes Wide Shut hovers in a Solarian dream-space, grounded in neither indexical reality nor iconic artifice. The no it says to the iconic is not simply an ironic or vacant no, but a no filled with death and horror. A world without reality or meaning is a void, and *Eyes Wide Shut* images that void in the female corpse. *Solaris*, too, shows us Hari's corpse on several occasions. In its deployment of both artworks and corpses, *Eyes Wide Shut* looks backward to *Solaris*, and forward to the more overt connection between art and murder in later films like Mary Harron's *American Psycho* (2000).

For Kracauer, film redeems reality. One of the ways it does this is by "challenging us to confront the real-life events it shows with the ideas we commonly entertain about them."[14] As Kracauer writes in a section called "The Head of Medusa," one of the challenges that cinema poses is that of horror. Kracauer argues that cinematic depictions of horror are "a mirrored representation, not the horror itself. But even though we see pictures of Nazi concentration camps, and not the camps themselves, this is still a salvific experience."[15] Kracauer wants cinema to ward off constructedness and artifice in order to allow us to experience the redemptive lessons of reality. Kracauer's premise is almost that of the mind programmers in Kubrick's *Clockwork Orange*, who think that by looking incessantly at violent horrors we will be free of them. Kubrick, by contrast, resists not only the iconic but also the redemptive. His films tell us much about the cinematic experience, about the reality and presence of the cinematic screen. But neither *A Clockwork Orange* nor *Eyes Wide Shut* dreams of redemption.[16]

Dissolution and Artifice: Bergman's *Persona*
and Altman's *Vincent and Theo*

Robert Altman refers to himself as an artist more consistently and more unashamedly than almost any other recent director of American film. In interviews, he inevitably falls back on intuition to explain why his films look the way they do. "Well, I don't have any goals," he says. "I consider myself an artist, and I don't have anything to say. I just show what I see."[17] He repeatedly points out that he does not like giving interviews, because his stated explanations might start to freeze his artistic instincts. "I'm not interested in analyzing myself," he says. "What I'm doing right now is a very dangerous thing for an artist to do."[18] Altman was a painter early in his career, and he has always insisted that his films need to be read carefully, "like paintings." He wants us to watch the films over and over again and not to be put off by ambiguity. For Altman, art is suggestive rather than direct. "I don't deal in propaganda, I never have; I think this is art."[19]

Altman inhabits not only the suggestive art of painting but also the arthouse cinema of Antonioni and Kurosawa. Altman makes art-house films that explicitly contrast themselves with Hollywood. *The Player* (1992) is Altman's most explicit savaging of Hollywood; there the producer Griffin Mill (Tim Robbins) gives a blatantly hypocritical speech promoting art films, and the audience pays no attention. Altman's anti-aesthetics is anti-Hollywood, and he follows instead in the line of Rossellini, de Sica (Griffin Mill commits his murder after watching *The Bicycle Thief*), Fellini, and Bergman. There are of course enormous differences between these European directors and Altman. Although the carnivalesque bustling of many Altman films can recall only Fellini, the two directors' attitudes toward sound design, for instance, is completely antithetical. Every sound in Fellini is dubbed in postproduction, often quite noticeably, whereas almost everything in Altman is recorded on the spot, including his trademark overlapping dialogue. Yet in his orientation toward the possibilities of film and in his relation to Hollywood, Altman remains close in spirit to Fellini, and to Bergman, as we shall see.

In this section I will attempt to characterize the chief elements and ramifications of Altman's cinematic art by looking at his 1990 film, *Vincent and Theo*. Artists make their appearances in other Altman films, in *Three Women* (1977) and *The Player*, for example, but *Vincent and Theo* is his most extended depiction of an artist. Vincent van Gogh has acquired by now a legendary status, so that *Vincent and Theo*, like Altman's *Buffalo Bill and the Indians, or Sitting Bull's History Lesson* (1976), takes a contemporary look at an essentially mythological figure. But it also takes the opportunity to reflect most explicitly of all of Altman's films on the nature of the artistic process. Even though it looks and feels wholly different from his comic, celebrity-studded *Player*, it is no coincidence that Altman issued these two films one after the other. After working through the eighties in the rather different world of theatre and video (*Come Back to the Five and Dime, Jimmy Dean, Jimmy Dean* [1982], *Streamers* [1983], *Secret Honor* [1984], *Fool for Love* [1985], *Beyond Therapy* [1987]), Altman returned to full-scale filmmaking in the nineties with two violently self-conscious meditations on art and cinema in *Vincent and Theo* and *The Player.*

What Altman is up to in *Vincent and Theo* can be understood most readily by comparing his biopic with those of Vincente Minnelli (*Lust for Life*, 1956) and Maurice Pialat (*Van Gogh*, 1991). Van Gogh is one of the most popular and well recognized of all the world's artists, and his life story has been told in film many times. Kurosawa even dresses up Martin Scorsese as van Gogh in a segment of his *Dreams* (1990) as a heartfelt tribute to the visual talents of his younger colleague. Van Gogh lived the tragic life of the artist, if anyone did, and because of his haunting expressionistic paintings, his story is much easier to visualize than the overly brief lives of writers like Shelley or Keats.[20]

Minnelli's *Lust for Life* works as an ideal star vehicle for Kirk Douglas. Douglas dominates the story from beginning to end, as he does in other films of the fifties, such as Wilder's *Big Carnival* (1951), Hawks's *Big Sky* (1952), and Kubrick's *Paths of Glory* (1957). Of all of Kubrick's films, only *Paths of Glory* and *Spartacus* (1960)—both with Kirk Douglas—show a star in all of his classically Hollywood dimensions. Minnelli's title, *Lust for Life*, emphasizes romantic vitalism, not morbid genius. Van Gogh begins as a Christian missionary, and all his work is seen in that light. His intensity, his passion, and his love of the common people originate in a Christian motivation. We are to see this van Gogh as more truly Christian than many more overtly religious practitioners. Thus, although van Gogh's paintings are imaginative, not realistic, there is a social realism at bottom. Van Gogh defends Millet to his brother because Millet showed the "dignity of toil." "Millet," says van Gogh, "uses paint to express the word of God."

When Gauguin (Anthony Quinn) appears on the scene, the effect is to make van Gogh seem comparatively naturalistic, since Gauguin is purposely inaccurate. Gauguin says he has spent a year cultivating a style with which he can convey "the idea without regard for concrete reality." "Art's an abstraction," he says, "not a picture book." Van Gogh objects to all this abstraction by asking, "What about the arrangement that exists in nature?" And Gauguin responds, "I choose to disregard nature." Van Gogh eschews the "scientific" pointillism of Seurat (although we see him imitating Seurat for a moment), but still maintains a strong attachment to nature and reality. His emotionalism seems healthy and attached to work, and his imaginative paintings still have their origins in nature. "The people I know," he says, "the earth I know." As we have seen on many occasions, film narrative often substantiates art's authority by appealing to nature, and Minnelli's biography partakes of the social realism that forms such an important strand of Kracauer's argument.

In *Lust for Life* there is almost none of the cinematic self-consciousness so evident in Minnelli's musicals, such as *The Band Wagon* (1953), or in his melodrama *The Bad and the Beautiful* (1952), which might be seen as a 1950s Hollywood version of *The Player*. And there is none of the play with artworks and paintings that so memorably makes the look of Minnelli's *American in Paris* (1951). Scenes in *Lust for Life* aim toward particular well-known paintings, but only to have one confirm the authenticity of the other. In *Lust for Life*, emotion and life are real, and the film does not attempt to accentuate the artificial.

Minnelli's most self-conscious gesture occurs when he shows van Gogh escalating into suicidal madness while a band plays outside. In this most musical sequence, crowds are gathered, the people dance in the square, and the band plays its inelegant oompahs, yet van Gogh claps his hands to his ears as if overwhelmed by the people and the sounds. Van Gogh's gesture here self-reflexively reads against self-reflexivity. That is, this is not a musical, in which people suddenly break into song, the sets are transparently paintings, and magic is all around. On the contrary, this is life, with all its agonies and ecstasies (that other Irving Stone book about an artist was shot by Carol Reed in 1965), and no magic will save van Gogh. Soon we see van Gogh walk out to a wheat field, paint his wheat field with crows, and then shoot himself in the side. But before he shoots himself he writes a suicide note, which we can read. In Minnelli, van Gogh's madness becomes a heightened and explicable version of artistic intensity. This van Gogh cuts off his ear because he is upset that Gauguin has left. Minnelli wants to give us a biography, and one that comes with causal explanation. Altman's van Gogh, in his turn, will not leave an explanatory note.

Maurice Pialat's *Van Gogh* (1991) appeared just after Altman's film. Unlike the classic Hollywood narrative of Minnelli's *Lust for Life*, Pialat's *Van Gogh* exhibits the free-flowing continuity of European art film. But Pialat has done more than open up the narrative, since he also softly but insistently revises our stereotypical senses of van Gogh's artistic character. This van Gogh is surprisingly gentle, and also surprisingly sensuous. This film concentrates in some detail on his sexual relations with women. Indeed, Pialat openly takes liberties with understood historical fact by expanding van Gogh's relationship with Marguerite, the daughter of Dr. Gachet. Thus the film becomes less centrally focused on the hero, van Gogh, and pays sustained attention to other characters, who are no longer his supporting cast. Marguerite plays the piano, and music plays a continually important role in the film. Whereas Minnelli essentially splits the serious music of Miklós Rózsa off from the bright melodies of film musical, Pialat's van Gogh takes a real interest in music, and the film offers music and song as complementary to all the paintings.

The musical and sexual themes culminate in an astonishing sequence toward the end of the film. After a fight with Theo, Vincent goes to a brothel, where a dance band serenades the prostitutes and their male clients. Theo and Marguerite go there to find Vincent, whereupon Theo immediately becomes a happy customer himself and Vincent alternates his affections between the prostitutes and Marguerite. The spinning dances and drinking go on all night, concluding with a final march and parade, all order restored. This sequence embodies the ideas of fluidity and restraint that the film has quietly associated with van Gogh's art. Earlier, van Gogh said that he did not paint water, because it was "too fluid." And his roommate, also a painter, criticizes van Gogh's painting because it is too thick and blocky, not fluid enough.

Dr. Gachet characterizes Vincent to Theo as monomaniacal and obsessive, and we might well see Vincent's paintings as reflecting a concentrated, obsessive life. But surely the movie shows us something richer than this diagnosis of monomania. Van Gogh is ill, certainly, but in the midst of a fluid, not concentrated, sensibility. Pialat objects to any simple diagnosis of van Gogh and to any easy connection between life and art. The people and things in van Gogh's life show up in his paintings, but we cannot explain the style of his paintings from his life. This van Gogh seems depressed and awkwardly related to society, but also multifarious, not concentrated, in his sensibility. In Pialat's telling, van Gogh simply returns from the woods with a bullet in his side, but with no particular cause for the action. The dance in which both Theo and Vincent respond flexibly to their surroundings is a nice synecdoche for the film as a whole.

Like Pialat's film, Altman's *Vincent and Theo* not only stages a revision of the myths surrounding van Gogh, but also enables us to rethink the myths surrounding art. As Altman himself puts it:

> My whole purpose there was to demythify art. If I have a van Gogh painting and I want to move it down to Christie's, six guys in white gloves and one guy with a gun will come in here to move it. But there was a time when he just painted the damn thing, and it fell on the floor, and people

stepped on it or left it out in the rain. I was trying to convey that the value of art is not in its existence, but in its doing.[21]

Vincent and Theo begins with a contemporary scene of an auction at Christie's with a van Gogh on the block. So we begin with one way of evaluating art— by money, institution, reputation, fame. But the film wants to reenact a more difficult way of evaluating art, outside of prestige or money. Altman intends that we see the merit in the doing of art, in the making, outside of whether it is sold or even exists. These emphases ask us to rethink our notions of aesthetic value. To celebrate an unfinished process instead of a finished success is to say no to most conventional ways of thinking about art.

Altman's films tend not to have the strong male protagonists of classic Hollywood film. On the contrary, his men tend to be either passive or in the process of dissolving.[22] Altman is known for films with a multitude of characters, with overlapping voices, and with camera shots that dart in and out, eccentrically. *The Player*, which expressly satirizes the star system, puts so many stars and celebrities in the film that the whole notion of the star is rendered nearly meaningless. *Gosford Park* (2001) is not as satiric, but it, too, powerfully reorients our sense of stardom, since every single character, from Helen Mirren and Derek Jacobi to Michael Gambon and Stephen Fry are really supporting characters. Nearly every actor and actress in *Gosford Park* has elsewhere had whole films to himself or herself, but here the celebrity is given over to the story of the film. Altman, like Woody Allen, can get practically anyone he wants to appear in his films. But whereas Allen's films tend to dissolve into one another, and to carry a similar wit and trajectory (and usually the Allen character), Altman's films appear and then vanish, as different from one another in feeling as works by the same director can be.

There is an even more specific dissolution of character that has attended Altman's work throughout his career, and that is the dissolution provided by Bergman's *Persona* (1966). In interviews, Altman frequently refers to Bergman, and *Persona* is one of Altman's most oft-referenced films. Altman is the opposite of the maniacal cinephile exemplified by Scorsese, De Palma, or Bogdanovich; on the contrary, he admits to seeing relatively few movies. But his favorites are overwhelmingly important to him. "*Images* [1972], I think, was an imitation of Bergman's *Persona*, which I was very impressed with."[23] *Three Women* (1977) is also obviously drawn from *Persona*, since the personalities of the women start to shift and blend. It is no coincidence that Bibi Andersson, who plays Alma in *Persona,* is also cast in a later Altman film, *Quintet* (1979). Altman films often present a decentralized canvas, and in those that put relatively few figures before us, even they start to blend together. This is what happens in Bergman's *Persona,* Altman's *Three Women,* and *Vincent and Theo.*

Bergman's *Persona,* like Tarkovsky's *Solaris,* explores the presence and absence of film through sequences that follow only the logic of dreams. At the beginning and end of *Persona* we see a boy who is in no particular place and who runs his hand over a screen. On the screen the cloudy faces of Bibi Andersson and Liv Ullmann change places slowly. Who the boy is will never be perfectly intelligible, but clearly a model for film and film watching is being portrayed. Whereas *Solaris* represents the absence and presence of cinema through the alien apparition of the dead wife Hari, *Persona* shows us a child watching and touching a ghostly screen. Whereas *Solaris* showed us a man dreaming of his dead wife, *Persona* shows us something more like a child dreaming of his mother, and so looks forward also to David's endless devotion in Spielberg's *A.I.* Both Sister Alma and Elisabeth Vogler have suffered maternal crises; Alma has had an abortion, and Elisabeth's child has died. So there is the strong sense that the child watching the women's faces on the screen is a kind of ghost child who belongs to them both, just as they themselves turn into each other. Just as Hari turns back and forth between alien and human, the women in *Persona* also change identities, and just as monstrously. They become cruel, nightmarish, insane. As in David Lynch, the unstable dream of cinema is precariously balanced at the edge of violence and nightmare. When Altman looks back toward Bergman's *Persona,* he sees therefore not only the dissolution of subjectivity, but also violence and horror.[24]

Vincent and Theo, like *Three Women,* is another version of *Persona.* The title itself shows that the expected hero, Vincent (Tim Roth), is inextricably linked to his brother Theo (Paul Rhys). *Vincent and Theo* deliberately wrecks the usual plot of biopic individualism by telling instead the crosscut tale of psychic twins. For half of the movie, Vincent and Theo actually live together, but for the other half we shift back and forth between brothers, who are clearly joined by fate, even if not by space. The crosscutting occasionally emphasizes an almost telepathic connection between the two men. In an early segment, their families fall apart simultaneously. Both women leave, and Altman crosscuts between the two men looking into mirrors and painting themselves. In Altman's retelling, Theo van Gogh is as substantial a figure as Vincent, as dramatic, as psychically compelling, equally worth the attention of the narrative. The characters do not actually turn into each other, as in *Three Women* or *Per-*

sona, but they together constitute an affront to the individualist protagonists of most Hollywood films. After Vincent dies, Theo kicks everybody out of the house, apparently to live in a room filled with Vincent's paintings. But this does not last too long, since suddenly we find ourselves looking at a matched pair of gravestones, side by side, Vincent and Theo. Vincent dies in 1890, Theo six months later in 1891. In the opening titles, there is no "and" between the painted names, "Vincent" and "Theo," and this lack immediately emphasizes the radical continuity.

Altman's signature techniques are indissociable from his notions of cinematic art. His overlapping sound does not emphasize realism so much as ambiguity. In his interviews he repeatedly speaks of training the audience to listen and to be satisfied with less. Overlapping dialogue often provides too much information, as well as insufficiently centralized information. The sound design of Altman's pictures corresponds to the decentered focus of their narratives. Altman's most overt visual technique, evident over the course of almost forty films, is his relentless use of the zoom. He tracks rarely and pans unremarkably, but he is always zooming, zooming out to begin a scene, zooming in on a face or an object. Films in the sixties and seventies zoomed more than those of the nineties, so it is even more evident, more palpable, as his career goes on. The zoom's focus cuts away at the world; as Robert Kolker says, "It offers more by showing less."[25] In Altman's view, the zooms always imply, "This is a movie." "So, the zoom lens," says Altman, "the attention to it, the moving in—many times I'm doing that to show you I'm doing that, so that I know that you know that's what I'm doing."[26] The zoom shot in Hollywood and television is generally used as a kind of underlining or intensification, a visual punctuation or emphasis, and indeed Altman does often zoom in on a face for an emotional response. But the zoom also says, "I am making this movie. You are watching this movie. We are together doing this thing called a movie." If art's value is in the doing, the zoom is Altman's visual and technical way of explaining what it means to be present in the making of art.

Altman begins *Vincent and Theo* with the auction at Christie's, that is, with our imagined goal of art: fame, fortune, success. But in his own life van Gogh exemplifies the artist without that end, and Altman deconstructs the narrative of artistic success at every turn. We might suppose that artists paint their paintings with a view to creating excellent paintings or even masterpieces. But van Gogh in this film rather frequently paints on other people. To paint onto another person is to emphasize the transience rather than the permanence of painting and to reroute the subject-object relationship. Van Gogh is constantly covered by what is either black soot or black paint. He licks the paintbrush and stains his teeth. This black indicates both a world of earth and a world of paint. Van Gogh's walls are covered with paintings, but also with drawings and paint. The standard plot in which an individual paints a picture with the intention of entering the art world is broken down into a world of paint, which sometimes goes onto a canvas, but just as often is spattered elsewhere. Van Gogh seems constantly to be practicing, in painting as in life. He proposes marriage while he sketches a model, and he reacts to her assent in an offhand way. Even marriage does not name a masterpiece for van Gogh. He will live with his new family, day by day, until he lives with them no more.

Vincent and Theo embodies an antiessentialist and antimonumental view of art. This art is not authenticated by society, nor is it even localizable in a painting, a painting that holds still to be appraised and interpreted. Nor is art localizable in an artist, suggests *Vincent and Theo,* since Theo is seen to be just as creative, stubborn, awkward, irrational, and incompetent in his role as gallery agent as Vincent is in his role as painter. Van Gogh, like Altman, has mainly an antipantheon, an anticanon, a group of painterly styles that he wants to avoid. Van Gogh is not an art lover, and Altman is not a movie lover; they each do what they do. What they make is obviously a construction, and a construction that runs counter to what already exists (this is not a Renoir; this is not another Bruce Willis movie). But it is not a construction that exists in a radically separate world from the world where other people live and work and interpret.

In Altman's earlier film *Three Women,* art seems in fact to have access to a powerful archetypal unconscious. Willie Hart (Janice Rule), the silent third woman and an artist, paints primitive-looking snake people at the bottom of swimming pools. The serpents rise up as if from a dream to revenge themselves on Willie's husband, Edgar (Robert Fortier). Yet instead of throwing themselves over a cliff, as in *Thelma and Louise* (Ridley Scott, 1991), these three women live happily ever after, like Griffin Mill in *The Player. Three Women* seems to be drawn from mysterious dreams and unconscious energies, and Altman here clearly associates art with telepathy, archetype, and dream. But *The Player*'s conclusion is Hollywood fantasy, the utopia of the dream factory, not the dream. June Gudmundsdottir (Greta Scacchi) in *The Player* is also an artist who paints serpentine pictures, but she is transparently a figment of cinematic imagination. She is too perfect, too amenable, too sexy, as Altman says in his interviews; she does not exist. *The Player* exposes not only the witless conventionality of Hollywood film productions, but also the magical powers of art. *The Player* thus becomes an implicit critique of Altman's own mythopoesis in *Three Women*.

Since Vincent and Theo are not joined magically, but psychologically, they are not linked telepathically, but through editing. The contingent association-ism that implies a higher power in Kieslowski's *Double Life of Veronique* (1991) is absolutely absent from *Vincent and Theo*. If Vincent resembles Theo, it is be-cause editing shows this to be the case, not because the world is full of coinci-dences and thus already edited ahead of time. Altman's sequences are always edited to reveal articulation and construction. Although the scene itself may proceed laterally or in an ambiguous relation to the scene behind or the scene ahead, Altman's scenes nonetheless have clear beginnings and ends. He likes a punch line or some conclusive punctuation. The accidents that connect Vincent and Theo do not imply a world where everything is overseen by God (as in another movie about an artist, William Dieterle's *Portrait of Jennie* [1948]); they only emphasize the power of editorial selection, emphasis, and crosscut-ting. *Vincent and Theo* never drifts into the dream world of *Persona* or David Lynch, where the dream may potentially remove the artifice from the arti-fact. *Vincent and Theo* never flinches from its status as an edited reconstruction in which the connections are found by the storyteller and signify no power beyond his own.

The two most extended sequences in which we see van Gogh paint are both scenes of self-destruction. In one scene he paints in a field of sunflowers, then smashes his canvas to pieces, returning home with a bouquet of sunflowers. The implication: why cannot I paint these flowers, as they are? But when we next see him, there are paintings of sunflowers all over the room, suggesting that maybe the work went better indoors than outdoors. In a final sequence, van Gogh prepares his canvas outdoors, but then manages to paint only a line across the middle before marching off into the cornfield and shooting himself in the side. Art in these scenes is made but also unmade, created and destroyed.

The process-oriented, antimonumental tendency of Altman's film is ac-cented by van Gogh's violence toward his own work and himself. Just as the liminal existence of Tarkovsky's *Solaris* is reinforced by the parade of suicides, the scenes of van Gogh cutting himself and shooting himself underline the impermanence of art. Van Gogh says no to his paintings and no to himself, with a frighteningly bloody violence. When he walks home at the end, soaked through with blood, we may well recall the figure of Tim Roth as Mr. Orange two years later, bleeding to death in Tarantino's *Reservoir Dogs*. From Ferrara to Scorsese, American cinema says no to art with the force of gangland violence. As we saw in Chapter Four, cinephilia can easily turn to horror, and as we saw in Kubrick, saying no to meaning can also welcome in the horror of the abyss. It is not surprising, then, that a serious attention to art in cinema may also open up an abyss of bloodshed and murder.[27]

Aesthetic Negation in the Serial-Killer Movie

The horror of absent meaning that runs throughout Kubrick is explored in a number of serial-killer films from the 1990s. The prestige of art sometimes accompanies and justifies the appearance of a serial killer. That is, while the serial killer may be a reprehensible maniac, he may also consider himself an artist. For example, the idea of the serial killer as artist builds the sympathetic ground for Jonathan Demme's *Silence of the Lambs* (1991). Dr. Hannibal Lecter (whose name combines the sounds of cannibalism and reading) is a charismatic, cultured connoisseur who quotes Shakespeare and sketches scenes of Florence in his cell. Anthony Hopkins descended from the world of classy films like *84 Charing Cross Road* (1987) and *The Good Father* (1985) to play a genius who also happens to kill people. Agent Starling (Jodie Foster) uses Hannibal Lecter to find another serial killer, Buffalo Bill, who in his turn makes clothing out of his victims' skin. In a ranked hierarchy of serial killers, Buffalo Bill is a craftsperson to Hannibal Lecter's artist. Lecter's wit and art give his gruesome murders a meaning, a significance. *The Silence of the Lambs* thus covers over its abyss, its horror, with the cloak of art.[28] But the truly horrific serial-killer films empty out art; they reject art's traditional signification and comfort.

Like *The Silence of the Lambs,* David Fincher's *Seven* (1995) also surrounds the serial killer with art and meaning. The serial killer in *Seven* kills his victims not just theologically but literarily. In a long sequence in a library, Detective Somerset (Morgan Freeman) looks for clues in volumes of Chaucer, Dante, and Milton. The murders are each horrific and gruesome, but clearly explicable by medieval allegory — the seven deadly sins. The killer (Kevin Spacey) purposefully leaves all kinds of signs around his murders — captions, fingerprints, quotations. The killer is insane, of course, but also a creative genius. He leaves behind notebook after notebook of maniacal prose, but also manages to lead around the cops according to his own plan. As Somerset says, "He's a preacher," and one who wants to mediate the wrath of God through his own murderous hands. Above all, the killer is an artist, who stages one killing after another in a weeklong production of homicide theatre.

The artistic metaphors attached to the serial killer in *Seven* are entirely explicit.[29] The killer arranges for his last two killings by saying, "You can't see the whole complete act yet." Somerset says, "He's two murders away from completing his masterpiece." The killer wants his acts interpreted and remembered, not just as religious messages but as works of art. All the major divisions of art are methodically touched on. The killer leaves behind a quotation from Milton at the first murder. At the second, he turns a painting upside down and then spells out "help me" in fingerprints (someone else's) on the wall behind the painting. Later one of the cops says that a corpse looks like "some friggin' sculpture or something." Many of the corpses are posed precisely as gruesome three-dimensional emblems. To illuminate the sin of pride, the killer cuts up a rich woman's face and glues a phone to one hand and a bottle of pills to the other. Instead of living with a disfigured face, the woman kills herself, and is thus discovered as a clearly readable, emblematic corpse. The killer punishes lust by forcing a man to wear a giant swordlike phallus and have sex with a prostitute; the maker of the monstrous phallus tells the detectives, "I thought he was a performance artist." The murders are staged, one after the other, and the crime scenes dressed by a homicidal art designer. The killer is a theologian, but he is also an aesthete.

Films like *Seven* not only use art to gain sympathy for their killers, but also use an outmoded definition of art. In this traditional version, the artist is a superior individual who creates art with meaning and significance. The meditations on art by Kubrick and Altman are powerful because they question these traditional descriptions of both artist and art. Kubrick, especially, seems to recognize a horror attached to the lack of meaning in art. Although it is a horror film, *Seven* revels in wit and good sense, from the first quotation of Milton to the final perfectly staged murder. But there are more powerful and convincing horror films that also connect the artist to serial killer, yet now without the consolations of meaning. In what remains of this chapter, I will look at two examples of such films, *American Psycho* (2000) by Mary Harron and *Office Killer* (1997) by the great art photographer, Cindy Sherman.

It is worth noting that the Cindy Sherman film was produced by Christine Vachon, who since 1992 has run a production company called Killer Films. Vachon has produced some of the most interesting American independent films of the 1990s, from Tom Kalin's *Poison* (1991) to Todd Haynes's *Velvet Goldmine* (1998). In her treatise on independent filmmaking, *Shooting to Kill: How an Independent Producer Blasts through the Barriers to Make Movies That Matter* (1998), Vachon scarcely mentions art at all. Most of the book is taken up with detailed account books and illuminating anecdotes from her extensive experience in low-budget filmmaking. But clearly both Larry Clark and Cindy Sherman get to make *Kids* and *Office Killer* in the first place because of their status as world-famous art photographers. Most of Vachon's films are swamped in art consciousness, but with the negative art consciousness of Kubrick. From Haynes's Kubrickian *Safe* to the Brechtian discomfort of Solondz's *Happiness* (which includes a slow-motion fantasy machine-gun massacre in a park), from Mary Harron's *I Shot Andy Warhol* to Cindy Sherman's *Office Killer*, Killer Films almost methodically articulates the art film's violent no to art.

In its equation of art and violence, Mary Harron's *I Shot Andy Warhol* (1996) looks directly toward her serial-killer film, *American Psycho*. Valerie Solanas is the one who shot Andy Warhol, and the film wants us to feel that she is just as much a revolutionary artist as Warhol. Both artists work against traditional high-art forms, but whereas Warhol luxuriates in glamour and cool, Solanas cultivates a truly radical negative aesthetics. Solanas wants Warhol to produce her play, *Up Your Ass*, and she sells copies of her feminist pamphlet, *The SCUM Manifesto*. Warhol's queer, drug-taking crowd is out of the mainstream, to be sure, but still relatively restrained compared to Solanas. "This is too disgusting, even for us," says Warhol of her work. At a Factory party, the two artists are aligned by the staging, as both of them become voyeurs, each superior and distant, watching other people dance and embrace. They even talk amicably at one point, and agree that sex is no big deal. But Solanas's "garbage mouth" violence deconstructs Warhol's aesthetics of glamour. In Warhol's Factory, all the hangers-on are their own movie stars, whereas the heroine of *I Shot Andy Warhol* tries to kill the star of stars.

I Shot Andy Warhol shows that all these artists—Solanas, Warhol, and everyone at the Factory—are pretty crazy, but the film does not idealize the "mad artist"—far from it. The film stands back, at a distance, and shows us the sequences of the story rather objectively. Stylistically, the film is neither Warhol nor Solanas, but a relatively detached study of the fate of Valerie Solanas. *I Shot Andy Warhol* is about different strands of radical aesthetics, but it does not claim in its telling to be organized by any aesthetic beyond the art-house film. In its conclusion, the film goes so far as to canonize the seemingly mad *SCUM Manifesto* by telling us that the book is "now a feminist classic." At which point the film has justified itself in a traditional manner by telling us that this misunderstood woman has turned out retrospectively to be an important person. Although Solanas undercut even avant-garde aesthetics with a murderous radicalism, she is nonetheless viewed as a historically significant figure. Harron's next film, *American Psycho*, will also deal with madness and murder, but will much more clearly embody the negative aesthetics that truly casts out these consolations of meaning and significance.

If *I Shot Andy Warhol* is a historical film that gives us insight into the connection between negative aesthetics and violence, *American Psycho* is a horror film that fully embodies the horror that attaches to an absence of meaning. Whereas the biographical caption at the end of *I Shot Andy Warhol* gives some intellectual context to Valerie Solanas, the psycho who tells us about his murderous existence says at the end of *American Psycho* that "this confession has meant nothing." The titular psycho is truly a maniac, who kills one person after another, but now without artistry, without significance. Even Dennis Hopper's maniac bomber in *Speed* (De Bont, 1994) gives a little speech about meaning and beauty: "You still don't get it, Jack. You don't get the beauty of it. A bomb is made to explode, that's its meaning, its purpose. Your life is empty because you spend it trying to prevent the bomb from becoming."

But for the murderer Patrick Bateman (Christian Bale), there is no plot that makes sense of his narrative, no metaphor that makes sense of the deaths. Even the Christian trajectory of confession and resolution eludes both him and the film as he looks out toward the camera at the end, entirely unpunished and unchanged: "But even after admitting this, there is no catharsis, and I gain no deeper knowledge of myself. No new knowledge can be extracted from my telling; this confession has meant nothing."

American Psycho is apparently a satire on the empty competitiveness of corporate offices, somewhat along the lines of *In The Company of Men* (LaBute, 1997). The macho office politics of *In The Company of Men* seems to breed extraordinary misogyny and cruelty, even if no actual corpses appear. To amuse themselves while on a six-week business stint away from home, two men conspire to torment romantically a deaf woman who also works in the office. The corporate suits look absolutely nasty, and the film seems to want us to enjoy (à la Tarantino) their sick transgressions of political correctness. The office workplace in LaBute's film breeds superficiality, emptiness, and cruelty, as in *American Psycho*, Soderbergh's *Schizopolis*, and Cindy Sherman's *Office Killer*. But one of the men in LaBute's company turns out to have scruples, and this allows the movie to split into two, into the shamed and the unashamed. Whereas *In The Company of Men* incorporates its own moral revulsion into the plot, *American Psycho* truly empties out the office and viciously underscores the *mean* in meaningless.

The art in *American Psycho* vacuums out the high-culture references in serial-killer movies like *The Silence of the Lambs* or *Seven.* During the opening titles, cartoon blood rains down in front of a white screen; the blood drips and pools like paint. It then flows down around a primped-up gourmet dish, and classical music comes in to show us a fancy restaurant. But one of the men in suits at the table says, "I hate this place. It's a chick's restaurant." Throughout the film, Bateman exhibits the vulgar tastes of the American mainstream. He is an elaborate music critic whose tastes run all the way from "I'm Walking on Sunshine" (Katrina and the Waves) to "Simply Irresistible" (Robert Palmer). Compared to the glamour aesthetics of Warhol, the trash aesthetics of John Waters, or the revolutionary aesthetics of Valerie Solanas, Bateman's aesthetics is nightmarishly populist, amounting to almost an absence of aesthetic criteria.

While he abuses two prostitutes, for example, Bateman shares with them his ideas about Phil Collins's career: "I also think that Phil Collins works better within the confines of a group than as a solo artist, and I stress the word 'artist.' " Bateman has a stylish apartment, dominated by an enormous modern-looking painting, but there is nothing beneath the stylishness except horrific violence. He is obsessed by his personal appearance, and we watch him groom elaborately in the shower. He scrutinizes and judges his coworkers' business cards; "Oh my God, he even has a watermark," thinks Bateman. But there is absolutely nothing else to him. On the one hand, he is made out of predetermined lifestyles and populist aesthetics; on the other hand, he is a vicious lunatic. In an opening voice-over, as he puts on his antiaging creams and moisturizers, he gives this description of his ghostly existence: "There is an idea of Patrick Bateman, some kind of abstraction, but there is no real me, only an entity, something illusory. And though I can hide my cold gaze and you can shake my hand and feel flesh gripping yours, and maybe you can even sense our lifestyles are probably comparable, I simply am not there."

The ghostliness of Bateman's murderous existence is developed by the trajectory of the narrative. In a film like *Henry: Portrait of a Serial Killer* (McNaughton, 1990), Henry eventually drives off down the road, escaping justice for now. But we do not doubt that the murders actually took place in the world of the film. Like Bateman, Henry is terrifically angry, and like Bateman, Henry likes to film his murders. But Henry has surely left a swath of destruction in his wake. *Henry: Portrait of a Serial Killer* is filmed naturalistically, not portentously, like *The Silence of the Lambs,* and the film explains the murders as the products of, above all, child abuse. In the film, Henry kills one person after another, mostly women, and then leaves the last body in a trunk by the side of the road. In its turn, *American Psycho* also lets its killer escape, but in this case we are not sure whether the murders actually happened.

After Bateman's final orgy of violence, his apartment is absolutely flooded in body parts and blood. There are heads in the refrigerator and bodies hung up in the closets. This sequence concludes as Bateman runs naked out into the hallway in pursuit of a fleeing woman. He manages to keep her from escaping by dropping a chainsaw on her from five floors up. To hit someone from that distance with a chainsaw is a cinematic idea, as well as a cinematic allusion (to *The Texas Chainsaw Massacre*), and scarcely related to any real world. And then we cut to Bateman drawing a picture of a woman with a chainsaw stuck in her side on the tablecloth of a fancy restaurant, followed by a pan over to another beautiful gourmet dish, in which an absent knife and fork have been outlined in the surrounding powdered sugar. Bateman's childlike drawing, and also the dessert, shows the absence at the heart of Bateman's horrific art. In a moment, when Bateman goes to the ATM, it tells him to "feed me a stray cat." And when he goes back to the apartment at the end, it has been entirely repainted.

There is the possibility that a lawyer has cleaned up the mess quite magically, but there is a much stronger sense that all of Bateman's murders have been one long hallucination. His office notebooks are filled with murderous doodlings, rapes, and decapitations, but it would appear that his anger has been entirely ineffectual in the real world and that nothing whatsoever has happened. In the last sequence, the men in suits watch President Reagan on television as he explains Iran-Contra, and an overwhelming sense of American emptiness and horror falls over everything. *American Psycho* empties out whatever meaning could attach itself to either art or cinematic murder. If *Solaris* haunts by conjuring up impossible loves, *American Psycho* horrifies by conjuring impossible deaths.

Cindy Sherman's *Office Killer* (1997) also leaves the impression of emptiness and horror. *Office Killer* shows some relationship with Sherman's work in photography, such as her series of untitled film stills and her more recent work with violently rent dolls. Most clearly, however, *Office Killer* is a deconstructive update of Hitchcock's *Psycho*. Whereas Hitchcock's Norman Bates keeps the body of his mother upstairs, Sherman's Dorine (Carol Kane) has a real mother upstairs and keeps the bodies of her victims downstairs. When her mother actually dies, Dorine sends the body away in an ambulance while continuing to play house with all the corpses downstairs. Whereas Norman Bates is charismatic and fiendish, Dorine is yet another absence, a barely recognizable bundle of timidity. Dorine is apparently so shy and withdrawn that she can only socialize with dead people. So her basement becomes an auditorium of ghosts who seem to emerge from their corpses in order to visit with one another and Dorine.

In contrast with films like *Seven* or *I Shot Andy Warhol*, *Office Killer* is not overtly about art, but the basement of corpses is implicitly a room full of photographs or sculptures, frozen images that have come under Dorine's control. Dorine thus becomes, metaphorically, a still-life photographer and gallery owner all in one. Whereas Norman Bates seems to act out a jealous, homicidal moralism on behalf of his mother (as Mrs. Bates does away with an attractive woman in a shower), Dorine's psychosis is completely amoral, and she kills not only nasty office managers, but also cute little girl scouts.

Office Killer is also shot as an exact antithesis to *Citizen Kane*. Whereas Welles repeatedly places both foreground and background objects in focus, Sherman shoots background and foreground out of focus with respect to each other. It is hard to think of another film where the foreground is so often blurry or the background so often out of focus. Even in a shot of only two hands typing, the up-screen hand may be in focus while the down-screen hand is not. Occasionally a rack focus will democratically allow both foreground and background to come into focus, but much more often the blur is there to stay. The blurs not only replicate a subjective psychosis that will eventually populate a room with ghosts, but also repeatedly call our attention to the surface of the screen. Just as Sherman's photographs always interrogate both the photographic subject and the photographic surface, so too does *Office Killer* quietly question cinematic representation and narration.[30] In both plot and technique, *Office Killer* thus offers itself as one more self-conscious address to the absence at the heart of the cinematic experience.

Tarkovsky's *Solaris* performs the elaboration of time—ongoingness and waiting—but in a narrative punctuated by violence. Kris rids himself of the first Hari by putting her in a spaceship and shooting her into space. The departing spaceship burns Kris with its flames. The second Hari still has on her arm the mark of the hypodermic with which she committed suicide. She bloodies herself tearing through a door to be near Kris. And then she is a horrible bloody mess after drinking liquid oxygen. If Hari embodies the philosophical traffic of cinematic absence and presence, she does so, indeed, with her wounded body, in a story that is one self-murder after another. Time in *Solaris* not only cures wounds but also repeats them, tormentingly. As in Kubrick, Altman, and Harron, violence in Tarkovsky is inextricably related to a meditation on cinematic art.

A Plague of Frogs: Expressionism and Naturalism in 1990s American Film   7

....

In Paul Thomas Anderson's *Magnolia* (1999) there is a now famous sequence in which all the main characters, one after the other, start singing along to an Aimee Mann song. They sing from entirely different locations, and two of them are nearly dead—it is an impossible moment. At which point Janet Maslin of the *New York Times* came quite unglued:

> The great uh-oh moment in Paul Thomas Anderson's "Magnolia" occurs about two-thirds of the way through this artfully orchestrated symphony of L.A. stories. A song bursts out: it is heard first from one character, then from another, until all the film's assorted lost souls are brought together by a single anxiety-ridden refrain. "It's not . . . going to stop," each one sings resignedly, signaling the approach of an impending group melt-down. But the effect is less that of a collective shiver than of directorial desperation.[1]

Even Anderson himself can only barely explain the outlandish improbability. For Anderson, the scene can be explained only as artistic license, creative intuitionism, as writing with his "gut."[2] The scene would be perfectly fine, even de rigueur, in a musical, but *Magnolia* is not a musical.

So if the scene does not make sense, it is because of our generic expectations. It must be that we are reading *Magnolia* as basically realistic, expecting the physical rules of our known world to obtain. *Magnolia* does not appear to be science fiction, horror, or musical comedy. The sequence is not a dream vision, and no character in the film ever levitates. The first character in the song sequence, Cynthia (Felicity Huffman), is snorting cocaine, but there is no indication that all the following characters are figments of her drug-altered imagination. At the end of the sequence the torrents of rain simply stop, as if switched off. But these things should not be there; there is not supposed to be, all of a sudden, a display of supernatural coincidence and musical telepathy. Surely the genre train has come off the tracks.

Yet earlier portions of *Magnolia* provided some foreshadowing for this expressionistic outburst. The title sequence showed us a whole series of oddball coincidences gathered directly from Charles Fort, a collector of paranormal phenomena. Some time after the telepathic song, a hailstorm of toads falls from the sky—another extremely improbable, even if not completely impossible, event. What is most strange, perhaps, is that although the frogs rain down improbably, no character in the film responds to the toads as anything out of the ordinary. People just push the dead frogs out of the way and try to go around them. No one says, "It certainly is mighty odd, isn't it, for a million frogs to fall out of the sky." So this is not a very realistic movie after all—or perhaps *Magnolia* wants to open up ideas of what is realistic and what is allowable in a narrative film. The whole structure of the film is based on a labyrinth of coincidences crossing between overlapping plots and unlikely connections between characters (two fathers are dying, for example, Earl Partridge (Jason Robards, in his last film) and Jimmy Gator (Philip Baker Hall), and there is not only a child currently playing on *What Do Kids Know?* there is also a former child star from that television show).

If Anderson is one of the cinematic sons of Robert Altman (known for his meandering ensemble pieces) or Martin Scorsese (known for his dramatic intensity and flying camera), then Anderson also helps us better locate the realism of these directors. *Magnolia,* in some ways, *is* a musical, as immersed in artifice and emotion as any production by Charles Freed. Recall the degree to which the musical always lurks around the edges of American New Wave film in the 1970s: Scorsese makes *New York, New York* (1977), *The Last Waltz* (1978), and gives the opening dream sequence of *Alice Doesn't Live Here Anymore* (1974) a set from 1950s Technicolor Hollywood; Coppola's first movie is *Finian's Rainbow* (1968, also Fred Astaire's last musical), and *One from the Heart* (1982) continues trying out the form; Altman does not have his characters actually sing until *Popeye* (1980), but Anderson latches onto that moment by replaying a song sung by Olive Oyl–Shelley Duvall in *Punch-Drunk Love* (2002).

The telepathic sing-along would not look peculiar in many other parts of the world. In a Bollywood film, musical numbers are expected to appear at regular intervals, no matter what the film genre—detective thriller, historical reconstruction, or political soap opera. In an art movie by Kieslowski or Wong Kar-Wai, we would not be put off by poetic coincidence; on the contrary, we would recognize in these coincidences the hand of the author. When Denis Lavant suddenly breaks into dance (although his character is dead) at the end of Claire Denis's *Beau Travail* (1999), or when all four characters in François Ozon's *Water Drops on Burning Rocks* (2000) abruptly start to dance with perfect choreography, we accommodate these flamboyant diversions under the sign of the art movie. One of the most brilliant genre-benders of recent years, Lars von Trier's *Dancer in the Dark* (2002), goes back and forth between handheld, grainy, realistic sequences and bouncy musical numbers performed by Bjork. Von Trier clearly intends to blow open the confines of what are especially American genres. For some critics, *Magnolia* (with Tom Cruise) can only barely get away with some poetic telepathy, whereas *Dancer in the Dark* usurps American terrain and goes on to win the Palme d'Or at Cannes.

Obviously the demise of the American musical is based on some fairly incoherent mass psychology.[3] If one argues, for example, that Americans are too cynical for musicals, or that musicals are too illogical for American minds, then most of what Hollywood produces would also have to go. John Woo's *Hard Target* (1993) readily transposes the contradictions of Hong Kong action movies to Hollywood by combining the most saccharine sentimentality with bloodthirsty violence. Action movies themselves might be seen as what musicals have evolved into: in both, cloying dialogue bridges the gap between the set pieces, whether the musical numbers of yesteryear or the special-effects fight sequences of today. The fights themselves often have dance music attached to them. *The Matrix*, for instance, lays down techno beats while Neo and the rest turn through digitally choreographed kickboxing stunts.

American movies may have given up on the musical, but not on the music, since most Hollywood films hope to appear with a CD sound track full of hit songs. When everyone in *Magnolia* starts singing along to Aimee Mann, then, the characters are really just breaking through the nondiegetic fourth wall. Aimee Mann has been singing during the whole movie anyway. But just as you are not supposed to look into the camera, you are not supposed to acknowledge the sound track. To turn *Magnolia* into a music video for four minutes is unusual for contemporary American film, but really just a creative acknowledgment of what most movies are doing already.

In this chapter, I will examine a range of American films in terms of self-reflexivity and artifice. In the final third of the chapter, I will provide more detail for my argument that naturalism without self-reflexivity is incoherent in 1990s American film. Many of the examples in this chapter are taken from independent film, and only Spike Lee among these directors maintained fitful connections to Hollywood. Independent film may be tempted to turn away from the artifices of Hollywood by attaching itself to reality and nature, but many of the decade's most promising directors realized that the most productive alternative to Hollywood's empty artifice is not nature, but a determinedly self-reflexive artifice of their own fabrication.

Todd Haynes and the Sons of Derek Jarman

As the years move forward, the importance of Derek Jarman in film history becomes more and more evident. Films are not important because critics approve of them, but because later artists enter into a dialogue with them. Jarman's independently produced British films of the 1980s have struck a chord with some of the most interesting American directors in the 1990s. Jarman's focus on homosexuality, in addition to his formal experimentation (particularly with home video), has made a significant impact on Gus Van Sant, Todd Haynes, and Harmony Korine. Jarman's representation of a lost generation, in a film like *The Last of England* (1987), has its American counterpart in Larry Clark's *Kids* (1995).

The films of Larry Clark are an apparent assault on Hollywood convention and artifice. Yet whereas Jarman's relentless self-reflexivity is carried on by Van Sant and Korine, Clark attempts to banish Hollywood artifice by realism. Clark intends his films to be representations of real life, and critics have tended to read the films as harrowing descriptions of the state of contemporary youth. In interviews, Clark likes to quote teenagers who have told him that—except for the murders—that is exactly how they are. No disaffected teens quote Shakespeare, as they might in Gus Van Sant (credited as executive producer on *Kids*); instead, we enter into a completely culture-free zone where neither director nor any character has the slightest artistic pretension. Roger Ebert, in fact, took this for one substantial element of the film's moral:

> Most kids are not like those in "Kids," and never will be, I hope. But some are, and they represent a failure of home, school, church and society. They could have been raised in a zoo, educated only to the base instincts. You watch this movie, and you realize why everybody needs whatever mixture of art, education, religion, philosophy, politics and poetry that works for them. Because without something to open our windows to the

higher possibilities of life, we might all be Tellys, and more amputated than the half-man on his skateboard.[4]

Some kids are really like those in this film, and we had better get them some poetry—we had better get them to school!

But the film itself is old, old school, taught by Aristotle and classic television. It is so carefully structured that any pretense to realism is exposed for what it is, a fabrication. The film takes place over the course of twenty-four hours—it goes from morning to morning. There is a main character, Telly (Leo Fitzpatrick), who is granted a little voice-over at the beginning and the end. He seduces a virgin at the very beginning of the film, and another one at the end. One of his previous "scores," Jennie (Chloe Sevigny), finds out that she is HIV-positive, and so goes looking for Telly the rest of the day. Is reality conveyed when the narrative is built into the hoary confines of a television script?

In *Kids* we are supposed to see irony everywhere, but this comes at the expense of reality. For instance, toward the beginning the film crosscuts between boys talking about girls, and girls talking about boys. They talk about the same topics simultaneously, although in different ways (the boys think that the girls like romantic sex, the girls say that girls actually like rough sex). The crosscutting does not give the impression of divine coincidence or authorial exuberance, as in *Magnolia*. Instead we simply hear the director saying, isn't this funny? This sort of irony appears also when Telly is scoring his second virgin of the day and the movie cuts back to show us a few moments of his first conquest. Yes, movie, we get it (as Mystery Science Theater 3000 would say), he did the same thing already.

At the end, one of Telly's friends chooses to have sex with a completely knocked-out Jennie. This is a very bad idea, and now the friend will get HIV. But it all comes off as a tragic plot contrivance. The episodes all seem representative: here is the drug buy, here is the fight, here is the boost at the convenience store, here is what Mom looks like. The movie affects to have no style, but there is no such thing. *Kids* does not want to be stylish and artificial, yet the film sets its scruffy nonactors into the most recognizable and readable narrative imaginable. The kids themselves may be able to think themselves into oblivion, but a movie cannot will itself into transparency. As Cassavetes and von Trier know, the only response to Hollywood artifice is other kinds of artifice.

The problematic transparency of *Kids* is made doubly apparent by setting it next to a film of Clark's own choosing, Cassavetes' *Shadows* (1959). Clark says that *Shadows* is his favorite movie, and in interviews he invariably brings up

Cassavetes as an influence, almost to the exclusion of anyone else. Warhol, for instance, is too knowingly "arty."[5] Cassavetes is, by contrast, "real." But *Shadows* combines its reality effects with endless bouts of self-consciousness. Cassavetes's realism—bequeathed through grainy visuals, ragged editing, scenes without conclusion, plots without direction—always appears inextricably enmeshed with every kind of cinematic self-consciousness. In *Shadows* almost all the characters are some kind of artist or performer; the characters often talk next to paintings and drawings. One scene takes place in a sculpture garden at the Museum of Modern Art. The theatrical, performative nature of Cassavetes's improvisational cinema is self-reflexively evidenced by making so many of the characters performers. Characters perform for audiences in the film; they perform for each other; they perform for the camera. There is, to be sure, a strong impression of reality, since the narrative, dialogue, and editing do not conform to Hollywood conventions. Yet Cassavetes could not be clearer about having chosen a different kind of artifice, a different sense of coherence, in order to make his art. Cassavetes's films are always made self-consciously in the mode of "theatrical realism."[6]

Shadows, like *Kids,* also boldly deals with a woman's loss of virginity. One can easily imagine why Clark would have seen himself as making another version of *Shadows.* Cassavetes's men are just as libidinal, just as angry as Clark's; we see the consequences of one of their seductions very soon after *Shadows* begins. In Cassavetes's film, Ben (Ben Carruthers) promises Lelia (Lelia Goldoni) that sex will be OK, but she is completely distraught after they make love. Similarly, the girls in *Kids* cry out how much it hurts, yet Telly keeps going. Since cinematic sexuality is usually so idealized, or violent to the point of rape, these scenes in Cassavetes and Clark are both unusual. But the way these scenes fit into what happens in the rest of the movie is strikingly different. In Clark, Telly is simply caught in a virgin-deflowering loop; that is all he does. In Clark, we see only apocalyptic consequences, that one of Telly's numberless scores of victims has gotten HIV. Obviously the dead-end quality of their teenage lives is the point, but it also leaves the impression of creative simplification. There is only orgasm and death in a world inhabited almost entirely by teens.

On the other hand, Cassavetes allows his characters to go somewhere. Lelia gets over the pain and surprise of her sexual initiation, only to find that Ben wants to drop her when he realizes that she is black. Cassavetes gives us a complex world of adult sexuality where reality emerges through self-conscious artifice. Clark gives us a cartoon world of repetitive teenage sexuality where conceptual incoherence emerges from the pretension to transparency. Cassavetes opposes Hollywood by brandishing a legitimately alternative style, whereas Clark opposes Hollywood by deploying, nonetheless, a framework of Hollywood legibility. The Aristotelian structure of *Kids* will soon be replaced by stars (James Woods, Melanie Griffith) and genre in Clark's *Another Day in Paradise* (1998), and by glossy, glamorous photography in Clark's *Bully* (2001).

Gummo (1997)—directed by Harmony Korine, the screenwriter for *Kids*—is another matter entirely. In a way it is the same idea—a much more realistic look at teenagers than any seen in Hollywood. Yet the execution is entirely different. For best reality effect, *Gummo* wins hands down over *Kids:* there are videotaped sequences here that are clearly unrehearsed slices of rural anthropology, like those in a documentary film. But other sequences seem just as clearly preconceived and rehearsed. The film cuts back and forth between home-video-style footage and 35 mm. The deployment of home video can remind us only of Derek Jarman's work in the 1980s, although he often could not afford the 35 mm to cut back to! Indeed, Van Sant, in a "forward" to *Gummo* for Fine Line pictures, finds Korine's strongest cinematic influences in Herzog, Cassavetes, Arbus, Fellini, Godard, Maysles, and Jarman.[7]

Narratively, *Gummo* wanders around, but no more so than movies by Fellini, Godard, or Jarman. It also repeatedly declares itself to be a film, just like the films of his masters. Simply to switch from video to 35 mm is to acknowledge the medium of film. It makes us wonder—Is this a documentary? Is this fiction? Although planted firmly in America, *Gummo* is a European art film. It travels out to the natural world of rural Tennessee, the diametric opposite of urban zones of *Kids*. Yet *Gummo* subtly acknowledges its artifice at every point. "I wanted it to come from every direction," says Korine, "to kind of fall down from the sky. But at the same time it's very constructed."[8]

When its characters are not looking into the camera and breaking down the documentary-fiction distinction in every way, *Gummo* is busily thematizing performance and theatricality with as much energy as a Cassavetes film. There are not any nightclubs or theaters around, but that does not mean that these nonactors cannot still perform and acknowledge their performances. One character repeats a monologue that he has heard somewhere else while standing on a table. Another listens to Madonna and lifts weights made out of silverware while looking into a mirror. His mother meanwhile does a tap dance in her dead husband's tap shoes. A motif throughout the film is that of a figure who shows his muscles to the camera. Two sequences are straight out masculinist performance pieces, and not far from those found in Jarman.

In one sequence, two burly teens pound on each other, seemingly for real. In another, after some arm wrestling, a man wrestles a chair to the ground while another man destroys it. Nonactors stomp around in the woods, but there is no transparent nature here. When the boys go out to sniff glue, seemingly in the middle of a forest, they lie back against graffiti-covered walls—against what is essentially a painting. Korine avoids the conventions of Hollywood while showing us that he is fully aware that one artifice must be replaced by another.

Korine's second film, *Julien Donkey-Boy* (1999), became the first American film to be granted a Dogma 95 certificate for obeying the "rules of chastity" set down by von Trier and Thomas Vinterberg.[9] The Dogma 95 movement—full of contradictions and absurdities, no doubt—in general stands as a vehement outcry against Hollywood special effects and artifice. Dogma demands all sound recordings to be in sync (no postproduction looping), using only diegetic (on-site) music. Visuals are shot only with a handheld camera (so no more elegant tracking shots), using only available light. No props may be brought in, and there are similar restrictions on costumes and makeup. Films are shot on location and in academy-ratio 35 mm. The director must not be credited. As von Trier said when he announced the rules: "The use of cosmetics has exploded. The 'supreme task' of the decadent film-makers is to fool the audience. Is that what we are so proud of? Is that what the '100 years' have brought us?"[10] Dogma rejects cinematic artifice.

Julien Donkey-Boy brilliantly reroutes Dogma by subverting its basic principles. Like *Gummo*, *Julien* knows that one replaces artifice by artifice. After the Dogma certificate is shown as the first image of the film, we see an ice skater spinning in staggered slow motion. Dogma rule number five is that "optical work and filters are forbidden," so Korine apparently breaks the rule in the first frame. But what has happened is that light digital-video cameras appeared in 1996 and became the Dogma camera of choice (originally 35 mm was required). Whatever else might be happening, digital cameras *are* their own optical effects, and Korine shows the viewer absolutely everything that his camera can do over the course of his second film. There are snapshots and slides (recalling Marker's *La Jetée*), stroboscopic collages, and painterly re-descriptions (we see a snowdrop blur into a white streak as it falls). When Julien (Ewen Bremner) walks down the street at the beginning, it looks exactly like the slick step printing associated with Wong Kar-Wai (as at the beginning of *Chungking Express* [1994]). As the Dogma certificate attests, Korine obeys the rules (the only rule he overtly breaks is that Chloe Sevigny is not actually pregnant), yet he surely violates the spirit. The movie is filled with special effects and self-consciousness. In one of the earlier scenes, Julien drives the camera down into the ground like a hammer. Attention may be drawn away from the uncredited director (the silliest of the rules), but it certainly is not drawn away from the camera.

Julien Donkey-Boy once again thematizes performance, and one sequence after another is built around displays and performances. A cigarette eater (whom we likely recognize from his appearances on television) does his thing, then a mildly retarded man dances on stage. Korine once again juxtaposes documentary and fiction. In an emblematic bout, a "real" wrestler (who wants to wrestle for real and wears an athletic wrestling uniform) wrestles Julien, shouting and preening dressed in a bra, who in his turn seems to want only to fake-wrestle, like the performers in the World Wrestling Federation.

The most self-conscious gesture of all comes from casting Werner Herzog as a tyrannical father. Herzog once said, "Cinema comes from the country fair and the circus," and his interest in oddballs and grotesques (such as Bruno S. in *The Mystery of Kasper Hauser* [1974]) is an obvious origin for Korine's menagerie.[11] To put Herzog in a Dogma movie—where the director is supposed to be absent—is, once more, brilliantly anti-Dogmatic. In the film, Herzog mainly does a dialogue loop, repeatedly telling his son (the wrestler) to be a winner, to be a "champion." There is perhaps some commentary here on Herzog himself, the insane taskmaster who made *Fitzcarraldo* (1982). But Herzog breaks out of the loop on a couple of occasions to give a long monologue (his face stuck up on the screen in a transcendentally cheesy special effect); he also explains to Julien how he hates Julien's "artsy-fartsy" poem and that the best of all film moments is the end of *Dirty Harry.* In Dogma films like Thomas Vinterberg's *Celebration* (1998), the characters all stay in character, but *Julien Donkey-Boy* shows all of its characters wavering back and forth between fictive constructions and real people. *Julien Donkey-Boy* is a stunning reply to Dogma theory.

Gus Van Sant's support and patronage of Larry Clark and Harmony Korine clearly feeds back into his own cinema, resulting in *Gerry* (2002) and *Elephant* (2003), his return to independent productions about young men. Before *Gerry,* his career seemed to be evolving away from the independently themed films of *Drugstore Cowboy* (1989) and *My Own Private Idaho* (1991) and toward the studio productions of *Good Will Hunting* (1997) and *Finding Forrester* (2000). But

Van Sant's studio films are by no means artistic sellouts. The concern with artifice as signaled by the Shakespearean quotation in *My Own Private Idaho* continues even more radically in his remake of Hitchcock's *Psycho*.

Van Sant's *Psycho* (1998) does not remake Hitchcock's film in the usual Hollywood sense, in which a few plot points are saved, but much else is transformed, updated, or quickened. Van Sant's *Psycho* remakes Hitchcock virtually shot for shot and word for word. Popular and critical response to this film was almost universally negative, since there seemed to be no plausible explanation for the exercise. Van Sant's own public rationale seemed none too helpful, either; he claimed that *Psycho* needed to be redone with modern actors and in color so that young people could experience the classic that they would not watch otherwise (since black-and-white is, apparently, an impenetrable obstacle for today's young moviegoers). Yet the film makes almost no attempt to update otherwise. The script is almost exactly the same; there is no more blood, and only a few extra frames of nudity. There are, in other words, none of the augmentations that would make this truly a contemporary suspense movie. On the contrary, Van Sant luxuriates in the anachronisms of speech and look, dressing the characters in '70s clothes (William Macy wears an impossible fedora) and refusing to show a cell phone.

In the same way that the success of Lynch's *Mulholland Drive* made earlier experiments like *Twin Peaks: Fire Walk* look retrospectively more convincing to *Cahiers du cinéma,* one might argue that the success and vigor of *Elephant* makes Van Sant's *Psycho* more worthy of reappraisal. In its enthusiastic overview of Van Sant's career up to *Elephant* (which would go on to win the Palme d'Or at Cannes), *Cahiers* in fact praises *Psycho* as offering one of the most "vertiginous" experiences in cinema.[12] The shadow film that is Van Sant's *Psycho* is, indeed, a remarkable experiment, as anyone with Hitchcock's *Psycho* in their heads hears these usurping contemporary actors mouthing lines that belong to Anthony Perkins and Janet Leigh.

The contemporary actors see themselves as making "more sense" than the originals; Anne Heche finds Janet Leigh's motivation too ambiguous in the early scenes, and sees her own Marion Crane as more clearly drawn.[13] Potentially, too, the charismatic couple formed by Viggo Mortensen and Julianne Moore might make the last third of the film more interesting than Hitchcock's parallel segment with Vera Miles and John Gavin. Yet surely no one can imagine that Anne Heche, Vince Vaughn, and even the redoubtable William Macy can step into the iconographic shoes of Janet Leigh, Anthony Perkins, and Martin Balsam without looking very small. The contemporaries are doomed to lose in any comparison. On the other hand, there they are, in color, alive. For the cinephile, the film may thus manifest an authentically weird, haunted power. The audience's response no longer has anything to do with suspense, but must entirely be concerned with the self-conscious embodiment of cinematic history. Even as *Psycho* comes to life again, it vanishes, doubling and splitting all the way through.

Van Sant's *Elephant* (2003) is one of the strongest American films in recent memory. It is fifteen times more real than Larry Clark's *Kids*, and a thousand times more real than anything in John Sayles. Acting and dialogue are flattened out to the minimum, to the quotidian. But at the same time, the film is completely self-reflexive. One of the main characters, Elias (Elias McConnell), is a photographer, and the film is entirely self-conscious about the degree to which we *look* at these young people, especially the young men. The film's camera is ostentatious, not hidden, never pretending that it transparently records this reality. As the teenagers act in their almost no-acting acting style, the camera moves glidingly around them, tracking ahead, framing things knowingly, reminding us that this is a movie. Since the plot is based on the Columbine shootings, the effect is constantly to move back and forth between documentary and fiction. The film begins with a gesture of purest cinephilia when it casts Timothy Bottoms as the drunken father of John McFarland (John Robinson). Yet Bottoms is the only recognizable star, and his son tells him to "get out of the car, Dad," since there will be no other stars in this picture. Timothy Bottoms as a washed-out drunken father is cast perfectly, since Bottoms's career washed out years ago. When he appears in this film about teenagers, we can only remember his transcendent promise in *The Last Picture Show* (Bogdanovich, 1971), one of that era's most powerful films about teenagers.

Unlike Larry Clark's *Kids*, whose teens all seem to be illiterate barbarians, *Elephant* is full of art and artists. Not only do we watch the photographer take and develop his pictures, we listen to one of the future gunmen play Beethoven's *Moonlight* Sonata at some length. That melody, in fact, becomes a main theme, and is heard at the beginning and end of the film. The two gunmen play shoot-'em-up video games and surf the Internet for guns, but their room is covered with drawings, one plays Beethoven on the piano (which the other boy says is "awesome"), and they are shown reading books. The presence of art and culture in *Elephant* not only complicates the role of art (art is not just aligned with good, interesting people), but also self-reflexively underlines the fact that *Elephant* is art. *Kids* does not let art in not only because Larry Clark thinks it is not true to the nature of the kids, but also because he does not want to be that kind of too arty artist. In its turn, *Elephant* situates itself as a realistic artifact, as a document of young people, but one self-consciously photographed and arranged. Films do not speak from nowhere, transparently; they speak from somewhere, and through the medium of film. Self-reflexivity is not postmodern decoration or a species of pleasant or ironic jargon; it is, at bottom, a situatedness. The film comes from somewhere.[14]

The way Van Sant wobbled between Shakespearean quotation and realistic homoeroticism in *My Own Private Idaho* was to a large degree authorized by the work of Derek Jarman. In the 1980s, Jarman made what he called "poetic documentaries," which continually experimented with the blending of the lyrical and the real. In *The Angelic Conversation* (1985), Judi Dench reads out Shakespearean sonnets while stroboscopic home movies show the dream world of the two male lovers. Jarman's *The Last of England* shows a lost boy, Spring, shooting up and wandering through urban ruins while a voice-over occasionally reads out apocalyptic poems. Van Sant's admiration for Jarman's films is well documented, and comes through in the look and approach of *My Own Private Idaho*.[15] But the 1990s film that was most rewardingly influenced by Jarman's cinematic example, and that appeared in the same year as *My Own Private Idaho*, is Todd Haynes's *Poison* (1991). In some ways, Haynes, of all American filmmakers, carries on Jarman's legacy most forcefully and deliberately.

Haynes's first feature film, *Poison*, grafts together three sections: "Horror," "Hero," and "Homo," each clearly distinguished by genre and look. "Horror" is a black-and-white horror film pastiche about an accused "leper murderer." "Hero" is a faux documentary about a boy, Richie, who shot his father and then flew out a window, up into the sky. "Homo" is a dark, claustrophobic prison drama based on the writings of Jean Genet. The stories are all visually distinct from one another, but they each work elliptically around images of homosexuality. The monster movie allegorizes societal response to HIV-AIDS. The Genet segment shows a very intense and complicated homoerotic world. And the mock documentary shows the collapse of heterosexual domesticity and the dream of escape.

"Homo" is an extraordinarily powerful synthesis of Genet and Jarman. The dark prison scenes, shot on a military base, revise and elaborate Genet's famous underground film, *Un chant d'amour* (1950). To these scenes, Haynes adds a bright, already artificial-looking dream world, which can only recall the soundstage Jarman of *War Requiem* (1989) and *The Garden* (1990). As in Genet, the men in prison interact in oblique, nonobvious ways. The male body is sensual and erotic, but the interactions between men are symbolic and not idealized. In one of the ritualized set pieces, a group of six or seven men take turns spitting in the mouth and on the face of another man. This kind of oblique torture is seen throughout the films of Jarman, and is very reminiscent of several performance-piece attacks in *The Garden*. Unlike Van Sant's *My Private Own Idaho*, in which dialogue is fulsome and narrative fairly continuous, Haynes pares back dialogue and plot to the more emblematic regions of Jarman and Genet.

The horror-film section looks forward to Haynes's *Far from Heaven* (2002) in the way that it seriously borrows from the genres of horror and melodrama. Although it collects all the right elements—mad scientist, chases, weird camera angles, noir lighting, and music—this is not just a parody, like Mel Brooks's *Young Frankenstein* (1974). Indeed, this section is in part a self-conscious reflection on the film that *Poison* actually is—a low-budget, cheap-looking movie— just like all those 1930s B horror movies. Thus we inhabit the monster movie not only with a sense of superiority (we are smarter than the stupid movie), but also with a sense of using all our resources, economic and otherwise. The "popular" monster movie then proceeds to collide generically with the "underground" Genet and the "contemporary" documentary. All are species of cheap filmmaking, but the hierarchies of old and new, art and trash, start to dissolve. All the sections are fabrications, yet all are in earnest. The monster movie is a gathering of cliches, but it is also clearly about HIV and the persecution of differences. *Poison* shows that self-conscious repetition and allusion do not necessarily turn into superficially clever forms of postmodernism. *Poison* sets Jarman and Genet next to bad James Whale and bad Errol Morris, not with postmodern irony, but with devastating, and situating, force.

If *Poison* is a remarkable transformation of films by Genet and Jarman, *Safe* (1995) is an equally remarkable working-through of films by Stanley Kubrick. In interviews, Haynes notes that the production team prepared by studying *2001*, and he mentions the influence of Kubrick in the DVD commentary. The influence of Kubrick is readily apparent in the film. The whole film is made out of master shots, long in duration and symmetrically framed. Carole (Julianne Moore) is observed from a distance (there are almost no close-ups) and very deliberately with respect to the edge of the frame (sometimes at the exact center of frame, sometimes hovering on an edge). The kind of distance and coldness that Kubrick became known for comes through in Haynes's approach. Within the deliberate frame of his camera, Kubrick typically stages a battle of nature versus culture, primitive versus technological, chaos versus order.

When the flying bone turns into the space station in *2001*, and Richard Strauss into Johann Strauss, the implicit question must be, is this progress? Is this technologically advanced civilization better off than the murderous apes? For soon enough the computer HAL itself will go around killing people. Kubrick's art repeatedly stages the dissolution of the nature-culture antithesis inside that steady frame.

Safe stages a similarly ambiguous dissolution of culture and nature within its own perfectly composed shots. *Safe* tells the story of a woman who grows progressively more ill, although we never know exactly why. Environmental toxins may be responsible for her nosebleeds, headaches, and nausea. The story moves from California suburbs and cities to the forested surroundings of Wrenwood. At Wrenwood, Carole and other people like her live in cabins in the woods and try to regain their lost health. But there is no natural world in *Safe*. The film is pervaded by ominous electronic music, even when Carole walks in the woods. The homes and offices are filled with pictures of plants, potted plants, and flowery wallpaper, but none of it gives the slightest impression of life. There are weird green lights in various scenes (emanating from a bedroom closet, for example), but they only imply a strange ambience, not organicism. When Carole walks around her garden at home, the lighting makes everything look plastic; on the DVD commentary Haynes says, "It is good when nature looks as artificial as possible." Finally, at the end, Carole moves into a round spherical hut that looks like one end of the spaceship to Jupiter in *2001*.

Safe feels like it ought to be an antimaterialist, proenvironmentalist film. But it is really a horror film, as Wes Craven, among others, have observed. Specifically, it is a Kubrickian horror film, in which the genre has been completely reinflected and slowed down. *Safe* is frightening because there is no safe place; there are no explanations for anything and no hope given. Carole gets sicker and sicker, is given every kind of test and counseling, and ends up moving into a spaceship. And in those moments when the camera moves slowly toward her, the film self-consciously acknowledges its collaboration with the mysterious entity that makes Carole sick. Many of the long-held shots are crawling zooms in which the screen slowly but inevitably collapses onto her. Thus while we can project whatever illness we would like onto Carole (bad marriage, too much money, urban toxins), the movie knows that it is itself not entirely innocent, that it too has placed Carole amid Kubrickian ambiguity, wherein she is treated both distantly and oppressively.

Velvet Goldmine (1998) is another audacious piece of cinematic ventriloquism that revels in its self-conscious artifice. Whereas *Poison* is knee-deep in Genet and Jarman, *Safe* in Kubrick, and *Far from Heaven* up to its eyes in Sirk, *Velvet Goldmine* does not borrow from any single director. But like Haynes's other films, it shows how one can collage together endless allusions without facile cleverness or irony. The 1970s songs, for example, are perfect recreations, and Haynes films the '70s sections with that characteristic technique of the age—the zoom. The London scenes recall something of the deft zaniness of Richard Lester, but the camera does not fixate on a style; instead, it moves around in time, bringing together a strange collision of glitter rock (à la David Bowie) and garage punk (à la Kurt Cobain) with the force of legend, not history. Allusions to *Citizen Kane* are thrown down everywhere to indicate the way that actuality (Hearst) has become legend (Kane). There is not much plot; instead, the musical numbers hold the movie together. *Velvet Goldmine* is, indeed, as much a musical as *A Star Is Born* or *Cabaret*; it is above all a celebration of the outlandish and the artificial.

Velvet Goldmine goes so far as to trace its own genealogy to Oscar Wilde, master of artifice. At the beginning, a rather dopey-looking spaceship comes down out of fakey stars to Oscar Wilde's Dublin, 1854. Little Oscar says, quite impossibly, "I want to be a pop idol." There is absolutely no narrative point to this pretitle prelude, except to indicate the presiding spirit of the film. The presiding spirit is one of self-conscious artifice. The 1970s ventriloquism is perfect, yet also continually self-conscious, reminding us that this is fiction, not history. Intertitles, lens flares, cinematic allusion, and impossible anachronisms (Bowie and Cobain as rivals and lovers) never let us forget that this is all a fiction. Like Van Sant's *Finding Forrester*, the movie frequently meditates on originality; here the issue is what rock star stole from whom. And it annotates its own self-consciousness by quoting Wilde; for example: "Every great century that produces art is so far an artificial century, and the work that seems the most natural and simple at the time is always the result of the most self-conscious effort."[16]

Like Jarman's films, *Velvet Goldmine* has to do not only with the artifice of queer sexuality (in contrast to the false "nature" of heterosexuality), but also the artifice of cinema. There is no natural sexual identity and there is no natural cinema. Jarman's last film was called *Glitterbug* (1994), and one imagines that he might have liked what Haynes did in *Velvet Goldmine*. Haynes chose as his production designer Christopher Hobbs, who worked in the same capacity on Jarman's *The Tempest* (1979) and *Edward II* (1991). *Velvet Goldmine* thus goes back not just to Wilde, but also to Derek Jarman.

From the point of view of academic criticism, most DVD commentaries are cluttered with anecdotes and tomfoolery. When Kevin Smith, Ben Affleck, and Jason Lee gather to watch *Chasing Amy* again, the boys are positively embarrassed by the sexual drama, and never stop cracking jokes. Presumably we do not listen to these kinds of commentary tracks for interpretive insight, but rather to spend more time in the company of Kevin Smith and his friends.[17] And one gets the feeling that Gus Van Sant might well have liked to talk more about *Psycho* as a cultural repetition, as an artistic artifact, but it is hard to do this with Vince Vaughan and Anne Heche yakking away (Vince asks Anne if Viggo became aroused during his nude scene). Todd Haynes, however, provides the DVD commentary to *Far from Heaven* (2002) by himself, and this absolves him from bantering with his actors or from engaging in some of the endless flattering that is now required by DVD-commentary etiquette (What a performance you gave, Julie! Only because of you, Todd). The DVD commentary for *Far from Heaven* is one of the most substantial director's commentaries I have come across, and Haynes unapologetically describes his project using terms of art and artifice.

On the commentary, Haynes quite frequently quotes out big chunks of Fassbinder and Sirk. You cannot do this with other actors around; for one thing, you don't want to make them feel stupid (Anne Heche had never seen Hitchcock's *Psycho* before she signed on to Van Sant's remake). Like Fassbinder before him, Haynes has found cinematic inspiration in the Technicolor melodramas of Douglas Sirk. Haynes explains at length how melodrama works, how the "condensation of narrative" and "transcendent artifice" of Sirkian melodrama nonetheless can lead to "social critique." *Far from Heaven* is a symphony of intense colors, and its locations are made to look like sets, not the other way around. As Haynes observes, everything is stylized—acting, language, setting. Almost all of Haynes's sources for 1950s culture—including the vexed topics of race and homosexuality—are 1950s movies. Even though some of the other cast members say that the film represents how things were in the fifties, Haynes himself is quite clear: this is how things were in 1950s films. Haynes quotes a meditation from Sirk on being "arty." "Don't be arty," someone says to the director. But Sirk replies that "arty" is a putdown that exists only in American culture and nowhere else. Sirk says that he is just trying to make "good pictures," with which Haynes wholeheartedly agrees. No reason to be afraid of art!

In *Far from Heaven,* Haynes revises Sirk even more insistently toward the artificial. One of Haynes' most substantial revisions of Sirkian melodrama is to take the Rock Hudson figure of nature and align him with art. The black groundskeeper, Raymond Deagan (Dennis Haysbert), is clearly the equivalent of the gardener in *Magnificent Obsession* (Sirk, 1954). But whereas Rock Hudson in Sirk is entirely aligned with nature, Haynes' groundskeeper is comfortable both in nature and in the world of art.[18] Raymond has even developed a preliminary theory of modern art, which he shares with Cathy (Julianne Moore) while standing before a Miró. The other people in the local art gallery seem to be interested only in playing games of cultural prestige, but for Raymond, an engagement with art is an important way of being in the world. Like *Velvet Goldmine, Far from Heaven* announces its own impossibility while it performs its own acts of ventriloquism. The fact that there is a Picasso, a Miró, and a van Gogh (*Starry Night!*) on tour in Podunkville is an outright impossibility. And when we arrive at the gallery, the local art critic is going on about a "counterfeit Rembrandt." *Far from Heaven* is Sirk all over again, but then it is not, because it has updated Sirk with far clearer representations of homosexuality and race. Like Hari in Tarkovsky's *Solaris*, and also like Haynes's *Velvet Goldmine, Far from Heaven* is a beautiful resurrection, but a self-consciously forged contrivance all the same.

Self-Reflexivity in Spike Lee and 1990s African American Film

So-called multicultural cinema might be expected to evidence social particularity—detailed cultural situatedness. Multicultural cinema might also be expected to appear in the context of realism, in which the reality of a given social collective is represented through film narrative. Yet some of the strongest examples of recent African American film combine social realism with personal, self-conscious expression. These films are not only particularized cultural representations; they are also self-reflexive cinematic representations. These films locate themselves with cultural specificity, and they also locate themselves with cinematic specificity. Spike Lee's films have always appeared as a kind of self-consciously artificial urban theater, and some of the most important African American films of the 1990s are likewise cinematically self-reflexive, knowingly artificial.

Spike Lee's films have always packed a political wallop. Lee's films deal unflinchingly with issues of race and racism and are almost inevitably set in an urban environment. Yet although Lee is interested in the various particularities of the African American experience, his approach is rarely to be characterized as simply realistic.[19] On the contrary, his films typically display an overt combination of expressionism and realism. His debut film, *She's Gotta Have It* (1986), introduces Lee's trademark device of talking directly into the camera. This in-your-face approach not only declines conventional invisibility, it goes hand in hand with politics by breaking down our comfortable expectations, along with the fourth wall. Lee's second feature film, *School Daze* (1988), adopts what is usually taken to be the most artificial genre of all, the musical, by blending the film's political comedy with full-scale song-and-dance numbers. A later work, *Clockers* (1995), is a realistically acted and plotted tale of a drug runner (the "clocker" moves between dealer and addict), but is shot as expressionistically as Soderbergh's *The Underneath*.[20] As Lee's cinematographer, Malik Sayeed, said: "We wanted to take a realistic approach to the lighting of the film. My expressionistic or interpretive elements were done with camera movement or the use of film stocks."[21] The look of *Clockers* complicates our sense of the film's realism. Lee intends to disorient a conventional take on urban squalor by showing that despite "this really messed up environment, there is still a beautiful culture within that environment."[22] The remarkable visuals decline anthropological objectivity; instead, the camera is personalized, visionary. Spike Lee's camera is able to see things that other cameras would not.

Do the Right Thing (1989) is Lee's early masterpiece of urban theater. Although it contains more social particularity than any hundred Hollywood movies, it is clearly and self-consciously staged. The dance by Tina (Rosie Perez) at the beginning is staged, for instance, on a completely artificial-looking set. She gives an incredible performance—"Fight the Power" blasting out all around—but the dance is deliberately staged as a performance. Even the actual streets in *Do the Right Thing* are dressed up to look like sets. Lee caught hell from critics for cleaning everything up ("those are the cleanest city streets I've ever seen"), but instead of being social euphemism, this is basic to the artificial, theatrical look of the movie. Lee complicates our sense that "this kind of story" is supposed to be told through handheld cameras and documentary-style realism. For music he uses not only hip-hop ghetto blasters, but also his father's Aaron Copland–like arrangements. *Do the Right Thing* refuses to be marginalized as urban realism, preferring to situate itself, through the deliberate and self-conscious use of artifice, as a cinematic construction. This self-conscious construction will continue in Spike Lee's films throughout the 1990s.

Girl 6 (1996) is Spike Lee's most deliberate examination of cinematic fantasy. Girl 6 (who has no other name, played by Theresa Randle) is a phone-sex operator who participates in the fantasies of her callers while generating substantial fantasies of her own. She wants to be a movie actress, and the film periodically shows her as the star of her own fantasies: as Dorothy Dandridge in *Carmen Jones*, as Pam Grier in a blaxploitation flick, as a member of *The Jeffersons* on television. In this way, *Girl 6* shows us the range of roles offered to black women—from the completely negative (as in this version of *The Jeffersons*, which turns into a racist sketch foreshadowing Spike Lee's later *Bamboozled* [2000]), to the more positive image of Dorothy Dandridge (whose star on the Hollywood Walk of Fame is shown at the end of *Girl 6*). Finding a good role for Girl 6 is difficult not only because of her race, but because of her sex. Moviemakers want her to take off her clothes, as we see at both the beginning and the end of the movie. But as a phone-sex operator she can at least control the fantasy somewhat; she is more of an agent and less of an object.

There are numerous cinematic references in *Girl 6*, some playful, some critical. At the beginning Girl 6 helps another woman with a crossword puzzle by suggesting the word "vertigo." And *Girl 6* is, indeed, another retelling of Hitchcock's *Vertigo*, as she changes from wig to wig and from role to role. But this is a collapsed, solitary *Vertigo*, without the Jimmy Stewart character. Vertigo also works in *Girl 6* as a metaphor. There is a somewhat strained subplot about a little girl who has fallen down an elevator shaft. Soon Girl 6 metaphorically falls into that elevator shaft herself by falling into a chaos of sexual fantasy. Whereas Hitchcock famously rendered vertigo by simultaneously zooming in and tracking back, Lee uses one of his patented "actor on the dolly" shots (so the actor moves with the camera, against a stable background) to render her fall into the abyss. Whereas the agency of Kim Novak in *Vertigo* is almost entirely opaque, *Girl 6* now shows us the interiority of a woman who is equally the product of male fantasy.

Spike Lee's cinematic references tend to be spare but pointed. In *Do the Right Thing*, Radio Raheem (Bill Nunn) wears knuckle rings with "LOVE" on one hand and "HATE" on the other. He even looks straight at the camera and gives a speech that revises Robert Mitchum's own "story of the right hand–left hand" from Charles Laughton's *Night of the Hunter* (1955).[23] In Laughton's film, Mitchum is a captivating but evil character, whereas in Spike Lee's film, Radio Raheem is a much more ambiguous figure. He tells Mookie (Spike Lee) that he loves him, and he certainly does not deserve to be strangled by the cops at the end. But Mookie yells "Hate!" when he throws a trash can through Sal's pizzeria window. In *The Night of the Hunter*, the story of love and hate shows what a lunatic Robert Mitchum's character is, but the story makes devastating sense in *Do the Right Thing*. *Do the Right Thing* closes with those famously antithetical quotations by Martin Luther King, Jr., and Malcolm X, and they carry the same complex of power and ambivalence as Radio Raheem's knuckle rings. In *Do the Right Thing*, Lee references a classic Hollywood moment, but also updates it and fills it out. The story of love and hate is no longer a great comic-book-genre speech by a noir villain, but a heartfelt monologue on racial injustice. Just as Public Enemy helps the inarticulate Raheem find the words, classic Hollywood has helped him find the images.

There are almost purely cinephilic references in early Spike Lee, such as an homage to *The Wizard of Oz* in *She's Gotta Have It*. But after *Bamboozled*, which so fiercely tears into the cultural representation of African Americans, Hollywood films are not likely to be revisited with naive admiration. In *He Got Game* (1998), for example, two of the most unlikable characters seem to be movie buffs. Jesus' Uncle Bubba (Bill Nunn) makes a number of allusions to films, referring to *The Shawshank Redemption, Escape from Alcatraz,* and *The Godfather: Part II.* Probably the most unlikable character of all, the pimp, Sweetness (Thomas Jefferson Byrd), says that the blond wig makes his call girl looks like "Kim Novak in *Vertigo*." *Vertigo*, beloved film of Chris Marker and David Lynch, is a pretty hip reference, but here it comes from the embodiment of everything corrupt and nasty in the world. If some of Lee's early works played around with movies and movie love, cinephilia turns out quite badly in *He Got Game* and *Bamboozled.*

25th Hour (2002) makes a less judgmental film reference when it puts a large poster of *Cool Hand Luke* in the apartment of drug dealer Monty Brogan (Edward Norton). The poster is ostentatiously noticeable, and present in many of the shots. On the DVD commentary, Lee says that they were looking for a '70s poster that had good graphics, that they could obtain the rights to, and that would have something to do with the movie and the character. Brogan has only twenty-five hours before he goes to prison, and the film watches him go through this last, terrifically anxious day. *Cool Hand Luke* (Rosenberg, 1967) begins with a drunken Luke (Paul Newman) sawing off the heads of parking meters. Luke spends the rest of the film trying to keep up his spirits while serving out his sentences; he is killed on his third attempt to escape. In *25th Hour,* we see in a flashback that the poster of *Cool Hand Luke* hangs in Brogan's apartment even before he is arrested: he has not bought the poster as a response to his jail sentence. For Brogan, *Cool Hand Luke* is about something larger than going to jail.

Seen somewhat more largely, then, and more self-reflexively, *25th Hour* is about being cool. Monty is named after Montgomery Clift, an actor almost as archetypically cool as James Dean. Everyone in the film tells Montgomery to keep cool: "When you are in jail, don't lose your temper until it is time to lose your temper." But everyone in the film is angry underneath; everyone is about to lose control. We are supposed to see the parallels between the cool stock-broker, the drug dealer, and the geeky English teacher, Jacob (Philip Seymour Hoffman), who is coming unglued over a high school student. Jacob is classi-cally uncool, but in the end it doesn't matter. All three men are lost in anger, lust, and obsession. And in this post-9/11 New York, hell is all around them.

At the end of *25th Hour* Montgomery asks his friends to beat him up so he won't be pretty in jail. Then as his father drives him to jail, Montgomery imagines an alternative fantasy life, one in which he does not report to jail, and instead starts a new life elsewhere, raising a family, growing old. As we watch the face of battered Edward Norton for the last ten minutes, we cannot help but recall his equally smashed-up face in *Fight Club* (Fincher, 1999). There the ultracool Brad Pitt starts up a comic-book revolution, and Edward Norton follows along. *25th Hour* consumes the cool, battered Edward Norton of *Fight Club*, and also the white supremacist Edward Norton of *American History X* (Kaye, 1998; Montgomery unleashes a racist diatribe in a bathroom in Lee's film) to critique the fundamental 1990s cinematic aesthetic of cool. When the city is wrenched apart in so many directions, and when there is a moon crater in part of it, nobody is really all that cool. *25th Hour* is a story about greed and anger, but it is also a substantial critique of recent American film.

After *Do the Right Thing*, Spike Lee's most powerful film in the 1990s is prob-ably *Summer of Sam* (1999). *Summer of Sam* leaves a rather Godardian impres-sion, in that it combines actuality and fictiveness with extraordinary effect. *Summer of Sam* shows how badly people in New York City responded to the Son of Sam killings during the record-setting summer heat of 1977. Vigilante squads scoured neighborhoods for suspicious looking undesirables. *Summer of Sam* tells a historical narrative, then, but in a completely self-conscious form. For this is nothing other than a Martin Scorsese movie.

Scorsese has always been one of the avowed influences on Lee, one of the few directors who were likely to come up in an interview with Spike Lee. In 1995 Scorsese gave over *Clockers* to Lee so that the older director could pursue *Casino*. *Summer of Sam* concentrates largely on an Italian American neighbor-hood, and the sparring macho dialogues alone will recall many similar scenes in Scorsese. But the film is set in 1977, during the decade in which Scorsese himself emerged as a major filmmaker. Thus *Summer of Sam* cannot fail to recall those landmark films of the 1970s, *Mean Streets* (1973) and *Taxi Driver* (1976). The crazy voice-over of David Berkowitz, although taken from his letters, cannot help but recall the homicidal insanity in the voice-over of Travis Bickle. Just as Bickle suddenly appears in a mohawk toward the end of *Taxi Driver*, the local punk, Richie (Adrian Brody), changes his spiked haircut to a mohawk as the film builds towards its climax. The scene in which Vinny (John Leguizamo) and Ruby (Jennifer Esposito) sleep with other people in an uptown orgy, and then Vinny blows up at Ruby with hypocritical jealousy, is a classic scene of Scorsesean male rage, straight out of *Raging Bull* (1980). Lee even underlines the Scorsesean context with a few spare but precise visual references: he puts a camera on the front fender of a moving car for an exact recollection of *Taxi Driver*; he quickly pushes the camera at people several times in a signature Scorsesean move; he uses a steadicam for a dramatic, long-take entrance into a club, as in *Goodfellas* (1990); after Vinny and Ruby enter the club for the first time, they dance in slow motion, then come back to their table slowed down—the overcranking is once again classic Scorsese. And the use of rock-and-roll music throughout to both date and annotate the events cannot but help recall films such as *Goodfellas* and *Casino*.

But *Summer of Sam* implodes Scorsesean violence, breaking the genre. Scorsese's films are often based on true stories, but none of them, not even *Gangs of New York*, has the incredibly awkward facticity of *Summer of Sam*. It is disturbing to watch a Scorsesean bloodbath, but none of his are as disturbing as watching a character called David Berkowitz shoot people in their cars. Rather as Godard pushed the genre of spy thriller beyond our expectations with the torture scene in *Le Petit soldat* (1963), Lee takes a Scorsesean morality play and freaks it out with actuality. We know that "violence is bad" is the message in *Gangs of New York*—why don't people just get along? But the nasty temper of Bob the Butcher seems a Shakespearean fiction compared to the insane howlings of Berkowitz. Lee works through the historical elements self-consciously; he does not attempt a documentary. A documentary effect is gained by having Jimmy Breslin, to whom Berkowitz wrote his letter, appear at the beginning and end of the film with contemporary comments. Yet Lee himself plays a 1977 television reporter, a portrayal that can only shatter any realist illusion. The music sometimes works for historical atmosphere, but is often even more jarring than anything in Scorsese, as when Abba accompanies Vinny and Ruby's most vicious argument.

Lee's film does not look any more real than a Scorsese film, but it does have a reality effect that pushes Scorsesean violence into an extraordinarily disturbing place. The intensity and pace of a Scorsese film (*Raging Bull, Goodfellas, Casino, Gangs of New York*) marks a dramatic, intense life, not a Spielbergian roller coaster, but *Summer of Sam* turns that same intensity into cinematic horror by naming that blood as death's blood in a way that few American films ever will. Lee's film does not just critique violence, as Scorsese's films also do; it critiques violent movies such as Scorsese's.

Other landmark African American films of the 1990s also combine cultural specificity with cinematic self-reflexivity. In an earlier chapter, I mentioned Julie Dash's *Daughters of the Dust* (1990), which brought before our eyes a very particular piece of American society and history at the same time that it never ceased to comment on its own status as a cinematic artifact. In what remains of this section I will look briefly at films by four other African American directors, Charles Burnett, John Singleton, Kasi Lemmons, and Mario Van Peebles.

Charles Burnett's *To Sleep with Anger* (1990) melds realism and allegory in one of the most arresting American films of the nineties. Henry (Danny Glover) comes to visit and also to annoy his relatives, and the narrative can be understood as a rather quotidian representation of family life in tension and crisis. Yet because *To Sleep with Anger* represents Henry as the localized cause of the family's difficulties, it makes one read Henry not just as an annoying in-law, but as the devil himself. The film crosscuts between coincidences (a woman giving birth in a hospital, a man dying in a hospital), stages the climactic crisis in a thunderstorm, and shows us various other telepathic moments. Hence the film moves back and forth between a realistic description of several generations in an African American family, and a magically framed, self-consciously constructed allegory of seduction, ruin, and salvation.

The beginning and end of *To Sleep With Anger* show most clearly the self-consciousness of the film. During the title sequence we see a carefully posed Gideon (Paul Butler) sitting in a chair, then the camera pans over to a picture of a woman (perhaps his mother) and finally down to a bowl of fruit on the table. The fruit catches fire. We are obliged such to read such a sequence allegorically and self-reflexively. There is a posed man, a photographed woman, and a still life — art is framed three times. But then everything starts burning. The fires of hell burns all through this film — the anger at the heart of African American experience, the evil brought by the devil. As the final credits roll, a boy who has so far been making only noise on his trumpet suddenly plays not just well but like a seasoned jazz professional. It is another magical, impossible artistic moment, but this time in the direction of salvation. The substance of *To Sleep With Anger* can be read in multiple ways: as a biblical allegory, as an amusing parable, as a symbolic memory of slavery and oppression, as a relatively realistic story of the relative who would not leave. The opening and closing credits are the most obvious ways that *To Sleep With Anger* frames its artful and artificial construction, inviting us to read the film as a painting or to hear it as a jazz melody, with all the various resonances and ambiguities that such reading and such listening imply.

Kasi Lemmons presents a historically and culturally specific environment in her critically acclaimed *Eve's Bayou* (1997).[24] Some of the characters speak Cajun French, while the sixties costumes and the surrounding swamp and forest give the film a very particularized sensibility. Yet the film is also relentlessly self-reflexive. Themes of artistry and expression go hand in hand with the narratives of childhood tumult and marital infidelity. Men tend to be artists—Harry, a character played by Branford Marsalis, is a photographer, and Julian Grayraven (Vondie Curtis-Hall) is a painter. In her turn, Aunt Mozelle (Debbi Morgan) plays the piano, but more importantly she is a visionary. Whereas the men practice more recognizable and institutionalized forms of art—with which we might include the physician Louis (Samuel L. Jackson)—the women often see into things, into the past and into the future. The telepathic women are like film projectors, and this ability to see clairvoyantly is clearly aligned with the ability to make films. Eve's closing monologue makes the parallel most memorably:

> Like others before me, I have the gift of sight, but the truth changes color depending on the light. And tomorrow can be clearer than yesterday. Memory is a selection of images, some elusive, others printed indelibly on the brain. Each image is like a thread, each thread woven together to make a tapestry of intricate texture, and the tapestry tells a story, and the story is our past.

With this feminine imagery of creation, Eve speaks for the director, who weaves and splices images together. Some moments are printed "indelibly," vividly, perfectly true, and other moments shift and change in the light. Film's photographed images are strong, and we receive them as a "gift," but they turn between presence and absence, sun and shadow, reality and ghost.

John Singleton's *Rosewood* (1997) presents itself as "based on a true story," but immediately gives signals that it will blend cinematic self-consciousness with historical reconstruction. Even the theme music changes, from a very contemporary mix to folk song, as we are given our first look at the houses of the town. At bottom, *Rosewood* is a powerfully transformed western. When the stranger, Mr. Mann (Ving Rhames), comes to town, riding a horse and chomping a thin cigar, we cannot help but think that this a kind of Clint Eastwood western, in which the mysterious lone rider will save the town from its difficulties. Rosewood happens to be in Florida, and an occasional car drives down these 1930s streets. But there are also traditional western genre indications all around: the sheriff, the horses, the people who need saving, the oppressors, the hero. In a Clint Eastwood film like *Pale Rider* (Eastwood, 1985), the stranger saves the poor tin-pan miners from the corrupt industrialized miners downstream. Meanwhile both the daughter and the mother of a local household fall in love with him, but he rides mysteriously away at the end of the film.

Mr. Mann is equally mysterious, although more human in his heroism. Yet he remains a cinematic entity, not a realistic one, and Ving Rhames brings with him the tough-guy machismo from previous roles in films like *Pulp Fiction*. Mr. Mann is more compassionate than the Pale Rider, and he eventually marries the daughter in the local household. Unlike the Pale Rider, he cannot kill twenty or thirty men by himself. "There's no way in the world," he says, "one man got enough bullets for all them crackers." Yet although more realistic than the Pale Rider in these respects, Mr. Mann is also shown as impossibly heroic. When the lynch mob tries to hang him, he is so strong that he hangs for minutes without strangling or breaking his neck. Eventually the mob is distracted, and he cuts himself down from the noose. John Williams's music at the end breaks into its most sentimental strains (which it never does in *Schindler's List*), so that the heroism surrounding this historical disaster is underscored in the most readily identifiable cinematic manner. The combination of realistic detail with cinematic self-consciousness in *Rosewood* is thoroughgoing and fascinating.

Mario Van Peebles's *Posse* (1993) is a much more direct revision of a cowboy movie. *Posse* educates the audience about basic historical facts; an end title says, "Although ignored by Hollywood and most history books, the memory of the more than 8,000 Black cowboys that roamed the early West lives on." At the same time that *Posse* reminds us of these black cowboys and black communities, it also puts these cowboys into an entirely recognizable set of generic fights and rides across the range. The film does not attempt to do real history; on the contrary, it teaches its history lesson by co-opting one generic sequence after another. Hence even though the scenes themselves are not innovative in their dialogue or narrative, the mere fact that black men stand in for all the usual white people is a powerful visual statement in itself. The shootout between blacks and whites at the end is a rather routine bit of violence, but a much more substantial showdown, nevertheless, than the usual good guys versus bad guys.

Van Peebles situates his film in cinematic history through very effective cinephilic casting. Van Peebles is the son of Melvin Van Peebles, one of the founding fathers of black filmmaking.[25] In *Posse*, Van Peebles casts his father, Melvin Van Peebles, the director of *Sweet Sweetback's Baadasssss Song* (1971), as his own character's father. By casting his father in this role, Van Peebles states figuratively that his film, too, is indebted to the films of the pioneers. Pam Grier, one of the greatest blaxploitation stars, is cast in a small part in *Posse*, although it would later be Tarantino in *Jackie Brown* (1997) who would develop her cinephilic presence most completely. The strongest cinephilic gesture of all occurs when Van Peebles frames *Posse* with the eighty-year-old Woody Strode, an African American actor who appeared in several westerns by John Ford. Strode's most significant acting role was undoubtedly as the title figure in Ford's *Sergeant Rutledge* (1960). In 1968, Sergio Leone put Strode at the beginning of *Once Upon a Time in the West* as his own cinephilic reference to all the westerns he was about to remake. For Woody Strode to introduce and conclude this black-focused western and American history lesson stands as an instructive and poignant act of self-reflexivity and positioning.

John Sayles and Indie Naturalism

Spike Lee, Van Sant, Korine, and Todd Haynes all happily complicate the relationship between realism and artifice, between nature and art. But there is an important strand of American independent filmmaking that wants only to rest in nature, and so avoid these essentially cinematic complications. John Sayles is surely the most significant independent filmmaker who has chosen to follow the path of nature. His films are celebrated for their naturalism, their detail, their multiculturalism. But this naturalism is extraordinarily problematic if thought through in any detail. In this final section, I will provide some of that detailed thinking, and this will lead us directly to the outright polemics of my last chapter. Saylesian naturalism is just as problematic a contribution to American cinema as Hollywood superficiality. Sayles's films look *situated;* the social landscape of these films is uniquely particularized in American film. Yet Sayles's films refuse to identify themselves as films. In fact, these films go out of their way to put down representation and artifice. The daily film reviewers fall over themselves to praise Sayles, whose films are undoubtedly more interesting than most mall movies. But compared to the best movies from around the world, which most American film reviewers will never review, Sayles's films are intellectually dubious. The misplaced emphases in Sayles' filmmaking are apparent from the very beginning.

John Sayles's career as a film director began with *Return of the Secaucus Seven* (1979), which he funded with money made from his novels and short stories. Many would agree with Gavin Smith's description of this film as "a milestone in the ongoing history of American independent filmmaking." Smith continues, "*Return of the Secaucus Seven* was a critical and commercial success and established Sayles as one of the most promising writer-directors of his generation."[26] *Return of the Secaucus Seven* foreshadows many of Sayles's concerns in later works, as it passes easily from natural surroundings (swimming naked in a forest) to frank discussions of society and politics. *Secaucus Seven* also looks forward to an intentionally anticinematic impulse in Sayles.

> The one thing I always try to achieve is that when people leave the theater, I want them to be talking about human beings, about their own lives and the lives of other people they know or could know, rather than thinking, "Oh, that was like *Citizen Kane*," or, "That was like *Raiders of the Lost Ark*." The references in the movies are references to historical things or personal things, not references to other movies.[27]

Very methodically, year after year, Sayles tries to make films disappear. He attacks not just the falseness of Hollywood, but the falseness of movies. He says in an interview that his model for *Return of the Secaucus Seven* was Altman's *Nashville* (1975), but it does not seem to matter that Altman's film, unlike *Secaucus Seven*, self-consciously foregrounds the issues of documentary and celebrity. Throughout his career, Sayles repeatedly invokes other movies to make the impossible point that the artifice you see before you is reality, not a movie.

Early on in *Secaucus Seven*, for instance, the characters all go to a Restoration comedy, which almost everyone agrees is quite bad. It is bad because it is badly acted, overplayed, and theatrical. The actress they visit afterward is also characterized as "stagey," which, in fact, she is, both onstage and in her dressing room. What Sayles wants us to conclude is that his story is, by contrast, "real," untheatrical. This is a dangerous comparison, since Sayles's actors (which is what they are) perform giant hunks of obviously written dialogue before a camera that (constrained by budget) hardly ever moves. Sayles, unlike his predecessors Altman and Cassavetes, wants to get at real life by working against theatricality.

In his films, Sayles repeatedly puts down television as a source of false, empty vision. Television programs offer us false dreams and oversimplifications. We are always to understand that Sayles's films are far truer and more complicated. This contrast, once again, is always hard to believe, since Sayles films manage to look like television programs — maybe something on PBS — in their deadpan shot–reverse shot editing and in their "good," completely functional dialogue. In *The Brother from Another Planet* (1984), television is seen to be as addictive and mind-numbing as video games. The Brother (Joe Morton) himself makes no particular judgment, and he happily repairs the broken game machines, but the movie makes an obvious judgment on these time wasters. By contrast, Sayles's own movie wants to be exempt from this critique, since it claims access to something much closer to the truth. The Brother has an eyeball that he uses as a VCR, to record things, and in a climactic scene he makes a rich white drug dealer look at the body of a black addict. My vision, my magic eyeball, tells us true things, says the movie, that television does not.

City of Hope (1991) is the ironic television slogan for a city much more complicated than slogans. We see a poster with these words on it, and we are supposed to see that no such bumper sticker can summarize the manifold particularity of Los Angeles. A main character in the film is a television store, where all the blaring televisions shout out with Mad Anthony's hyperactive sales pitch. There is also an authentically crazy person, who goes around repeating phrases and slogans from television. At the end, this mentally ill person suddenly starts saying, "Help, we need help, we need help," as we see once and for all that his television slogans and the "City of Hope" poster must give way to a deeper truth. But the idea that Sayles can think more deeply simply because his characters speak paragraphs instead of slogans is pretty dubious. Why is it that Godard matches the slogans of television with his own slogans, fragments, and posters? If "more talking" is better, then we had better just write books instead of making movies. Since films are so caught up in what films are — in representation, in buying and selling — Godard continually critiques his own superiority to television or books or film. Sayles never gives the appearance of thinking through what he is indicating about representation or argument.

Sayles's flight from cinematic self-consciousness is evidenced most clearly, perhaps, in *Passion Fish* (1992). *Passion Fish* is another version of Bergman's *Persona*, in which a nurse helps a sick actress recover. But Sayles mainly sees the relationship as having to do with ironies of power, not with ideas about theatricality. The irony is that the "servant" is the healthy one, and the "master" is debilitated. As Sayles puts it: "My idea was like *Persona* where there was a woman in a wheelchair in some kind of power struggle that turns out to be friendly. And I always felt in the American version, they would be different races, the woman who was pushing the wheelchair around would be black. In my experience in hospitals, that was pretty much the story."[28]

In *Persona,* the fact that Elizabeth Vogler (Liv Ullmann) is an actress makes theatricality an overwhelming theme; everything in the film turns on issues of artifice, performance, and reality. *Persona* is one of the key documents of cinematic modernism, and from time to time we see images of film projected and burning. Thus the psychological conundrum—who is who?—is mapped onto questions of cinematic identity. But Sayles has no interest in the cinematic questions; he wants to look only at the power struggle of patient to caregiver. May-Alice (Mary McDonnell) is a soap-opera actress in Sayles's film apparently only to allow him to cast someone pretty in the part. As a celebrity, she can now become more self-righteously a bitch than an ordinary woman. But compared to the complications of *Persona,* issues of role-playing and theatricality seem a thousand miles away here. *Passion Fish* stages only an obvious contrast between the glamorized problems of television soap operas and the real-life problems of the people in Louisiana Cajun country. Television is silly, and the outdoors is good. May-Alice makes no progress while sitting inside, watching television, and drinking, whereas going outside is a good thing. According to Sayles,

> When you're looking at TV you're not looking at anything else. She's closed the blinds. She's on the lawn for two seconds and then the nurse carries her in. She doesn't go out after that. But then she's starting to resee something that she ignored and wanted to get away from when she was a kid, which is why I had her get back into photography. And eventually that leads to her coming back to the world, hoping to be happy again.[29]

May-Alice becomes interested in photography during her recovery, but Sayles almost goes out of his way to make sure that there is nothing self-conscious about that. In his outline above, photography stands for antinarcissism; taking pictures means looking at what is around oneself. Another director might stress the fact that the female object of photography, the soap-opera actress, has now become the master of her medium, the subject. But photography in *Passion Fish* seems merely an interchangeable occupation that allows May-Alice to take some pleasure in life. Sayles is mostly subtle; he has no speech in which his heroine says: "I'm glad I'm outside on the dock watching the beauties of nature instead of sitting around watching the fakeries of American TV." But when a producer comes to offer May-Alice a chance to return to her role on television, she refuses, and the soap-opera plot sounds sillier than ever (one character, whose presence looms large in the soap-opera plot, is a space alien). So she refuses television, and then shares that refusal later with Chantelle (Alfre Woodard) in a boat out in the middle of a river.

Lone Star (1996) is Sayles's anti-*Solaris*, in which he attempts to show most decisively that the cinema does not exist. There are numerous discussions in the film about the way that history is constructed differently, depending on who tells it; the teachers at a school debate traditional and revisionist histories of Texas. Yet the film itself offers complete access to a history that is incontestable. One of Sayles's most striking visual effects in this film is the way that flashbacks occur simply by panning, without any dissolve or cut whatsoever. If a character tells a story about Buddy Deeds (Matthew McConaughey) in the bar, the camera just pans from that character straight over to Buddy, moving from present to past without a boundary. Sayles explains his technique: "I wanted the past, those stories about his father, to be so much more present than when you play a harp and do the lap dissolve."[30] Playing a harp certainly does seem absurd, but at the same time it does insist on the difference between past and present by implying that it takes divine power to cross the divide.

But despite the contested histories — of Texas and of peoples — that fathers and teachers pass on to sons and students, history in Sayles's film seems completely accessible. The flashbacks themselves are all implied to be the truth; no one's memory is faulty. When we learn the true story at the end, there are two witnesses to supply the truth, and both apparently agree. There are now two stories in the world, the true story and the cover story, but we know the truth, and there is no ambiguity at all about that. The final flashback is rendered more subjectively than the others, in that dialogue vanishes from the sound track. Yet this effect, finally, does not seem to imply that this memory is distorted, but instead the soundlessness underlines the drama of crisis and revelation. All other flashbacks are visualized as quite simply the truth — this is what happened.

Hand in hand with our complete access to history is an anti-*Solaris* story. Whereas in *Solaris* the past returns in a hopelessly ungraspable ghost, in *Lone Star* Sheriff Sam Deeds (Chris Cooper) and Pilar Cruz (Elizabeth Peña) renew their childhood love as if nothing has changed whatsoever. They were child-hood lovers, but could not marry because of the racial prejudices of their par-ents. Now that their marriages to other people are over, due to death and di-vorce, they get back together. After they make love, Pilar says that it "feels the same." They start over exactly where they left off. A major obstacle is thrown up at the end, however, when they find out that Buddy was also her father, which makes her Sam's half-sister. Yet she dismisses this problem, and our impression is that they will be able to fulfill the romantic promise of their youth.[31] It is telling that Sayles stages this last scene in a dilapidated drive-in theater, in the place where they were torn from each other's arms. The screen is now an empty board, and the parking lot is overgrown with green weeds and trees. What a perfect emblem for a Sayles film!—nature wins out over artificial cinema. Sam Deeds's ex-wife, Bunny (Frances McDormand) is a hyperactive Dallas Cowboys fan, straight out of a Coen brothers movie. No wonder Sam left her—the television-addicted, sports-obsessed crazy woman.[32] How much better to sit in the quiet overgrown parking lot with a far more naturalistic actress and rekindle our childhood love. Let the movie screen stay an empty wooden board, since the divine contrivance known as a movie camera does not exist anyway.

Sunshine State (2002) makes many of the same uncritical gestures, but it does allow the theatrical to survive to some extent. Like "City of Hope," "The Sun-shine State" is another idealistic slogan that we are supposed to see through. A few moments into the film we see a man trying to hang himself in the for-est, and his repeated suicide attempts make it clear that all is not sunshine on (the pointedly named) Plantation Island. The man's wife, Francine Pick-ney (Mary Steenburgen), spends her days promoting the island at the mall and at a parade. But these performances take place under a mask; she hates the fact that she has to "invent a tradition." The developers and the politicians are mostly pretty evil and corrupt, as in *City of Hope* and Victorian melodrama, although a real estate agent, Jack Meadows (Timothy Hutton), seems like a reasonable person (the name helps). As in *Passion Fish*, nature helps recon-cile opposites, and Jack rides down a lovely river with one of the prospective sellers, Marly Temple (Edie Falco). For the moment, developer and denizen cease their struggle.

Even though the stage villains and the hypocrisy must give way to truth and complex reality, theatricality still survives intact in *Sunshine State*. Whereas the theatre seemed like the repository of staged fakiness in *Secaucus Seven*, *Sunshine State* grants it respectability. At least it would seem so. Marly

Temple's mother, Delia (Jane Alexander), has run a community theater on the island for twenty-five years. She allows troubled youth to help her work on her plays, and she is clearly not in the business for the money. So she is an independent, socially conscious artist, just like John Sayles. When introduced to us, she is giving a long monologue from *As I Lay Dying*, which she has adapted for the stage from Faulkner's novel. We have just heard a completely reactionary monologue from her husband (where he talks about all the things that "aren't natural"), then we hear this staged monologue from Delia, after which she tells her fellow players to "freeze yourself into an interesting but comfortable position" during her monologue. It is possible that we are supposed to be a bit skeptical about her project, but I do not think so. Elsewhere she seems permanently wise and authentic, even if strangely matched with her reactionary husband. It is later noted that two of Delia's most formidable productions were *Mother Courage* and *Electra*. Surely Sayles's accommodating, entirely transparent film wants to credit itself by allowing this socially conscious woman to perform Brecht. But the abyss between Brecht and Sayles is instructive. Brecht and Sayles are both socially conscious and even didactic, but only Brecht is medium-conscious. To my mind, that difference amounts to everything.

Sayles is not the only director, of course, who works through cinematic naturalism, and I will close this section by looking at a few more films. Some share Sayles's belief that the camera can simply be set aside to better represent life as it is lived, but others demonstrate that the most convincing naturalism is often obtained through self-reflexivity and self-conscious artifice.

A director who shares Sayles's penchant for naturalism is Victor Nunez. *Ruby in Paradise* (1993), which won the Sundance Grand Jury Prize in 1993, shows a young woman making her way alone in Panama City, Florida. The local scenery and people are depicted in some detail: we see the Indian workers at the hotel; we watch women fold and press sheets at a local laundry. The seasons change from the emptiness of winter to the hubbub of spring break. There are postcard-like pictures of the sunset beach, but also some not very glamorous shots of strip malls and highways. Ruby (Ashley Judd) has moved down from Tennessee, and she just tries to get by.

Ruby in Paradise shows us these realistic details in a low-key manner, but the naturalism is conflated with didacticism and blatant structure. Compared to that of a Hollywood detective thriller, the plot here seems nearly to have vanished, yet the constructedness of the narrative becomes more and more palpable nonetheless. For example, Ruby has two choices for candidate boyfriends, and they contrast with one another like night and day. One deals in the stock market and is a notorious womanizer. Eventually he nearly rapes her, and since he is the boss's son, he has her fired from her job. As a complete contrast, the other man works in an agricultural concern, gives her plant advice, reads books, and has lots of ideas about the environment. The two men form a transparent opposition—sleazy goldmonger versus literary gardener.

The movie resolves the opposition somewhat interestingly, but only by invoking more didacticism. Eventually Ruby gets her job back, and the sleazeball apologizes; he is not completely evil, and he is not allowed to wreck her life. While Rudy is out of work she distances herself from the gardener; she wants to have a job, she says, before she throws herself deeper into a relationship. But eventually she comes to find his philosophizing too negative, and ends up by herself, yet happily so. We discover, then, a quietly feminist didacticism that works outside of either of these potential boyfriends, and that is associated with the divorced female storekeeper. Managing the store by herself, the owner embodies a solitary female strength, although her lesbianism is implied when we see her exchanging loaded glances with other women at a convention. In a summary speech at the end, she tells Ruby that she didn't really need to hire her, but saw something in Ruby, a "fire," a desire, that she recognized from her own youth.

Thus, female independence and solidarity win out over male literariness. Ruby's desire to say that it is OK to work in this store (the critical gardener wonders how she can) and to think that these things are OK is just like the movie's desire—to merely show things as they are, with affection and without judgment. But the film's naturalism—the impulse to let things be—is undermined by its own ideas and constructions. *Ruby in Paradise* wants to appear as an account of a typical young woman's life while pretending that it isn't making one highly tendentious choice after another.

Victor Nunez's second film, *Ulee's Gold* (1997), is equally unwilling to show us "real life" without legible plot conventions. Ulee (Peter Fonda) is a beekeeper, and there are numerous scenes of him working at his job, and also at home with his family. But a movie plot is called for: two scruffy hoodlums make Ulee tell them where money from an armed robbery is stashed. Peter Fonda does indeed give a refreshingly naturalistic performance, but in the midst of a gangster movie. The hoods even come over to Fonda's home and wave their guns around in the living room. When they threaten the family, we find ourselves in a less melodramatic version of *Desperate Hours* (Wyler, 1955) or *Cape Fear* (J. Lee Thompson, 1962). To show pictures of Ulee working with bees in the woods apparently does not seem enough to justify a contemporary American movie with a star, so Fonda is flung into a moderated version of a cops-and-robbers plot.

That there is a plot at all might be thought problematic. Does not the need to explain things—sequentially, by cause and effect—stand at odds with all the attempts at naturalism? Everything makes sense from the perspective of cinematic genre and convention, even while characters deliver their quite credibly authentic speeches in an unglamorously lit world. Even the music participates in a contradictory way. It refuses to annotate "suspense" in any conventional way during the gangster sequences—that would be too vulgar. But it is happy to support the understatement of the film with New Age piano and quietly melancholy flutes. This music does not annotate Hollywood-style, but it is still a much more legible, conventional choice than no music at all. In the end, after the mess of the hoods (who stab Ulee but are caught), there is a friendly, smiling scene of the family back in the house. And Ulee goes up to dinner with his new female doctor friend for about the most conventional ending imaginable. The final shot then takes us into the woody swamp to as-sure us, once and for all, that all this is "nature." *Ulee's Gold* and *Ruby in Paradise* look pretty good compared with standard Hollywood fare, but they are not forthcoming about their contradictory deployment of the natural and the ar-tificial. Unconscious naturalism is too incoherent to think about, and calls for an equally unconscious spectator.

By contrast, one of the most convincingly naturalistic films of recent years, Kimberly Peirce's *Boys Don't Cry* (1999), is also one of the most self-reflexive. *Boys Don't Cry* tells us the "true story" of Brandon Teena (Teena Brandon), a Nebraska woman who chose to live her life as a man, and who was eventually murdered. The film's mise-en-scène often obeys the classic tenets of cinematic realism: scenes are shot on location, and a detailed sense of rural Nebraska is imparted; relatively unknown actors are used (Chloe Sevigny still early in her career); there is not much shape to the narrative, other than to give one the impression that Brandon repeatedly "fucks up." There is no Hollywood genre anywhere around, even though guns come out in a late sequence. When the film tells us the fates of the various protagonists at the end, it is not too hard to think back and say, that *was* a true story.

On the other hand, the film is shot subjectively, and the story is told very thematically. Much of the film takes place at night. Rock-and-roll music not only provides historical detail, but also underscores the intoxicating, halluci-natory quality of these characters' lives. The young people live for the night, to escape the boredom of the day. They drink and speed around in cars. The film shows what an imaginative landscape the characters live in through blurred streetlights, a sudden whiting out of the screen, and speeded-up motion. Nearly all the scenes combine on-location detail with determinedly expressionistic light, especially at night. Brandon (Hilary Swank) tells the police that he has a "sexual identity crisis," and the movie sets us down in a world that is fluid, dreamlike, and only occasionally holds still. As one of his colleagues puts it, "You don't need drugs. You just hallucinate twenty-four hours a day."

The film is also relentlessly self-conscious. It argues, visually, that a crisis of sexual identity is also a crisis of imagery. Nearly every sequence is worked out as a discussion of looking and celebrity — of film, in other words. The very first scene shows Brandon's brother cutting his hair; he calls him a "superstar." Brandon is an actress-actor, putting on a show and lying through the whole film. He makes his first appearance at a roller-skating rink, beneath rotating disco lights. One of his lies is that his mother lives with his sister in Hollywood; his sister is supposedly a model. We watch him looking in the mirror, making himself up. He falls in love with Lana (Chloe Sevigny) while watching her sing karaoke; later they dream of going to Memphis and making money by singing karaoke. What is on television is often briefly shown to us, and this allows us to see the world of images in which all of them are immersed. For the last half of the movie Brandon takes photographs of everyone with his Polaroid; when he is finally found out, he burns the photographs.

Who is he? What should he look like? The film's self-conscious and expressionistic elements are perfectly appropriate to the tumultuous life we see before us. These elements not only support the imaginative world of the protagonist and all its characters, but also authenticate the discourse of naturalism by cinematic self-consciousness. In one of the most surrealistically staged scenes, Lana prepares to tell her mother that she has seen for herself that Brandon is a male (which she has not). She rehearses the scene with Brandon in her bedroom, but then the lighting and sound change, and we are suddenly in the living room again, with everyone swearing at Brandon. Brandon and Lana seem to have teleported from private to public with no visible editing. As the chaos ensues, we see another Brandon appear in a spotlight, looking on. The scene wants to get at psychological division, but in a way that is self-consciously staged. Brandon's sexual dilemma has not come upon him out of nowhere, but in a world of intoxicating imagery. The story is true, and told naturalistically in many respects, but all the more convincingly for its self-consciousness. Cinematic naturalism is grounded in both detail and self-reflexivity. The American film of the 1990s that pretends that this has not been staged, that this is not a film, represents naivete, not the world.

In the next and final chapter, I will argue that self-reflexivity in contemporary American film is necessary not only because this is film, but also because this is American film. In our age of American imperialism, American film must confess not only its mode of representation, but also it provenance, its place of origin. American film must acknowledge its place in the global system. One of the many brilliant aspects of Van Sant's *Gerry* (2002) is that it refuses to moan and coo over nature's sublimities. The landscape that the two men walk through is not particularly anything—not beautiful, not sublime, not symbolic—just endless. The landscape is also completely impossible, in that the two men will go to sleep in one place and wake up somewhere else. The different landscapes they walk through—marching relentlessly, silently —are palpably too different; the spaces have been brought together by magic. And indeed, the end credits observe that the film has been shot partly in Utah, partly in Death Valley, and partly in Argentina. In *Gerry*, the American desert, which stands at the heart of the western and so many other American films, is blown up into unrelated, meaningless parcels of land. The only plausible nature that remains in American film is an impossible nature.

Situating American Film in Godard, Jarmusch, and Scorsese 8

Nonvirtual America in a Virtual Age

This book's presiding spirits have been Andrei Tarkovsky and Jean-Luc Godard. These two masters may seem to approach film from entirely opposite directions, but as the years go by it becomes more and more apparent that this is not the case. Descriptions of Godard's most recent films—meditative, mystical, full of beautiful pictures—make it look as though Godard has developed through time into another kind of Tarkovsky. If I have shown that Tarkovsky is often as modern, as self-reflexive, and as knowing about his medium as Godard, then let me also emphasize the degree to which films like Godard's *Hélas pour moi* (1993) and *JLG/JLG* (1995) are brooding and philosophizing, quite close to the borders of Tarkovsky's cinematic zone. Both directors show us characters wandering around with books; in either case, there are discussions about time, life, and memory. Both directors constantly think about the relationship of film to the other arts while showing their immense and ongoing love for the possibilities of cinema.

Yet perhaps their clearest commonality is the way that their works show that the beauty of film is always juxtaposed with the wretched violences of human history. The wars that ravaged both France and Russia in the twentieth century haunt nearly all of their films; the wars that mankind is capable of waging flings the shadow further. The boxcars in Tarkovsky's *Stalker* and the nuclear apocalypse in *The Sacrifice* have their counterparts in the Vietnam of Godard's *Weekend* and the Yugoslavia of *For Ever Mozart*. The devotion to film, the love of film, is always counterbalanced by a sense of the weightlessness of film. The Solaris effect, the absent presence of film, is not only a psychological event, or a trick of visual perception, since it is at bottom a historical understanding.

The barely perceptible plot of Godard's *In Praise of Love* (*Éloge de l'amour*, 2001) concerns Hollywood producers who are negotiating for the rights to tell the story of a French resistance fighter. The film pretends to find its occasion by discussing the four stages of love, but this is a false lead.[1] The narrative of love is soon replaced by the narratives of history and of cinema. The recurring idea in the film is that America has no history of its own and so must purchase the histories of others. This political criticism is leveled most explicitly at Steven Spielberg and his production of *Schindler's List*, but it is aimed more broadly at all Hollywood filmmaking.

In the late 1950s, Godard and the rest of his colleagues at *Cahiers du cinéma* famously rerouted our sense of the cinematic pantheon by juxtaposing Ingmar Bergman with Nicholas Ray, and Robert Bresson with Howard Hawks, but for some time now Godard has shown no patience whatsoever with Hollywood's imperialism. When he films a scene in front of side-by-side posters of Bresson's *Pickpocket* and the Wachowski brothers' *The Matrix*, it is very clear which film he sees as the thief. Later on a woman reads quotes from Bresson's *Notes on Cinematography* ("be sure to have exhausted everything that you can communicate through immobility and silence" [p. 115; my translation]) while someone notes that there is an attempt to translate *The Matrix* into Breton (120; parenthetical page numbers are to *Éloge de l'amour: Phrases* by Godard).[2] When this last remark is spoken, the screen splits into two so that ocean waves seem to occupy the same sunset orange room as a man. In this manner, Godard modestly but pointedly shows us his "special effects." Godard's effects consist of digitally altered color and conventionally simple dissolves, and each effect stands as a silent comment on the world-beating, hyperactive *Matrix*, whose end-of-the-world spectacle did indeed conquer the global world market.

What Godard always emphasizes, in contrast to Tarkovsky, is the money behind art, behind film. Godard and Tarkovsky are equally programmatic about philosophy, questions of existence, the role of art, the horrors of war. Tarkovsky does not make the camera invisible, but he does often make the market for art invisible. We see the physical labor and time that goes into art in *Andrei Rublev*, but that film is set in a feudal society, and the icons rise triumphantly above that society at the end. By contrast, Godard is always as money-conscious as the Bresson of *L'argent* (1983), which traces the fate of money with a merciless eye. Art surrounds the characters in *In Praise of Love*, partly as objects of memory, but more emphatically as objects to be bought and sold. "I found the Corot at Vollard's, a Lichtenstein at Cazzilli's in New York, but too late; I was able to purchase a small Brueghel, but in my opinion it is a copy" (19–20). When Kris and Hari float up in front of the brightly lit Brueghel in Tarkovsky's *Solaris*, the ontological problem of the copy—since *she* is a copy—is up in the air too. But no one in Tarkovsky will wonder who will pay for Hari or where the Brueghel came from.

Like Arthur Danto, who believes in the category of the masterpiece, Tarkovsky does not see art as part of a global market.[3] Instead, Godard resembles an art historian like Benjamin H. D. Buchloh, who always insists on the relationship of art to the "culture industry." Buchloh reads all of American postwar culture as a kind of bulldozer Hollywood. He writes, for instance, "This could provide a possible explanation of the fact that the secret and latent ground of American popular culture has increasingly been determined by the hegemonic exclusion typical of economic competition among global corporations rather than by competing models of national cultures that had previously, however falsely, determined cultural difference in European nation-states."[4]

One of the earliest critical descriptions of film in a global economic context is Fredric Jameson's *Geopolitical Aesthetic* (page references to the book are in parentheses).[5] I have mentioned this book before; *The Geopolitical Aesthetic* contains a chapter, "Soviet Magic Realism," that celebrates Sokurov at the expense of Tarkovsky. *The Geopolitical Aesthetic* begins with a long section working around the genre of the conspiracy thriller (*All the President's Men*, *Three Days of the Condor*) and also contains a chapter on Godard ("High-Tech Collectives in Late Godard"). Jameson is more than willing to celebrate a good movie ("Abdrashitov's wonderful film" [37]) and put down a bad one, but in general he is more interested in mapping out complex relationships between cultural artifacts and economic and political indicators. Thus he is not particularly interested in finding good movies, and thereby creating his own version of the *Cahiers* pantheon, but rather in looking at how various movies throughout the world respond to "late capitalism." Jameson thus examines *Cahiers* favorites like Godard and Cronenberg, but he is not particularly drawn to the *Cahiers* American canon except for a few mentions of De Palma. Films are chosen primarily for the way they point beyond themselves and toward a description of contemporary international society. Thus, when Godard is, at last, praised for his originality, it is because he has opened a window onto the world system: "This is now the task with which *Passion* confronts us, as a peculiar signifying artifact of a wholly new sort, which nonetheless, like a meteorite fallen from outer space, bears within it that promise and the suggestion that grasping its structure—were that really ever possible!—would also lead to grasping the structure of the modern age itself" (184).

In Jameson's description, the existence of international banking conglomerates proceeds to erase any vestige of national boundaries. Although his book seems to be broken up by country (Russia, France, United States, the Philippines, Taiwan), his theory is always consistent—there are no nations. Jameson always insists on the "disappearance of specifically national cultures, and [also on] their replacement, either by a centralized commercial production for world export or by their own mass-produced neotraditional images" (3). In his introduction to Jameson's book, Colin MacCabe writes that "the complicated search for a European culture seems more pertinent in a world where the political dominance of America is now equal to the cultural dominance that Hollywood achieved over a half century ago" (xvi). But Jameson never talks like that. Hollywood is not a particular entity, but rather one effect among many. Instead, "late capitalism weighs on the globe like a doom" (111), and Cronenberg, Godard, and Sokurov each inhabit and reveal the multiple features of this world system.

Jameson thus reads the pan-European casting of Godard's *Passion* (1982) as an emblematic collective that occurs at the boundary of fantasy. "Whether these various organs of Europe's *corps morcelé* [divided body] are thereby envisioned as coming together in some healed and transformed post-1982 body, the various local speech impediments all somehow miraculously cancelling each other out, cannot here be decided" (171). But clearly Godard's pan-European allegory insists on two things: the reality of Poland's political situation (the Polish director returns to his country at the end), and its opposition, all the way, to Hollywood. Among other things, Godard has arranged his film to look like all those European films that can exist only by banding together collectively. Just as *In Praise of Love* insists on the harsh reality of French history along with the cinematic monopoly held by Hollywood, *Passion* insists on the reality of work and Polish Solidarity while repeatedly staging an opposition to Hollywood. For Colin MacCabe and Godard, America never vanishes under the tide of global capital; America and American film are localizable entities. In my turn, I do not ask that American films look like Godard films. But I do ask that American films stage their own sense of global consciousness as explicitly as Godard's *Passion*.

Before we turn to a more detailed description of American film in a global market, I will indicate here one more important critical text. Recall the 1972 conclusion to Peter Wollen's *Signs and Meaning in the Cinema*, which shows an astonishingly abrupt impatience with Hollywood (page references to the book are in parentheses).[6] The suddenness of Wollen's remarks results from the fact that his conclusion was discovered several years after the rest of the book was published and now nearly, indeed, controverts the previous structure of the entire book. For the whole logic of the body of the book resides in an insistence that film critics need to be able to work with complicated works of art and theory (in this instance, Eisenstein) at the same time that they treat critically the productions of Hollywood. Thus Wollen writes early on:

> The main stumbling block for film aesthetics, however, has not been Eisenstein, but Hollywood. Eisenstein, as we have seen, was a part of a general movement which included not only film directors, but also poets, painters and architects. It is relatively easy to assimilate the Russian cinema of the 1920s into the normal frame of reference of art history. Hollywood, on the other hand, is a completely different kind of phenomenon, much more forbidding, much more challenging. (10)

Thus the tripartite structure of *Signs and Meaning in the Cinema* begins with a survey of Eisenstein's writings and films ("Eisenstein's Aesthetics"), turns to a discussion of the auteur theory with respect to Hollywood, while rounding things out with a discussion of semiology, a film semiotics that will allow us to look critically at both European art films and the cinema of Hollywood. The structure of the book makes beautiful sense, and Wollen's text is still one of the most lucid presentations of film theory in English. But in the 1972 conclusion, three years after the 1969 first edition, Wollen abruptly turns away from Hollywood, and thus the whole premise of his book.

Wollen's 1972 conclusion suddenly verges on a retraction, since it now concludes the book by disagreeing with it. "Looking back over this book," writes Wollen, "I feel that its most valuable sections are those on Eisenstein and semiology, even though I have now changed my views on the latter" (173). But the emphasis on equal time for Hollywood is no longer present. "I do not believe that the development of *auteur* analyses of Hollywood films is any longer a first priority," he writes, continuing:

> This does not mean that the real advances of *auteur* criticism should not be defended. Nor does it mean that Hollywood film should be dismissed out of hand as "unwatchable." Any theory of cinema, any film-making, must take Hollywood into account. It provides the dominant codes with

which films are read and will continue to do so for the foreseeable future. No theory, no *avant-garde* director can simply turn their back on Hollywood. It is only in confrontation with Hollywood that anything new can be produced. Moreover, while Hollywood is an implacable foe, it is not monolithic. It contains contradictions within itself, different kinds of conflicts and fissures. (173)

What has happened, in the meantime, is that Wollen has reversed himself and taken a stand against Hollywood by siding with Godard. In Wollen's description, Godard's films interrogate filmmaking and challenge cinematic codes. And film criticism, too, according to Wollen, needs to work as forcefully and as testingly as Godard. "To go to the cinema, to read books or to listen to music is to be a partisan. Evaluation cannot be impartial" (172).

Wollen's principled refusal to clump Hollywood together with Godard, to celebrate analysis over its objects, was inspirational at the time and even more to the point now. It is true that we can analyze anything, whether it is Godard or grilled chicken, whether it is the Met's latest *Trovatore* or the most recent season of *24*. But we need to acknowledge what we are doing. Movies that are the products of deals between agents and producers, that have budgets running into the tens of millions, and that rely more and more on speed and special effects are products that need be treated no differently from automobiles and cell phones. Indeed, some of the most useful analyses of contemporary Hollywood films rely extensively on economic information, distribution statistics, and promotion strategy—in other words, these readings treat the film as a business product. Such films are interchangeable and have little to do with film as an art. An art historian need not spend much time worrying about the fact that millions of people buy prints by Thomas Kinkade. Neither should historians of film worry too much about Vin Diesel in *XXX* (2002). Most Hollywood films are business arrangements that happen to be projected on screens; films by Godard and Rossellini are also projected on screen. But this is merely a coincidence of form. Students of poetry do not need to read the poems of Jimmy Stewart, although these also take the shape of poems and are printed in books, just like other books of poetry. We are so good these days at blurring boundaries (where does Hollywood begin and end?) and at wanting to ward off privilege and elitism that we do not like to rule automatically against popular forms of American culture. But by choosing not to decide, by choosing to analyze and tolerate all films equally, we conspire with American imperialism and meanwhile fail to promote a foreign film that needs to be promoted. For criticism is also promotion and counterpromotion.

The critique of Hollywood is nothing new, and Wollen began his book by arguing against such regular criticisms. Hollywood has always been formulaic, and it has always been globalized. But the scale of Hollywood's imperialism is unprecedented since the 1990s. The bloated American blockbusters that circle the globe have become more and more disturbing and unacceptable, conjoined as they are with a single-superpower, unilateral foreign policy that, among many other manifestations, invaded Iraq in 2002. The Hollywood that *Cahiers* defended in the late 1950s not only was made up of arguably better movies, but also took place in a less obviously expansionist cold-war world. But 1990s Hollywood is a central force behind the global Americanization of everything. Not only is there a McDonalds everywhere, there is also a *Matrix*. On Wednesday, November 5, 2003, *The Matrix Revolutions*, the third installment of the series, became the first film in history to open globally, showing simultaneously worldwide in forty-three languages and on more than 10,000 screens.[7] *The Matrix* franchise is hegemonic, not revolutionary, and we need to follow it with the heightened impatience of Godard.

Because we are so good at seeing hybridization and deconstruction at the edges and centers of everything, descriptions of cultural imperialism have recently given way to the seemingly much more complicated critical landscapes of postcolonial global media studies.[8] Michael Hardt and Antonio Negri's *Empire* (2000) speaks of a decentered Empire, without boundaries, and Daniel T. O'Hara writes in *Empire Burlesque* (2003), that "given the power of the telecommunications industry, the rise of the Internet, and the emergence of the new tech-based economy, the postmodern form of empire may remain mostly virtual, except for projects and operations, scenes of instruction and entertainment."[9] Yet after Bush's invasion of Iraq, you do not have to be Gore Vidal or Noam Chomsky to call U.S. aggressiveness imperialistic. Empire in this case is now not virtual, hybridized, or blurred. The United States has staked out territory with an explicitly "forward strategy of Freedom to promote democracy in the Middle East."[10] The fluid, unlocalizable powers of capital in Jameson seem now to be concretely situated. Actual nations continue to exist; some prosper at the expense of others.[11]

Godard knows as much about deconstruction as anyone. His work of the late 1960s and the 1970s overlaps exactly with the interrogation of writing and methodology in the French journal *Tel Quel*.[12] *Le Gai savoir* (*The Gay Science*, although released under the English title *Joy of Learning*, 1969) has a Nietzschean title and a Derridean project, which is to investigate the origin and ground of his medium. Yet even though Godard practices a thorough familiarity with postmodern disjunction, evasion, and self-consciousness, he does so in the service of thinking through and investigating the situation of film. Where is the film coming from? Who is making this film? Who is speaking? Where are the various sites of film and of film production? Thus whereas Jameson and others virtualize the United States out of existence, Godard persists in pointing a complicated finger at Hollywood and the United States. All of Godard's films are investigations of situation, and American films need to continue the many possible forms of this investigation.

In this concluding chapter, I argue that the future of American film depends on its openness to the rest of the world. Such an argument is staged in part as prophecy, perhaps, but more practically it stands as a method of reading recent American film. Independent American film ought to be conscious of its place both alongside the gargantuan monster of Hollywood and as resident on planet Earth. But the right attitude is not so much *against* Hollywood as it is *for* the rest of the world. American film, if it wants to be anything, if it aspires to art, if it wishes to take a place in film history, must listen to the world that Hollywood steamrolls. The most interesting American films of the 1990s open themselves to the world beyond the United States. Such films neither follow Hollywood as a model of success nor do they embody provincial American know-nothingism. These films open their ears to history and to other cultures. The best contemporary American films are those that listen to other cinematic voices. The U.S. films that go crashing around, at once deafening and deaf, able to hear nothing but their own loud self-satisfied voices, are films that we need not listen to either. Why spend too much of your life with someone who is all monologue and no conversation?

Jim Jarmusch and the Evaporation of America

Maybe New York City directors have better ears, all the better to hear beyond Hollywood. Martin Scorsese's *Mean Streets* and *Taxi Driver* are steeped in European film — de Sica, Visconti, Bresson. Woody Allen's *Interiors* (1978) and *Stardust Memories* (1980) hear Bergman and Fellini too directly, no doubt, but it is European influences that have kept Allen's films so distinct in form and tone from so much of what is produced in the United States. More recently, Hal Hartley has repeatedly worked through a global consciousness in his New

York City films. *No Such Thing* (2001) moves from New York City to Iceland, and *Flirt* (1995) takes place in three cities, New York, Tokyo, and Berlin. *Amateur* (1994) stars the great French actress Isabelle Huppert across from the Hartley regular, Martin Donovan. Abel Ferrara's *New Rose Hotel* (1998) is an explicit and brutal representation of global capitalism, while his *'R Xmas* (2001) and *Bad Lieutenant* (1992) are savage critiques of America and American ideals. In Ferrara's *Bad Lieutenant*, surely one of the masterpieces of 1990s American film, the World Series goes on, baseball game after baseball game, while the bad cop (Harvey Keitel) gambles and drinks his life down the gutter. The films of Jim Jarmusch methodically open themselves to the global currents. They render American locales in vigorous detail, even as the boundaries of America are reseen by international eyes. Jarmusch's films are exemplary listening posts, attuned both to film history and to voices outside the United States. His films implicitly stage a global consciousness and attentiveness that seek to subvert Hollywood's global monopoly.

Stranger than Paradise (1984) is emblematic of the way Jarmusch reroutes America through the world. As the film begins, Eva (Eszter Balint) stands next to her bags on an outcropping of dirt, watching an airplane take off. She has just landed in New York to visit her cousin, Willie (John Lurie). Willie's real name is Bela Molnar, and while he understands Hungarian perfectly well, he tells his cousin Eva and his Aunt Lottie to speak English, not Hungarian. The first section of the film is titled "The New World," but the ongoing joke is that this America looks as grey and industrialized as any Eastern European country. The film travels from New York City to Cleveland and from Cleveland to Florida, but each new place seems equally desolate. At the end Willie quasi-randomly flies off to Hungary while Eva flops down in her hotel room on the beach. Everyone is a stranger and nowhere is paradise.

The first third of *Stranger than Paradise* was shot on film left over from Wim Wenders's *State of Things* (1982), and it was financed in part by German television. *Stranger than Paradise* looks in many ways like a European art film peopled with American characters. "I have a lot of influences," said Jarmusch in a 1984 interview. "Anything that moves me influences me somehow. I take from European and Japanese films and also from America. The characters [in *Stranger than Paradise*] are really American."[13] Jarmusch himself is completely immersed in European art film, having spent much of his senior year in college watching movies at the Cinémathèque in Paris. But American filmgoers have too often removed themselves from the history of film and from a consciousness of film outside the U.S. So we cannot be too surprised when we run across embarrassing moments like this one, from a 1985 interview with Jarmusch, when the cinematic illiteracy of the American reviewer becomes all too apparent:

Q: So you saw a lot of these films?
JJ: Yeah. That's where I first saw a lot of films that I had only read about before, especially European films or Japanese films.
Q: Can you name a few of those films?
JJ: Well, films by Vertov, Vigo, films by Bresson, short films by Raul Ruiz. I don't know—you probably don't know most of these people.
Q: I'm not aware of them. They're more art filmmakers?[14]

This is pretty much what Godard has in mind when he puts Bresson next to *The Matrix* in *In Praise of Love*. Although an American journalist from San Francisco can consider himself prepared to talk about movies without ever having heard of Vigo or Vertov, Jarmusch brings a much wider range of films to the table. But his knowledge is never self-righteous. In *Stranger than Paradise*, Eva argues with Willie on behalf of the music of Screamin' Jay Hawkins, and she sometimes blasts a Screamin' Jay tape that she has brought over from Hungary. We might well support this level of "Americanization" and congratulate her on her good taste. But when offered the possibility of going to see a "foreign flick," *Days without Sun*, she opts instead for a kung fu movie. And then we watch all four of them (Eva, her date, Willie, and Eddie) watch the kung fu movie for a while. The Americans are a bit dense, but Eva, the Hungarian, is not an idealized alternative to them.

The connection between Wenders and Jarmusch originally established by sharing film is worth reflecting on a bit further. The two directors not only shared film, they shared cinematographers, since one of Wenders's favorite directors of photography, Robby Müller, also worked with Jarmusch on a regular basis (*Down by Law* [1986], *Mystery Train* [1989], *Dead Man* [1995], *Ghost Dog: The Way of the Samurai* [1999]). Both directors repeatedly put into play an intense self-consciousness about cinema in a global context. While Wenders assembled international casts for films like *Wings of Desire* (*Der Himmel über Berlin*, 1987) and *Until the End of the World* (1991), Jarmusch sent Roberto Benigni into the U.S. South (*Down by Law* [1986]), told the story of a Japanese couple in Memphis ("Far from Yokohama" in *Mystery Train* [1989]), and cut back and forth between California and Finland in *Night on Earth* (1991). Wenders's *Paris, Texas* (1984), which stars Natassia Kinski opposite Harry Dean Stanton (French actress Aurore Clément plays Dean Stockwell's wife), is another emblematically global investigation. The casting in these films is only in part an attempt to speak English on behalf of better financing. Wenders's international casts appear not just for the bankers, but also to embody the complexities and the interrelationships of global cinema. Both Jarmusch and Wenders show a consciousness of interpenetrating global space, in contrast to an American sensibility that evaporates the rest of the planet. But what has happened over the years is that Wenders wants to see the whole globe the way God sees it.

Wenders' *End of Violence* (1997), for example, describes the state of global interdependency, but from the point of view of God. The movie producer (Bill Pullman) crosses class and ethnic boundaries when he drops out of the high life and lives with poor Hispanics; in another plot, a gangster rapper learns to write poetry, but without the violence. A foreign director, Zoltan Kovacs (Udo Kier), seems to be a rather lewd voyeur, but the movie forgivingly rises above mere nationalities. That is what all the helicopter shots mean, those angel shots from high in the air that carry over from *Wings of Desire*. Wenders's globalism has become more and more the globalism of angels, and one whose Bible says things like this: "There are no enemies or strangers, just a strange world." At the end, the movie producer speaks over the final rising helicopter shot, "I can see China now. I hope they can see us." Thus Wenders's global consciousness is partly a banking decision (and *The End of Violence* is basically an American movie, with American stars, financed by European producers, CIBY 2000), but more substantially a religious decision. Despite a gestural critique of government conspiracy, politics has almost entirely vanished in *The End of Violence*, and religion has taken its place. *The End of Violence* asks us to change our individual lives, and then ride up into the sky on Jacob's helicopter. By contrast, Jarmusch's globalism is still symbolic rather than literal or analytic, and it has not blown up into God.

So yes, there are overhead shots in Jarmusch's *Ghost Dog: The Way of the Samurai*, but they do not imply the point of view of angels. At the beginning and in the middle of the film we slowly float over the city with what is literally a bird's-eye view. Ghost Dog (Forest Whitaker) raises pigeons on his roof, and in a film that takes seriously the existence of birds, dogs, and bears, the camera is thus birdlike overhead, not godlike. In the penultimate sequence, the camera shoots down onto the now dead Ghost Dog from a height of twenty feet. But an angelic perspective is certainly not implied at any point, since the film is steeped in an archaic Eastern wisdom that we can never take completely straight. The film mixes up cultures as a black man, Ghost Dog, learns the ancient ways of the samurai, but attaches himself to an Italian mobster. The Mafiosi in their turn meet in a Chinese restaurant, and one of their bosses loves listening to black gangster rap. Ghost Dog's best friend is a French immigrant who does not speak or understand any English.

There is a mild Kieslowskian sense of benign coincidence in the world, since Ghost Dog is always guessing exactly what his French-speaking friend says, and since whatever cartoon the gangsters are watching is a perfect annotation of what is happening at the time. But this mild sense of intuitionism, interconnectedness, or telepathy never attains the certainty of belief. If there is any religion at the center of *Ghost Dog*, it is the Eastern sense that existence is unreal amid an abyss of nothingness. And so an intertitle card reads: "Our bodies are given life from the midst of nothingness. Existing where there is nothing is the meaning of the phrase 'Form is emptiness.' That all things are provided for by nothingness is the meaning of the phrase 'Emptiness is form.' One should not think that these are two separate things."

Ghost Dog floats through a world that is clearly at war. On the one hand, the film is playful and artificial, messing around with movie genres — the gangster movie, the cool killer movie — and Ghost Dog shoots the rapping gangster up through a sink in a direct quotation of Seijun Suzuki's great yakuza thriller *Branded to Kill* (1967). The movie is cartoonish often enough that we do not take the killings too seriously, and Ghost Dog twirls his gun around like a cowboy. Yet *Ghost Dog* is not so cartoonish that it has become *The Matrix* or *Kill Bill*. Ghost Dog passes by another black man, who wears army fatigues, and the scene in which Ghost Dog confronts white hunters who have shot a bear is straight-out about race, undiluted by Lynch's dreamy weirdness or Tarantino's escalation for its own sake. The gangsters console themselves by watching cartoons, whose violence does not matter, but the violence in *Ghost Dog* clearly does matter. Violence in Godard is almost always unreal, even ridiculous, and this is his way of admitting that movie violence is worlds away from the violence and suffering of the real world. Yet Godardian violence always comes from the real world and points back to where we are. *Ghost Dog*, too, circulates through cartoon violence and genre violence back to the real world.

Dead Man (1995) is also a description of violence and war in a global market. In a long sequence at the beginning of the film, William Blake (Johnny Depp) is shown riding a train west; we understand him to be traveling farther and farther away from the civilization of the American East. But at the end of the line, apparently in the middle of nowhere, is a town called Machine. In the middle of the desert, in other words, looms up the industrial nightmare of Victorian England, billowing smoke and loudly grinding its gears. When William Blake seeks to claim his job as an accountant at the offices of John Dickinson, he walks into a clerk's office straight out of Charles Dickens. Dickinson himself is played by Robert Mitchum in his final role—a determined bit of cinephilic casting that remembers Mitchum's career-long display of all-American masculinity and toughness. But his Dickensian company is overseen by a clerk played by John Hurt, who appeared previously in another black-and-white Victorian industrial nightmare, David Lynch's *Elephant Man* (1980). Dickinson's factory combines English industrial machinery with American ruthlessness, and proceeds to turn the city and the country all around into a graveyard. Eventually, Dickinson will use his wealth to pursue Blake all the way out to the Pacific coastline. So that by the end we see that it is really all one vast, monstrous machine, which stretches from England across the Atlantic to the Pacific Northwest. It is the machine of money and death.

Cultures circulate and crisscross oceans in *Dead Man,* as English industry suddenly appears (as it were) in the Mojave Desert, and as the Native American, Nobody (Gary Farmer), goes on a grand tour through Canada and Great Britain. We learn that in England, Nobody was exhibited as a curiosity, but he was also educated. The most important artifact of British civilization for Nobody was the poetry of William Blake, and he treats Depp's Blake as if he were the poet himself. Great Britain is thus associated with horrific machinery, but also with beautiful poetry. Native American culture is treated as wise and dignified, but also ridiculous and forlorn. In the same way that we cannot entirely trust the archaic Eastern wisdom of Ghost Dog, we are often equally suspicious of Nobody's aphoristic wisdom. Jarmusch pointedly shows us that the Native American town at the end is also a boneyard, which looks just as ruined and depressed as Machine itself. Presumably this is because even though cultures move back and forth, over the continents and across the oceans, there is still the overwhelming fact of America. For America is a killing field. Early on, Blake asks Thel (his newfound female acquaintance, with a name from the real Blake; played by Mili Avital) why she has a gun. "Because this is America," she says. America is full of immigrants; Mr. Olafsen (John North) has taken Blake's job at the factory, and British rock-and-roller Iggy Pop plays one member of a sorry trio of backwoodsman. But America stands over them all like Robert Mitchum with a gun, foregrounding money and violence and killing everything in its path. America seems to turn everyone into murderers and cannibals. As Nobody says to William Blake, "Your poetry will now be written with blood."

Martin Scorsese, Cinematic Art, and the Inclusion of the Foreign

American films need to acknowledge their place in the global marketplace. American films must not only acknowledge their transience as cinematic artifacts, but also open themselves to global currents. Cinematic art may be the result of these acknowledgments. Without such determined self-descriptions, American film becomes a blind agent of empire. These days, European influences are salutary, not limiting. Eurocentrism is clearly a cultural problem, but compared to American imperialism, it may seem positively a virtue.

In recent years, Martin Scorsese has made many films that deliberately examine America in a global context and that deliberately examine art. Scorsese's most forthright portrait of the artist occurs in "Life Lessons," the first section of the anthology *New York Stories* (1989). Scorsese's *Age of Innocence* (1993) is equally inundated with art, since every room in the costume film is filled floor to ceiling with paintings, some clearly appropriate to the time, some just as clearly anachronistic and impossible. Scorsese thinks through his own relationship to the wider world in films like *Kundun* (1997), which tells the story of Tibet's Dalai Lama, and in *Gangs of New York* (2002), a parable of interethnic struggle shot entirely at the famous Italian studios of Cinecitta. Scorsese's films ambitiously aim toward art, but only by humbly passing through world history and film history. We can refine yet again our sense of cinematic art and cinematic presence by surveying some of the recent films of this American master.

In interviews and documentaries, Scorsese is quite insistent about the idea that cinema can be an art. For Scorsese, cinematic art is always characterized by personal expression. He has what amounts to an auteur theory of film in which the most interesting directors, no matter who the producers, actors, or scriptwriters are, put their obsessive themes and visions on the screen. In *A Personal Journey with Martin Scorsese through American Movies* (Scorsese and Michael Henry Wilson, 1995), Scorsese doubly underlines the personal expressiveness of the finest films by selecting his own favorites, which are often B movies that have allowed a director's personal vision to come through. "Less money, more freedom," says Scorsese of the low-budget film. Scorsese has directors like Coppola, Eastwood, and De Palma speak of cinema as an art, yet notes that "most American directors never claimed to be artists." He closes the first section of the film with a clip from Peter Bogdanovich's documentary on John Ford; Ford refuses to say a word about any of his films. Most Hollywood directors and producers have been similarly tight-lipped about cinematic art.

In *A Personal Journey*, Scorsese shows how the greatest studio directors would take hackneyed genres and make them dark and difficult. Scorsese calls these directors "iconoclasts" and "smugglers" who sneak in social issues and criticize the status quo. Scorsese is drawn to the tragic doom of Ford's *Searchers* (1956) and the darkness in Anthony Mann westerns like *The Furies* (1950) and *The Naked Spur* (1953). Gangster films by Raoul Walsh and Howard Hawks are really savage critiques of the American dream; these films show family values, patriotism, loyalty, and business in a totally "twisted" light. Allan Dwan in *Silver Lode* (1954) shows the "frailty of our democratic institutions" in the age of McCarthyism. Douglas Sirk skewers small-town Americana in his Technicolor melodramas, in which the "subtext is as important as the subject matter." And Sam Fuller overtly aims his energetic theater at American social wounds in films like *Shock Corridor* (1963). Scorsese quotes last from Kazan's *America, America* (1963), a story of immigration to the United States, although Scorsese reads the film in this case in both a personal and figurative sense: "I kind of identified with it and was very moved by it. I later saw myself making this same journey, but not from Anatolia, rather from my own neighborhood in New York, which was in a sense a very foreign land. I made that journey from that land to movie-making, which was something unimaginable." Scorsese's cinematic artists are strong figures whose individuality refuses to conform not only to the studios but also to American society. In this view, an American film artist is in some sense always a foreigner, always an immigrant, and a sense of perpetual displacement will necessarily coexist with the process of making American films.

In "Life Lessons," Lionel Dobie (Nick Nolte), a successful painter, instinctively arranges his life to ensure his foreignness. He works best isolated and in difficult circumstances; as Scorsese says, "what interested me was the pain of this situation, how much of it is needed for his kind of work, and how much he creates himself."[15] When an art gallery agent comes to visit his studio, Dobie talks to him only through the elevator grille, and shortly sends him back where he came from. During the art parties, Dobie is gruff and obnoxious, telling off-color jokes to the wine-drinking crowd. But above all, he has arranged for a young assistant, Paulette (Rosanna Arquette), to live in his studio with him. At this point in the story she has agreed to stay only if she does not have to sleep with him. So his difficulties are guaranteed. We see point-of-view shots of her underwear and of her bare feet (with a likely allusion to Kubrick's *Lolita*); his young assistant obviously fills him with lust. For a moment we drift into an imaginary blue-tinted world, where they make love, a fantasy world of his own making. The window to her room is always present to him while he works, a framed light of hope and hopelessness, an omnipresent picture. Dobie has thus arranged for himself a psychological torture chamber that literally divides his house in two. His art is stronger, in this telling, for his having alienated himself and for having let in the foreigner.

The artist as foreigner is made explicit at several points. The film begins by having Dobie pick up Paulette at the airport. Paulette is never at home with Dobie and spends most of the film expressing her desire to go home. She comes in on an airplane at the beginning, and she leaves with her brother at the end. But the metaphor of the foreigner is played out most explicitly when Paulette brings home a Hispanic man, Reuben Toro (Jesse Bourego). Dobie's reaction to this man verges on racism; he tells Paulette that Toro is a "greasy-haired kid." Dobie himself underlines the foreignness of Toro by playing Italian opera at the couple tucked away in Paulette's room. Otherwise we have heard Dobie play only American rock and roll. Later Paulette and Dobie go to see a performance artist, Gregory Stark (Steve Buscemi), whose standup caters to the hip black-leather-jacketed crowd. "I felt really strange," says Stark, and everyone seems to identify with him.

But the film suggests that Dobie is the real artist and that his estrangement is the more authentic. In this parable of artistic creation, art prospers and flourishes when the artist allows in the foreigner. The foreigner does not appear as a benign influence, but rather as an inspiring difficulty. The artist becomes less and less likeable (Dobie is a loathsome prick by any reckoning), even as his art soars. We feel a clear irony when we turn from the self-destructive arrangements of his life to the artistic result of these divisions. For his masterwork appears to be a huge picture of a bridge. The parable of "Life Lessons" thus suggests that you build the bridge of art by throwing up walls.

The Age of Innocence is also, among other things, a parable of art and the foreigner. In the story Archer (Daniel Day-Lewis) yearns to escape from his marriage to May (Winona Ryder) in order to live with the foreign princess, Countess Olenska (Michelle Pfeiffer). The paintings that surround these characters associate the foreign with promise and fantasy. Here Scorsese, unlike Kubrick, does want his paintings to mean, and the pictures hang significantly next to particular characters, in particular scenes. Paintings in *The Age of Innocence* tell us about their owners; they are visual indications of the owners' interiority. These characters make rooms for themselves where they are surrounded by pictures of their own dreams. The extremely satisfied Mrs. Mingott (Miriam Margolyes), for instance, lives in a room with one picture of herself and dozens of paintings of dogs. And there are already numerous dogs jumping all over her. The pictures of dogs and the actual dogs imply that there is absolutely no distance between desire and satisfaction.

Whereas Mrs. Mingott shows no gap between her actual life and the life portrayed in pictures, the sitting room of Archer is covered with dreamscapes. His walls are made out of seasides, boats on water, ruins with aqueducts. His paintings convey a world elsewhere, and this is the whole tendency of his mind. He dreams of escaping to a country where he can be together with the countess, and toward the end of the film we see him reading a book on Japan (with large illustrations). For Archer, the real world is somewhere else. As he says to the Countess: "You gave me a glimpse of a real life, and then you told me to carry on with a false one." At the end there hovers a great sadness in the air when the voice-over says of his room: "It was the room in which most of the real things of his life had happened." The voice-over speaks here of things like the baptism of his son and the marriage of his daughter. His son and daughter have come into the world precisely because he did not go on any of the voyages, because he did not run away with the Countess, because he stayed in his room covered by boats and seascapes.

The paintings in the Countess's rooms are even more obviously symbolic and impossible. Whereas Mrs. Mingott and Archer have arranged their rooms to reflect satisfied and unsatisfied desire, the film has arranged the countess's paintings like those in an impossible museum. The paintings in her rooms could not have existed in the 1870s; they are palpably modern. They are not visually extreme in their modernism—they are not abstract or cubist—but stylistically they are much more open, more impressionistic, and less realistic than the nineteenth-century paintings elsewhere. When Archer waits for the countess in her rooms early on in the film, the camera pulls back from a painting of a woman without a face. The picture's outlines are blocky, and the landscape begins to turn into a Cézanne. Clearly the countess is not only of another place, another world, but also of another time. In the future, one might say, when class snobbery declines and women's rights increase, this romance might take place. Since she is moving from one house to another, her rooms are also scattered with empty picture frames. In some spots there are the blank outlines of pictures on the wall, the spaces where paintings used to be. In these instances the gallery is thus hung with nothing, a museum of emptiness.

In *The Age of Innocence*, Scorsese jokes with the paintings, in witty and astonishing asides. In the ballroom dance sequence, there is a wonderful trompe l'oeil when the elegantly dressed partygoers pose in front of a huge painting that could be of them (J. J. Tissot, *Too Early*, 1873). Later in a conservatory, a servant comes to tell them the whereabouts of the countess. We cut from a family sitting nearly outdoors to the servant standing in front of a painting by Alma-Tadema. This is another impossibly anachronistic painting (*Expectations*, 1885), and another symbolic painting, in that the solitary red-haired woman in the picture can only recall the countess. One of the most amazing paintings is panned over quickly in Archer's room; it is a Turner, *The Fighting Temeraire*.[16] At this point the narrator sums up the life of Archer's room, and she says over the Turner: "Thus it was here that Archer and his wife discussed the future of all their children." This is a sunset monologue, in fact, taking the long view of his life, even as the steamship in the picture moves ahead. But that Archer has a Turner is almost as fantastically implausible as those Picassos on James Cameron's *Titanic*, and it helps drive the wedge further between the life Archer lived and the life he could have lived, but did not.

Like "Life Lessons," *The Age of Innocence* is a tale of claustrophobia in which passion and art emerge from the collision of native and foreign. Dobie lives in a self-destructive box with young women stuck inside with him, and Archer is trapped in Victorian New York with impossible Turners on the wall and a countess from the future. The foreign represents an opening, and it changes the sense of the American self. But the foreign is in either case not so easily grasped and is, finally, rejected. The openness to a world beyond America results in a passionate critique of America. The foreign allows one to find what is personal, beyond the conformity of things as they are.

Scorsese's *Gangs of New York* shows that fiery apocalypse is the result of rejecting the foreign. Bill Cutting (Daniel Day-Lewis), aka Bill the Butcher, is the bloodthirsty self-appointed guardian of America. The sign on his wall says "Native Americans Beware of Foreign Influence," and his gang, or tribe, is called the Confederation of American Natives. He prays to an American flag and sometimes speaks with an American flag draped around him like a robe. He represents the sheer, homicidal hatred of the foreign, and he is clearly the devil of this underworld.

But *Gangs of New York* also shows that the gang wars of New York City, ones that set the "natives" upon the "foreigners," are only a microcosm of American self-division and self-loathing. Throughout *Gangs of New York* Scorsese crosscuts between gang violence and larger news of the American Civil War. At the same time that Amsterdam Vallon (Leonardo DiCaprio) marches out in vengeance against Bill and his "native" gangs, the film crosscuts to draft riots breaking out simultaneously in uptown New York. The implication is clear: it is not just Bill the Butcher who is steeped in homicidal hate, but also thousands of like-minded citizens, who blow up just as murderously under the right provocation. Blacks are lynched and soldiers massacre the poor. The city that is put together out of all the world's immigrants is a powder keg waiting for a spark. The gangs of New York represent only the most transparent embodiment of violence and venom.

Like the Hollywood films that Scorsese loves, *Gangs of New York* combines a withering attack on race and ethnic prejudice with recognizable film conventions and form. Audiences are given their two young stars (DiCaprio and Cameron Diaz), and also a love story between the two that seems to be there only so that we will know this is a movie. Cinephiles will recognize the way that Scorsese's epic sweeps through the same space as films like D. W. Griffith's *Birth of a Nation* (1915) and Victor Fleming's *Gone with the Wind* (1939). With its brawls and frontier justice, *Gangs of New York* is also Scorsese's version of a western, a spaghetti western made in Italy. But Scorsese's historical epic undermines cinematic landmarks and causes American genre and substance to evaporate. Scorsese's epic flies up out of the Italian studios and then buries itself in darkness.

The concluding sequence is not unimportant, then; on the contrary, it is the moral of Scorsese's cinema. New York City, says Vallon in voice-over, was "born of blood and tribulation." But "for the rest of time, it would be like no one knew we were ever here." Then there are a series of archeological dissolves, from the Victorian graveyards of New York, to a grass-covered riverside, to a skyline crowded with more and taller buildings, which eventually include the Twin Towers of the World Trade Center. By showing the Twin Towers in 2002, the film dissolves its own cinematic epic into ghosts and causes us to reflect one more time on the provincial native and the problematic of the foreign.

Bringing Out the Dead (1999) is Scorsese's Solaris masterpiece of the 1990s. The story follows a paramedic, Frank Pierce (Nicolas Cage), as he makes his exhausted, delirious way from one emergency call to the next. His patients are bleeding, dying, or dead, and he is barely half alive himself, unable to sleep and haunted by ghosts. The whole film is bathed in an impossible white light — sheer, subjective expressionism — which shows what a liminal, ghostly world this is — and for everyone, not just those calling 911. As Frank says, "We're all dying." With Scorsese voicing the ambulance dispatcher, *Bringing Out the Dead* offers itself as an always-vanishing film, impossibly lit, which, like the ambulance driver, does not save anybody, but bears witness to transience and death.

Bringing Out the Dead, like many of Scorsese's films, also foregrounds an openness to the foreign. Frank is haunted by a girl named Rose (Cynthia Roman), who died in his care. Using the same CGI technology that allowed John Malkovich to appear everywhere in *Being John Malkovich* (Jonze, 1999), Rose appears on every street corner in *Bringing Out the Dead*, and sometimes as every person in a crowd. Rose is Hispanic, and at the coffee shop El Toro de Oro, Spanish music causes Rose to appear. Frank's last ambulance partner, the aptly named Tom Wall (Tom Sizemore), frequently reverts to racial comments and slurs, reminding us of the tensions always present in the multicultural city. In his despair, Frank does not care whether Rose is dark-skinned or light; "The city does not discriminate," he says, "it gets everybody." But Wall goes after a Hispanic man he generically calls "Pedro," saying, "Your first lesson is how to be an American." Not everyone tolerates or welcomes difference.

The most striking invocation of the foreign in *Bringing Out the Dead* comes in the form of the rock-and-roll songs that fire up each time the ambulance goes charging down the road. These songs are all chosen to underline the foreign. Two songs are reggae classics by UB40 and Melodian. Two songs are by the archetypically British rock band the Clash (one of the songs is "I'm So Bored with the USA"). Two other songs are "Rivers of Babylon" and "I Am a Japanese Sandman." The most programmatic selection of all, perhaps, is Van Morrison's "T.B. Sheets," a mournful epic about a hospital ward. One set of lines goes: "You're a little starstruck, innuendos, inadequacies, and foreign bodies." Scorsese lifts out "foreign bodies" so we hear it two different times, ten minutes apart, even though the phrase occurs only once in Van Morrison's song. Tuberculosis is an onset of foreign bodies that need to be killed. But *Bringing Out the Dead* represents the cinema as an otherworldly welcoming of the foreign, for better or for worse. When the bright lights come on at the beginning of the film, we realize immediately that everyone is already dead, that all of this takes place somewhere else, on another world.

Theoretical criticism in the 1970s argued that films needed to take into account their existence as films. Godard always takes into account the origins of cinema in money, and he self-reflexively broods over the consequences, for example, of filming beautiful women. Tarkovsky's films relentlessly examine the metaphysical nature of the cinematic artifact, its precarious aesthetic. Scorsese's films, as we have seen, repeatedly stage the confrontation of the native and the foreign, with implications for both cinema and nation.

Not every film need imitate Godard or Tarkovsky or Scorsese. But in the twenty-first century, when, for the foreseeable future, America is the self-appointed administrator of the planet, American films must be especially conscious of their place in history and of their place in the world. Without this self-consciousness, most simply, movies become unwatchable, just as McDonalds hamburgers become inedible. We want at least to know that these films know where they are coming from. Godard rises up superior to Spielberg, but he is never superior to movies. He knows that he is implicated in the problematic. The Solaris effect emerges when a film acknowledges its troubling origins in money, history, and imagery. What this cinematic self-consciousness will look like is entirely open. Godard's *Histoire(s) du cinéma* cuts back and forth between a Hollywood glamour queen and a concentration-camp victim for the most straightforward kind of commentary, but there are elsewhere in these histories many less obvious kinds of juxtapositions. Godard's *Passion* cuts back and forth between a film studio and a factory, but the result of that juxtaposition is far from clear. Tarkovsky and Godard are relentlessly self-conscious about their medium, about their place in cinematic history, but each of their films leaves a different impression from the last. Both give us the clear sense that a film that comes into the world without self-consciousness would belong to another kind of cinema.

I want American films to adopt a stance of transience and humility before history and the world. I want American films to represent themselves as aliens. I want films to acknowledge their artifice but to connect to reality. I want films to stage a confrontation between "America" and the "foreign," since that is what happens when a film appears in a global market overseen by an imperialist United States.

This is prescriptive, no doubt, but far from a radical or militant aesthetics. A truly radical aesthetic would promote an agenda characterized by third-world cinema, documentary, television, and revised forms of anthropology — an agenda, in other words, similar to those found in the 1970s, in the issues of *Cahiers du cinéma* and in the films of Godard. But both *Cahiers* and Godard returned to feature filmmaking in the 1980s, allowing themselves to think more deliberately about cinema and more openly and metaphorically about politics. Godard made one of the most moving and illuminating gestures in the history of film when he issued *Sauve qui peut (la vie)* in 1980. After the searing radicalism and militancy of films like *Le Gai savoir* (1969), *Pravda* (Dziga Vertov Group, 1970), *Le vent d'est* (Dziga Vertov Group, 1970), and *Tout va bien* (Godard and Jean-Pierre Gorin, 1972), his return to feature filmmaking at the end of the 1970s demonstrates a trust in fiction that Godard would never again leave behind. Unlike avant-garde or experimental film, which refuses to hold a dialogue with other films, Godard's radicalism after 1980 always takes place as part of a conversation with the history of cinema.[17]

By his example, Godard encourages us to think that a self-consciously metaphorical approach to the world is ultimately more powerful than a more literal-minded militancy. The aesthetics described in this book similarly allows for—and celebrates—the continuing existence of the fiction feature film. A more radical aesthetics would cut the ground out from under Van Sant and Jarmusch.[18] In this book, however, these directors are important not just for their multicultural politics, but above all for the way that they reflect on the possibilities and practice of American film.

Art in an age of Americanization and globalism often adopts either of two strategies. On the one hand, it becomes culturally specific, site specific. For example, Philippe Vergne, a curator of the exhibition How Latitudes Become Forms: Art in a Global Age, explains the title: "Its an awareness about where we're coming from, our roots in a specific field, and our working methods. It is a marker and a point of reference. In giving ourselves latitudes we don't want to forget or deny our own history."[19] Or, just as likely, an artist may wish to comment on America's ever-increasing omnipresence in the world, what Lawrence Rinder calls the "American effect." "In this age of American empire," writes Rinder, "the image of the United States has taken on almost mythic dimensions, symbolizing, consciously or unconsciously, deeply held fantasies and fears."[20] American films ought to align themselves with the artists in these collections by contemplating explicitly the site of their emergence in film history and in the United States.

But even more then tracing their emergence, American films ought to trace their disappearance. Nobody wants to be told about "ought," but with empire comes responsibility. In "The Artist's Responsibility," Tarkovsky insists on the moral responsibilities of the artist:

> I therefore find it very hard to understand it when artists talk about absolute creative freedom. I don't understand what is meant by that sort of freedom, for it seems to me that if you have chosen artistic work you find yourself bound by chains of necessity, fettered by the tasks you set yourself and by your own artistic vocation.[21]

What is the responsibility of the American filmmaker toward film? What is our own responsibility as critics of film? What is Kris's responsibility when he faces Hari, his alien beloved? His duty is both certain and unclear. And then she vanishes, and vanishes again, always differently. We must watch over our theater of disappearance with care, rejecting both the simulacral and the natural, in hopes that American film's elusive metaphors will help us see a place to land.

Notes

....

Preface

1. Robert Kolker, *A Cinema of Loneliness: Penn, Stone, Kubrick, Scorsese, Spielberg, Altman*, 3rd ed. (New York: Oxford Univ. Press, 2000).

2. For a critical description of private and public spaces in Hitchcock, see Jonathan Freedman and Richard Millington, eds., *Hitchcock's America* (New York: Oxford Univ. Press, 1999).

Chapter 1

1. A characteristic description of Lacanian "lack" that seems only a few refinements away from the absent presence of the film screen is given by Francesco Casetti: "In short, like linguistic structure, psychic structure is defined through opposition and lack (represented by the phallus and the fear of castration). Such differentiality and subtraction may either be accepted and made to act or hidden and compensated for. It is typical of the *imaginary register* to create an impression of illusory fullness. One can think of those (mental, iconic, etc.) representations that seems to offer us a world, while in reality they deprive us of it." *Theories of Cinema, 1945–1995*, trans. Francesca Chiostri and Elizabeth Gard Bartolini-Salimbeni, with Thomas Kelso (Austin: Univ. of Texas Press, 1999), 163.

2. Jean-Louis Baudry, "Ideological Effects of the Basic Cinematographic Apparatus" in *Narrative, Apparatus, Ideology: A Film Theory Reader*, ed. Philip Rosen, 286–298 (New York: Columbia Univ. Press, 1986); Marc Vernet, *Figures de l'absence: De l'invisible au cinéma* (Paris: Éditions de l'étoile, 1988).

3. See especially, Richard Allen, "Dream, Fantasy, and Projective Illusion," in *Projecting Illusion: Film Spectatorship and the Impression of Reality* (New York: Cambridge Univ. Press, 1995), 122–126. Allen's work criticizes contemporary film theory, but still finds psychoanalysis—properly deployed—to be crucial to understanding the cinematic experience. What I call the "Solaris effect," Allen calls "projective illusion," and so describes the medium-aware spectator: "Contemporary film theorists construe the

film spectator as a passive observer of the image who is duped into believing that it is real. In fact, as I shall argue, the film spectator knows it is only a film and actively participates in the experience of illusion that the cinema affords" (3).

4. Steven Shaviro, *The Cinematic Body* (Minneapolis: Univ. of Minnesota Press, 1993), 257.

5. Compare, for example, Christian Metz's characterization of film: "The cinema is a body (a *corpus* for the semiologist), a fetish that can be loved." *The Imaginary Signifier: Psychoanalysis and the Cinema*, trans. Celia Britton, Annwyl Williams, Ben Brewster, and Alfred Guzzetti (Bloomington: Indiana Univ. Press, 1982), 57. In the same volume, see also "Loving the Cinema," 14–16.

6. Vernet, *Figures de l'absence*, 5. The quotation from Jean Mitry comes from *The Aesthetics and Psychology of the Cinema*, trans. Christopher King (Bloomington: Univ. of Indiana Press, 1997), 34.

7. For a complete survey of the ways critics and theorists have treated this phenomenon, see Jacques Aumont, *The Image*, trans. Claire Pajackowska (London: British Film Institute, 1997), particularly those sections dealing with cinema, such as "The Cinematographic Situation," 128–129.

8. D. N. Rodowick, "Modernism and Semiology," in *The Crisis of Political Modernism: Criticism and Ideology in Contemporary Film Theory*, 2nd ed. (Berkeley and Los Angeles: Univ. of California Press, 1994), 42–67.

9. As Robert Stam describes the difference: "Fully capable of charming their audience, they [Brecht, Buñuel, and Godard] choose, for a variety of reasons, to subvert and undermine their tale. Their central narrative strategy is one of discontinuity. While illusionist art strives for an impression of spatio-temporal coherence, anti-illusionistic art calls attention to the gaps and holes and seams in the narrative tissue." *Reflexivity in Film and Literature: From "Don Quixote" to Jean-Luc Godard* (New York: Columbia Univ. Press, 1992), 7. Stam's work on reflexivity has led logically and beautifully to *Literature through Film: Realism, Magic, and the Art of Adaptation* (Malden, Mass.: Blackwell, 2005), a profound description of places where reflexivity and realism combine rather than contrast. Stam's characterization of "reflexive realism," embodied above all in Latin American film (see *Literature through Film*, 307–370), may be placed next to the final chapters of *The Solaris Effect*, in which I argue that realism in American film only makes sense if framed by self-consciousness.

10. Richard Allen, *Projecting Illusion*, 37. In "Not What is Seen through the Window but the Window Itself: Reflexivity, Enunciation, and Film," Warren Buckland writes that "Christian Metz was preoccupied—either directly or indirectly—with reflexivity in film" (*The Cognitive Semiotics of Film* [New York: Cambridge Univ. Press, 2000], 52). Buckland notes, however, that Metz uses the term "enunciation" rather than "reflexivity," which is at some distance from my emphasis. All films eventually enunciate, but not all films are equally self-reflexive. The self-reflexivity of Fellini's *8 ½*, which Metz wrote about in *Film Language: A Semiotics of the Cinema* (trans. Michael Taylor [Oxford: Oxford Univ. Press, 1974; Chicago: Univ. of Chicago Press, 1991], 228–234; citations are to the Chicago edition), and which Buckland points to as a "key

moment" (*Cognitive Semiotics*, 52) in Metz, is very different from the disruptive Brechtian self-reflexivity in Godard. Metz's clearest description of cinematic reflexivity as enunciation occurs in "The Impersonal Enunciation, or the Site of Film," trans. Béatrice Durand-Sendrail and Kristen Brookes, in *The Film Spectator: From Sign to Mind*, ed. Warren Buckland (Amsterdam: Amsterdam Univ. Press, 1995), 140–163. By this time (1987), Metz had dropped almost entirely the psychoanalytical paraphernalia.

11. Metz, *Imaginary Signifier*, 44–45.

12. See the section "Theatre Fiction, Cinema Fiction" in Metz, *Imaginary Signifier*, 66–68. It is in this section that Brecht makes his first and only appearance.

13. Actually there is one reference, in which Metz notes a brief look at *Pierrot le fou* in his previous book, *Film Language* (1974).

14. Gilles Deleuze, *Cinema 1: The Movement-Image*, trans. Hugh Tomlinson and Barbara Habberjam (Minneapolis: Univ. of Minnesota Press, 1986); *Cinema 2: The Time-Image*, trans. Hugh Tomlinson and Robert Galeta (Minneapolis: Univ. of Minnesota Press, 1989).

15. *Cinema 2*, 172.

16. Ibid. "Thinking is a matter of affirmation, not determination," writes D. N. Rodowick in *Gilles Deleuze's Time Machine* (Durham, N.C.: Duke Univ. Press, 1997), 133. For a fuller account of affirmation in Deleuze, see 132–138.

17. Jean-Pierre Oudart, for example, speaks of the "tragic and vacillating nature of the image," as quoted in Stephen Heath, "On Suture," in *Questions of Cinema* (Bloomington: Indiana Univ. Press, 1981), 89.

18. The title of the collection edited by David Bordwell and Noël Carroll sums up well the general condition: *Post-Theory: Reconstructing Film Studies* (Madison: Univ. of Wisconsin Press, 1996).

19. According to Philip Fisher, "The act of painting is a self-historicization, an interpretation, and a prediction. An object is produced whose *content* is not an image but the instructions for setting it in historical terms." *Making and Effacing Art: Modern American Art in a Culture of Museums* (New York: Oxford Univ. Press, 1991), 35.

20. *Japón* looks like an astonishing feat of cinematic naturalism, but one that also frames its nonactors and authentic locations with references to Tarkovsky through and through, as Reygadas is the first to admit: "There's much about your film that's reminiscent of Tarkovsky. Was he an influence?" "Yes, the only one I'd mention" (Carlos Reygadas, interviewed by Demetrios Matheou, "A Good Place to Die," *Sight and Sound* 13 [Feb. 2003], 12).

21. This is what *Cahiers du cinéma* implied when, in an overview of recent American film, it put an article on McTiernan next to pieces on Soderbergh, Van Sant, and Todd Haynes (577 [March 2003], 18–25).

22. Tarkovsky's film was adapted from the novel *Solaris* by Stanislaw Lem (trans. Joanna Kilmartin and Steve Cox [New York: Walker, 1970; New York: Harcourt, 1987; citations are to the Harcourt ed.]); see 42 for the epigraph to this subsection. On "poetry" in cinema, see Tarkovsky, *Sculpting in Time: Reflections on the Cinema*, trans. Kitty Hunter-Blair (Austin: Univ. of Texas Press, 1986), especially 15–35.

23. Mark Le Fanu, *The Cinema of Andrei Tarkovsky* (London: British Film Institute, 1987), 59.

24. Ibid.

25. In the words of Donald Richie: "Here, then [in *Rashomon*], more than in any other single film, is found Kurosawa's central theme: the world is illusion, you yourself make reality, but this reality undoes you if you submit to being limited by what you have made." *The Films of Akira Kurosawa* (Berkeley and Los Angeles: Univ. of California Press, 1984), 76.

26. Le Fanu, *Tarkovsky*, 68.

27. Ibid., 60.

28. Vida T. Johnson and Graham Petrie, *The Films of Andrei Tarkovsky: A Visual Fugue* (Bloomington: Indiana Univ. Press, 1994), 104–105; the authors also note "a certain woodenness in the acting, especially that of Donatas Banionis as Kris" (110).

29. Andrei Tarkovsky, *Collected Screenplays*, trans. William Powell and Natasha Synessios (London: Faber and Faber, 1999), 184.

30. On painting and film in Tarkovsky, see Angela Dalle Vacche, "Andrei Tarkovsky's *Andrei Rublev:* Cinema as the Restoration of Icon Painting," in *Cinema and Painting: How Art Is Used in Film* (Austin: Univ. of Texas Press, 1996), 135–160.

31. An interview with composer Eduard Artemyev reveals that Tarkovsky intended to create "depths of time" through his selection of music and paintings (interview included on the DVD of the Criterion Collection *Solaris* [2002]).

32. I refer to the DVD commentary on the Criterion Collection *Solaris*.

33. Jameson, *The Geopolitical Aesthetic: Cinema and Space in the World System* (London: British Film Institute, 1992), 100.

34. Jean Baudrillard, "The Murder of the Real," in *The Vital Illusion* (New York: Columbia Univ. Press, 2000), 62.

35. On Harold Russell's hooks in *The Best Years of Our Lives*, see Kaja Silverman, "Historical Trauma and Male Subjectivity," in *Psychoanalysis and Cinema*, ed. E. Ann Kaplan (New York: Routledge, 1990), 110–127.

36. I do not linger too much on the often vexed relationship between independent film and Hollywood film, often linking small distribution companies somehow (sometimes quite directly) to Hollywood financing. My pantheon of independent filmmakers is basically the same as that found in Emanuel Levy, *Cinema of Outsiders: The Rise of American Independent Film* (New York: New York Univ. Press, 1999). Levy provides much detail about the different degrees of financial and creative independence available to particular filmmakers.

37. See, for example, Jon Lewis, ed., *The End of Cinema as We Know It: American Film in the Nineties* (New York: New York Univ. Press, 2001).

38. For examples of more complicated phenomenological descriptions, see Vivian Sobchack, *The Address of the Eye: A Phenomenology of Film Experience* (Princeton, N.J.: Princeton Univ. Press, 1992), and Kaja Silverman, *The Threshold of the Visible World* (New York: Routledge, 1996).

Chapter 2

1. Jameson, "On Soviet Magic Realism," in *The Geopolitical Aesthetic*, 87–113. In the paragraph that follows, page numbers in parentheses refer to this text.

2. Vida T. Johnson and Graham Petrie, *The Films of Andrei Tarkovsky: A Visible Fugue* (Bloomington: Indiana Univ. Press, 1994), 153.

3. Peter Ettedgui, *Cinematography Screencraft* (Boston: Focal Press, 1998), 42. Other examples of tinting from this excellent collection are Gordon Willis's "dirty, brassy, yellow" filtration for the Robert De Niro sections of *The Godfather: Part II* (120), and Roger Deakins's desaturating process for Michael Radford's *1984* (165).

4. *Andrei Rublev* turns to color at the very end, when the camera pans all around the finished icons.

5. For example, Donald Lyons, "Lubricating the Muse," in *Film Comment* 28 (Jan.– Feb. 1992), 14–16.

6. Nicolas Saade, "La métamorphose de Soderbergh," *Cahiers du cinéma* 454 (Apr. 1992), 52.

7. Nick James, *Sight and Sound* 4 (Mar. 1994) 43.

8. Saade, "La métamorphose," 50; Lyons, "Lubricating the Muse," 15.

9. As Soderbergh himself puts it: "I'm not a visionary artist; sometimes I would like to be, but I don't belong to that category of filmmakers like Kubrick, Altman, or Fellini, let alone share their talent. These artists have changed the cinematic vocabulary; their films are unlike any others. I am more like those who respond to a certain kind of subject matter, and who look for the best style to express it. I am not trying to impose my style." *Steven Soderbergh: Interviews*, ed. Anthony Kaufman (Jackson: Univ. Press of Mississippi, 2002), 60.

10. "Godard is a constant source of inspiration," says Soderbergh. "Before I do anything, I go back and look at as many of his films as I can, as a reminder of what's possible." *Soderbergh Interviews*, 140.

11. "Tainted with nostalgia," *Soderbergh Interviews*, 62.

12. Wilmington's top 10 list, which appeared in the *Chicago Tribune*, was as follows: 1. *Three Colors* (Kieslowski), 2. *Forrest Gump* (Zemeckis), 3. *Sunday's Children* (Daniel Bergman), 4. *Pulp Fiction* (Tarantino), 5. *Hoop Dreams* (Steve James), 6. *To Live* (Zhang Yimou), 7. *Ready to Wear* (Altman), 8. *Natural Born Killers* (Stone), 9. *Naked* (Mike Leigh), 10. *Interview with A Vampire* (Neil Jordan).

13. Mark C. Carnes, "Past Imperfect: History According to the Movies," *Cineaste* 22, no. 4 (Fall 1996); reproduced online at *www.lib.berkeley.edu/MRC/pastimperfect.html*; accessed September 22, 2005.

14. *Oliver Stone: Interviews*, ed. Charles L. P. Silet (Jackson: Univ. Press of Mississippi, 2001), 31.

15. Carnes, "Past Imperfect."

16. Ibid.

17. Kolker (*Cinema of Loneliness*, 66) aligns Stone's editing with Eisenstein's.

18. Zizek, *The Fright of Real Tears: Krzysztof Kieslowski between Theory and Post-Theory* (London: British Film Institute, 2001), 66. One of Zizek's examples in this description is Siodmak's *Criss Cross*.

19. Ibid.

20. In McTiernan's *Rollerball* (2002) there is a long sequence that is, in fact, green due to night-vision goggles.

21. Stanley Cavell, *Pursuits of Happiness: The Hollywood Comedy of Remarriage* (Cambridge, Mass.: Harvard Univ. Press, 1981).

22. Soderbergh, *Getting Away with It: Or, the Further Adventures of the Luckiest Bastard You Ever Saw,* (London: Faber and Faber, 1999).

23. Roger Ebert writes, "The costume design sinks this movie. Roberts is a sensational-looking woman, and dressed so provocatively in every single scene, she upstages the material." *Chicago Sun-Times,* March 17, 2000. Accessed September 22, 2005, on rogerebert.suntimes.com.

24. To describe the layering of time in *The Limey,* Soderbergh called his film "*Get Carter* as made by Alain Resnais" (*Soderbergh Interviews,* 115).

25. Andrew O'Hehir, review of *Traffic, Sight and Sound* 11 (Feb. 2001), 54.

26. Soderbergh comments on Dogma and its relation to *Traffic* in *Soderbergh Interviews,* 159–160. I will talk more about the austere principles of Dogma in Chapter Seven.

27. Soderbergh describes the filters and the rest of the technical apparatus in *Soderbergh Interviews,* 150.

28. Patrice Blouin, "Frontière mexicaine," *Cahiers du cinéma* 555 (Mar. 2001), 74.

29. On his DVD commentary Soderbergh says exactly that.

30. On the presence of water and rain in Tarkovsky, see Antoine de Baecque, *Andrei Tarkovski* (Paris: Cahiers du cinéma, 1989), 21–34.

31. On the tradition of including poems in films, see Steven Dillon, *Derek Jarman and Lyric Film: The Mirror and the Sea* (Austin: Univ. of Texas Press, 2004).

32. After the titles, the very first thing we see in *Breathless* is a newspaper advertisement with a picture of a sexy woman in a bathing suit. The apartments in *Breathless* are papered over with posters and photographs. Over the course of his filmmaking career, Godard has never stopped collecting and analyzing images.

33. See note 24 to this chapter.

34. Wheeler W. Dixon, *It Looks Back at You: The Returned Gaze of Cinema* (Albany: State Univ. of New York Press, 1995).

Chapter 3

1. For an excellent survey of American films with an environmental emphasis, see David Ingram, *Green Screen: Environmentalism and Hollywood Cinema* (Exeter, UK: Univ. of Exeter Press, 2000). A powerful attempt to characterize the "nature movie" as a genre in 1980s American film is found in Leo Braudy, "The Genre of Nature: Ceremonies of Innocence," in *Refiguring American Film Genres: Theory and History,* ed. Nick Browne (Berkeley and Los Angeles: Univ. of California Press, 1998). For a very useful collection of articles on the role of nature in twentieth-century thought, see *The Green Studies Reader: From Romanticism to Ecocriticism,* ed. Laurence Coupe (New York: Routledge, 2000).

2. Darren Aronofsky, *Pi: Screenplay and the Guerilla Diaries* (London: Faber and Faber, 1998).

3. Thierry Jousse, *"Frankenstein contre Dracula,"* *Cahiers du cinéma* 463 (Jan. 1993), 16. Here Jousse argues for the signal influence of Romero's *Night of the Living Dead* on John Carpenter, Joe Dante, and Oliver Stone.

4. Abigail Crispin and Sam Haaz, students in my 2002 course in contemporary American film, demonstrated how well π corresponds to the elements of horror film as characterized by David Bordwell and Kristin Thompson (*Film Art: An Introduction* [New York: McGraw-Hill, 2001], 102–105).

5. Gibson is still very much around and weighing in on the information revolution. In a recent film, *William Gibson: No Maps for These Territories* (Mark Neale, 2000), Gibson delivers a feature-length monologue on cyberculture.

6. Both π and *The Matrix* rely overwhelmingly on a mystical, intuitive sensibility to cancel out or tranquilize a technological apocalypse.

7. Jameson, *Geopolitical Aesthetic*, 100.

8. Kenneth Turan, *Sundance to Sarajevo: Film Festivals and the World They Made* (Berkeley and Los Angeles: Univ. of California Press, 2002), 36.

9. *www.sundancechannel.com/family* (accessed Sept. 25, 2000). Redford's entire Academy Award acceptance speech is reproduced on the page that collects the various organizations that constitute the "Sundance Family."

10. Janet Maslin, *New York Times*, Feb 1, 1998.

11. Turan, *Sundance to Sarajevo*, 40.

12. *www.sundancechannel.com/family* (accessed Sept. 25, 2005).

13. *www.sundancecatalog.com/jump.jsp?itemID=348&itemType=Artist_Community& iMainCat=132&iSubCat=136&page=20* (accessed Sept. 25, 2005).

14. Robert Redford, interview with Patricia Troy, "Robert Redford Talks Scripts, Independent Film, and Sundance," *Written By*, Jan. 1996, *www.wga.org/WrittenBy/1996/ 0196/redford.htm* (accessed June 15, 2003; now unavailable).

15. The first of Redford's Sundance films, those with an environmental emphasis, was *The Milagro Beanfield War* (1988). The first film that Redford directed was *Ordinary People* (1980).

16. Robert Redford, interview with James Mottram of the BBC, www.bbc.co.uk/ films/2001/02/20/robert_redford_baggervance_200201_interview.shtml (accessed Sept. 26, 2005).

17. For example, Pauline Kael criticizes *Broadcast News* for taking a superior attitude toward television in "Fakers" (in *Hooked* [New York: Dutton, 1989], 416–420).

18. The circle is completed when we realize that Harvey Keitel was originally cast as the Martin Sheen character in *Apocalypse Now;* Keitel was fired by Coppola after only a few days of work. See the entry on Harvey Keitel in Karl French, *Apocalypse Now* (London: Bloomsbury, 1998), 123–124.

19. Gavin Smith, "Going Pro," *Film Comment* 36, no. 2 (Mar./-Apr. 2000), 44.

20. Although not everyone will be able to understand the poetry, as the following exchange suggests.

CUZ: So after smoking this, I'll understand some of that shit you be talking about in your rhymes, right?
RAY: Probably not.

Slam: The Book, ed. Richard Stratton and Kim Wozencraft (New York: Grove Press, 1998), 176.

21. Solondz's first film is actually *Fear, Anxiety, and Depression* (1989), although that film has essentially fallen off the map of his career.

22. In an interview the artist Barbara Kruger says that she feels closer to certain films than gallery art: "*Happiness, Welcome to the Dollhouse*, Kevin Smith's *Clerks*, Spike Lee's *Do the Right Thing*, Vincent Gallo's *Buffalo 66*, Neil LaBute's *In the Company of Men*—I feel very close to that kind of address. But most critics compared the Deitch show to other art world practices, which is never my baseline at all." Barbara Kruger, *Thinking of You* (Cambridge, Mass.: MIT Press; Los Angeles: Los Angeles Museum of Contemporary Art, 1999), 195.

23. Review of *Requiem for a Dream, Sight and Sound* 10 (Dec. 2000), 26–28.

24. "Introduction: An Interview with Darren Aronofsky by Miles Fielder," in *Requiem for a Dream*, screenplay by Darren Aronofsky and Hubert Selby, Jr. (London: Faber and Faber, 2000), vii, x. That Faber and Faber published the scripts of both of Aronofsky's films gives a sense of the critical regard for Aronofsky in 2000. The prestigious house has also published scripts by the Coen brothers, David Cronenberg, and David Lynch, in addition to screenplays by the most interesting younger American directors, such as Rebecca Miller, Paul Thomas Anderson, and Neil LaBute.

25. Hubert Selby, Jr., *Requiem for a Dream* (New York: Playboy Press, dist. by Simon and Schuster, 1978), 89.

26. Aronofsky, *Requiem for a Dream*, xiv.

27. Ibid., xv.

28. Ibid. Harry and Marion, 123; Tyrone, 124.

29. Ibid., 126–127.

30. Erwan Higuinen, review of *Requiem for a Dream, Cahiers du cinéma* 555 (Dec. 2001), 88. After showing π at Sundance and *Requiem for a Dream* at Cannes, Aronofsky was widely regarded in 2000 as at least masterful enough to write his own Hollywood meal ticket. Yet the shooting of *The Fountain* broke down in 2002 when Brad Pitt left to film *Troy* (Petersen, 2004). Later Aronofsky worked on a Batman project that would eventually be given to Christopher Nolan. As of this writing (June 15, 2005), Aronofsky's *Fountain*, a time-travel film now starring Hugh Jackman, looks to be released in 2005 by Warner.

31. Truffaut's famous essay "A Certain Tendency of the French Cinema" argued against a "tradition of quality" on behalf of films like Bresson's *Diary of a Country Priest*, Cocteau's *Orpheus*, and Tati's *Mr. Hulot's Holiday*. The essay is reprinted in Bill Nichols, ed., *Movies and Methods*, vol. 1 (Berkeley and Los Angeles: Univ. of California Press, 1976), 224–237.

Chapter 4

1. Ebert, review of *Mulholland Drive*, *Chicago Sun-Times*, Oct. 12, 2001. rogerebert .suntimes.com (accessed 6/15/2005).

2. See *Cahiers du cinéma, 1969–1972: The Politics of Representation*, ed. Nick Browne (Cambridge, Mass.: Harvard Univ. Press, 1990).

3. Kolker, *Cinema of Loneliness*, 177.

4. Armond White, "Brian De Palma, Political Filmmaker," *Film Comment* 27, no. 3 (May–June 1991), 72.

5. Howard Hampton, "Mission," *Film Comment* 32 (July–Aug. 1996), 48. De Palma finally found his way back onto the cover of *Film Comment* (Nov.–Dec. 2002) for *Femme Fatale*.

6. *Cahiers du cinéma* 492 (June 1995), 18ff.

7. Scorsese, "Notre Génération," *Cahiers du cinéma* 500 (Mar. 1996), 37–39.

8. Roger Ebert, review of *Mission to Mars*, *Chicago Sun-Times*, Mar. 10, 2000. rogerebert.suntimes.com (accessed 6/15/2005).

9. This is in complete contrast to the polls in *Film Comment*, which do not list the movie even once.

10. *Cahiers du cinéma* 546 (May 2000), 38.

11. Ibid., 36.

12. Ibid., 42.

13. Ibid., 46.

14. Ibid., 50.

15. Ibid., 51 (my translation).

16. See, for example, Michel Chion, *The Voice in Cinema*, trans. Claudia Gorbman (New York: Columbia Univ. Press, 1999).

17. Michel Chion, *David Lynch*, trans. Robert Julian (London: British Film Institute, 1995).

18. "Sus au mystère," *Cahiers du cinéma* 457 (June 1992), 44.

19. The decade poll was included in *Cahiers du cinéma* 542 (Jan. 2000). There is a small ambiguity in the phrasing, insofar as "*Twin Peaks* (Lynch, 1992)" took the spot, not *Twin Peaks: Fire Walk with Me*. The title was given this way in the ranking because although Thierry Jousse and Erwan Higuinen voted for *Twin Peaks: Fire Walk* on their lists, Jérôme Larcher voted for both "*film et série*," for both the film and the television series, in his list. So the title given in the decade poll is a kind of average, to take into account Larcher's elevation of the *Twin Peaks* television series.

20. "When David Lynch tells us, as he does in every public statement, that he makes his films to give his audience a place to dream, he is not waxing metaphorical" (Martha Nochimson, *The Passion of David Lynch: Wild at Heart in Hollywood* [Austin: Univ. of Texas Press, 1997], 16).

21. *Lynch on Lynch*, ed. Chris Rodley (London: Faber and Faber, 1997), 15.

22. Nochimson, *Passion of David Lynch*, 14, 13. "Lynch seeks to avoid the Hollywood trap of creating substitutes for life. Rather he seeks to use the power of Hollywood to make film narrative a subconscious bridge to real perceptions of life" (13).

23. Ibid., 14.

24. Ibid., 197.

25. As Tarkovsky himself put it: "I find poetic links, the logic of poetry in cinema, extraordinarily pleasing. They seem to me perfectly appropriate to the potential of cinema as the most truthful and poetic of art forms. Certainly I am more at home with them than with traditional theatrical writing which links images through the linear, rigidly logical development of the plot." *Sculpting in Time*, 18, 20.

26. Frédéric Strauss, "Tempête sous un crâne," *Cahiers du cinéma* 509 (Jan. 1997), 24.

27. Ibid.

28. Chion, *David Lynch*, 150–151.

29. Nochimson describes the antics of Lil very well: " 'Her' face is covered with theatrical white make-up; 'she' wears a patently artificial red wig, black stockings and red high heels, and a loosely fitted, cartoony red dress to which is pinned an artificial blue rose" (*Passion of David Lynch*, 178). But in her discussion, Nochimson emphasizes not artificiality, but rather gender decoding and semiotic confusion.

30. The imagery of dream theater goes all the way back to Lynch's *Eraserhead* (1976), in which Henry Spencer (John Nance) dreams himself right onto a cur-tained stage.

31. Chion, *David Lynch*, 158–159.

32. Greg Taylor, *Artists in the Audience: Cults, Camp and American Film Criticism* (Princeton, N.J.: Princeton Univ. Press, 1999), 157.

33. Thierry Jousse, "L'amour à mort," in *Pendant les travaux, le cinéma reste ouvert* (Paris: Cahiers du cinéma, 2003), 200.

34. Ibid.

35. Amy Taubin offers one of the most detailed explications of who is who in *Mulholland Drive* ("In Dreams," *Film Comment* 37, no. 5 [Sept.–Oct. 2001]). I completely agree that "Betty is Diane's fantasy alter ego" (54). But Taubin does not give a central role to the woman in apartment 12, an omission that to my mind misses the "reality" of that romance. Just as Betty is Diane's alter ego, Rita is the woman in apartment 12's alter ego, as it were.

36. Jousse, *Pendant les travaux*, 196.

37. Thierry Jousse, "Les dandys du câble," in *Critique et cinéphilie* (Paris: Cahiers du cinéma, 2001).

38. Ibid., 184.

39. Serge Daney, *La rampe* (Paris: Cahiers du cinéma, 1996); *Ciné Journal 1: 1981–1982* (Paris: Cahiers du cinéma, 1998); *Ciné Journal 2: 1983–1986* (Paris: Cahiers du cinéma, 1998)

40. Daney's nearness to Godard is made explicit by Godard himself when he films a long and rather surrealistic dialogue-interview between himself and Daney for *Histoire(s) du cinéma: Seul le cinéma* (1997). The phrase "cinema alone" (*seul le cinéma*) originates with Daney and refers to film before television.

41. In July 2003, *Cahiers du cinéma* changed its editorial board from one headed by Tesson to one headed by Frodon. The approach of the magazine seems basically unchanged, although there are some different departments ("Le cinéma retrouvé" is now a regular feature, for example).

42. Serge Daney, "La fonction critique," in *Critique et cinéphilie*, 99–122. The section heading that follows Daney's set of essays is "Retours de cinéphilie," which dates, in effect, the return of cinephilia to *Cahiers du cinéma* to 1977.

43. Ibid., 109.

44. Serge Daney, *L'exercice a été profitable, monsieur*, ed. Jean-Claude Biette and Emmanuel Crimail (Paris: POL, 1993).

45. All of these references come from Daney, *Ciné Journal 2*.

46. Daney wrote a whole series of articles under the rubric "Le cinéma voyagé."

47. *Stalker* as realist: *Ciné Journal 1*, 90. *Vertigo* as human: *Ciné Journal 2*, 95.

48. Daney, *La rampe*, 209. Georges Sadoul, one of the most important film critics in midcentury France, was the author of many works, including *Histoire général de cinéma*, the first volume of which appeared in 1946. Daney was born in 1944.

49. Daney, *La rampe*, 201.

50. Deleuze weighs in on Daney's voyages in "Letter to Serge Daney: Optimism, Pessimism, and Travel," in *Negotiations, 1972–1990*, trans. Martin Joughin (New York: Columbia Univ. Press, 1995), 68–80. This essay originally appeared in French as the preface to *Ciné Journal 1*.

51. Other "effects" in *L'exercice* include the *Ordet*-effect (83) and the Hitchcock-effect (269).

Chapter 5

The quote by Chris Marker comes from Michel Ciment and Laurence Kardish, eds., *"Positif" 50 Years: Selections from the French Film Journal* (New York: Museum of Modern Art, 2002), 159.

1. Serge Daney reads this and similar passages in Bazin as a demand that human beings risk their lives for cinema ("L'écran du fantasme [Bazin et les bêtes]," in *La rampe*, 36–47).

2. "Digital images are truly revolutionary," writes Ollivier Dyens (*Metal and Flesh: The Evolution of Man; Technology Takes Over*, trans. Evan J. Bibbee and Ollivier Dyens [Cambridge, Mass.: MIT Press, 2001], 85). According to William J. Mitchell, "The emergence of digital imaging has irrevocably subverted [the certainties of photographs], forcing us to adopt a far more wary and more vigilant interpretive stance, much as recent philosophy and literary theory have shaken our faith in the ultimate grounding of written texts on external reference" (*The Reconfigured Eye: Visual Truth in the Post-Photographic Era* [Cambridge, Mass.: MIT Press, 1992], 225). Peter Lunenfeld, *Snap to Grid: A User's Guide to Digital Arts, Media, and Cultures* (Cambridge, Mass.: MIT Press, 2000), tends to emphasize the differences between old and new media. In "Moving the Center: The Reconfiguration of the Moving Image" (in *The Transparency of Spectacle: Meditations on the Moving Image* [Albany: State Univ. of New York Press, 1998], 1–46), Wheeler Winston Dixon contrasts the empty artifice ("non-reality") of CGI Hollywood with the "humanist rawness" of Iranian and African cinema (44). Yet a number of writers emphasize a gradual continuity between analog and digital cinema, and this is my position as well. Jay David Bolter and Richard Grusin question the novelty of new media in *Remediation: Understanding New Media* (Cambridge,

Mass.: MIT Press, 1999). Toby Miller and Robert Stam write, "This is simply one more moment in the history of film and illusion. Digitization makes the appearance of a person look actual when it is not. Is the intent or effect different from matting-in or rear projection? No, the degree of spectacle is what differs, and doctrines of verisimilitude and customer expectations shift along with them" ("The Image and Technology: Introduction," in *Film and Theory: An Anthology*, ed. Robert Stam and Toby Miller [Malden, Mass.: Blackwell, 2000], 97). Philip Rosen, "Old and New: Image, Indexicality, and Historicity in the Digital Utopia," in *Change Mummified: Cinema, Historicity, Theory* (Minneapolis: Univ. of Minnesota Press, 2001), 301–349, is also more balanced in his weighing of old against new.

3. Thomas Elsaesser and Warren Buckland, *Studying Contemporary American Film: A Guide to Movie Analysis* (London: Arnold, 2002).

4. Jean-Pierre Oudart, "Cinema and Suture," in Browne, *Cahiers du cinéma*, 45–57. In his 1969 article, Oudart observed that Bresson's *Au hasard, Balthazar* (1966) would not suture. Heath took Oudart's work beyond the shot–reverse shot motif to account for more cinematic elements. But the result generally works to map continuous suturing onto classical narrative. See Heath, "On Suture," 76–112.

5. Lev Manovich, *The Language of New Media* (Cambridge, Mass.: MIT, 2001).

6. David Bordwell and Kristin Thompson, "Technological Change and Classical Film Style," in *Grand Design: Hollywood as a Modern Business Enterprise, 1930–1939*, ed. Tino Balio (New York: Scribner's, 1993), 132–133.

7. David Bordwell, Janet Staiger, and Kristin Thompson, *The Classical Hollywood Cinema: Film Style and Mode of Production to 1960* (New York: Columbia Univ. Press, 1985), 258.

8. Ibid., 258.

9. Ibid., 21.

10. Stam, "Post-Cinema: Digital and Theory and New Media," in *Film Theory*, 316.

11. The only substantial discussion of Godard in Manovich is of the video series *Histoire(s) du cinéma* (1989–), which develops "a unique aesthetics of continuity that relies on electronically mixing a number of images together within a single shot" (Manovich, *New Media*, 151). Despite this extraordinary experiment in montage, which now seems to be one of Godard's most lasting achievements, Manovich does not elect Godard to his slender pantheon. And Godard's radical film co-op of the 1970s was called, precisely, "Dziga Vertov"!

12. I leave to one side the small-scale independent films that use digital cameras, since that history is even more abbreviated, as well as foreign films made with digital technology.

13. Raymond Bellour, "L'instant de voir," in *L'entre-images 2: Mots, images* (Paris: POL, 1999), 267–279.

14. Quoted in Bellour, *L'entre-images 2*, 161.

15. Marker's CD-ROM *Immemory* is distributed by Exact Change (5 Brewster Street, Cambridge, Mass., 02138), and runs on a Macintosh. Bellour's essay on *Immemory* appears in *L'entre-images 2* (335–362), and also in a special volume, *Qu'est-ce qu'une*

madeleine? A propos du CD-ROM *"Immemory" de Chris Marker* (Paris: Centre Georges Pompidou, 1997), which contains two essays, one by Laurent Roth and the other by Bellour.

16. Manovich mentions Marker's CD-ROM as an example of a "project investigating database politics and possible aesthetics" (*New Media*, 221), but that is the only mention of Marker in the book.

17. Bellour, *A propos du* CD-ROM *"Immemory,"* 147.

18. Ibid., 147–148.

19. Ibid., 142.

20. Manovich, *New Media*, 325.

21. Gilliam's barely begun film on Don Quixote is documented in *Lost in La Mancha* (Louis Pepe and Keith Fulton, 2002).

22. Sergei Eisenstein, *Eisenstein on Disney*, trans. Alan Upchurch (London: Methuen, 1988), 23.

23. Eisenstein, quoted in Michael O'Pray, "Eisenstein and Stokes on Disney: Film Animation and Omnipotence," in *A Reader in Animation Studies*, ed. Jayne Pilling (Sydney: John Libbey, 1997), 201. For Eisenstein's response to Disney in particular, see See Esther Leslie, "Eisenstein Shakes Mickey's Hand in Hollywood," in *Hollywood Flatlands: Animation, Critical Theory, and the Avant-Garde* (New York: Verso, 2002), 232–234.

24. O'Pray, "Eisenstein on Disney": "plasmatic," 201; "fragility of the image," 200.

25. Maureen Furniss, "Defining Animation," in *Art in Motion: Animation Aesthetics* (Sydney: John Libbey, 1998), 6. Furniss thus begins her book by complicating the distinction between live-action and animated film, but the rest of the examples in the book are drawn from what we ordinarily think of as animated film.

26. *Computer Gaming World*, June 2003, 43.

27. These genres are the main game categories that organize Kate Berens and Geoff Howard, *The Rough Guide to Videogaming* (New York: Rough Guides, 2002). For a full-scale analysis of the relationship between movies and videogames, see Geoff King and Tanya Krzywinska, eds., *ScreenPlay: Cinema/Videogames/Interfaces* (London and New York: Wallflower, 2002).

28. Kevin Smith, *The Green Arrow: Quiver* (New York: DC Comics, 2002), 117–118.

29. Tarantino talks about the comic books and posters in *Reservoir Dogs* in his interview with Michel Ciment and Hubert Niogret ("Interview at Cannes," in *Quentin Tarantino: Interviews*, ed. Gerald Peary [Jackson: Univ. Press of Mississippi, 1998], 20).

30. As Laura M. Holson reported: "'As long as it was cartoonish and fun they were fine with it,' Mr. Weinstein said." "Studies Killing (But Carefully) So They Can Get an R Rating," *New York Times*, Oct. 21, 2003.

31. The torture scene in *Pulp Fiction* is taken directly from *Deliverance* (Boorman, 1972), in which the violent rape in the woods is fantastically extreme yet played realistically.

32. Tarantino self-reflexively comments on the acting style of *Reservoir Dogs* in

the speech of Holdaway, the cop who trains Mr. Orange: "An undercover cop has got to be Marlon Brando. To do this job you got to be a great actor. You got to be natural-istic. You got to be naturalistic as hell." *Reservoir Dogs and True Romance* (New York: Grove, 1994), 70.

33. *Tarantino Interviews*, 7.

34. There is one post–New Wave reference to Godard. In an interview, Tarantino says he put Godard's *King Lear* (1987) on his résumé because "nobody would ever see the film" (*Tarantino Interviews*, 27).

35. Deleuze, *Cinema 2*, 37.

36. Alain Badiou, *Deleuze: The Clamor of Being*, trans. Louise Burchill (Minneapolis: Univ. of Minnesota Press, 2000), 61.

37. Drehli Robnik, "Saving One Life: Spielberg's *Artificial Intelligence* as Redemp-tive Memory of Things," *Ejumpcut, http://www.ejumpcut.org/archive/jc45.2002/robnik/* (accessed Sept. 28, 2005).

38. Karen Alexander, "Interview with Julie Dash," in *American Independent Cinema*, ed. Jim Hillier (London: British Film Institute, 2001), 44.

39. Mark Williams, "Real-Time Fairy Tales: Cinema Prefiguring Digital Anxiety," in *New Media: Theories and Practices of Digitextuality*, ed. Anna Everett and John T. Caldwell, 159–178 (New York: Routledge, 2003).

40. See Michael Heim, "The Erotic Ontology of Cyberspace," in *The Metaphysics of Virtual Reality* (New York: Oxford Univ. Press, 1993), 83–108.

Chapter 6

1. On reading the combines, see Branden W. Joseph, *Random Order: Robert Rauschenberg and the Neo-Avant-Garde* (Cambridge, Mass.: MIT Press, 2003), 157–171.

2. Rosalind E. Krauss, "Sculpture in the Expanded Field," in *The Originality of the Avant-Garde and Other Modernist Myths* (Cambridge, Mass.: MIT Press, 1985), 282.

3. David Lubin calls the anachronism of this scene "wonderfully campy" (*Titanic* [London: British Film Institute, 1999], 34).

4. On nature and art in *Titanic*, see Lubin, *Titanic*, 28–36.

5. An example of such a film, which bends its visuals into the contorted figures of its hero's paintings, is John Maybury's brilliant study of Francis Bacon, *Love is the Devil* (1998).

6. Siegfried Kracauer, *Theory of Film: The Redemption of Physical Reality* (New York: Oxford Univ. Press, 1960; rept. Princeton, N.J.: Princeton Univ. Press, 1997).

7. Initially Kubrick and Raphael intended to make the wife a painter, according to Frederic Raphael, *Eyes Wide Open: A Memoir of Stanley Kubrick* (New York: Ballantine, 1999), 60, 73.

8. Michel Chion, *Eyes Wide Shut*, trans. Trista Selous (London: British Film Insti-tute, 2002), 25.

9. On parroting, see Chion, *Eyes Wide Shut*, 76–80.

10. Kracauer, *Theory of Film*, 20.

11. Kracauer, *Theory of Film*, 1–11.

12. Chion, *Eyes Wide Shut*, 41.

13. Raymond Durgnat, *Films and Feelings* (Cambridge, Mass.: MIT Press, 1971), 232.

14. Kracauer, *Theory of Film*, 305.

15. Ibid., 306.

16. At the end of Kubrick's *A Clockwork Orange*, Alex simply announces that he is cured, which seems to mean that he has regressed right back to being the ultra-violent maniac he was when the film began. Kubrick deliberately omits the events contained in the final chapter of Anthony Burgess's novel *A Clockwork Orange*, showing Alex developing into a humane citizen. Burgess found Kubrick's conclusion stultifying, whereas Kubrick found Burgess's conclusion idealizing and inconsistent. See Anthony Burgess, "Introduction: *A Clockwork Orange* Resucked," in *A Clockwork Orange* (New York: Norton, 1986), v–xi.

17. *Robert Altman: Interviews*, ed. David Sterritt (Jackson: Univ. Press of Mississippi, 2000), 110.

18. Ibid., 41.

19. Ibid., 118.

20. Ken Russell likes to accept the challenge of telling the stories of writers and musicians, in films like *The Music Lovers* (1970; about Tchaikovsky), *Mahler* (1974), *Lisztomania* (1975), *Gothic* (1986; Mary Shelley), and *Salome's Last Dance* (1988; Oscar Wilde).

21. *Altman Interviews*, 204.

22. Kolker, *Cinema of Loneliness*, 386.

23. *Altman Interviews*, 194.

24. Recalling the way that Elisabeth sucks Alma's blood like a vampire, and also the interpolated silent film featuring a running skeleton, Lloyd Michaels notes that "*Persona* may be fairly regarded as a kind of modernist horror movie" ("Bergman and the Necessary Illusion," in *Ingmar Bergman's "Persona"*, ed. Lloyd Michaels [New York: Cambridge Univ. Press, 2000], 17). Altman's *Images* (1972), which is most explicitly drawn from *Persona*, has its hallucinating heroine, Cathryn (Susannah York), kill her ghosts one after the other. The dissolution of subjectivity goes hand in hand with violence.

25. Kolker, *Cinema of Loneliness*, 342ff.

26. *Altman Interviews*, 145.

27. Art that wants to sabotage all vestiges of "high culture" often runs into the trashy, sleazy grounds of horror. See Joan Hawkins, *Cutting Edge: Art-Horror and the Horrific Avant-Garde* (Minneapolis: Univ. of Minnesota Press, 2000).

28. Commenting on the "iconic" crucifixion of Lieutenant Boyle, Yvonne Tasker calls *The Silence of the Lambs* an "arty slasher" (*The Silence of the Lambs* [London: British Film Institute, 2002], 32).

29. In his monograph on *Seven*, Richard Dyer comments a few times on the artistic figurations in the film; most explicitly, he argues that if religious salvation is not represented in the film, at least a vision of high culture is: "*Seven* addresses us as people familiar with high culture" (Richard Dyer, *Seven* [London: British Film Institute, 1999], 73). On art and high culture, see also 46, 53, 71–73.

30. On screen and subject in Sherman's photographs, see Hal Foster, *The Return of*

the Real: Art and Theory at the End of the Century (Cambridge, Mass.: MIT Press, 1996), 148–149.

Chapter 7

1. Janet Maslin, review of *Magnolia*, *New York Times*, December 17, 1999.

2. Paul Thomas Anderson, *Magnolia: The Shooting Script* (New York: Newmarket Press, 2000), viii.

3. A very few live-action musicals appeared in the 1990s, such as *Evita* (Parker, 1996) and *Moulin Rouge* (Luhrmann, 2001). *Chicago* (Rob Marshall, 2002), which won the Academy Award for best picture in 2002, does not foretell the return of the theatrical musical to film, unless those films, too, will simply appear as transposed advertisements for Victoria's Secret. *Chicago*'s opening song, "All That Jazz," unintentionally acknowledges its far more inventive predecessor, *All That Jazz* (Fosse, 1979), which outperforms *Chicago* in every respect — choreography, wit, drama, sensuality. Many animated films, of course, are musicals.

4. Roger Ebert, review of *Kids*, *Chicago Sun-Times*, July 28, 1995. rogerebert.suntimes.com/apps/pbcs.dll/article?AID=/19950728/REVIEWS/507280301/1023 (accessed Sept. 29, 2005).

5. In an interview with Van Sant, Clark says, "When I came back to New York around '68, after being in the army, I went to a movie theater to see [Warhol's] *Chelsea Girls* [1966], and I remember thinking, What the fuck is this? But I also thought, They know what they're doing. They're all doing drugs, but they know where the camera is. I grew up in the generation just before the Warhol people; by the time Warhol was making his films, everyone was self-aware and living their lives like they were on a stage. It was like they were performing." "Larry Clark: Shockmaker," *Interview*, July 1995. The article was reproduced on *www.harmony-korine.com/paper/int/clark/shockmaker.html* (accessed Sept. 29, 2005).

6. See the definitive study by Ray Carney, *The Films of John Cassavetes: Pragmatism, Modernism, and the Movies* (New York: Cambridge Univ. Press, 1994).

7. *www.finelinefeatures.com/gummo/about.html* (accessed Sept. 29, 2005).

8. Interview with Korine (*www.finelinefeatures.com/gummo/inter01.htm*; accessed Sept. 29, 2005).

9. For the rules, see "The Birth of Dogma and *The Idiots*," in Jack Stevenson, *Lars von Trier* (London: British Film Institute, 2002), 102–137.

10. Charlotte Garson, "Dogme, mensonges, et vidéo numérique," *Cahiers du cinéma*, special issue, April 2003, 22.

11. The quote comes from Paul Cronin, ed., *Herzog on Herzog* (New York: Faber and Faber, 2002), 139.

12. Jean-Marc Lalanne, "Filmographie/Gus Van Sant," *Cahiers du cinéma* 579 (May 2003), 28.

13. According to commentary by Anne Heche on the *Psycho* DVD.

14. As Michael Kustow affirms: "This, therefore, is the question that must be put to every blazing prophet, evangelistic reformer, or indeed, crusading artist: where do you stand, you who say all this? Where did you find the vantage-point from which to

speak your communications or cries of warning?" Introduction to Jean-Luc Godard, *Made in USA: Screenplay* (London: Lorrimer, 1967), 19.

15. The admiration comes through most clearly in "Freewheelin' Gus Van Sant Converses with Derek Jarman," in *Projections 2: A Forum for Film-Makers*, ed. John Boorman and Walter Donohue (Boston: Faber and Faber, 1993), 89–99.

16. The quotation is from Wilde's essay "The Critic as Artist."

17. Many people must enjoy spending more time with Kevin Smith, since Sony has recently released a two-disc set of Smith's monologues, *An Evening with Kevin Smith* (J. M. Kenny, 2002).

18. "Raymond's natural habitat is not the wilderness but the art gallery," writes Richard Falcon. "Magnificent Obsession," *Sight and Sound* 13 (Mar. 2003), 13.

19. In "Black American Cinema: The New Realism" (1993), Manthia Diawara distinguishes between two tendencies in black American film, a more "realistic," linear style, and a "symbolic, reflexive, and expressive" style (in Stam and Miller, eds., *Film and Theory*, 242–243). Diawara sets *Do the Right Thing* in the "realist" camp (243). Wahneema Lubiano complicates the sense of realism in Spike Lee's films in her article "But Compared to What? Reading Realism, Representation, and Essentialism in *School Daze, Do the Right Thing,* and the Spike Lee Discourse," in *Representing Blackness: Issues in Film and Video,* ed. Valerie Smith, 97–122 (New Brunswick, N.J.: Rutgers Univ. Press, 1997).

20. Lee takes the cross-processing method used in Soderbergh's *Underneath* and elaborates and multiplies it in *Clockers.* See *Spike Lee: Interviews*, ed. Cynthia Fuchs (Jackson: Univ. Press of Mississippi, 2002), 104.

21. Ibid., 111.

22. Ibid., 105.

23. There is a good discussion of Lee's reference to *Night of the Hunter* in Ed Guerrero, *Do the Right Thing* (London: British Film Institute, 2001), 56–58.

24. Roger Ebert ranked the film as the best of 1997.

25. See, for example, Melvin Donalson, "The Pathmakers," in *Black Directors in Hollywood* (Austin: Univ. of Texas Press, 2003), 18–24.

26. *Sayles on Sayles*, ed. Gavin Smith (London: Faber and Faber, 1998), xii.

27. Ibid., 52.

28. Ibid., 194.

29. Ibid., 196.

30. Ibid., 230.

31. Julianne Burton-Carvajal sees more ambivalence in the conclusion of *Lone Star* than I do: "The romantically inclined [in the audience] will opt to believe that Sam and Pilar can manage to pull up stakes and start fresh elsewhere, leaving Frontera and their entangled personal histories behind. Less sanguine viewers will ponder how the pair could live out their attachment to one another under the shadow of this unwelcome new knowledge." "Oedipus Tex/Oedipus Mex: Triangulations of Paternity, Race, and Nation in John Sayles's *Lone Star,*" in *Multiculturalism, Postcoloniality, and Transnational Media,* ed. Ella Shohat and Robert Stam (New Brunswick, N.J.: Rutgers Univ. Press, 2003), 141.

32. Sayles talks about how each character in *Lone Star* is part of a "tribe." "And Bunny's tribe is the Dallas Cowboys," says Gavin Smith. "Absolutely," replies Sayles, "But it's a very artificial thing" (*Sayles on Sayles*, 226). Sayles wants to emphasize how false and illusory Bunny's life is, since she is so tied to sports and television.

Chapter 8

1. Charles Tesson, "Et l'age de l'amour," *Cahiers du cinéma* 557 (May 2001), 38.

2. Jean-Luc Godard, *Éloge de l'amour: Phrases* (Paris: POL, 2001). Many of Godard's recent films have been turned into these phrase books, which are not scripts in any usual sense, but simply a recording of all the words spoken in the film, irrespective of context or speaker.

3. See, for example, Arthur C. Danto, "Masterpiece and the Museum," in *Encounters and Reflections: Art in the Historical Present* (Berkeley and Los Angeles: Univ. of California Press, 1990), 313–330.

4. B. H. D. Buchloh, *Neo-Avantgarde and the Culture Industry: Essays on European Art and American Art from 1955 to 1975* (Cambridge, Mass.: MIT Press, 2000), xviii. One of the first books to connect American cultural imperialism with art was Serge Guilbaut, *How New York Stole the Idea of Modern Art: Abstract Expressionism, Freedom, and the Cold War*, trans. Arthur Goldhammer (Chicago: Univ. of Chicago Press, 1983).

5. Jameson, *Geopolitical Aesthetic*.

6. Peter Wollen, *Signs and Meaning in the Cinema* (London: Thames and Hudson, 1972).

7. *New York Times*, unsigned editorial, "The Matrix: Global Opening," Nov. 7, 2003.

8. In their introduction to *Global Media Studies: Ethnographic Perspectives* (New York: Routledge, 2003), editors Patrick D. Murphy and Marwan M. Kraidy note that several recent books on global media warn against the dangers of this turn away from "cultural imperialism." James Curran and Myng-Jin Park note in the introduction to *De-Westernizing Media Studies* (New York: Routledge, 2000) that "the nation is still a very important marker of difference" (12). Nancy Morris and Silvio Waisbord state in the introduction to *Media and Globalization: Why the State Matters* (New York: Rowman and Littlefield, 2001) that "states retain important functions and are not likely to disappear" (ix).

9. According to Michael Hardt and Antonio Negri, "In contrast to imperialism, Empire establishes no territorial center of power and does not rely on fixed boundaries or barriers." *Empire* (Cambridge, Mass.: Harvard Univ. Press, 2000), xii. Daniel T. O'Hara, *Empire Burlesque: The Fate of Critical Culture in Global America* (Durham, N.C.: Duke Univ. Press, 2003), 3–4.

10. *www.whitehouse.gov/news/releases/2003/11/20031106-11.html* (accessed Sept. 29, 2005).

11. See the powerful critique by Atilio A. Boron in *Empire and Imperialism: A Critical Reading of Michael Hardt and Antonio Negri*, trans. Jessica Casiro (New York: Zed Books, 2005).

12. Godard published a version of the script for *Letter to Jane* (1972) in *Tel Quel* 52 (Winter 1972). For a description of the magazine's various projects, see Patrick

Ffrench, *The Time of Theory: A History of "Tel Quel"* (New York: Oxford Univ. Press, 1995). Godard and *Tel Quel* both turned Maoist at the beginning of the 1970s.

13. *Jim Jarmusch: Interviews*, ed. Ludvig Hertzberg (Jackson: Univ. Press of Mississippi, 2001), 13.

14. Ibid., 23

15. *Scorsese on Scorsese*, ed. David Thompson and Ian Christie (Boston: Faber and Faber, 1989), 148.

16. The complete impossibility of this painting existing in Archer's room is underscored by the fact that this Turner was never sold. "[Turner] had kept many of his pictures together there [in his London house], even buying back some works and, in the case of *The Fighting Temeraire*, refusing to sell 'my darling' " (Richard P. Townsend, *J. M. W. Turner: "That Greatest of Landscape Painters"* [Tulsa, Okla.: Philbrook Museum of Art, 1998], 12).

17. Note that even a director like Derek Jarman, who is profoundly indebted to underground filmmakers like Kenneth Anger and Jean Genet, determinedly makes feature films, not underground films. Jarman thus insists on a centrality for his radical visions. At exactly the same time that Godard returned to fiction film, Andrew Sarris argued that narrative films are much more successful and interesting than experimental films at rendering politics ("Avant-Garde Films Are More Boring Than Ever," in *Politics and Cinema*, 196–206 [New York: Columbia Univ. Press, 1978]).

18. For descriptions of such radical aesthetics, see *Underground U.S.A.: Filmmaking beyond the Hollywood Canon*, ed. Xavier Mendik and Steven Jay Schneider (New York: Wallflower, 2002). See also Malcolm Le Grice, *Experimental Cinema in the Digital Age* (London: British Film Institute, 2001).

19. *How Latitudes Become Forms: Art in a Global Age*, ed. Philippe Vergne (Minneapolis, Minn.: Walker Art Center, 2003), 131.

20. Lawrence Rinder, ed., *The American Effect: Global Perspectives on the United States, 1990–2003* (New York: Whitney Museum of American Art, 2003), 16.

21. Tarkovsky, *Sculpting in Time*, 179–180.

Bibliography

··

Alexander, Karen. "Interview with Julie Dash." In *American Independent Cinema*, edited by Jim Hillier. London: British Film Institute, 2001.

Allen, Richard. *Projecting Illusion: Film Spectatorship and the Impression of Reality.* New York: Cambridge Univ. Press, 1995.

Anderson, Paul Thomas. *Magnolia: The Shooting Script.* New York: Newmarket Press, 2000.

Aronofsky, Darren. *Pi: Screenplay and the Guerilla Diaries.* London: Faber and Faber, 1998.

Aronofsky, Darren, and Hubert Selby, Jr. *Requiem for a Dream,* screenplay. London: Faber and Faber, 2000.

Aumont, Jacques. *The Image.* Translated by Claire Pajackowska. London: British Film Institute, 1997.

Badiou, Alain. *Deleuze: The Clamor of Being.* Translated by Louise Burchill. Minneapolis: Univ. of Minnesota Press, 2000.

Baudrillard, Jean. "The Murder of the Real." In *The Vital Illusion.* New York: Columbia Univ. Press, 2003.

Baudry, Jean-Louis. "Ideological Effects of the Basic Cinematographic Apparatus." In *Narrative, Apparatus, Ideology: A Film Theory Reader,* edited by Philip Rosen. New York: Columbia Univ. Press, 1986.

Bellour, Raymond. *L'entre-images 2: Mots, images.* Paris: POL, 1999.

Bellour, Raymond, and Laurent Roth. *Qu'est-ce Qu'une Madeleine? A propos du CD-ROM "Immemory" de Chris Marker.* Paris: Centre Georges Pompidou, 1997.

Berens, Kate, and Geoff Howard. *The Rough Guide to Videogaming.* New York: Rough Guides, 2002.

Blouin, Patrice. "Frontière mexicaine," *Cahiers du cinéma* 555 (Mar. 2001).

Bordwell, David, and Noel Carroll. *Post-Theory: Reconstructing Film Studies.* Madison: Univ. of Wisconsin Press, 1994.

Bordwell, David, Janet Staiger, and Kristin Thompson. *The Classical Hollywood*

Cinema: Film Style and Mode of Production to 1960. New York: Columbia Univ. Press, 1985.

Bordwell, David, and Kristin Thompson. *Film Art: An Introduction.* New York: McGraw-Hill, 2001.

Boron, Atilio A. *Empire and Imperialism: A Critical Reading of Michael Hardt and Antonio Negri.* Translated by Jessica Casiro. New York: Zed Books, 2005.

Braudy, Leo. "The Genre of Nature: Ceremonies of Innocence." In *Refiguring American Film Genres: Theory and History,* edited by Nick Browne. Berkeley and Los Angeles: Univ. of California Press, 1998.

Browne, Nick, ed. *Cahiers du Cinéma, 1969–1972: The Politics of Representation.* Cambridge, Mass.: Harvard Univ. Press, 1990.

Buchloh, Benjamin H. D. *Neo-Avantgarde and the Culture Industry: Essays on European Art and American Art from 1955 to 1975.* Cambridge, Mass.: MIT Press, 2000.

Buckland, Warren. *The Cognitive Semiotics of Film.* New York: Cambridge Univ. Press, 2000.

Burgess, Anthony. "Introduction: *A Clockwork Orange* Resucked." In *A Clockwork Orange.* New York: Norton, 1986.

Burton-Carvajal, Julia. "Oedipus Tex/Oedipus Mex: Triangulations of Paternity, Race, and Nation in John Sayles's *Lone Star.*" In *Multiculturalism, Postcoloniality, and Transnational Media,* edited by Ella Shohat and Robert Stam. New Brunswick, N.J.: Rutgers Univ. Press, 2003.

Carnes, Mark C. "Past Imperfect: History According to the Movies," *Cineaste* 22, no. 4 (Fall 1996).

Carney, Ray. *The Films of John Cassavetes: Pragmatism, Modernism, and the Movies.* New York: Cambridge Univ. Press, 1994.

Casetti, Francesco. *Theories of Cinema, 1945–1995.* Translated by Francesca Chiostri and Elizabeth Gard Bartolini-Salimbeni, with Thomas Kelso. Austin: Univ. of Texas Press, 1999.

Cavell, Stanley. *Pursuits of Happiness: The Hollywood Comedy of Remarriage.* Cambridge, Mass.: Harvard Univ. Press, 1981.

Chion, Michel. *David Lynch.* Translated by Robert Julian. London: British Film Institute, 1995.

———. *Eyes Wide Shut.* Translated by Trista Selous. London: British Film Institute, 2002.

Coupe, Laurence, ed. *The Green Studies Reader: From Romanticism to Ecocriticism.* New York: Routledge, 2000.

Cronin, Paul, ed. *Herzog on Herzog.* New York: Faber and Faber, 2002.

Curran, James, and Myng-Jin Park, eds. *De-Westernizing Media Studies.* New York: Routledge, 2000.

Dalle Vacche, Angela. "Andrei Tarkovsky's *Andrei Rublev:* Cinema as the Restoration of Icon Painting." In *Cinema and Painting: How Art is Used in Film.* Austin: Univ. of Texas Press, 1996.

Daney, Serge. *Ciné Journal 1: 1981–1982.* Paris: Cahiers du Cinéma, 1998.

———. *Ciné Journal 2: 1983–1986.* Paris: Cahiers du Cinéma, 1998.

———. *L'Exercice a été profitable, monsieur,* ed. Jean-Claude Biette and Emmanuel Crimail. Paris: POL, 1993.

———. "La fonction critique." In *Critique et cinéphilie,* 99–122 (Paris: Cahiers du Cinéma, 2001).

———. *La rampe.* Paris: Cahiers du Cinéma, 1996.

Danto, Arthur C. "Masterpiece and the Museum." In *Encounters and Reflections: Art in the Historical Present.* Berkeley and Los Angeles: Univ. of California Press, 1990.

De Baecque, Antoine. *Andrei Tarkovski.* Paris: Cahiers du Cinéma, 1989.

———. "Sus au mystére," *Cahiers du cinéma* 457 (June 1992).

Deleuze, Gilles. *Cinema 1: The Movement-Image.* Translated by Hugh Tomlinson and Barbara Habberjam. Minneapolis: Univ. of Minnesota Press, 1986.

———. *Cinema 2: The Time-Image.* Translated by Hugh Tomlinson and Robert Galeta. Minneapolis: Univ. of Minnesota Press, 2001.

———. "Letter to Serge Daney: Optimism, Pessimism, and Travel." In *Negotiations, 1972–1990.* Translated by Martin Joughin. New York: Columbia Univ. Press, 1995.

Dillon, Steven. *Derek Jarman and Lyric Film: The Mirror and The Sea.* Austin: Univ. of Texas Press, 2004.

Dixon, Wheeler H. *It Looks Back at You: The Returned Gaze of Cinema.* Albany: State Univ. of New York Press, 1995.

Donalson, Melvin. *Black Directors in Hollywood.* Austin: Univ. of Texas Press, 2003.

Durgnat, Raymond. *Films and Feelings.* Cambridge, Mass.: MIT Press, 1971.

Dyens, Ollivier. *Metal and Flesh: The Evolution of Man; Technology Takes Over.* Translated by Evan J. Bibbee and Ollivier Dyens. Cambridge, Mass.: MIT Press, 2001.

Dyer, Richard. *Seven.* London: British Film Institute, 1999.

Eisenstein, Sergei. *Eisenstein on Disney.* Translated by Alan Upchurch. London: Methuen, 1988.

Elsaesser, Thomas, and Warren Buckland. *Studying Contemporary American Film.* London: Arnold, 2002.

Ettedgui, Peter. *Cinematography Screencraft.* Boston: Focal Press, 1998.

Falcon, Richard. "Magnificent Obsession." *Sight and Sound* 13 (Mar. 2003).

ffrench, Patrick. *The Time of Theory: A History of "Tel Quel."* New York: Oxford Univ. Press, 1995.

Fisher, Philip. *Making and Effacing Art: Modern American Art in a Culture of Museums.* New York: Oxford Univ. Press, 1991.

Foster, Hal. *The Return of the Real.* Cambridge, Mass.: MIT Press, 1996.

Freedman, Jonathan, and Richard Millington, eds. *Hitchcock's America.* New York: Oxford Univ. Press, 1999.

French, Karl. *Apocalypse Now.* London: Bloomsbury, 1998.

Fuchs, Cynthia, ed. *Spike Lee: Interviews.* Jackson: Univ. Press of Mississippi, 2002.

Furniss, Maureen. *Art in Motion: Animation Aesthetics.* Sydney: John Libbey, 1998.

Garson, Charlotte. "Dogme, mensonges, et vidéo numérique." *Cahiers du cinéma,* special issue, Apr. 2003.

Godard, Jean-Luc. *Éloge de l'amour: Phrases.* Paris: POL, 2001.

Guerrero, Ed. *Do The Right Thing.* London: British Film Institute, 2001.

Guilbaut, Serge. *How New York Stole the Idea of Modern Art: Abstract Expressionism, Freedom, and the Cold War.* Translated by Arthur Goldhammer. Chicago: Univ. of Chicago Press, 1983.

Hampton, Howard. "Mission." *Film Comment* 32 (July–Aug. 1996).

Hardt, Michael, and Antonio Negri. *Empire.* Cambridge, Mass.: Harvard Univ. Press, 2000.

Hawkins, Joan. *Cutting Edge: Art-Horror and the Horrific Avant-Garde.* Minneapolis: Univ. of Minnesota Press, 2000.

Heath, Stephen. *Questions of Cinema.* Bloomington: Indiana Univ. Press, 1981.

Heim, Michael. *The Metaphysics of Virtual Reality.* New York: Oxford Univ. Press, 1993.

Hertzberg, Ludvig, ed. *Jim Jarmusch: Interviews.* Jackson: Univ. Press of Mississippi, 2001.

Higuinen, Erwan. Review of *Requiem for A Dream. Cahiers du cinéma* 555 (Dec. 2001).

Hillier, Jim, ed. *American Independent Cinema.* London: British Film Institute, 2001.

Jameson, Fredric. *The Geopolitical Aesthetic: Cinema and Space in the World System.* London: British Film Institute, 1992.

Johnson, Vida T., and Graham Petrie. *The Films of Andrei Tarkovsky: A Visible Fugue.* Bloomington: Indiana Univ. Press, 1994.

Jousse, Thierry. "Les dandys du câble." In *Critique et cinéphilie.* Paris: Cahiers du Cinéma, 2001.

———. "Frankenstein contre Dracula." *Cahiers du cinéma* 463 (Jan. 1993).

———. *Pendant les travaux, le cinéma reste ouvert.* Paris: Cahiers du cinéma, 2003.

Kael, Pauline. *Hooked.* New York: Dutton, 1989.

Kaufman, Anthony, ed. *Steven Soderbergh: Interviews.* Jackson: Univ. Press of Mississippi, 2002.

King, Geoff, and Tanya Krzywinska, eds. *Screenplay: Cinema/Videogames/Interfaces.* London and New York: Wallflower, 2002.

Kolker, Robert. *A Cinema of Loneliness.* New York: Oxford Univ. Press, 2000.

Kracauer, Siegfried. *Theory of Film: The Redemption of Physical Reality.* Princeton, N.J.: Princeton Univ. Press, 1997.

Kruger, Barbara. *Thinking of You.* Edited by Ann Goldstein. Cambridge, Mass.: MIT Press, 1999.

Lalanne, Jean-Marc. "Filmographie/Gus Van Sant." *Cahiers du cinéma* 579 (May 2003).

Le Fanu, Mark. *The Cinema of Andrei Tarkovsky.* London: British Film Institute, 1987.

Lem, Stanislaw. *Solaris.* Translated by Joanna Kilmartin and Steve Cox. New York: Walker, 1970; rept. Harcourt, 1987.

Leslie, Esther. "Eisenstein Shakes Mickey's Hand in Hollywood." In *Hollywood Flat-lands: Animation, Critical Theory, and the Avant-Garde*. New York: Verso, 2002.

Levy, Emanuel. *Cinema of Outsiders: The Rise of American Independent Film*. New York: New York Univ. Press, 1999.

Lewis, Jon, ed. *The End of Cinema as We Know It: American Film in the Nineties*. New York: New York Univ. Press, 2001.

Lubiano, Wahneema. "But Compared to What? Reading Realism, Representation, and Essentialism in *School Daze*, *Do The Right Thing*, and the Spike Lee Discourse." In *Representing Blackness: Issue in Film and Video*, edited by Valerie Smith. New Brunswick, N.J.: Rutgers Univ. Press, 1997.

Lubin, David. *Titanic*. London: British Film Institute, 1999.

Lunenfeld, Peter. *Snap to Grid: A User's Guide to Digital Arts, Media, and Cultures*. Cambridge, Mass.: MIT Press, 2000.

Lyons, Donald. "Lubricating the Muse." *Film Comment* 28 (Jan.–Feb. 1992).

Manovich, Lev. *The Language of New Media*. Cambridge, Mass.: MIT Press, 2001.

Mendik, Xavier, and Steven Jay Schneider, eds. *Underground U.S.A.: Filmmaking beyond the Hollywood Canon*. New York: Wallflower, 2002.

Metz, Christian. *Film Language: A Semiotics of the Cinema*. Translated by Michael Taylor. Chicago: Univ. of Chicago Press, 1974, 1991.

————. *The Imaginary Signifier: Psychoanalysis and the Cinema*. Translated by Celia Britton, Annwyl Williams, and Ben Brewster. Bloomington: Indiana Univ. Press, 1982.

Michaels, Lloyd. "Bergman and the Necessary Illusion." In *Ingmar Bergman's "Persona,"* edited by Lloyd Michaels. New York: Cambridge Univ. Press, 2000.

Mitry, Jean. *The Aesthetics and Psychology of the Cinema*. Translated by Christopher King. Bloomington: Indiana Univ. Press, 1997.

Morris, Nancy, and Silvio Waibord, eds. *Media and Globalization: Why the State Matters*. New York: Rowman and Littlefield, 2001.

Murphy, Patrick, and Marwan M. Kraidy, eds. *Global Media Studies: Ethnographic Perspectives*. New York: Routledge, 2003.

Nochimson, Martha. *The Passion of David Lynch: Wild at Heart in Hollywood*. Austin: Univ. of Texas Press, 1997.

O'Hara, Daniel T. *Empire Burlesque: The Fate of Critical Culture in Global America*. Durham, N.C.: Duke Univ. Press, 2003.

O'Pray, Michael. "Eisenstein and Stokes on Disney: Film Animation and Omnipotence." In *A Reader in Animation Studies*, edited by Jayne Pilling. Sydney: John Libbey, 1997.

Peary, Gerald, ed. *Quentin Tarantino: Interviews*. Jackson: Univ. Press of Mississippi, 1998.

Raphael, Frederic. *Eyes Wide Open: A Memoir of Stanley Kubrick.* New York: Ballantine, 1999.

Richie, Donald. *The Films of Akira Kurosawa.* Berkeley and Los Angeles: Univ. of California Press, 1984.

Rinder, Lawrence, ed. *The American Effect: Global Perspectives on the United States, 1990–2003.* New York: Whitney Museum of American Art, 2003.

Rodley, Chris. *Lynch on Lynch.* London: Faber and Faber, 1997.

Rodowick, D. N. *The Crisis of Political Modernism: Criticism and Ideology in Contemporary Film Theory.* Berkeley and Los Angeles: Univ. of California Press, 1994.

———. *Deleuze's Time Machine.* Durham, N.C.: Duke Univ. Press, 1997.

Rosen, Philip. *Change Mummified: Cinema, Historicity, Theory.* Minneapolis: Univ. of Minnesota Press, 2001.

Saade, Nicolas. "La métamorphose de Soderbergh." *Cahiers du cinéma* 454 (Apr. 1992).

Sarris, Andrew. *Politics and Cinema.* New York: Columbia Univ. Press, 1978.

Scorsese, Martin. "Notre génération." *Cahiers du cinéma* 500 (Mar. 1996).

Selby, Hubert, Jr. *Requiem for a Dream.* New York: Simon and Schuster, 1978.

Shaviro, Steven. *The Cinematic Body.* Minneapolis: Univ. of Minnesota Press, 1993.

Silet, Charles L. P., ed. *Oliver Stone: Interviews.* Jackson: Univ. Press of Mississippi, 2001.

Silverman, Kaja. "Historical Trauma and Male Subjectivity." In *Psychoanalysis and Cinema,* edited by E. Ann Kaplan. New York: Routledge, 1990.

———. *The Threshold of the Visible World.* New York: Routledge, 1996.

Smith, Gavin. "Going Pro." *Film Comment* 36 (Mar./-Apr. 2000).

———, ed. *Sayles on Sayles.* London: Faber and Faber, 1998.

Smith, Kevin. *The Green Arrow: Quiver.* New York: DC Comics, 2002.

Sobchack, Vivian. *The Address of the Eye: A Phenomenology of Film Experience.* Princeton, N.J.: Princeton Univ. Press, 1992.

Soderbergh, Steven. *Getting Away with It: Or, the Further Adventures of the Luckiest Bastard You Ever Saw.* London: Faber and Faber, 1999.

Stam, Robert. *Literature through Film: Realism, Magic, and the Art of Adaptation.* Malden, Mass.: Blackwell, 2005.

———. *Reflexivity in Film and Literature from "Don Quixote" to Jean-Luc Godard.* New York: Columbia University Press, 1992.

Stam, Robert, and Toby Miller, eds. *Film and Theory: An Anthology.* Malden, Mass.: Blackwell, 2000.

Sterritt, David, ed. *Robert Altman: Interviews.* Jackson: Univ. Press of Mississippi, 2000.

Stevenson, Jack. *Lars von Trier.* London: British Film Institute, 2002.

Stratton, Richard, and Kim Wozencraft, eds. *Slam: The Book.* New York: Grove Press, 1998.

Strauss, Frédéric. "Tempête sous un crâne." *Cahiers du cinéma* 509 (Jan. 1997).

Tarantino, Quentin. *Reservoir Dogs and True Romance.* New York: Grove Press, 1994.

Tarkovsky, Andrei. *Collected Screenplays.* Translated by William Powell and Natasha Synessio. London: Faber and Faber, 1999.

Tasker, Yvonne. *The Silence of the Lambs*. London: British Film Institute, 2002.

Taylor, Greg. *Artists in the Audience: Cults, Camp, and American Film Criticism*. Princeton, N.J.: Princeton Univ. Press, 1999.

Taubin, Amy. "In Dreams." *Film Comment* 37 (Sept./-Oct. 2001).

Tesson, Charles. "Et l'age de l'amour." *Cahiers du cinéma* 557 (May 2001).

Thompson, David, and Ian Christie, eds. *Scorsese on Scorsese*. London: Faber and Faber, 1989.

Truffaut, François. "A Certain Tendency of the French Cinema." In *Movies and Methods*, edited by Bill Nichols. Berkeley and Los Angeles: Univ. of California Press, 1976.

Turan, Kenneth. *Sundance to Sarajevo: Film Festivals and the World They Made*. Berkeley and Los Angeles: Univ. of California Press, 2002.

Vergne, Philippe, ed. *How Latitudes Become Forms: Art in a Global Age*. Minneapolis, Minn.: Walker Art Center, 2003.

Vernet, Marc. *Figures de l'absence: De l'invisible au cinéma*. Paris: Éditions de l'étoile, 1988.

White, Armond. "Brian De Palma, Political Filmmaker." *Film Comment* 27, no. 3 (May–June 1991).

Williams, Mark. "Real-Time Fairy Tales: Cinema Prefiguring Digital Anxiety." In *New Media: Theories and Practices of Digitextuality*, edited by Anna Everett and John T. Caldwell, 159–178. London: Routledge, 2003.

Wollen, Peter. *Signs and Meaning in the Cinema*. London: Thames and Hudson, 1972.

Zizek, Slavoj. *The Fright of Real Tears: Krzyzstof Kieslowski between Theory and Post-Theory*. London: British Film Institute, 2001.

Index

··

Age of Innocence, The (Scorsese), 224–226
A.I. (Spielberg), 120–123, 130–140
Allen, Richard, 1, 3, 233–234n
Allen, Woody, 216
Altman, Robert, 156–166
American Beauty (Mendes), 69–70
American History X (Kaye), 193
American Psycho (Harron), 169–171
Amistad (Spielberg), 133–134
Another Day in Paradise (Clark), 179
Apocalypse Now (Coppola), 63
Araki, Gregg, 75

Badlands (Malick), 64
Basquiat (Schnabel), 145–148
Baudrillard, Jean, 16
Baudry, Jean-Louis, 1
Bazin, André, 105–106
Beau Travail (Denis), 175
Bellour, Raymond, 114–118
Black Hawk Down (Scott), 35
Blackout, The (Ferrara), 11
Blade Runner (Scott), 10, 49
Blow-Up (Antonioni), 11
Bordwell, David, 110–111
Boys Don't Cry (Peirce), 206–208
Branded to Kill (Suzuki), 220
Breathless (Godard), 28
Bresson, Robert, 210, 216

Bringing Out the Dead (Scorsese), 227–228
Brother from Another Planet, The (Sayles), 200
Buchloh, Benjamin H. D., 211
Buckland, Warren, 108–109
Bully (Clark), 179
Burnett, Charles, 195–196

Casetti, Francesco, 233n
Cassavetes, John, 74, 177–179
Cavell, Stanley, 30–31, 122
Celebration, The (Vinterberg), 181
Chasing Amy (Smith), 126
Chion, Michel, 83–84, 87, 91, 150–151, 153
Citizen Kane (Welles), 172, 187
City of Hope (Sayles), 200
Clockers (Lee), 22, 190, 193
Clockwork Orange, A (Kubrick), 156
Close Encounters of the Third Kind (Spielberg), 121
Cool Hand Luke (Rosenberg), 192
Criss Cross (Siodmak), 30
Cronenberg, David, 25, 48–49, 75

Dancer in the Dark (von Trier), 175
Daney, Serge, 97–103
Dangerous Lives of Altar Boys, The (Care), 119
Daughters of the Dust (Dash), 134–136

Days of Eclipse (Sokurov), 21–22
Dead Man (Jarmusch), 11, 220–221
Deleuze, Gilles, 5, 131
Deliverance (Boorman), 245n
De Palma, Brian, 77–83
Do the Right Thing (Lee), 190–191
Durgnat, Raymond, 155

Ebert, Roger, 77, 80, 176
Ed Wood (Burton), 80
Eisenstein, Sergei, 123–124
Element of Crime, The (Von Trier), 29
Elephant (Van Sant), 183–184
Elephant Man (Lynch), 221
Elsaesser, Thomas, 108–109
End of Violence, The (Wenders), 219
Eraserhead (Lynch), 242n
Erin Brockovich (Soderbergh), 33–34
E. T. the Extra-Terrestrial (Spielberg), 106–107
Eve's Bayou (Lemmons), 196
Eyes Wide Shut (Kubrick), 105, 149–156

Far From Heaven (Haynes), 188–189
Ferrara, Abel, 217
Fight Club (Fincher), 193
For Ever Mozart (Godard), 141
Full Frontal (Soderbergh), 36–37
Full Metal Jacket (Kubrick), 151–152

Gangs of New York (Scorsese), 63, 194, 226–227
Genet, Jean, 184–185
Gerry (Van Sant), 208
Ghost Dog: The Way of the Samurai (Jarmusch), 11, 119, 219–220
Ghost World (Zwigoff), 11
Gibson, William, 49, 239n
Gilliam, Terry, 25, 49, 119
Girl 6 (Lee), 190–191
Girlfight (Kusama), 65–67
Godard, Jean-Luc, 1, 5, 7, 22, 28, 116, 129–130, 141–142, 209–216
Gordon, Douglas, 115

Gosford Park (Altman), 161
Great Expectations (Cuarón), 143
Greenaway, Peter, 113–114
Gummo (Korine), 179–180

Happiness (Solondz), 50
Hard Target (Woo), 175
Hartley, Hal, 216–217
Haynes, Todd, 184–189
Heath, Stephen, 108
He Got Game (Lee), 192
Henry: Portrait of a Serial Killer (Mc-Naughton), 170–171
Herzog, Werner, 181
Hitchcock, Alfred, xi–xii
Horse Whisperer, The (Redford), 57–58
Hunter, Holly, 64–65

Images (Altman), 247n
Indian Runner, The (Penn), 64
In Praise of Love (Godard), 1, 115, 142, 210–211
In the Company of Men (LaBute), 169
I Shot Andy Warhol (Harron), 168–169

Jackie Brown (Tarantino), 198
Jameson, Fredric, 15, 21–22, 52, 211–212
Japón (Reygadas), 6
Jarman, Derek, 66–67, 146, 176, 179, 184–185, 187
Jarmusch, Jim, 216–221
Jay and Silent Bob Strike Back (Smith), 126
Jetée, La (Marker), 116, 118, 180
JFK (Stone), 27–29
Johnson, Vida, 14
Jost, Jon, 75
Jousse, Thierry, 92–93, 96–97
Julien Donkey-Boy (Korine), 180–181
Jurassic Park (Spielberg), 105, 107–109, 112, 114

Kafka (Soderbergh), 25–26
Kids (Clark), 176–179
Kill Bill, Volume 1 (Tarantino), 128

King of New York (Ferrara), 90
King of the Hill (Soderbergh), 26–27
Kolker, Robert, ix, 79, 150, 163
Korine, Harmony, 179–181
Kracauer, Siegfried, 149–156
Krauss, Rosalind, 141
Kruger, Barbara, 240n
K Street (Soderbergh), 37–39
Kubrick, Stanley, 13, 149–156, 185–186

Last Picture Show, The (Bogdanovich), 183
Lee, Spike, 189–195
Le Fanu, Mark, 9–10, 11–12
Legend of Bagger Vance, The (Redford), 57
Lemmons, Kasi, 196
Leone, Sergio, 128, 198
Lester, Richard, 22, 32
Limey, The (Soderbergh), 34–35
Lion King, The (Allers and Minkoff), 123
Lone Star (Sayles), 202–203
Losing the Thread (Nossiter), 148–149
Lost Highway (Lynch), 87
Lost World, The (Spielberg), 109
Love Is the Devil (Maybury), 246n.
Lubin, David, 145
Lust for Life (Minnelli), 158–159
Lynch, David, 84–103

Magnificent Obsession (Sirk), 189
Magnolia (Anderson), 173
Manovich, Lev, 109–114, 118
Man Who Wasn't There, The (Coen), 11
Man with a Movie Camera, The (Vertov), 113
Marker, Chris, 105, 115–118, 125
Maslin, Janet, 173
Matrix, The (Wachowski brothers), 51, 105, 175, 210
McTiernan, John, 7
Metz, Christian, 3–5, 234n, 235n
Mildred Pierce (Curtiz), 39
Minority Report (Spielberg), 15, 46, 106
Mission to Mars (De Palma), 80–82
Mulholland Drive (Lynch), 36, 91–103

Natural Born Killers (Stone), 27–29
Night of the Hunter, The (Laughton), 191
Nixon (Stone), 28–29
Nochimson, Martha, 86
No Such Thing (Hartley), 11
Numéro deux (Godard), 115
Nunez, Victor, 204–206

Ocean's Eleven (Soderbergh), 33
Office Killer (Sherman), 171–172
One Day in the Life of Andrei Arsenevitch (Marker), 117
O'Pray, Michael, 124
Orpheus (Cocteau), 11
Out of Sight (Soderbergh), 33

Passion (Godard), 141, 212
Passion Fish (Sayles), 200–202
Persona (Bergman), 23, 161–162, 200–201
Petrie, Graham, 14
π (Aronofsky), 15, 45–53
Player, The (Altman), 36, 157, 164
Plympton, Bill, 128
Poison (Haynes), 184–185
Pollock (Harris), 142–143
Posse (Van Peebles), 197
Psycho (Hitchcock), 171, 182–183
Psycho (Van Sant), 39, 182–183
Pulp Fiction (Tarantino), 128–130
Punch-Drunk Love (Anderson), 174
Purple Rose of Cairo (Allen), 8

Quiz Show (Redford), 59–61

Raiders of the Lost Ark (Spielberg), 121–122
Rauschenberg, Robert, 141
Redford, Robert, 53–61
Requiem for a Dream (Aronofsky), 70–74
Reservoir Dogs (Tarantino), 127, 129
Return of the Secaucus Seven (Sayles), 199–200
River Runs Through It, A (Redford), 58–59
Rosewood (Singleton), 196–197

Ruby in Paradise (Nunez), 204–205
Russian Ark (Sokurov), 22

Safe (Haynes), 185–186
Sayles, John, 198–204
Scenes from the Life of Andy Warhol
  (Mekas), 147
Schindler's List (Spielberg), 133
Schizopolis (Soderbergh), 32–33
School Daze (Lee), 190
Scorsese, Martin, 80, 147, 193–195, 222–228
Seven (Fincher), 166
sex, lies, and videotape, 23–25
Shadows (Cassavetes), 177–179
Shaviro, Steven, 1
Sherlock, Jr. (Keaton), 8
Sherman, Cindy, 171–172
She's Gotta Have It (Lee), 190
Signs and Wonders (Nossiter), 148–149
Silence of the Lambs, The (Demme), 166
Singleton, John, 196
Sirk, Douglas, 188–189
Sixth Sense, The (Shyamalan), 11
Slam (Levin), 67–68
Smith, Kevin, 125–127
Soderbergh, Stephen, 21–27, 29–44
Solaris (Soderbergh), 39–44
Solaris (Tarkovsky), 2, 8–19, 40–43, 81
Solondz, Todd, 32, 50, 147
Speed (De Bont), 169
Spiderman (Raimi), 120, 124
Spielberg, Steven, 106–109, 120–123,
  130–140
Stalker (Tarkovsky), 22, 101, 116
Stam, Robert, 234n
Star Wars: Episode I—The Phantom Men-
  ace (Lucas), 113
Stone, Oliver, 27–29
Storytelling (Solondz), 69–70
Stranger Than Paradise (Jarmusch), 217–
  218
Summer of Sam (Lee), 193–195
Sunshine State (Sayles), 203–204

Tarantino, Quentin, 127–130
Tarkovsky, Andrei, 2, 21–22, 39–40, 52,
  117, 130–131
Taste of Cherry, The (Kiarostami), 6
Taxi Driver (Scorsese), 194
Three Seasons (Bui), 61–63
Three Women (Altman), 164
Titanic (Cameron), 144
To Sleep with Anger (Burnett), 195–196
Toy Story (Lasseter), 120
Traffic (Soderbergh), 35–36
Tsukamoto, Shinya, 48–49
Turan, Kenneth, 53
25th Hour (Lee), 192–193
Twin Peaks: Fire Walk with Me (Lynch),
  84–91, 241n
2001: A Space Odyssey (Kubrick), 9, 40, 49,
  81, 185–186

Ulee's Gold (Nunez), 205–206
Ulysses' Gaze (Angelopolous), 62
Underneath, The (Soderbergh), 29–31
Under the Sand (Ozon), 11

Vachon, Christine, 167–168
Van Gogh (Pialat), 159–160
Van Peebles, Mario, 197–198
Van Sant, Gus, 181–184, 208
Velvet Goldmine (Haynes), 186–187
Vernet, Marc, 1–3
Vertigo (Hitchcock), 11, 89, 101, 116, 125,
  191, 192
Vincent and Theo (Altman), 157–166
Voyage to Italy (Rossellini), 154–155

Waking Life (Linklater), 106
War Room, The (Hegedus and Penne-
  baker), 38
Weekend (Godard), 23
Welcome to the Dollhouse (Solondz), 68–69
Wenders, Wim, 218–19
White, Armond, 79
Wilde, Oscar, 187

Williams, Mark, 137–138
Wilmington, Michael, 27
Wollen, Peter, 212–214

You Can Count On Me (Lonergan), 63–65

Zizek, Slavoj, 29

Milton Keynes UK
Ingram Content Group UK Ltd.
UKHW030658220824
447225UK00001B/19

9 780292 713451